THE FEDERAL LANDS ❦ Their Use and Management

THE FEDERAL LANDS:

THEIR USE AND MANAGEMENT

BY MARION CLAWSON AND BURNELL HELD

UNIVERSITY OF NEBRASKA PRESS
LINCOLN

Copyright © 1957 by The Johns Hopkins Press, Baltimore 18, Md.
Library of Congress Catalog Card Number 57–12121
Manufactured in the United States of America

RESOURCES FOR THE FUTURE, INC., Washington, D. C.

Resources for the Future is a nonprofit corporation for research and education to
advance development, conservation, and use of natural resources, primarily in the
United States. It was established in 1952 with the cooperation of The Ford Foundation and its activities have been financed by grants from that Foundation. The
main research areas of the resident staff are Water Resources, Energy and Mineral
Resources, Land Use and Management, Regional Studies, and Resources and
National Growth. One of the major aims of Resources for the Future is to make
available the results of research by its staff members and consultants. Unless otherwise stated, interpretations and conclusions in RFF publications are those of the
authors. The responsibility of the organization as a whole is for selection of
significant questions for study and for competence and freedom of inquiry.

*Bison Book edition reproduced from the 1957 edition by arrange-
ment with Resources for the Future, Inc. and The Johns Hopkins
Press.*

Foreword & Acknowledgments

THIS STUDY RESTS UPON THREE MAJOR FOUNDATIONS: (1) the personal experience and knowledge of the senior author, derived from several previous research studies but primarily from five years' experience from March, 1948, to April, 1953, as Director of the Bureau of Land Management of the Department of the Interior, and from the published sources of information with which that type of experience provides a familiarity; (2) a detailed study, by the junior author, of federal land management agency records to obtain data on uses of land, revenues therefrom, and expenditures thereon, which form a major section of the book and the statistical appendix; and (3) a rather extensive review of a first draft by persons in the federal agencies concerned and elsewhere.

We have made an effort to be as factual and as objective as possible. No attempt has been made to present a critical over-all appraisal of federal land management in its entirety, although some of the data included should be helpful in such an appraisal. At the close of the book, some problems of the future are considered as well as alternative means of dealing with the problems. Advocacy of any of these alternatives is not intended, nor is there a desire to promote any particular program.

We hope that consideration of the facts presented herein, and of the ideas advanced, will lead to discussion and debate as to the best future program for federal land management. If our efforts help to stimulate such discussion, and provide some of the important basic

AUG 5 1970

data needed for intelligent decision, then they will have been well worth while.

The agencies and persons who have offered comments are as follows:[1]

Bureau of the Budget, Management and Organization Division

Bureau of the Budget, Resources and Civil Works Division

Fish and Wildlife Service

Forest Service

Geological Survey

National Park Service

Office of the Secretary, Department of the Interior

Office of the Solicitor, Department of the Interior

Murray R. Benedict, Professor of Agricultural Economics, University of California

J. H. Beuscher, Professor of Law, University of Wisconsin

Henry Clepper, Executive Secretary, Society of American Foresters

Albert M. Day, Director, Waterfowl Research Project, Arctic Institute of North America

William A. Duerr, Chairman, Department of Forest Economics, State University of New York

Ernest A. Engelbert, Department of Political Science, University of California

Philip M. Glick, attorney, Washington, D. C.

---

[1] Copies of the first draft report were provided to the Bureau of Land Management, and its comments solicited. The following letter from the Director of the Bureau of Land Management, U.S. Department of the Interior, dated October 8, 1956, explains why the requested comments could not be given:

"My dear Mr. Clawson—Supplementing my letter to you of July 31, and your more recent visit to my office, concerning comments to be made by the Bureau on the draft of the report entitled 'Federal Land Use and Management' prepared by you and Mr. Burnell Held, I am still of the opinion that to make the analysis suggested by you would require a considerable amount of time, and our present workload is much too heavy for such an undertaking.

"I appreciate the courtesy you have extended to me and members of my staff to make comments on your manuscript. As you are aware, some of the topics are controversial, and in some we differ in our personal interpretation. Clarification of these differences would require a great amount of detail, resulting in a voluminous reply. I feel that it is your report and, as such, should reflect your point of view. By your past experience you are, of course, familiar with the Bureau's operations, and with the same statistics available to both of us the only differences that can be resolved would be on our personal interpretation of them.

"To save time, and to insure thorough coverage, I believe it would be more beneficial to review the various items on an informal basis. I have no objection to discussing these items with you, or you may discuss informally with the various Staff Officers those parts of the manuscript which apply to their particular functions. —Sincerely yours, Edward Woozley"

Christopher M. Granger, formerly Assistant Chief, Forest Service

Paul A. Herbert, formerly professor of Conservation, Michigan State University

Herbert Kaufman, Assistant Professor of Government, Yale University

M. M. Kelso, Dean of Agriculture, Montana State College

James A. Lanigan, Counsel, Public Works and Resources Subcommittee, House Committee on Government Operations

Charles McKinley, Professor of Political Science, Reed College

E. Louise Peffer, Food Research Institute, Stanford University

Raymond J. Penn, Professor, Department of Agricultural Economics, University of Wisconsin

William Pincus, Associate General Counsel, House Committee on Government Operations

Theodore W. Schultz, Chairman, Department of Economics, University of Chicago

Howard R. Tolley, Consultant in Agricultural Economics, Washington, D. C.

Peter F. Watzek, President, The Crossett Company, Crossett, Ark.

Norman Wengert, Professor of Political Science, University of Maryland

Robert E. Wolf, formerly Consultant, Subcommittee on the Legislative Oversight Function, Senate Committee on Interior and Insular Affairs, 84th Congress

The assistance of these various agencies and persons has been extremely valuable. Errors have been pointed out to us, and have been corrected; omissions have been called to our attention, and additions have been made. On many matters exception was taken to our interpretations and statements. Some of these criticisms have been met, we hope, by new and more clearly worded statements. In some cases we have modified our views as a result of facts or arguments brought to our attention; in others, where we have disagreed with the comments offered or where suggestions have been made that are contrary to others, the views of commentators have not been met. Accordingly it must be emphasized that none of the agencies or individuals named is committed to the statements made in the report. The authors alone are responsible. With the exception noted, the data have been checked for accuracy by each of the agencies concerned; but even here the authors, and not the agencies, are responsible.

To the many persons who have helped in the preparation and review of this book, our sincere thanks.

Most of the work on this study was done during 1956. Data are brought up to the end of fiscal or calendar 1956, depending upon the basis of their compilation. Just before the manuscript went to the printer, the President's Budget for fiscal 1958 was available; a few pertinent items from it have been cited in footnotes but our analysis was not reworked to include it. The Forest Service report, *Operation Outdoors,* was also available just at the close of the study; reference is made to it, but our analysis was completed before it was available. Several other reports or studies will be available in the next few months: the Forest Service is making a study of wildlife on national forests, the Bureau of Sport Fisheries and Wildlife is formulating a long-range program, the Bureau of Land Management is studying the abolition or modification of its marketing areas for timber in western Oregon, the Senate Committee on Interior and Insular Affairs is making a study of oil and gas leasing practices on the public lands, and others, including perhaps some of which the authors are unaware. Federal land administration is changing and dynamic, and a picture at any date is shortly modified by new developments. It is believed, however, that recent and pending reports and studies do not basically modify the situation as it has been described herein.

Washington, D. C.   *Marion Clawson*

March, 1957   *Burnell Held*

Contents

LIST OF TABLES

Text Tables

Appendix Tables

III DATA RELATING TO NATIONAL PARKS, NATIONAL
MONUMENTS, AND OTHER AREAS ADMINISTERED BY THE
NATIONAL PARK SERVICE

IV DATA RELATING TO WILDLIFE REFUGES

V SUMMARY DATA FOR ALL FEDERAL LANDS

LIST OF FIGURES

THE FEDERAL LANDS ❧ Their Use and Management

THE LANDS

The scenic splendors of Yellowstone, the arid lands of the Desert Game Range in Nevada, sand dunes on the Pea Island National Wildlife Refuge in North Carolina, a mountain meadow in the Deschutes National Forest in the Pacific northwest—these are typical of the contrasting nature of land types held by the federal government. Some lands were reserved from general disposal; others were purchased for particular purposes; and still others remained in public ownership when otherwise available to private owners, because of their low apparent value. Diverse as are the lands themselves, the laws governing them, even for lands generally similar as to physical characteristics and location, are often as strikingly different.

Photo by George A. Grant, courtesy of National Park Service

Photo by E. P. Haddon, courtesy of U.S. Fish and Wildlife Service

Photo by Rex G. Schmidt, courtesy of U.S. Fish and Wildlife Service

Photo by Ray M. Filloon, courtesy of U.S. Forest Service

Photo by Dan O. Todd, courtesy of U.S. Forest Service

❦
THEIR USE

Vegetation, timber, water, mineral deposits, geological formations and the like have values that suggest a variety of uses for the land on which they are found. Some tracts of land may be managed to yield satisfaction and values in ways as various as their resources. The national forests, for instance, provide opportunity for recreation, as well as for watershed management and the production of timber. In some of the forests, as in the Ozark National Forest in Arkansas, the recreational facilities are in heavy demand.

The magnificent stands of mature timber, such as the Douglas fir in Oregon, are unlikely to be duplicated again, but the harvest of this and subsequent crops of timber on federal lands, cut and manufactured by private companies and operators, contribute substantially to the timber requirements of the United States.

Courtesy of Bureau of Land Management

The surface resources of most of the land found in grazing districts are of extremely low value but do provide forage that supports thousands of head of cattle and sheep belonging to ranchers.

Sharing the range resources, within and without the game ranges specifically provided for them, are the various species of wildlife. The prong-horned antelope is an example.

Photo by E. P. Haddon, courtesy of U.S. Fish and Wildlife Service

Beneath the surface of the federal lands, mineral deposits, whether oil in Kansas or Wyoming or elsewhere . . .

Photo by Rex G. Schmidt, courtesy of U.S. Fish and Wildlife Servi

. . . or potash in New Mexico, are developed privately under lease from the federal government.

REVENUES & INVESTMENTS

Photo by Bluford W. Muir, courtesy of U.S. Department of Agriculture

The sale of timber, receipts from grazing . . .

. . . and revenues from mineral royalties and the lease of mineral lands (which have been particularly spectacular with respect to offshore lands beneath the Gulf of Mexico) totaled to over $330 million in 1956.

Courtesy of Pure Oil Company

Even greater revenues are in prospect but their attainment will require large investment outlays for timber and range management activities, particularly for forest roads.

Photo by Paul S. Bieler, courtesy of U.S. Forest Service

Introduction

FEDERALLY OWNED AND FEDERALLY ADMINIS-
tered lands are an important part of the economic
and social life of the United States. They include 24 per cent of the
nation's total land area and contribute from their resource base something like 9 per cent of the gross national product. In recent years
particularly, their use for forestry, mineral production, recreation,
and other purposes has been growing rapidly, and there is every reason
to believe that the lands will continue to increase in usefulness.

Federal lands are also important in less tangible ways. Throughout
our history they have been the testing ground for many policies. In
the first instance, debate and decision over the public lands were
important in the evolution of our particular kind of rural society
and our national character. Throughout the nation's great period
of expansion the existence of the public lands along the frontier
was a major formative influence. Later the public lands figured
prominently in the growth of the conservation movement. The concept of sustained yield management of forests, for example, was first
put to major use on the national forests. More recently, practices
on the best private forest holdings have been patterned on those
used in the national forests, and sometimes have improved on them.

The concept of retaining in permanent federal ownership land
for which, it was believed, private ownership could not achieve the
same purposes began and developed in the last quarter of the nineteenth century and the first quarter of the twentieth. The United

3

States has changed greatly since those days, no less in its methods of government administration than in its striking economic growth.

Has administration of the federal lands kept pace with the dynamics of the economy and society? Would other methods of management be better adapted to demands of the present and increasing demands of the foreseeable future? Is it possible that modern techniques of administration and management are not used as fully as they might be?

This study examines such questions from an economic viewpoint. In recent years management of the federal lands has become big business. Now is the time for a critical reconsideration of their management. Attention, consequently, is focused on the revenues the federal government receives from these lands and the use made of those revenues, and the management expenditures and investments on these lands. The larger question of the federal lands in relation to the national welfare is not dealt with directly. Nor is an attempt made to describe or analyze all the technical problems of management and of the interrelations among uses of the federal lands. The problems of management of the privately owned lands intermingled with the federal lands receive some general consideration, but only where the use and management of the privately and the federally owned lands are so closely interwoven that they cannot be considered separately.

But a number of social, political, and technical considerations are necessary to an understanding of the economic aspects of the federal lands. The present inquiry seeks to take them into account.

Thus, management problems of the federal lands and the governmental procedures by which such management problems are decided are examined when they affect the use and returns from the land. The impact of major policies and the operation of laws and regulations are described insofar as they bear upon economic issues. The technical possibilities and problems that affect the economic use and administration of the lands are considered, although for many aspects of federal land management it has been assumed that the technical problems could be met if it is desired or economic to do so. A high degree of technical competence has been built up in the federal agencies, and it is assumed that this will continue and be adequate to meet the problems that will arise.

Discussion of the economic use and management of the federal lands must be built upon some assumptions as to the role of the federal lands in relation to the role of privately owned lands. Continued growth in the population of the United States, rising per capita incomes, and an increasing demand for most kinds of natural resources have been assumed. These general assumptions of demand for resources do not mean that every increase in output from federal lands, no matter at what cost, is desirable. Rather, we have assumed that prices for merchantable outputs and demonstrated past trends for services will provide some measure of the future demand for the use of federal lands, and that the economic analysis of the management of the federal lands could be built on this basis.

A Basic Assumption: Continuation of Federal Landownership Policy

One assumption is basic to the entire study: that for an indefinite period into the future the acreage of land in federal ownership will show no major change from the present—377 million acres, excluding Indian lands which are not federally owned, and military reservations. This assumption rests on the belief that the basic policy issue as to the role of federal lands in our national economy and society has been settled, and that the people of the United States will not agree to major additions to federal land holdings nor to major disposition of them.

It is necessary to define the word "major" in this connection. Net changes in total acreage of the magnitude of 5 million, 10 million, or possibly even 25 million acres are not excluded. Even the latter is only 5 per cent of the area of all federal lands (excluding military lands). This is not considered "major." The basic assumption does not preclude transfer of specific tracts of land from federal to private ownership, nor acquisition by the federal government of other specific tracts by sale, purchase, or exchange. Neither does it exclude transfer of specific tracts of land from one type of federal land management unit to another—from national forest to national park, from grazing district to national forest or the reverse, or any other change in designation of the federal area. In other words, we are assuming that the net acreage of federal land holdings will not change greatly for many years, if ever, and that at least 95 per cent of the land now in federal ownership will remain there and in unchanged status.[1]

---

[1] The possibility of federal purchase of farm lands as a means of coping with the farm problem may exist; it has not been included in our assumption.

This assumption is based upon our analysis of events of the past thirty years. During this period there has never been in the numerous official and semiofficial studies, commission reports, and other documents relating to federal lands, a serious suggestion that any major part of national park or national forest land should be passed to private ownership. And in only a few instances have any private groups made such proposals. Several proposals to turn public domain lands to state or private ownership have been made, but these have each aroused so much opposition that they have been rejected. Such an effort was made in 1931 by a commission appointed by President Hoover. The commission proposed to grant the lands, after reserving the mineral rights, to any state choosing to take them. Although bills to implement this were introduced, opposition was so great they were never reported out of committee. Again in 1947 bills were introduced providing for the sale of grazing lands within and outside of grazing districts and within national forests to livestock men under new terms and a new formula. But the bills died as a result of violent opposition from many quarters. As recently as 1953 bills were introduced to provide different legal authorization for grazing, especially on national forests. They failed of passage because they were alleged to be the first step in actual transfer of the lands from public to private ownership.

A rather minor, but recent, instance is also indicative of Congressional attitude toward the disposal of federal land. Bills were introduced in the 83rd Congress to authorize the sale by the Forest Service of certain scattered parcels of national forest lands that lay at some distance from the bulk of other national forest lands, and as a result could not be administered efficiently.[2] The Department of Agriculture submitted somewhat different bills to the same end. As S. 1079 of the 84th Congress, the latter passed the Senate and, with some amendments, was reported on favorably by the House Committee on Agriculture and Forestry. But when twice brought up for House action in the summer of 1956, various Congressmen objected to its passage and the bill was stricken from the Consent Calendar. Several members of the Congress, who may reflect the attitude of some conservation groups, object to the disposal of *any* national forest land. Thus it would seem that prospects for ultimate passage of a similar measure are not bright.

The Department of Agriculture also proposed a program for dis-

---

[2] H. R. 2725 and H. R. 2105, 83rd Congress.

position to states, private nonprofit groups, and individuals, of the Land Utilization lands (those purchased during the depression of the 1930's because they were judged submarginal).[3] This proposal has not yet received favorable action and, again because of the general sentiment against federal land disposal, is not likely to be acted upon favorably at any time. On the other hand, Public Laws 447, 846, and 891 of the 84th Congress did provide for abolishment of three national monuments in South Carolina, North Dakota, and South Dakota. It appears that a certain part of the public is opposed to disposition of federal land, except for state or nonprofit association ownership, and is able to make its opposition effective.

We recognize there is a body of opinion favoring large-scale disposal of federal lands, especially of the remaining public domain. We also recognize the argument that in some respects the present policy is irrational: it is not always possible to achieve desired objectives through federal ownership; other means of attaining these goals may be equally or more effective. We doubt, however, if those who hold these views will have much success in changing the attitude of the supporters of federal ownership. The vigor with which proposals interpreted as disposing of federal lands or weakening control in their management have been fought is a convincing expression of popular will. The issue has been decided, and further discussion is fruitless so long as this attitude remains. The minority opinion, however, may well prevent substantial increases to federally owned land. Popular support for additional land is vastly less than for retention of the land now owned.

Thus in our opinion the real problem for the future is development and management of substantially the existing area of federal lands, rather than a consideration of large-scale disposal or acquisition.

Appropriate Goals for Federal Land Management

What are the most appropriate goals for management of the federal lands? If all products and uses of the federal lands were of a type to which price or other monetary expression might readily be given,

[3] H. R. 5088, 84th Congress.

then one goal might be maximization of their contributions to the national product. For example, the contribution of grazing or timber production from national forests or grazing districts could be measured to take into account the value of these products. For grazing, an accurate measurement would apply a commercial price rather than the existing fees which are generally agreed to be below the commercial rental level. From these estimates of gross output, the value of inputs from other sectors, such as machinery purchased, etc., would have to be deducted. But these deductions would not ordinarily include the cost of labor used in the administration of the lands. Labor cost would remain as part of the gross output of this sector of the economy.

However, serious problems arise when we consider, on such a basis, those products from the federal lands for which there is no normal price association. Recreation is one of these. Most recreational use of federal lands is free or is available for a nominal fee. It would be extremely difficult to estimate its market price. Further problems arise when we consider the watershed values of federal lands. Can we accurately estimate the effect of federal land management on water supply? How can the values of water be assessed at the point of origin when they are usually included in products produced elsewhere? Wildlife on the federal lands presents yet another problem. Its value is not commercial and to put a monetary measure on it would be difficult. In addition to these separate problems, there is the overriding one that the values of these various items are not usually included in national income accounting; to do so for the federal lands would introduce some confusion of concepts.

Perhaps a better general goal is maximization of the public welfare, insofar as the federal lands can affect such welfare. This would involve, for salable products, getting the most out of their contribution to the national product and, for nonsalable products, making them as fully available as is compatible with cost. A major complication arises when maximization of the national product from salable resources conflicts with maximization of the availability of other resources.

One goal in management of federal lands should be economy. This involves such considerations as maximum output per man through better organization of work, labor-saving devices, and the like; the most economical and efficient use of machinery; and other cost factors. This is an old and familiar matter of efficiency in operations. Regardless of the intensity of management of the federal lands, which might be decided upon various grounds, efficiency to obtain the desired results at minimum cost is desirable.

On those aspects of federal land management which produce salable products it should ordinarily be desirable to apply another test of economic efficiency—the use of labor and other inputs up to the point where marginal or additional revenues are barely sufficient to meet marginal costs. If gains from tree pruning, or forest replanting, or range reseeding, or any other federal land management practices are more than enough to pay the full costs of the practice, then economic analysis would indicate that such a practice is desirable. But, as will be shown later, there are serious obstacles to the application of this test on the federal lands. Gross national product will be increased as long as returns to marginal expenditure on the federal lands are greater than returns to marginal expenditure on other lands, or elsewhere in the economy.

Unfortunately, it is not possible readily to apply the test of marginal revenue equalling marginal cost to those products or services of the federal land which are not ordinarily salable, simply because there is no easily determined price or value for them, or perhaps no price or value that could be determined in any way. There often will be good reasons why investments or current inputs of labor and machinery should be greater on federal land than on privately owned land. In some cases it may be appropriate to use a lower interest rate for discounting to present value the amount of future additions to income from federal land. In other cases the value of goods and services which cannot be readily valued on a market basis may be considered so important by officials and the public as to warrant expenditures which economic analysis would not justify for privately held lands. Decisions of this kind are often debatable, but a greater investment would often be defensible. In general, it is safe to say that investment and expenditure for current operation should not be less than the usual private accounting of marginal cost and marginal revenue would indicate, unless it can be shown that this intensity of management to produce salable products would be harmful to the production of other benefits and values. That is, ordinarily management should be carried to the intensity that calculations and considerations of private business would indicate, often a good deal farther, and only rarely to a lower intensity of management. As will be shown later, in practice this general principle is often difficult to apply.

The federal lands produce large revenues to the federal govern-

ment from the sale of timber, oil royalties, etc.; but maximization of
these revenues does not seem an appropriate primary goal in the
management of the federal lands. The federal government is a landowner in a proprietary as well as in a governmental sense; if its interests as a land proprietor were dominant, then it might seek
maximum revenue from the products and uses of its land. Even here,
as an enlightened landowner, it should seek maximum income over
a long period of time rather than on a short-run basis. But the federal government's interest in management of its lands is basically
more that of a government concerned with the people's welfare;
its interest as a landowner in a proprietary sense should be, and
generally has been, subordinated to its general governmental responsibilities. This has often meant greater consideration than an enlightened private owner would give to those products or uses of federal land which do not yield salable products. It may mean
subordination of its interest to that of owners of private land, or
subsidies of various kinds. For these and perhaps for other reasons,
the federal government has not sought, and often should not seek,
to maximize revenue from its lands.

But, to the extent that other conscious objectives of federal land
management are not interfered with, attainment of maximum or near
maximum revenues from federal land would seem to be a reasonable
objective. In the nature of things, the use of the federal land is
available to some citizens and not to others; this is especially true
for those uses which produce salable products. Those who enjoy the
gains from federal land use should pay a reasonable price for that
use. Such payment on their part is equitable inasmuch as their competitors must bear the cost of similar resources from private land;
and it is also equitable because the general public must appropriate
funds for the management of the federal lands. Within some limits,
and to the extent it does not conflict with other more important objectives of federal land management, maximization of revenues from
federal lands seems an appropriate goal.

Types of Federal Land

Of the several different types of federal land—national forests,
national parks, grazing districts, and others—all are subject to certain

general laws. An additional body of special laws exists relating to each type. These have been built up over a considerable period of years and reflect the interest, pressures, and objectives of the time when they were passed or modified. As long as land stays in a particular category it is subject to the laws and regulations relating to that category. Land can be shifted from one category to another, by Presidential order in some cases, but only by legislation in others. For example, the President can transfer land from public domain to national monument status. In some states he can transfer from public domain to national forest status. Under the Taylor Grazing Act, he can transfer land from national forest to grazing district status. But national parks can be created only by Congressional action. The fact that lands, after transfer, are subject to a different set of laws and regulations, and hence that different classes of users are affected differently, is often a bar to their transfer even beyond the complexities of the legal process.

It would have been desirable to study each type of federal land separately in order to obtain the most satisfactory picture of its use and management. To some extent this has been done, but mostly for groups of types of federal land rather than for individual types. For instance, funds for insect control work, on both national forest lands and other federal lands, have been included in the data and discussion for national forests. Accounting and budgetary systems frequently inhibit consideration of types of federal land apart from the work of the federal agency primarily responsible for their management. The administration of the grazing districts, of the public domain outside of the grazing districts, and of the revested and reconveyed Oregon and California railroad grant lands, for instance, is so intertwined and intermingled in the total operations of the Bureau of Land Management that it would be unrealistic to present all the data and discussion for each type of land separately. A similar consideration holds as to national parks, national monuments, and the other units of the national park system. Thus it has been necessary to consider all the lands under the jurisdiction of the Bureau of Land Management as one unit of federal land administration, all the lands under the National Park Service as another, and so on. As far as possible, all significant data and matters relating to each group of federal lands have been considered in the discussion relating primarily to that group. But there are exceptions. Leasing of minerals on lands not primarily under the jurisdiction of the Bureau of Land Management, for instance, has been considered in the discussion of

that agency because it would be impractical and unrealistic to separate this leasing from other mineral leasing.

We definitely do not try to consider the full scope of activities of
each of the federal agencies, but only its management activities
on federal land. Each of the agencies has some responsibilities other
than federal land management—for some agencies, these are relatively minor, for others they are major. Considerable attention is
given to the work of five federal agencies—the Forest Service of the
Department of Agriculture, the National Park Service, the Bureau
of Land Management, the Fish and Wildlife Service, and the Geological Survey of the Department of the Interior—and some attention to the work of other agencies. Of these, the National Park
Service and the Bureau of Land Management have only relatively
minor responsibilities in addition to land management. Under the
Recreation Act of 1936 [4] the National Park Service is authorized to
make comprehensive recreation planning studies in co-operation with
the states. The Bureau of Land Management has certain cadastral
survey and land title record functions that apply to all lands, not
merely to those now under its jurisdiction. The Forest Service has three
major functions: the administration of the national forests, research,
and co-operative activities with states, especially on fire control. The
Fish and Wildlife Service through fiscal 1956 had important functions to do with commercial fisheries, research, and enforcement of
certain game laws, as well as with land management. The Geological
Survey is primarily concerned with topographic mapping and hydro-
logical and geological studies but its Conservation Division is concerned with operations of the Mineral Leasing Act.

A full consideration of all the functions of these federal agencies
would lead this study too far afield from its central purpose. At the
same time it is not possible to ignore these other activities. Some
attention will be paid to them in the discussion of future alternatives
in chapter six. Certain of the data, especially those on expenditures,
may not relate solely to the land management function of an agency,
but may also include parts of other functions. In the complex operations of a large federal bureau where programs are often closely
interconnected, it may be impossible to eliminate all traces of a secondary activity from data relating to another. However, the authors
believe these overlaps to be minimal.

[4] 49 Stat. 1894.

Federal Land Defined

A variety of terms have been built up applying to the lands owned by the federal government, the meanings of which are not fully agreed upon by all workers; neither is common usage consistent.[5] The origin of some of the more generally used of these terms is explained in the next chapter, but at this point it may be useful to identify briefly the lands that will be considered throughout the book.

As used here, "federal land" includes substantially all nonurban land, title to which is held by the federal government and for which the main purpose of ownership is the management of natural resources. This definition obviously excludes such urban land as post office and other building sites. It also excludes land owned by Indians, whether in reservations or elsewhere and whether owned individually or tribally. These lands are managed to a considerable degree by the federal government but they are held in trust for the Indians who own them and are not owned by the federal government. Moreover, at least theoretically, their management is not solely in the hands of the federal government, but is subject to approval by the Indians. This definition also excludes military reservations of all kinds, since even though they contain substantial areas of land and considerable resources, the primary purpose of federal ownership in such cases is not resource management but national defense. Some miscellaneous small areas of land also are excluded, either because they are in the hands of agencies other than the major land managing agencies or because they have various special features.

In the case of Alaska no detailed treatment is included. To do so would involve a full-scale study of the special conditions relating to the territory. While nearly all the land in Alaska is federally owned, situations exist there that are at variance with those in the United States. Physical conditions, particularly climatic conditions, are different; the territory's economy does not rest upon use of large areas of land in the same sense as does the economy of the States, but access to water and to mineral deposits is most important. There is a considerable body of federal land law that applies only to Alaska. In some instances, however, pertinent data for the territory are included in the data on types of land available from federal land management

[5] Peffer, E. Louise, *The Closing of the Public Domain*, Stanford: Stanford University Press, 1951, especially references p. 5.

agencies; to this limited extent, Alaska is included among the lands considered in this study.

The lands of the continental United States that are the main sub-ject of this study account for 80 per cent of all federally owned or federally administered land (including Indian land and military reservations) of nonurban character, and an almost equally high per-centage of the area of all federally owned or federally administered land, urban and nonurban alike, since the area (but not necessarily the value) of federal urban land is small compared with the area of nonurban land. If Indian and military lands are excluded, the lands dealt with here account for nearly 97 per cent of all federally owned nonurban land.

The Legal Background

Federal law dealing with the public lands tends to be quite par-ticularized. Not only are there a large number of private laws re-lating to individual tracts and persons, but many of the more gen-erally applicable laws have been drawn with specific problems and situations in view. Consequently, some attention to the background of laws and regulations is necessary to a broad understanding of a great many problems of federal land management.

Even a brief survey of the large body of law and administrative regulations governing use of the public lands is well beyond the scope of this study, but some discussion of the legal background and iden-tification of the most important laws are essential. These are to be found in Appendix A. There are, of course, many additional refer-ences in the course of the text to particular laws and how they have worked.

CHAPTER ONE

Federal Lands

in American Society,

Past and Present

THE FEDERAL GOVERNMENT OF THE UNITED States is and always has been the largest proprietor of land in the nation. A mixture of government and private ownership of land has characterized the American economy from the beginning. Federal holdings have been predominantly of rural and noncrop land; they have been especially large for forested and grazing land and for certain types of waste land such as deserts. Large-scale federal ownership of land has not been in major conflict with the dominant ideology of private enterprise, for the federal lands have been used by private individuals and businesses and the products of the federal lands have been harvested and transformed into economic output through private efforts.

Federal lands have certain rather special characteristics, not only as to their physical features, but also in that they have often served as a mirror of the goals and ideals of the nation. Before considering the uses and management problems of these lands, it is useful to review their background, both historical and current. Several aspects of federal land management are understandable only against the background of their particular history; several situations that today

appear illogical have a history which at least accounts for their origin
if it does not explain their rationale.

The Origin of Federal Landownership [1]

It has been usual to identify the major eras of federal landownership as four: "acquisition," "disposal," "reservation," and "management." The first three referred to historical phases, the fourth spanned
the immediate past with the present and foreseeable future. But in
recent years the nature of the federal land management job has
changed and bids fair to change still further as time goes on. The kind
of management given the federal lands in most of the past fifty years or
so is very different from that given them today and foreshadowed for
tomorrow. The former was in the nature of custodial management;
the latter might best be termed intensive management. And so in
figure 1 and throughout this book, the eras of federal landownership
are designated as five: "acquisition," "disposal," "reservation," "custodial management," and "intensive management."

These periods, naturally, do not have sharply defined beginnings

---

[1] This section presents in brief, simplified form the complicated history of the
federal lands in the United States. Readers who are interested in greater detail
are referred to studies dealing specifically with this subject. In addition to the
following books, others mentioned in their pages will be found useful.

Cameron, Jenks, *The Development of Governmental Forest Control in the United
States*. Baltimore: Johns Hopkins Press, 1928.

Clawson, Marion. *Uncle Sam's Acres*. New York: Dodd, Mead & Co., 1951.

Dana, Samuel T. *Forest and Range Policy—Its Development in the United States*.
New York: McGraw-Hill Book Co., 1956.

Hibbard, Benjamin H. *A History of Public Land Policies*. New York: Macmillan
Co., 1924.

Ise, John. *The United States Forest Policy*. New Haven: Yale University Press,
1920.

Peffer, E. Louise. *The Closing of the Public Domain*. Stanford: Stanford University Press, 1951.

Pinchot, Gifford. *Breaking New Ground*. New York: Harcourt Brace & Co., 1947.

Robbins, Roy M. *Our Landed Heritage*. Princeton: Princeton University Press,
1942.

Stegner, Wallace. *Beyond the Hundredth Meridian*. Boston: Houghton Mifflin
Co., 1954.

Webb, Walter P. *The Great Plains*. Boston and New York: Ginn & Co., 1931.

and endings; some overlap considerably. Within each major era of federal land history there have been minor periods when trends characteristic of earlier or later eras have accompanied the dominant trends of the era. But the major forces and nature of the federal land problem differ so greatly between one period and another as to provide a reasonably firm basis for division of the long flow of history into parts.

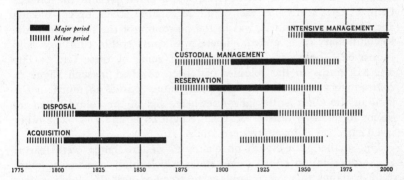

FIGURE 1. *Chart of major eras in federal landownership and land management in the United States, 1800-2000.*

In the first period the problem was to acquire for the United States the central band of the North American continent before any other power could acquire it. In the second period the chief concern was to get federal land into the hands of the nation's citizens without too much regard for process or results. A reaction against the abuses of these disposal practices led to the reservation of extensive areas of federal land for continued federal ownership and ushered in the third period. But lands cannot be merely reserved; they must be managed in some degree—protected against fire and trespass at the minimum. Such caretaking activities characterized the next era. Now, a rapidly developing national economy requires the full output of federal as well as of private lands, thus requiring a much more intensive management—the new era. Although the history is much more complicated than these one-sentence characterizations suggest, the essence of the federal land management problem clearly has changed greatly from era to era.

PERIOD OF ACQUISITION

The period of acquisition of the federal lands began even before the formation of the Union and continued until 1867 when Alaska was purchased from Russia. Nearly 76 per cent of the land within the continental United States has been or is still part of the public domain. The last major purchase within continental boundaries came in 1853.

Land claims of original thirteen states. That part of the present United States which lies east of the Mississippi River, except Florida and certain minor tracts, was in the possession of the states when the Revolutionary War ended. There was considerable confusion and controversy, however, as to who owned some of these lands. The original grants to the colonies had been couched in such vague or contradictory terms that overlapping claims existed to much of the land in the Ohio Valley and elsewhere. Six of the colonies had no claims to territory outside of their recognized boundaries. The other seven each had claims to western lands.

The smaller states, with no claims to western lands, were fearful of the domination of the larger states which might grow even larger if their claims to western lands were accepted. Finally, for a variety of reasons, the states with western land claims ceded their claims to the Confederation. New York ceded her claims to western lands as early as 1781, and Georgia was the last in 1802. Some of the states reserved certain lands to meet the grants that they had made to their soldiers, or received certain indemnity payments from the common funds. But a substantial public domain had been created.

Political and policy issues arose at once, and two important decisions were made which were to have an important effect upon the form of American government and daily life. First, the Ordinances of 1785 and 1787 provided that the territory would ultimately be divided into new states on an equal basis with the older ones. Thus any idea of a colonial or provincial government was rejected. Second, provision was made for the granting of a part of the land in support of common schools, thus giving a powerful boost to universal free education.

Louisiana Purchase. In 1803 President Jefferson agreed to buy the Louisiana territory from France for $15 million, thus acquiring an immense new area and free use of the Mississippi to its mouth. This one purchase almost doubled the area of the United States and includes today some of the best farm and other lands of the country.

Florida Purchase. A second purchase was made in 1819 when Spain ceded her claims to Florida for about $6 million. Although this worked out to a price per acre about three times what was paid for the Louisiana Purchase, the higher price reflected not better land, but chiefly a desire to clear the eastern half of the country of foreign powers.

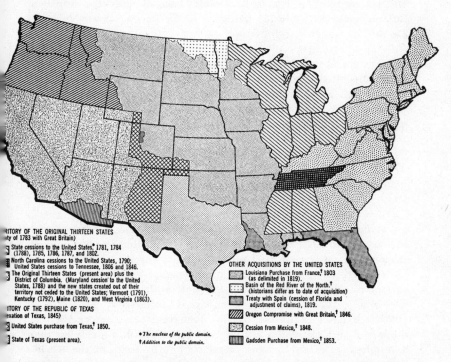

RITORY OF THE ORIGINAL THIRTEEN STATES
ty of 1783 with Great Britain)

State cessions to the United States, 1781, 1784 (1788), 1785, 1786, 1787, and 1802.

North Carolina cessions to the United States, 1790; United States cessions to Tennessee, 1806 and 1846.

The Original Thirteen States (present area) plus the District of Columbia. (Maryland cession to the United States, 1788) and the new states created out of their territory not ceded to the United States; Vermont (1791), Kentucky (1792), Maine (1820), and West Virginia (1863).

RITORY OF THE REPUBLIC OF TEXAS
exation of Texas, 1845)

United States purchase from Texas, 1850.

State of Texas (present area).

* *The nucleus of the public domain.*
† *Addition to the public domain.*

OTHER ACQUISITIONS BY THE UNITED STATES

Louisiana Purchase from France, 1803 (as delimited in 1819).

Basin of the Red River of the North. † (historians differ as to date of acquisition)

Treaty with Spain (cession of Florida and adjustment of claims), 1819.

Oregon Compromise with Great Britain, † 1846.

Cession from Mexico, † 1848.

Gadsden Purchase from Mexico, † 1853.

FIGURE 2. *Acquisition of the territory of the United States and origin of the public domain, exclusive of Alaska and island possessions.*

Texas. The next major acquisition of territory was the annexation of Texas. Following some American settlement in Texas, the Texans revolted from Mexico and won their independence in 1836. The controversy over slavery delayed her annexation until 1845. When it did occur, her land remained her own. Thus there never has been federal public domain in Texas. In this respect Texas resembles the original thirteen states, rather than the states created out of purchased or other acquired territory. There was some doubt about the exact boundaries of Texas, and in 1850 she ceded a substantial area to the west and north of her present boundaries for a price of $15 million. This land became United States property and was public domain.

Treaty with Mexico. Failure to agree upon boundary lines and resentment over the war with Texas led the United States to go to war with Mexico in 1846. In the peace treaty of 1848 the United States acquired the Pacific Southwest, from roughly the center of Colorado and New Mexico westward to the Pacific. A total price of $16 million was paid to Mexico.

Pacific Northwest. At a slightly earlier date, in 1846, the Pacific Northwest was annexed to the United States following prolonged and somewhat bitter negotiations with Great Britain. Both countries claimed the area, basing their claims upon earlier discovery and settlement. At one time war was threatened, but the issues were settled by negotiation and mediation.

Gadsden Purchase. The last purchase in the present area of the United States was the Gadsden Purchase, in 1853, for $10 million. This is a fairly large tract along the southern side of Arizona, valued in part because it contained what was then believed to be the most feasible route for a railroad to the Pacific Coast.

Other acquisitions. The purchase of Alaska in 1867 from Russia, for about $7 million, was the last major purchase of territory which has been considered part of the original public domain and to which the public land laws of the United States have applied. Later acquisitions of territory, in the sense of governmental jurisdiction, as in the case of Hawaii and other areas, did not result in their inclusion as part of the public domain in the sense used in this book.

Perhaps never in history has so much valuable territory been acquired for so little money and so little blood. Within much less than a hundred years an immense area, containing some of the world's best farmland, many rich oil lands, and much mineral wealth was acquired for the people of the United States!

Two additional points must be made about these land acquisitions. First, in each of the areas acquired some land was already privately owned or claimed under the laws of the previous government. All clearly established ownerships and all legitimate claims were recognized, together with many claims that were shady or perhaps even fraudulent; only the remainder of the land became public domain, subject to disposition under the land laws. Second, although purchases were made from or treaties made with foreign powers, the land was in fact the home of American Indians, lived on by them

TABLE 1. *Summary of Origin of Original Public Domain* [1]

Land	Date of acquisition	Total area (land and water)	
		million acres	*% of U.S. total*
Original public domain:			
Cessions by original states	1781–1802	237	12.2
Louisiana Purchase [2]	1803	560	28.9
Florida Purchase	1819	46	2.4
Oregon Compromise	1846	183	9.4
Mexican Treaty	1848	339	17.5
Purchase from Texas	1850	79	4.1
Gadsden Purchase	1853	19	1.0
Subtotal		1,462	75.5
Never public domain:			
Original states [3]		305	15.7
Texas		170	8.8
Subtotal		475	24.5
Total area of United States		1,937	100.0
Alaska	1867	375	

[1] These data relate to the origin of the original public domain; they should not be confused with means whereby the United States acquired territory in a governmental sense. For instance, by treaty with Great Britain in 1783, the states acquired their independence and also all the territory listed here as part of the original states and as ceded by them to the national government. Likewise, by annexation of Texas, all the land now within Texas and within the purchase from Texas was acquired as territory.

[2] Including Red River Basin of North.

[3] Includes area within states later created out of territory of original states. See figure 2.

and claimed by them. Following each of the major acquisitions of territory, treaties had to be entered into with the Indians. Indian concepts of landownership differed greatly from the white man's, and out of this difference arose many misunderstandings and tragedies. The Indians were pushed out of their original homes, mostly westward, and gradually were confined to reservations, the areas of which were sharply reduced from time to time. Substantial sums were paid the Indians, and in very recent times lawsuits have enabled some of the Indians to obtain large additional sums. It is impossible to estimate the total sum paid to the Indians for their interests in the land. It certainly exceeds many times the amount paid to the foreign powers, and further even larger payments seem probable.

National policy in the early days of our country revolved around land to a degree not readily appreciable now. Lawmakers and officials were critically concerned over the territorial acquisitions. They recognized that the use made of this land would markedly influence the nature of the country. Policies with regard to the establishment of new states and the encouragement of schools have already been mentioned. The concept of public land as the basis for an agrarian democracy was rather widely held. After all, one of the major motives bringing people to the new country was to acquire land—to escape the landed estates and the systems of land inheritance in the old country which had made landownership so difficult for the masses. The economic and political significance of the new lands was fully appreciated. There were some differences of opinion, of course, and the divergence between Hamilton, who viewed the public lands as a means of raising revenue and thus of supporting the national currency, and Jefferson, who viewed them primarily as a place of settlement for people lacking capital, has often been described.

There was a great popular hunger for land in those days, and an immense supply of the new public domain and of land belonging to the states, as well as of land acquired earlier in large private grants.

Although the term "public domain" has at times been applied to any publicly owned land, its most common use in the United States for many years was to describe the lands acquired by the nation in the various ways outlined above. Later, when tracts of public domain were exchanged for tracts of privately owned lands, the land acquired in exchange was usually considered as public domain also, and the laws applicable to public domain extended to it. As that part of the public domain which remained in federal ownership was gradually split up into special land management categories, such as national forests and national parks, the term "public domain" came to mean the unreserved and unappropriated parts, and the term "original public domain" came to be applied to the areas acquired by the United States from other countries.

ERA OF DISPOSAL

Disposal of the federal lands began even before the first stage of their acquisition—the cession of claims by the states—was completed. The various colonies had given land to settlers upon the frontier, both as a means of expansion and as a buffer against Indian attacks, and the new Confederation and Union gave land as rewards and payment to its soldiers. Almost immediately, land was offered for sale by the new nation. Although serious policy debates had preceded this action, and although those who advocated the sales of land entertained high hopes of the revenues that would be forthcoming, in general federal land sales were small in the early years of our national history. They completely failed to meet the early revenue needs of the new country; indeed, they were virtually nil until after 1800 and income from land sales did not reach 10 per cent of total federal revenues until 1814, by which time the worst financial stringency was over.

From the beginning there was a constant struggle as to the place where land was to be sold, the size of tracts, and the terms of sale. The settlers favored sale in cities relatively near the land itself and the speculators favored sale in larger cities. On the minimum unit of sale, settlers wanted small areas and speculators wanted larger ones. As to the terms of sale, the settlers sought low prices, low down payments, and easy credit to a greater degree than did the speculators. The terms of sale gradually shifted in favor of the settlers and increasing assistance was given to promote the actual settlement of the land, first through pre-emption acts which gave the occupant various advantages, and in later years through the Homestead Law and its various extensions and ramifications.

During the more than a century that disposal was a major objective of federal land management, many different laws were enacted providing for various means of disposal. It has sometimes been said that there are five thousand land laws. There are indeed a relatively large number of land disposal laws, but the great majority of them are private land measures in the sense that each relates to a specific tract of land. But there are perhaps a hundred or more land laws of more or less general applicability still upon the statute books, the chief of which are described very briefly in Appendix A. The applicability of some laws, such as the Homestead Act, is now greatly reduced because land suited to its provisions has become scarce.

One measure taken at the beginning of the land disposal era has left its mark on all the land included in the original public domain. That was the system of rectangular land survey. It provided a ready means of identification and description of land, which is basic to most land titles today. At the same time it imposed rigid boundaries which often did not fit topographic and other natural features—a square survey for a rounded countryside, it has been described. Ownership boundaries today generally coincide with the original land survey lines and sometimes seriously complicate the control of erosion and the attainment of good land use.

The net area of public domain rose to a peak in 1850, with acquisitions of territory exceeding disposals up to that time. Thereafter,

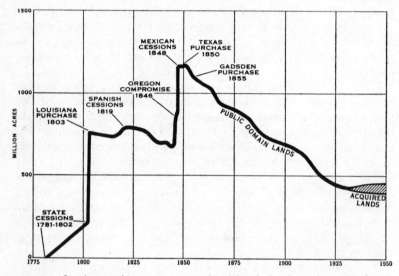

FIGURE 3. *Approximate area of federal lands in the states, 1781-1950, with dates of important acquisitions. The areas of "acquired land" prior to 1930 were too small to appear on the scale used.*

the area of public domain declined steadily, although land acquisitions in recent years have increased the total area of federal lands.

Land disposal selective in character. The process of land disposal permitted individuals to exercise a high degree of selection. Given the transportation and other conditions of the time, and the knowledge of the settlers, each settler chose the land he thought best suited to his needs. Although efforts were made by the government to keep settlement within the bounds of the surveyed areas, they were largely unsuccessful, and settlers spread onto the frontier much as their judgment and tastes dictated. At any given time a would-be settler could choose between less attractive land relatively close to a settlement and better land in more remote parts. Judged by present conditions and present knowledge, some settlers made mistakes, but at the time the land they chose looked like the best. This highly selective land disposal system, over which the federal government had virtually no control, left the federal lands at any date in patterns not ideal for good land management. Generally, the higher and more distant mountain areas were not taken, so that much of them could later be set aside in relatively solid tracts as national forests and national parks. But even these lands often contained enclaves of private property, and other types of federal land often were more notable for their "holes" than for the land that was in federal ownership. As long as ultimate disposal was the objective of federal land management, the scattered nature of the federal lands was relatively unimportant, since in time the remaining tracts would also go into private ownership. But once continued federal ownership and management became the objective, this pattern of federal holdings was a serious obstacle to efficient land management.

Grants to states and railroads. Disposal of public domain to individuals through sale or by homesteading was by no means the only method of disposal used by the federal government. Grants of land were made for many purposes. Most of the grants were made to the states (either for such public purposes as common schools, agricultural colleges, hospitals, etc., or in the naive hope that the states would reclaim swamp and other land) and to railroads and other transportation companies. With so much land to be settled and with so great a need of transportation facilities, it was only natural that the nation should seek to encourage railroad construction by means of land grants to railroad builders.

Disposal of minerals. Disposing of mineral land or of minerals from the federal land has involved several special features not found for other types of land. After an initial and unsatisfactory experience in trying to provide for extraction of minerals under lease by the federal government, provision was made in 1866 for the mining laws under which miners could obtain title to metal-bearing land. In general, the area of land taken under the mining laws has been small compared with that taken under the various agricultural land laws, but some of these areas have been highly important and have produced large incomes.

In 1920 the Mineral Leasing Act was passed, applying particularly to petroleum and other nonmetallic minerals. Under this act, title to the surface of the land remained in the federal government and use was often made of the surface for other purposes, but the minerals were extracted under lease. This was disposal not of land, but of certain of its products and of a certain part of it. Somewhat of a companion to this exists in the authority to dispose of the surface rights of certain lands for agricultural purposes, while retaining title to the subsurface minerals. These minerals may then be extracted by other private persons holding leases from the government.

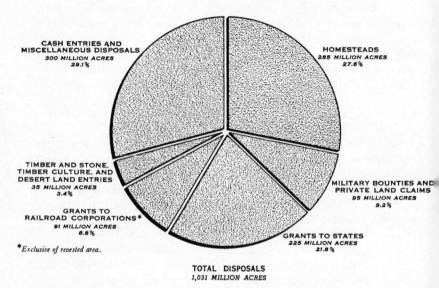

CASH ENTRIES AND
MISCELLANEOUS DISPOSALS
300 MILLION ACRES
29.1%

HOMESTEADS
285 MILLION ACRES
27.6%

TIMBER AND STONE,
TIMBER CULTURE, AND
DESERT LAND ENTRIES
35 MILLION ACRES
3.4%

GRANTS TO
RAILROAD CORPORATIONS*
91 MILLION ACRES
8.8%

Exclusive of revested area.

MILITARY BOUNTIES AND
PRIVATE LAND CLAIMS
95 MILLION ACRES
9.2%

GRANTS TO STATES
225 MILLION ACRES
21.8%

TOTAL DISPOSALS
1,031 MILLION ACRES

FIGURE 4. *Approximate area of the public domain disposed of under the public land laws.*

Emergence of a new era. The processes described above were largely indiscriminate and were certainly headlong. Much land was disposed of in the first half of the nineteenth century, and in the latter half the process was accelerated. Very little concern was given to physical characteristics and suitability for private uses. It was assumed that the whole purpose was to transfer the ownership of these lands from public to private hands, but not much attention was paid to the kind of private ownership that resulted. Fraud and trespass, even with the extremely lenient land laws prevailing, were common. Perhaps never in history has so much really good land, as well as much that was inferior, been available to the common man on terms he could meet. The opportunity was seized to the full.

Concern grew throughout the nineteenth century that the land disposal practices were not working as well as had been hoped. Even earlier many leaders had deplored the cycle of clearing land, cultivating it until it was exhausted, abandoning it, and moving, usually westward, to clear new land. But the process had been on a relatively small scale until the nineteenth century. Then vast areas of lands were cleared, forests were cut in ways not conducive to their regrowth, fire was rampant in the woods, and the plains began to be plowed in areas where they should not have been. The census of 1880, which first obtained information on farm tenancy, shocked the nation by showing that the ideal of the independent landowner tilling the soil he owned had not been achieved to the extent that had been fondly hoped. One-fourth of all farmers were tenants, even in this period of generally free public domain.

In 1877 Carl Schurz, Secretary of the Interior, proposed a system of landownership under which permanent forests would remain in public hands with the timber harvested by private persons. Congress established a public land commission in 1879, and its report a year later was monumental. It urged repeal of many of the least suitable land laws, a system of classification of public land and selective disposal suited to the character of the land, and other reforms, few of which were adopted. The American Forestry Association and the American Association for the Advancement of Science, each of which had studied the problem, made suggestions for better administration of these lands. Several other studies and reports were made, generally less well known and less influential. But the general public was quiescent, as yet unaware or unconcerned with the waste and disposal of public land.

THE ERA OF RESERVATION

The next major stage in the history of the federal lands, the reservation era, emerged from a growing concern over the land disposal process and its consequences. The first major reservation had taken place in 1872, when Yellowstone National Park was set aside by special Act of Congress to serve as "a public park or pleasuring ground for the benefit and enjoyment of the people." Significant as this reservation was in breaking with the tradition of unrestricted land disposal, it was not part of a system of federal land reservations and for many years the area was not managed in any way. In fact, because of its isolation and the difficulties of travel, little use was made of it. The beginning of a system of federal land reservation came nineteen years later in 1891, when the forest reserves—now the national forests—were authorized. The act which authorized the President to reserve land for this purpose dealt with general land matters. The provision pertaining to the forest reserves was added at the last minute, when the bill was in conference. The bill was passed in the closing days of the Congress on an oral presentation of its terms, no printed version being available. It is highly doubtful if the Congress knew what it had done. Certainly the public did not; still less was there general public understanding and support. This was the humble beginning of one of the most important land administration measures ever undertaken in the United States.

By the time he left office in early 1893, President Harrison had withdrawn some 13 million acres for national forest purposes, but no funds had been available for even their most elemental administration. Fires raged until they burned themselves out and trespassers took what they wished. President Cleveland strove to get the necessary appropriations and made only moderate additional withdrawals until near the end of his administration when, largely at the recommendation of a group of eminent scientists, he established thirteen additional forests. His action took the country by surprise and aroused a good deal of criticism. The basic act providing for the administration of the forests was passed in 1897 after much debate and serious consideration. In some ways this act marks the real beginning of the national forest system; certainly the whole idea now was supported by popular knowledge and understanding in a way that it had not been ten years earlier.

The major growth of the national forest system occurred under President Theodore Roosevelt, largely under the intellectual leadership of Gifford Pinchot. In 1905, 33 million acres were added to the forests, almost doubling the area previously in existence; another 30 million acres were added in 1906. These withdrawals aroused so much opposition that an act was passed prohibiting additional withdrawals in many states without specific Congressional approval. Roosevelt signed the bill, but first—rumor says on the same day—he established twenty-one additional forests. Although this aroused a storm of criticism the withdrawals remained, partly because by that time popular support for the national forest system had become widespread.

The reservation process was, in its way, nearly as selective as the disposal process. That is, individuals and corporations throughout the disposal era had selected for private ownership the best lands available to them within the limits of their knowledge. So the federal agencies, the President, and the Congress selected for permanent federal management the best lands available to them, given the characteristics of the areas remaining in federal ownership, their knowledge of the land and its resources, and their objectives for management. The most unusual scenic areas available were set aside as national parks; additional areas were added as they became better known or as demand increased, but always the superior areas were sought. Forested, watershed, and key grazing areas from the available public domain were put into national forests during the period of major expansion and an effort was made to acquire the best, or even all, of the commercial forest lands still remaining in the public domain. The result of this selective process by the public agencies was to leave in unreserved public ownership usually only those tracts not desired for other public purposes.

New definition of "public domain." One consequence of the establishment of permanent types of federal land units by reservation of public domain was to create some confusion as to the meaning of the latter term. The national parks were known as parks from the beginning. What are now known as national forests were first called "forest reserves," and this name continued in popular use long after it was no longer correct. Thus these two major types of federal land management units were no longer called "public domain," although they had been created out of the original public domain and as public property might have been considered such. Instead, this term gradually came to be applied to the land not yet reserved or set aside for continued management. For many years it was generally modified to "unreserved and unappropriated public domain," to distinguish the lands it described from those parts of the original public domain which had been reserved for continued federal ownership or appropriated for one use or another. With the passage of the Taylor Grazing Act, even this land is in a sense reserved. These lands have now gradually come to be called simply the "public domain," and throughout the remainder of this book this is the term that will be applied to them.

ERA OF CUSTODIAL MANAGEMENT

The fourth major era of federal land management history followed quite shortly after the reservation era began. Although it is difficult to fix a definite date, there are good reasons for choosing 1905 as the beginning of the custodial management era. The Forest Service was created in that year and the forest reserves were transferred from the Department of the Interior to the new Service in the Department of Agriculture. Two years later the name "forest reserves" was changed to "national forests."

The Forest Service immediately began to extend to the national forests as good management as was possible with the technical knowledge and appropriations at its disposal. Efforts centered on fire control, prevention of trespass, and positive measures for good use of lands for grazing, timber harvest, recreation, and the like. Gradual development of such management took place over the years, particularly as the uses of the national forests for various purposes increased.

A beginning was made during these years on the program of waterfowl and wildlife refuges when the first refuge was established in 1903. Such areas were small at first and little management was provided them; nevertheless, important areas were set aside and the idea was planted, to bear more fruit in the early 1930's.

By 1909 the area of national forests had reached the approximate level it has since maintained, although considerable modifications in boundaries have occurred. National parks and national monuments have been established at fairly regular intervals, and the area in them has expanded steadily and slowly, with a period of rapid growth in the latter 1930's. Those established since about 1900 have to a large extent come out of the national forests.

Purchase of land for management purposes. Hardly had the national forest system become established by the reservation of public domain, than a movement started to add to it by purchase of land. This culminated in the Weeks Act in 1911 and the Clarke-McNary Act in 1924, which also contained authority to purchase land. Under these two acts, some 18 million acres of land have been purchased for the national forests. About half of this area was authorized for purchase during the three years 1934 through 1936. Purchases since about 1942 have been very small. Under the authorization of other acts, purchases have been made for additions to national parks, to wildlife refuges, and for other purposes.

In the midst of the Great Depression of the 1930's and its droughts, a program for purchase of submarginal lands was set up to relieve bad land-use situations existing in the areas of purchase. A substantial part of the nearly 11 million acres of land purchased under this program was subsequently added to wildlife refuges, national parks and monuments, national forests, and the grazing districts yet to be discussed.

In addition to buying land for federal management, the federal government in recent years has bought substantial areas of land for defense purposes, and some for incidental purposes. In total, the government has acquired some 50 million acres of land from private owners, much of it part of the original public domain. About half of this was purchased for national forests.

Acquired lands. Lands the federal government obtains through purchase from individuals or from states, regardless of whether or not they have been part of the original public domain, are generally known as "acquired lands." This title covers them regardless of their present management. Thus the national forests include acquired land as well as land transferred from the original public domain; so do national parks and monuments, wildlife refuges, and grazing districts.

Most of the land laws relating to the disposal of federal land, and some other laws, too, do not apply to acquired lands. Although acquired lands may be leased for mineral development under the Mineral Leasing Act, they are not available under the mining laws. Neither are they available for forest or other homesteading, for purchase under the public sale provisions of the Taylor Grazing Act nor under the Small Tract Act, nor in many other ways open to disposal of the original public domain. On the other hand, so far as actual management of the land and its resources is concerned, there is little to distinguish the treatment of acquired and original public domain lands now included in the same kind of federal land management unit.

Land exchanges. During the years when custodial management was perhaps the dominant objective of federal land administration, two other developments occurred which deserve mention. One was the General Exchange Act of 1922, whereby tracts of federal land could be exchanged for private land of at least equal value. The purpose of this act was to provide a legal means of simplifying the complex land-ownership pattern resulting from application of the various older land laws. The existence of scattered tracts certainly complicates the administration of federal lands, and it often appears that the private landowner would gain by consolidation of his holdings.

A significant number of exchanges have been made with material benefit to the federal government and, presumably, to private landowners as well, since they have been free to refuse exchange if they could perceive no benefit. Nevertheless, the basic pattern of federal ownership has not materially been modified by exchanges, nor does it appear likely that it will be. In the first place, many private land-owners prefer to own lands intermingled with federal lands; they gain advantages, sometimes very substantial advantages, in competition with other landowners for the use of intermingled federal lands or for their products. In the second place, land exchanges are a particularly difficult form of barter, and barter is always more complicated than sale and purchase of property for money. A land exchange requires that each party to it should be better off after the exchange than before, yet each will seek equal value in the land he wants for the land he gives. There are situations when each party will consider he has benefited by an exchange of tracts, but such situations are rare. More frequently a satisfactory exchange is found to be difficult to negotiate.

O & C lands. The other event deserving special mention is the repossession by the federal government of certain lands it had granted to a railroad. A grant had been made in 1866 to the Oregon and California Railroad Company to build a line southward from Portland, Oregon to California cities. This company was later taken over by the Southern Pacific Railroad, and the line was built. Beginning in 1908, legal action was taken to have the grant forfeited and the lands returned to the United States. Two terms of the grant had been that the railroad company would sell its grant land in parcels not greater than 160 acres to any settler and at a price not greater than $2.50 per acre. It was charged that both these terms, and others, had been violated.

After long and complicated legal and legislative action, approximately 2.5 million acres of land were repossessed by the federal government. These lands are termed "revested and reconveyed Oregon and California railroad grant lands," but are more commonly known as O & C lands. Another smaller area, the Coos Bay Wagon Road grant lands, has had a somewhat similar history. In much popular discussion, and that which follows in this book, the Coos Bay lands are included with the O & C lands.

The O & C lands today have some of the finest stands of virgin Douglas fir forest to be found in the United States and are extremely valuable.

Taylor Grazing Act. By the early 1930's the process of reservation of parts of the original public domain had largely run its course;

there was little suitable land left. But there remained something over 180 million acres of the "unreserved and unappropriated" public domain. Very little of this was suited to crop production; with few exceptions it had been available for transfer to private ownership via one of several relatively generous and easy paths. The flow of land from the public domain to private ownership, mostly for grazing uses, continued, but as a trickle compared with the flood of earlier years. From about 1850 to about 1925 transfers from public to private ownership had averaged roughly 10 million acres a year and in some years had been far greater; in 1933 they were less than 1 million acres.

For many years proposals had been made for some form of administration of these remaining lands or for transfer to private ownership other than by ways then available. In the Public Land Commission inquiry of 1879, Major John Wesley Powell had proposed a system of land classification, disposition of strictly grazing land in units large enough to support a family, and government administration of both grazing and forested lands for private use. Pinchot, after the national forests became firmly established, strove to arrange for retention in federal ownership and management, but private use, of the strictly grazing lands, especially those in the Great Plains which were then being homesteaded and plowed. In this endeavor he had the active alliance of the cattlemen but the opposition of the sheepmen. At the time, general opposition to further extensions of federal reservation prevented acceptance of the idea. But in the 1920's special legislation provided for co-operative public and private administration of public domain for one area in Montana and one in California.

The situation on these remaining lands was extremely bad. Throughout the period of white man's occupancy these lands had been used for grazing domestic livestock without legal provision and also without serious efforts to stop the practice. Under these circumstances, any man was equally entitled to the use of the lands. Through ownership of watering places and of hay-producing land for winter feed, some cattle ranchers were able to maintain a measure of control over "their" public range. But this control was incomplete, at best, and in many instances it virtually did not exist. Land was often used to the point where no grass was left. Unseasonal use, with its serious ill effects, was the rule.

By the later 1920's it had become obvious to all that the situation was unsatisfactory and that the existing legal framework was inadequate to meet it. Various bills were introduced in the Congress, lead-

ing in 1934 to passage of the Taylor Grazing Act. The act provided
for the creation of grazing districts within which grazing would be
permitted under management and control, and for the leasing for
private use of land outside of districts. Its provisions also established,
for the first time in public land history in the United States, general
land classification authority. The act permitted selective disposal of
public lands, partly by providing for continued operation of the
homestead, desert land entry, and other land disposal laws where
land was classified as suitable for disposition under them, and partly
by providing for sale of isolated tracts of public land which did not
fit into a management program. It placed administration of the
grazing districts in the Department of the Interior, rather than in
the Forest Service. In large part, the Congress was moved to do this
because of promises by the Department of the Interior for low-cost
administration and low grazing fees that would just cover costs—
promises which were later to embarrass the department seriously in
its efforts to get adequate appropriations.

In general, the Taylor Grazing Act was a major piece of land legislation, comparable to those providing for the establishment of the
national forests and other major federal land management units.
However, it contains one uncertain note: The preamble states, "pending the final disposition" of the public domain, the things authorized
in the act are to be done. This phrase was rather clearly a political
compromise, necessary to alleviate the opposition of those who did
not want permanent federal ownership of land. It has repeatedly
been cited to suggest that these lands are at some time to be transferred to private or to state ownership, but this has not so far seriously
affected their actual administration and conservation.

Custodial management in retrospect. In many ways the era of
custodial management was highly important. A policy of reservation
alone, without use of the reserved resources, would have been unpopular; in fact, criticism on this ground occurred between 1890 and
1905. Custodial management opened the reserved areas for use; it
prevented the most serious wastage, especially from fire; and it reduced
losses from theft and trespass. Perhaps its greatest accomplishment was
in the devising and improving of techniques of federal resource management—techniques which will have their greatest test in the decades
ahead. During this era, also, substantial popular support was developed for the various forms of federal land management. At first use
of the reserved lands was small, but gradually use for nearly all purposes grew much greater. Management throughout this era was exten-

sive, in the economic sense of the word. This will become clearer as we consider the characteristics of intensive management. For some federal lands, especially in Alaska, management is still extensive and will probably remain so for many years.

ERA OF INTENSIVE MANAGEMENT

What an economist means by "intensive" can perhaps be described best by a quotation from *Webster:* "Designating, or pertaining to, a method of cultivating land designed to increase the productivity of a given area by the expenditure of more capital and labor upon it." The essence of the idea is the proportion between land, as one factor of production, and the other factors such as labor and capital, and current inputs such as fertilizer.

This definition fits closely the management practices recently applied to federal lands or now in the process of being applied to them. Today the area of federal lands is more or less fixed; no more, or little more, original public domain remains to be reserved for different types of management. There is substantial opposition both to large-scale purchases of more federal land and to large-scale disposal, and changes in acreage through exchange and selective disposal are comparatively small. At the same time a major program of investment in all types of federal lands is under way. Investments have been particularly large in roads, but have also included buildings and various facilities, especially recreational facilities. They have also included land improvement such as range and forest reseeding or replanting. Inputs of labor, machinery, and other factors are now higher for land management and are being used for insect and disease control; to increase sales, especially of timber; to increase inventorying and other management planning; to provide increased service to the public, especially for recreation; and for other purposes. All of this has required an increased expenditure of funds, but at the same time, partly because of current economic conditions, it has produced even greater increases in revenues from the federal land.

The change from custodial management to intensive management has been gradual so far, but the pace is quickening. The tempo of management since World War II has been greatly speeded up compared with prewar days. Many of the distinguishing characteristics of intensive management have not yet, apparently, reached their peak, nor even a new level. Considerable as investments have been in timber

management and access roads, the continuing need for further investment is much greater. Although revenues from federal lands are now
several times what they were before the war, further major increases
seem certain. The application of intensive management has also
varied on different areas or tracts of land within each major land
management type.

The years 1947 through 1950 seem to mark the transition from
predominantly custodial to predominantly intensive management,
with 1950 as the best single date. A good argument might be advanced
for 1946, or for 1942, or even for a later year such as 1954. No legislative or administrative act dramatizes this change from one era to
another in the sense that the creation of the Forest Service dramatized
the beginning of the era of custodial management, or the purchase
of Alaska dramatized the end of the era of acquisition. The upsurge
in investments that commenced with the close of World War II, however, provides one indication of the change, and increases in revenues
during the same period provide another, even when both are deflated.
Gross cash revenues exceeded total direct appropriations for all purposes, on all federal lands combined, for the first time in fiscal 1951.
How this occurred is explained in chapter five. Most of the data in
this book relate, either directly or indirectly, to these last two eras.
How management has developed through the major era of custodial
management and the shift to intensive management is important to
understanding the likely pattern of management in the future.

Federal Landownership Today

AREA OF FEDERAL LANDS

In 1950 federally owned lands and federally administered reservations amounted to 456 million acres, or almost exactly 24 per cent
of the total land area of the United States. This excludes Alaska,
where nearly all of the 365 million acres of land are still owned by
the federal government. Of the total in the United States, slightly
more than 10 per cent was acquired land, the rest original public
domain. If the Indian lands are omitted, the federal holdings are
398 million acres; and if the lands under the defense agencies are also
excluded, there remain 376 million acres of rural land or 19 per cent
of the total land area under civilian agencies.

Although some federally owned land is to be found in every state, it is concentrated for the most part in the eleven western states where nearly 54 per cent of the area is federal land.

Outside of the West, South Dakota with 18 per cent of its land (largely Indian reservations) under federal administration, and New Hampshire with 12 per cent, are the only states with more than 9 per cent of their area in federal ownership or administration. In the Lake States from 6 to 8 per cent of the land falls in this category; in most of the southern states the percentages range from 4 to 8; and in most of the Corn Belt and eastern states, they are less than 1. Administration of federal land is thus of concern to all states, but of far more concern to some than to others.

Although a score or more federal agencies administer some land, often as one of the less important features of their operations, more than 99 per cent of all federal land is administered by three departments—Interior, Agriculture, and Defense; and about 95 per cent of it in 1950 was administered by seven bureaus or services within Agriculture and Interior. Listed in order of importance as measured by total area of land, these were: Bureau of Land Management, Forest Service, Office of Indian Affairs, National Park Service, Bureau of Reclamation, Soil Conservation Service, and Fish and Wildlife Service. In 1954 nearly all of the land administered by the Soil Conservation Service was transferred to the Forest Service for administration. This does not change the ranking of the Forest Service in the above list, but does eliminate the Soil Conservation Service.

The distribution of federal lands under the control of the various agencies shows considerable geographical variation. (Their distribution in 1950 according to states and regions is detailed in appendix table 1.) The Forest Service has land in all but three states—New Jersey, Kansas, and Delaware—but the area in some states is comparatively small. The Fish and Wildlife Service has land in every state but Alabama, with holdings of less than 500 acres in nine states. The National Park Service has land in thirty-seven states, although in several of these the area is less than 500 acres. These are the organizations that most nearly approximate national coverage. In several states the types of land they administer are almost the only federal rural lands, and the experience of people in those states with federal landownership and management is largely limited to these types of land. At the other extreme, the Bureau of Reclamation has land only in seventeen states of the West and Great Plains. The Bureau of Land Management, the largest land managing agency of all measured in

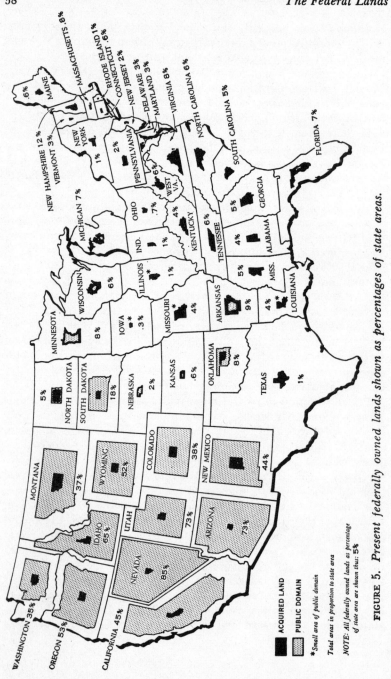

FIGURE 5. Present federally owned lands shown as percentages of state areas.

ACQUIRED LAND

PUBLIC DOMAIN

Total areas in proportion to state area

*Small area of public domain

NOTE: All federally owned lands as percentage of state area are shown thus: 5%

MAINE .6%

MASSACHUSETTS .8%

RHODE ISLAND 1%

CONNECTICUT .6%

NEW JERSEY 2%

DELAWARE 3%

MARYLAND 3%

VIRGINIA 8%

NORTH CAROLINA 6%

SOUTH CAROLINA 5%

FLORIDA 7%

NEW HAMPSHIRE 12%

VERMONT 3%

NEW YORK 1%

PENNSYLVANIA 2%

WEST VA. 6%

GEORGIA 5%

MICHIGAN 7%

OHIO .7%

KENTUCKY 6%

TENNESSEE 6%

ALABAMA 4%

WISCONSIN 6%

IND. 1%

ILLINOIS 1%*

MISS. 5%

LOUISIANA 4%*

MINNESOTA 8%

IOWA .3%*

MISSOURI 4%

ARKANSAS 9%

NORTH DAKOTA 5%

SOUTH DAKOTA 18%

NEBRASKA 2%

KANSAS .6%

OKLAHOMA 8%

TEXAS 1%

MONTANA 37%

WYOMING 52%

COLORADO 38%

NEW MEXICO 44%

IDAHO 65%

UTAH 73%

ARIZONA 73%

WASHINGTON 35%

OREGON 53%

CALIFORNIA 45%

NEVADA 85%

terms of area, is largely confined to the same states. The Bureau of Indian Affairs, and the Soil Conservation Service prior to the transfer of its lands to the Forest Service, occupied a somewhat intermediate position.

In its general outlines the situation had not changed greatly by 1955. In that year the General Services Administration began to make an annual inventory of all federal lands and real estate, urban as well as rural. Its data are based upon reports from the various agencies. In spite of care in assembling these data, the possibility exists that certain tracts of land may be listed by two or more agencies as being under the jurisdiction of each. Double counting of this nature has always been one of the complicating factors in assembling accurate comparable data on those lands which are managed for a variety of purposes by more than one agency. The inventory excludes Indian

TABLE 2. *Federally Owned Land by Principal Managing Agencies and by Method of Acquisition, June 30, 1955*

(in millions of acres)

Agency	Method of acquisition		Total
	Public domain	Purchase, donation, transfer, etc.	
Department of Agriculture: Forest Service	139.4	28.1	167.5
Department of the Interior:			
Bureau of Land Management	177.8	0.3	178.1
National Park Service	10.6	4.3	14.9
Fish and Wildlife Service	5.3	2.8	8.1
Bureau of Reclamation	8.2	1.6	9.8
Department of Defense	14.2	11.2	25.4
All other agencies [1]	1.7	2.4	4.1
Total	357.2	50.7	407.9

[1] Including bureaus, other than those named, in the departments of Agriculture and the Interior.

Source: Inventory Report on Federal Real Property in the United States as of June 30, 1955, Senate Document No. 100, 84th Congress, 2nd Session. Prepared by the General Services Administration at the request of the Committee on Appropriations of the United States Senate. Data are taken from reports supplied by land managing agencies. Data include urban as well as rural land, but exclude federally administered land, such as Indian land.

and other land under federal administration but not under federal ownership. For these reasons, the data in table 2 are not precisely comparable with those in appendix table 1, although the differences for the major federal land managing agencies are not large.

Table 2 shows that 12.4 per cent of the total federal land, as defined in the General Services Administration study, had been acquired; the remainder had been originally public domain. Slightly more than half of the total acquired lands are national forests, most of them having been acquired during the mid-1930's. The next largest area of acquired land comes under the Department of Defense. These two types of federal land account for nearly four-fifths of all acquired land.

CONTRIBUTION OF FEDERAL LANDS

The contribution of land to the nation's resource base is not easily measured, particularly when the lands are as varied in character as those owned by the federal government. Acreage alone clearly gives an exaggerated picture of their importance, since the areas most valuable for agricultural, mineral, and other private use have generally been taken into private ownership. As we are using the term "federal lands," slightly more than 19 per cent of the total area of the United States is included. No one would assert that 19 per cent of the resource base of the United States is to be found on the federal lands, but a figure of 7 per cent seems within reason.[2] One may conclude that the federal lands have too many resources to be neglected, but too few in total to be a dominant factor in the national prosperity or lack of it.

Forests on federal land. Slightly less than one-fifth of all commercial forest land in the United States is owned by the federal government. (Table 3.) In the West, where most of the federal forest land lies, more than half the forest land is federally owned. With regard to live saw timber, the contribution of the federal lands is more important still; the lands contain nearly 40 per cent of the national total,

---

[2] Adequate data for accurate measurement are lacking. However, in unpublished calculations made in 1952 by the senior author and others in the Bureau of Land Management, it was estimated that the lands under that agency's jurisdiction were the resource base for possibly 3 per cent of the gross national product. Since these lands account for about 9 per cent of the total land area, it may conceivably be estimated that the federal lands, as we use the term, are the resource base for 6 to 8 per cent of the gross national product. The total for federally owned and federally administered lands would be higher.

TABLE 3. *Summary of Importance of Federal Lands for Forestry*

Region [1]	Commercial forest area		Live saw timber volume		Growing stock	
	Total	Federally owned [2]	Total	Federally owned [2]	Total	Federally owned [2]
	Million acres		*Billion bd. ft.*		*Billion cu. ft.*	
North	174	12	266	15	111	7
South	193	14	357	30	114	9
West	117	66	1,345	722	273	147
Total	484	92	1,968	767	498	163

[1] Forest Service division of continental United States into three major regions by types of growth. North includes whole Great Plains area south through western Texas and Oklahoma. South includes eastern Texas and Oklahoma and extends north through Arkansas, Tennessee, and Virginia.

[2] Area and volume of Indian forests have been deducted from summary totals as reported, in order to get figures nearly comparable to our definition of "federal lands." Alaska also excluded from all figures.

Source: U. S. Forest Service, "Timber Resource Review," preliminary review draft, subject to revision, 1955.

and well over half of all the live saw timber in the West. In growing stock of all sizes, the federal lands have about a third of the total, and again about half in the West. Since a large part of the saw timber on federal lands is virgin timber of relatively large sizes and high quality—in contrast to that usually found on land of other ownerships —the forests on the federal lands are more important to the general economy than even these percentages would suggest.

Recreation on federal land. Comprehensive figures for outdoor recreation, comparable to those quoted for forestry, are not available, and data on this use of grazing districts and other public domain are entirely lacking. As far as can be estimated, in 1955 more than 75 million visits for specific recreational purposes, including hunting and fishing, were made to federal lands as we define the term. This compares with 162 million visits to all state parks in 1954,[3] and with 500 million visits to local and county recreation areas in 1950.[4] In addition, private outdoor recreation areas and federal reservoir areas

[3] National Park Service, *State Park Statistics, 1954,* August 1955.

[4] National Recreation Association, *Mid-century Edition, A Review of Local and County Recreation and Park Developments, 1900-1950, Recreation and Park Yearbook,* New York, 1951.

provided facilities for an unknown number of visitors. On this basis, recreation on federal land would appear minor in the total picture. However, on the average, the travel time, length of visit, and money spent en route and on location are probably several times greater per person for federal than for state and local recreation areas. The present state of knowledge about outdoor recreation prevents us from being more specific than this.

Federal lands as watersheds. Summary figures on watershed use are as sparse as those for recreational use. It is sufficient here, perhaps, prior to lengthy discussion in chapter two, to quote the Forest Service: "In the 11 Western States the national forests yield about 53 per cent of the total runoff although they occupy only 21 per cent of the area . . . . The national forests are a major source of water for some 1,800 cities and towns."[5] But the national forests are not the only type of federal land important as watersheds in the West, and elsewhere in the nation the federal lands play a smaller but still important role in this capacity.

Grazing on federal lands. Davidson has estimated that in 1949, 15.5 per cent of all forage-consuming livestock in the United States grazed on federal land; for the eleven western states, his estimate is 64 per cent.[6] But most of these livestock find only a part of their total feed supply from federal lands. Much of the grazing is seasonal and therefore is highly important to the livestock operator, even though it may supply only a small part of the total yearly feed. For the nation as a whole, it is estimated that only 4.5 per cent of all feed required for forage-consuming livestock comes from federal lands, but for the West the figure is as high as 19 per cent.

THE FEDERAL LAND ADMINISTERING AGENCIES

Since the various types of federal land cannot always, for analytical purposes, be separated from the agencies administering them, some idea of the processes by which the agencies have developed their land managing functions is helpful to an understanding of federal land management as a whole.

[5] U. S. Department of Agriculture, *Report of the Chief of the Forest Service*, 1953, p. 20.

[6] Davidson, R. D., *Federal and State Rural Lands, 1950, with Special Reference to Grazing*, U. S. Department of Agriculture Circular No. 909, May 1952.

Why should the administration of the various lands be split up among bureaus or agencies and between departments? The physical types, or mixtures of physical types, of land administered by each agency are quite similar; so are the use patterns of the various types of land, and the methods of organization and administration among the various agencies.

The explanation is to be found in the history of the federal lands. For many decades, from 1812 until after 1900, the federal lands were under the administration of the General Land Office, whose major function was disposal of the lands to private ownership. When the forest reserves were first created they too were placed under the management of this agency.

At the same time, a small Bureau of Forestry existed in the Department of Agriculture. A dominant figure in the latter was Gifford Pinchot. Alarmed at the General Land Office's inadequate, incompetent, and politically minded administration of the forest reserves, he prevailed upon President Theodore Roosevelt, and through him the Congress, to establish a new agency, the Forest Service, out of the old Bureau of Forestry, and to transfer the administration of the forest reserves to the new agency.

When a separate agency to manage the national parks was established, it was placed in the Department of the Interior. The management of wildlife refuges of various types was placed in the Bureau of Biological Survey, a specialized agency concerned with wildlife which was then in the Department of Agriculture. In 1939 this agency was transferred from Agriculture to Interior and the Bureau of Fisheries was transferred from the Department of Commerce to Interior. The two bureaus combined the next year to form the Fish and Wildlife Service.

When the Taylor Grazing Act was passed in 1934, a new Interior agency was established to administer the grazing and some other functions within the new districts. First called the Division of Grazing, it was later known as the Grazing Service. But even within grazing districts the General Land Office continued to administer mineral leasing laws and laws for disposal of land, and to exercise other powers. It also leased for grazing the lands outside of districts. The resultant confusion between the functions of two agencies in relation to the same land led, in 1946, to their amalgamation as one: Interior's Bureau of Land Management.

Numerous students of public administration and various public commissions have criticized this multiple organization of federal land management. Overlapping, duplication, and inefficiency have been noted or alleged. Many critics have suggested various forms of reorganization or combination, but, as will be discussed in chapter six, these proposals have by no means met with unanimous approval.

While undoubtedly there are objections to change on the part of the several land bureaus, there are also substantial groups within the general public which have opposed and will continue to oppose changes affecting the bureaus to which their interests are attached. During the past fifteen years the only major changes in organization have been the consolidation of the General Land Office and the Grazing Service into the Bureau of Land Management and the transfer of the "land utilization" or "submarginal purchase" lands from the jurisdiction of the Soil Conservation Service to that of the Forest Service.

CHAPTER TWO

Uses of the Federal Land

THE PECULIAR CHARACTER OF THE FEDERALLY owned lands—the fact that they have been available for the use of private individuals and groups but not used by government enterprise as such—has resulted in a pattern of use compatible with both private and public landownership. Each form of landownership in the United States has stimulated and benefited the other. This is not to say that major management problems have not emerged as a result of the mixed pattern. The user of the federal lands is often a user and an owner of private lands, and his use of the one must be closely related to his use of the other. The fact, too, that federal land units are variously interspersed with private land units has often presented problems for the federal land administrator. Such problems, and those arising out of increasing competition among the various users of the land, are dealt with in connection with the decision- and policy-making procedures discussed in chapters three and four. While these institutional arrangements and the financial factors discussed in chapter five do affect the uses of the land, it is first necessary to understand the conditions that give rise to them. The institutional arrangements have developed, in part at least, to provide a bridge between the use potentials and the needs and desires of the people. Similarly, the kind of expenditures made and revenues derived from the federal lands depends on the one hand on use potentials, and on the other, on the actual use made of the land.

The uses we are considering in this chapter occurred during the latter part of the disposal era, during nearly all of the reservation era, through the era of custodial management into the beginning of the era of intensive management, and can be expected to continue into the future.

Prior to roughly 1900, use of the federal land was without specific legal authority in the great majority of cases. Until the national forests were brought under constructive administration following the Act of 1897, little or no legal authority existed by which the federal lands could be used or their products harvested. There was authority for land disposal, although this was often ill-suited to the types of land and the uses sought; but authority to use the federal land itself was lacking. While the federal government had never provided specific legal authority for many of the uses, neither had it made a serious attempt to stop them. This is true of the grazing of livestock on federal land, especially in the pioneer days. In other cases, as in the building of roads across public land, the law was vague and constituted an open invitation to the public to avail itself of the federal land without specific authorization. In still other cases, as in the extensive cutting of timber in trespass, especially in the Lake States, the federal government made sporadic and generally ineffectual attempts to stop the trespass. The General Land Office tried repeatedly and with great courage to stop trespass; but the Congress and the people generally were either indifferent or positively encouraged it. Congress was willing to provide neither funds to enforce action, nor legal means whereby lumbermen could get land or cutting rights suited to their needs.

The essential point is that in these earlier years, with few exceptions, the federal lands were not kept from use by the public. In more recent years the use has been regulated primarily to conserve the lands' resources. Some trespass or other legal violation has occurred, but for the most part use has been kept within the law and the regulations.

Because the federal lands are to be found in all parts of the United States, they include some land of almost all the physical types common to the country and contain a wide variety of resources. Differing locations with respect to centers of population lead to differing uses of similar tracts. Good cropland is relatively uncommon today among federal lands; when Indian reservations and military lands are excluded, it is extremely rare.

Uses of the federal land by private individuals can be classified broadly as follows:

1. Uses yielding commodities or services of direct commercial value to the user. These include chiefly:
   a. timber harvest;
   b. mineral production, including oil and gas, coal and other leasable minerals, as well as metals;
   c. forage harvest by domestic livestock;
   d. occupancy for various business purposes, such as resort hotels, service stations, and many others.

2. Uses yielding directly consumable services and satisfactions to the user, on the site. Because of custom, history, or for other reasons, many of these are available free of charge or for nominal charges. These include chiefly:
   a. recreation uses by individuals, in all aspects, including vacation residence;
   b. scenic uses;
   c. wildlife, for enjoyment as it is or for hunting and fishing.

3. Uses yielding commodities and services that are primarily consumed off the site, and for the most part noncommercial. The chief use here is as watershed; the water may be valuable, but the watershed use generally does not yield direct revenue to the landowner.

4. Miscellaneous uses of all kinds, of which rights of way for many purposes are perhaps the most important.

Each of these general purposes can, of course, be subdivided further. For instance, timber harvest can be for lumber production, for pulp wood, for poles, for plywood bolts, for Christmas trees, or for other uses. And the harvest may be undertaken by many different types of users, from the small operator who works mainly with his own labor, through a wide variety of arrangements up to the branch processing plant of a large integrated wood-using organization. The harvest of forage plants may be by cattle or by sheep, at different seasons, and by livestock owned by different types and sizes of ranches. Recreation may take many forms, from the packer or hiker enjoying a distant wilderness area to the highly urbanized use of popular outdoor areas. There are literally innumerable uses and variations of use, each with its distinctive characteristics and its clientele.

These various uses of federal land are available to private persons or groups under a range of terms and conditions. Some products or uses are available only on the basis of commercial sale: nearly all timber from federal land is sold on a competitive bid basis, with the contract awarded to the highest bidder. In many cases the resource or the use is available to the first comer, with or without a price more or less at the market. For instance, most leases of land for oil and gas development are issued noncompetitively to the first applicant, but he pays a royalty, if he is fortunate enough to strike oil, at more or less the commercial rate. Visitors to the national parks and other recreation areas are admitted freely in order of appearance, with payment of only limited fees. Mining claims can be staked by the first person, and obtained after meeting the requirements of the law. In still other instances only applicants who meet certain requirements, sometimes rather exacting ones, are allowed to use the federal lands. Chief among the uses on this basis is grazing; the rancher who seeks to use federal land for grazing must ordinarily own complementary ("commensurate") property nearby, and in many instances preference is also given among the latter to those with a record of prior use of this land. In some cases distinction is made between local or nearby residents as compared with more distant ones. This may be true even for timber sale, or for grazing use, or for hunting. In the latter case, a state may sell hunting licenses freely to its citizens and less freely to nonresidents, or at one price to residents and at a much higher price to others.

How Intermingled Private Lands Affect the Use of Federal Lands

The various types of federal land management units, such as national forests, national parks, and grazing districts, are not solid units of wholly federally owned land. Within their boundaries are larger or smaller areas of nonfederal land, both privately owned and state owned, which affect the use and management of the federal lands they adjoin. Their origin goes back to the long disposal era when private individuals, companies, and the states each selected choice land from the available public domain. Generally speaking, the unit of selection was small relative to the total area of federal land in a state or county. Homesteads under the original Homestead Act were 160 acres, for instance, and most land selections were of units of 640 acres or less. Settlers, states, and others were not required to take any available land within a township or county or other geographical unit, before being allowed to select land in another unit, sometimes in a distant one. The result was that landownership at any given time formed a variable and somewhat erratic pattern, some tracts being privately owned, others remaining in federal ownership.

Ranchers often wanted ownership of only hay-producing lands or lands containing waterholes; such ownership often gave them substantial control over the intervening federal lands without the cost of private landownership. In many of the mountain areas the valley bottoms would pass into private ownership, leaving the steeper hills in federal ownership. Lumbermen often bought only the finest and most accessible stands of timber, leaving the others in federal ownership. Some bought only occasional tracts in order to have the appearance of legality while logging the federal lands in trespass. In other cases large, solid blocks passed into private ownership. The miner was interested in mineral-bearing lands; these are the only types of land available under the mining laws.

The extent of privately owned land within the boundaries of federal land management units depends largely upon the date the federal unit was established in relation to the history of settlement and economic development of the area, and also upon the policy followed in drawing its boundaries. At one extreme is Yellowstone Park—established at a very early date when there was almost no agricultural or lumbering development, and hence very little privately owned land, in the general locality. At the other extreme are most grazing districts—established comparatively late in western history when all the best lands had already passed into private ownership, and with their boundaries so drawn as to include all major areas of remaining public domain in the general locality. Most other types of federal land fall between these extremes.

More than one acre in five of the total area within the boundaries of national forests is in state or private ownership; there are 167.2 million acres of federally owned land and 47.3 million acres of non-federal land. In the entire national park system only 671,000 acres are not federally owned, an area equal to 3 per cent of the 22.3 million acres in federal ownership. Grazing districts present a sharp contrast: 97.3 million acres, an area over half as large as the 168.5 million acres in federal ownership, are nonfederal land. Comparable data are not available for the wildlife refuges and similar lands.

However, to consider these nonfederal lands only in terms of area underrates their importance both to the private landowner and to the federal land managing agency. It must be emphasized again that the most productive, valuable, and strategically located lands have passed to private ownership. In a part of a grazing district where much less than half of the land area is federally owned one does not have to see the federal land to know that it will be the driest, rockiest, steepest, least productive part of the whole area.

Ownership of the intermingled private lands often brings substantial advantage to the owner who is in competition with other landowners in obtaining the use of federal land or its products. The owner of private land within a national park may possess a choice site for a dude ranch or a summer resort: the national park lies at his very door for the easy enjoyment of his guests. Grazing on both national forests and grazing districts is usually easier and more profitable for the owner of nearby or intermingled land than for the distant landowner. Ownership of intermingled timbered lands and investment in a road system for their exploitation may be very advantageous to a lumberman bidding for the timber from federal lands. There are times, indeed, when an owner of intermingled land may enjoy nearly all the advantages of ownership of the adjoining federal lands without the accompanying responsibilities and costs.

These intermingled private lands can present the federal land administrator with serious problems. First of all, he must know where the boundaries of the private land are, in order to prevent trespass on the part of users of the federal land on the private land, and on the part of private landowners on the federal land. In view of the chaotic condition of many land surveys, especially for mountainous areas, this in itself is no easy job. The federal government has never denied access to the intermingled private lands, although it has prescribed reasonable conditions for passage over its land; and it cannot deny the owner the right to use his land as he sees fit, although it may prevent him from injuring the federal land in the process. The use he makes of his land may not be in harmony with the uses of the federal land, or may be different from that sought by the federal agency were the land under its management. There may be problems arising out of fire, disease, or insect hazards, requiring special cooperative efforts between private owner and federal agency. Erosion control on land of one ownership may be difficult or impossible without its control on the land of the other ownership. Thus, in a great many ways the presence of the intermingled privately owned land affects federal land management.

Single, Multiple, and Dominant Uses

Federal land may be administered so as to be used under a variety of arrangements with respect to other uses of the same land. There is the so-called single-purpose use. The national parks, reserved for recreational use only, are one of the better examples of this. Or an area which is the watershed for a municipal water supply may be excluded from all other use in order to protect the purity of the water supply. At the other extreme is multiple-purpose use, by which the lands are administered to make possible some degree of use for all the purposes to which the land is physically adapted and for which there is a demand. This latter situation prevails on most national forest, grazing district, and some other types of land. The administrators of such lands try to fit one use into another so as to minimize or eliminate conflict and competition between them. It is often true that an area can be used for timber production with some livestock grazing, while at the same time it serves well as a watershed and provides considerable recreation and wildlife value as well. Minerals in the land may often be developed with only moderate or even no conflict with surface uses.

Actually, "single" and "multiple" uses represent the extremes of a continuum of methods of use and administration. There is virtually no land with only a single use; all land upon which rain or snow falls is watershed, all land except the most extreme desert has some wildlife, nearly all land has some recreation and scenic value, and most land has some forage or tree growth that can be harvested. Even if the latter uses are excluded, as from most national parks, watershed and wildlife values remain along with recreational values. This situation applies also to privately owned land; however selfishly the lumberman or rancher might manage his land in his own interest, some of its watershed and wildlife values remain, though perhaps in greatly diminished stature. As a matter of fact, private owners of land are coming increasingly to consider land uses other than the dominant one in the management of their lands.

The essence of multiple-use management is the conscious management of the land to the end that it will provide several uses at the same time. The process is not haphazard; it is deliberate. But no matter how assiduously "multiple" purpose use is sought in federal land administration, there must be some scale of preferences for choice among uses in those situations where full use for one purpose interferes with full use for another. There may be situations in which the best management for watershed purposes is also the best management for wildlife, or when the best management for timber production and harvest is also the best management for watershed, and so on. When this is true there is clearly no need for a scale of preferences among uses. But in the more common case full enjoyment of one use means some loss of another. Then the question arises: Which use, or which degree of one use, should be sacrificed to another use, or to some degree of another use?

This latter situation may be illustrated by a hypothetical example.[1] Figure 6 is a graphical representation of all the possible combinations of deer and cattle that a particular range will support. If the land

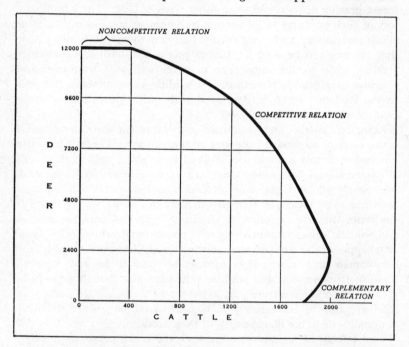

FIGURE 6. *Interrelations of cattle and deer grazing—a hypothetical example of the production possibilities of a tract of range land.*

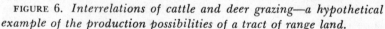

[1] An extensive use of this form of analysis, as applied to management of grazing and forest lands, has been made by John A. Hopkin, "Use of Economics in Making Decisions Relating to Range Use," *Journal of Farm Economics*, Vol. 38, No. 5, December, 1956. See also his doctoral dissertation, Iowa State College.

were given over entirely to deer it would support, for the season it was usable by them, 12,000 deer; or if used primarily for cattle it would support for the same season 2,000 cattle. This suggests that six deer replace one cow, or one cow replaces six deer; each increase in deer means a constant and proportionate decrease in cattle, and vice versa. However, this is contrary to common experience with cattle and deer. Because of differences in forage preferences of the two classes of animals and the variety of plants on the land, and differences in preferences for terrain, some deer can be present without interfering at all, or in any major way, with cattle and some cattle can be present without interfering importantly with deer. Thus, up to 400 head of cattle can be added without any reduction in number of deer. At only one point, where there are 1,200 cattle and 9,600 deer, will one additional head of cattle substitute for six deer and vice versa (although the ratio between total numbers of deer and total numbers of cattle is not 1:6 but rather 1:8). With a large number of deer and a small number of cattle on the range, additional cattle may be run without displacing large numbers of deer. For instance, with 800 head of cattle it is necessary to cut deer numbers by 2.9 to provide grazing for an additional head of cattle. On the other hand, as the numbers of cattle increase and the numbers of deer decrease, more and more deer must be displaced to make room for each additional head of cattle—9.7 deer to one head of cattle when there are 1,600 head of cattle. The more cattle there are, the more they replace deer at the margin; and the more deer there are, the more they replace cattle at the margin. At the extremes there is no competition. A few cattle may graze without affecting deer numbers, and conversely a few deer may even mean more cattle because they will hold brush in check which would otherwise crowd out some of the grass upon which cattle feed.

This illustration of the choices posed by cattle and deer could be adapted to many other types of joint or competitive uses of the same area at the same time—or multiple use. There is competition between sheep and cattle for forage resources; between domestic livestock and game animals, also for forage; between grazing of all kinds and timber production of all kinds; between production of pulpwood and saw timber, at least in some situations, within the forest use of land; possibly between either grazing or timber production, or both, and water yield from the area; between grazing, forestry, and perhaps other uses on the one hand, and recreation on the other; between the wilderness type of recreation and the more popular and intensive recreational uses of land; and many more pairs of uses or groups of uses. Kelley has listed some thirty-one types of competition for land, under a multiple land-use program.[2]

Multiple use of federal land creates some difficult management and choice problems which are considered in chapter three. There are also many difficult technical problems, which are not considered because they lie outside the scope of this study. It should be recognized, however, that the uses of federal land discussed in the following pages of this chapter fall somewhere in the continuum between single use and multiple use. That is, in some cases a particular use of a particular tract of land may so dominate the use of that tract, and so effectively exclude other uses in any important degree, as to be virtually single-purpose, even though some other uses actually do occur. In other cases a number of uses may take place upon the identical area of land. Or the various uses of land may take place upon separate tracts, at least to some degree, but the boundaries of the tracts may be so adjusted and the tracts so intermingled that the area as a whole is used for multiple purposes. Some of the uses described in the remainder of this chapter occur as the major or single use of the land in question; but for other areas the same use may be but one of several. Data are generally lacking to show the areas of land used for the different purposes and the areas with different combinations of use on the same tracts. The data presented are total uses of the total areas within each category, such as national forests or national parks, and do not deal specifically with this matter of single, dominant, and multiple uses of land.

Diffusion and Concentration of Various Uses over the Land

In some cases a use of federal land may be spread more or less evenly over the entire area of land allotted to it; in other cases a use may be highly concentrated in certain well-adapted areas. Where use is concentrated, special problems of administration and management are involved.

The watershed use, or value, of land applies more or less equally

[2] Kelley, Evan W., "Problems of Land Management and Administration Arising from Associated Uses of Land for the Various Services which the Public Seeks from the National Forests," *Proceedings of the Western Farm Economics Association, Eleventh Annual Meeting, 1938.*

to all the land in a federal land management unit; after all, the rain and snow fall on all the land, though not equally. But land on which precipitation is relatively great is, from one viewpoint, unusually important as a watershed area. Erosion hazard also differs; some areas have a greater erosion potential than others. From this viewpoint, areas with high erosion potential are important watershed lands. In some areas the balance between vegetation and other forces holding soil in place is so precarious, as against the rainfall and other forces leading to soil movement, that relatively slight changes in land management methods and practices may lead to seriously accelerated erosion. These "brittle" areas may be highly localized or widespread. In other areas there has never been a balance between soil-moving and soil-holding forces during white man's occupancy of the United States; active erosion has been under way for centuries. When floods occur, whether because of land mismanagement or for other reasons, the damages are likely to be highly localized also. Thus, in general, watershed is a "use" of land widely dispersed in total but with localized spots of greater importance.

Wildlife tend to use large areas of federal land since the animals and birds are able to govern their own movements. Man can influence their distribution in various ways, but always within some limits. Animals and birds will go where food and water and shelter adapted to their needs are to be found, and where disturbances from man and predators are at a minimum. Yet, on the whole, this use of federal lands tends to be a widely dispersed one.

The grazing of domestic livestock is also more or less proportionately distributed, in relation to available forage, over the entire area allotted to this use. In fact, one of the objectives of good range management, seldom completely achieved, is a uniform distribution of grazing, in proportion to available feed, over the entire area. Where water, whether from natural or man-made sources, is to be found at relatively long intervals and only at specific locations, livestock must trail to the water, with consequent unavoidable damage to the immediately adjacent land. Such areas are almost sure to be overused; the only practical management problem is to limit the area and the extent of the overuse. There may well be remote, steep, rocky areas, and other areas onto which domestic livestock will not naturally go as long as they can find enough to eat elsewhere. Herding sheep, or even driving cattle, may lead to greater use of such areas, in some cases approaching uniform use; or through the use of salt the animals may be induced to graze on areas that otherwise they would find unattractive.

Forestry, in the sense of positive management of land to produce forest products, may be practiced over relatively large areas. Fire control and disease and insect control, for instance, are necessary for the entire area. On the other hand, the timber harvest from such lands is almost sure to be concentrated on a relatively small part. On federal lands particular tracts of timber land are put up for harvest either on a clearcut basis, as is usually the case in the Douglas fir type, or on a selective-cut basis, as in most of the pine areas. In both cases the timber is cut over a period of several months or perhaps a few years on a particular tract. Timber harvest operations then proceed to other areas, perhaps within the same federal land administrative unit. Harvest upon the first area will again be possible at some future date, the precise time varying from as few as ten years, where pine is selectively cut, to as long as a hundred or more years, when Douglas fir is clearcut.

Recreational use of most federal lands is highly concentrated. Most people actually use only very small areas in the sense that they walk over them, camp upon them, and hunt or fish upon them. Usually the larger areas are used only to look at from a distance, and as buffer strips to give value to intensively used areas. There are a few people who use the larger areas, but this generally involves hiking or riding horseback for considerable distances, and the great bulk of visitors do not want to do this. It has been estimated that nearly all the use of national parks occurs on 5 per cent of their total area, and a generally similar situation exists within national forests. This concentration of use creates many problems, first of all in connection with the resource itself—trampling within the best camping areas may in time kill the trees and shrubs which make them good camping sites—and secondly in connection with the safety and comfort of visitors—safe water supply and sewage and sanitation facilities are the bare essentials of any attractive recreational area within federal lands, if it is at all accessible. Roads and other facilities can often open new areas for recreation, and thus spread the load somewhat.

Actual mineral development of federal lands is also likely to be highly localized. Mineral occurrence is usually confined to specific areas and in many situations the surface use of land for mineral production is quite small, even when the value of the minerals is great. In other situations, however, mineral use may be destructive to surface values. For example, placer mining for gold, by use of dredges, completely destroys the surface values for many years. To some extent the surface of the land may be restored after such destructive mining by application of suitable techniques. Those who seek minerals may do so throughout the federal land area, except in national parks and other areas withdrawn from mining, and to this extent use wider areas. Mining claims cover a much larger area of federal land than does actual mineral development; and these claims often limit, if not exclude, other uses of the land.

Use Pattern on National Forests

The relationships among uses of the federal land are brought into sharper focus when we consider these uses as they apply to a specific type of federal land. The national forests have had the longest record of constructive land management, and the concept of multiple land use has been applied to them rather fully. They contain a wide variety of physical conditions; in addition, pressures of nearby populations accentuate public need.[3]

GRAZING[4]

One of the major uses of national forests is for grazing of domestic livestock. Of the total area of 161 million acres in national forests (excluding Alaska), 62 million acres are used for grazing, of which 25 million acres also grow commercially valuable timber. The area within western national forests had, with few exceptions, been fully used for grazing of domestic livestock prior to the establishment of the national forests. In fact, it had generally been overused for this purpose. Well before 1900 settlement had extended throughout nearly every section of the West, and the grazing livestock industry had pushed into nearly every corner of the land. With no control or management of the federal lands to prevent their use, it was only natural that the ranchers should graze their herds and flocks upon the land later to be included in the national forests. With no control over use, excessive use and improper seasonal use inevitably were widespread. Many a rancher used the land in ways he knew were not

[3] Throughout this section totals and averages applying to the national forests as a whole are used; the situation in some areas may differ considerably from that characteristic of the national average.

[4] Specific data on grazing are to be found in appendix table 2.

proper because he was aware that if he did not, someone else would. It is also true that knowledge about grazing land use was less common in those days, and often the ill-effects of improper grazing practices on the plant cover and the soil resource itself were not foreseen.

The early administration of the national forests largely legalized the grazing uses which had grown up previously. The new Forest Service had many problems in getting into operation and it could only gradually extend constructive management to the national forests. Moreover, there was a great need for more and better information about how to use the types of land included in the forests. In particular, new methods for estimating forage productive capacity of grazing lands had to be developed and new methods of livestock management evolved. It took time to convince the general public of the advantages and necessity of new methods of land use, and of the ability and authority of the Forest Service officials to work out and enforce the necessary regulations. But a substantial beginning was made in the first decade of national forest administration.

Unfortunately, events over which the Forest Service had no control were largely to nullify the good results of its early work and to create problems which have plagued it to the present. In World War I, "food will win the war" became the slogan of the day, and strenuous efforts were made to increase all types of food output, including that of beef cattle and sheep. One undesirable effect of this pressure was an unwarranted plow-up of much submarginal land for wheat production, especially in the Great Plains. Another was a major increase in livestock grazing on the national forests as well as on other range lands, both public and private. From about 1.5 million cattle and 7.5 million sheep grazing on these lands before the war, numbers increased to about 2,250,000 cattle and 8.5 million sheep. Total grazing load upon land is usually measured in terms of animal-unit months, or the number of months that animals, on the basis of a cow equivalent, are upon the land.[5] The number of animal-unit months increased from about 15 million prewar to over 20 million at the war peak. (Figure 7.) This one-third increase came upon ranges which were fully stocked or overstocked before the war, and on which the positive management programs of the Forest Service had only begun.

In retrospect, this wartime increase in grazing upon the national forests was a serious mistake. There is considerable evidence that it

---

[5] For further discussion of the meaning of animal-unit months (AUM), see section in this chapter dealing with grazing in grazing districts, p. 87.

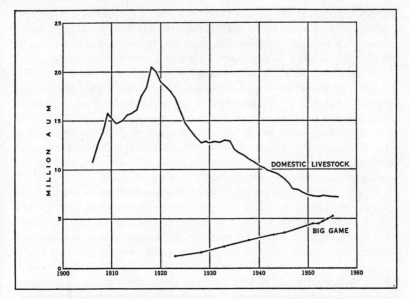

FIGURE 7. *Domestic livestock and big game animals grazing on the national forests, 1906-56.*

failed of its immediate purpose to increase livestock output; the larger number of livestock did not produce proportionately more output because the feed simply was not there to support it. The effect on the range was serious. It may be argued now that these unfavorable effects should have been foreseen more clearly and been more stoutly resisted at the time, but perhaps, in view of the pressures exerted, this was impossible.

Since 1918 there has been a continuous and almost uninterrupted decline in grazing of domestic livestock on the national forests. By the latter 1920's total grazing load was below the prewar level, and it briefly seemed stabilized at that point, but major further reductions have been made since then. By 1956 total grazing load was down to 35 per cent of the World War I peak and to roughly half of the pre-World War I and late 1920 plateaus. Since 1950 the rate of decline has been slower than previously. In speaking specifically about the national forests, the Chief of the Forest Service has said, "The problem of bringing about a proper balance between livestock numbers and the forage supply constitutes a serious present-day problem in many parts of the West."[6]

If the rate of decrease in grazing on national forests which prevailed from 1933 to 1956 (slightly less than the rate which prevailed from 1918 to 1956) were to continue, all grazing on national forests would cease in about 1982. It is improbable that this will occur; the 1953 annual report of the Forest Service, which deals in some detail with grazing, makes it clear that grazing by domestic livestock is a major and important continuing use of national forests.

During these same years the total grazing of domestic livestock in the West, on all types of land of all ownerships, has been roughly constant, with some fluctuations because of climatic or economic conditions, but with no clear trend either up or down.

The Forest Service estimates that the number of national forest grazing permittees is about 3½ per cent of the total number of livestock growers in the West, that about 11 per cent of the beef cattle and about 22 per cent of the sheep in that region graze upon national forests, and that the national forests provide about 7 per cent of the total feed requirements of western livestock.[7] This latter figure understates the importance of these lands in the western livestock economy. In general, national forest grazing is seasonal, usually summer, grazing. Although it may provide but a small part of the total feed required for a livestock operation, that feed may be a critical part of the total annual operation.

The Forest Service has evolved certain new concepts in its administration of grazing on the national forests. Livestock owners are given permits to graze specified numbers of livestock during a specified season on a specified area or tract of land. Some of their management practices with the livestock, such as salting of cattle or bedding of sheep, are also specified. In order to qualify for national forest grazing, the applicant must own ranch property and livestock, and he must need the national forest forage as part of his livestock operation. When management of the national forests was begun, preference was given to those livestock operators who had been using this land. If additional grazing was available it was generally extended to nearby settlers and ranchers. At the beginning licenses or permits to graze were issued annually, but since 1925 they have generally been for a ten-year term.[8]

[6] U. S. Department of Agriculture, *Report of the Chief of the Forest Service, 1953*, p. 4.
[7] *Ibid.*
[8] The fees charged for grazing livestock in the national forests and in grazing districts are discussed in chapter four, pp. 220-23.

GAME AND OTHER WILDLIFE[9]

The national forests have important game and wildlife values which the Forest Service seeks to protect and develop. In many states Forest Service employees are also local game wardens with power to arrest violators. The numbers of game on national forests have increased greatly in the last thirty years, as they have also on other types of land. The population of some game animals, deer in particular, is greater today than it was thirty or forty years ago, and in many areas is in excess of the available feed supply. While many game species have not adapted so well to white man, the primary reason for the large increase in deer and other game in recent years has been the protection of animals from overhunting and from predators, although logging and other uses of land have often increased the feed for some game animals. As is evident from figure 7, the total amount of forage on national forests used by game animals has increased fourfold since 1923. Although the statistics do not go back as far as 1918, it is likely that in that year, when livestock grazing was at its height, game used perhaps 5 per cent as much forage from national forests as did domestic animals; by 1955 they used 81 per cent as much as domestic animals, or 45 per cent of the total forage use. If past trends continue, big game animals will be using as much forage as domestic livestock before 1960. The decrease in animal-unit months of grazing by domestic livestock for the 1918-55 period was offset to the extent of 27 per cent by the increase in grazing by game animals; for the 1933-55 period, it was offset to the extent of 41 per cent.

These comparisons, however, may overdramatize the competition between game and domestic animals. Part of the increase in game animals has been upon national forests where few if any domestic livestock graze. Thus about one-fifth of the total increase in game animals between 1921 and 1955 was on national forests in the eastern half of the United States, where grazing by domestic livestock is relatively unimportant. Much of the increase in game animals in the western national forests has been upon areas not well suited and in some cases not used for domestic livestock, because of inaccessibility, heavy timber, remoteness from water, or other reasons. Even on the areas used by both game and domestic livestock, differences in feed preferences may mean limited competition between the two types of animals. On the basis of evidence available to the authors, it is im-

[9] The specific data for this section are to be found in appendix tables 2 and 4.

possible to estimate the degree to which increases in game animals have required forage that otherwise could have been available to domestic livestock for grazing.

Since 1924 the forage taken by game animals on national forests has increased about fourfold; during the same years, as will be shown later, total recreational use of national forests has increased nearly tenfold. The increase in game and the better hunting opportunity this affords have been factors in increased recreational use of the national forests. The number of deer and other big game killed by hunters on national forests has more than doubled since 1940, and in 1955 came close to 480,000 head.

In many local areas game animals have increased to the point where they do substantial damage to the vegetative cover and to the land itself. Overgrazing by game animals is just as possible, and just as destructive, as overgrazing by domestic livestock. Increased kill by hunters may be the answer in such situations, and in recent years the number of states where a two-deer kill or a doe kill is authorized has considerably increased.

TIMBER HARVEST[10]

Timber harvest from national forests was small in the early years of their administration, but rose gradually and steadily. (Figure 8.) By 1910 only about 0.5 billion board feet of timber were removed from the national forests annually. At that time most national forest timber was relatively remote and there was little demand for it. An ample supply of old-growth timber existed in private ownership, generally in more accessible locations, and often of higher quality, so that timber owners had little incentive to bid for national forest timber. Timber processors who did not own timber could usually buy all they wanted at low prices from private owners.

The volume of timber sold rose at a regular pace during World War I, hardly dropped at all in the depression of the early 1920's, and then rose again steadily and at the same relative rate to a peak in 1930, at which time sales were up to about 1.5 billion board feet annually. By and large, during these years all the timber was sold from national forests for which there was a market even at relatively

---

[10] The specific data for this section are to be found in appendix table 3.

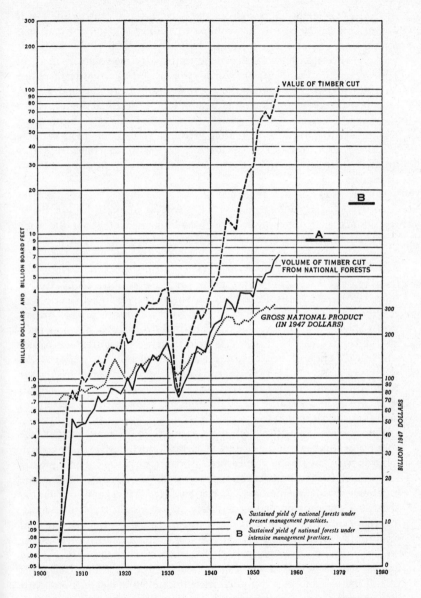

FIGURE 8. *Timber sales from the national forests, 1905-56 and projections for 1960 and 1980.*

low prices; demand for timber set the pace in sales. During the Great Depression of the 1930's the volume of timber sold off the national forests declined sharply, to about half of the 1930 peak. While it was also true that harvest of private timber declined sharply in these same years, the Forest Service during this period as a matter of policy held much timber off the market. Timber sales from national forests, as a percentage of total lumber manufacture, declined somewhat in these years. Private timber owners were often in distress, liquidation was proceeding rapidly and often without regard for good forestry practices, and the Forest Service did not wish to complicate this unsatisfactory situation in the private industry by pushing sales of its timber.

Sales rose again after 1933, and by 1940 had nearly regained a level in line with the trend from 1910 to 1930, at about 2 billion board feet. Since that date timber sales have increased at about the same percentage rate of increase as in 1908-30, reaching a level of just over 7 billion board feet in fiscal 1956. A strong demand for timber products of all kinds during World War II and since, especially for housing, has been one major factor in these rapidly rising timber sales. Perhaps equally important has been the decline in supply of readily available old-growth timber of good quality in private ownership. Most of the latter, which had existed up to 1940, has now been cut, and much of what remains is held by large integrated companies which will not sell because they want to process the timber themselves. In parts of the West there is now a demand for more timber than the Forest Service can sell, because of lack of access roads in some areas, and because of limitations of allowable cuts set up to maintain sustained yield.

Throughout the entire period of national forest management, the volume of timber cut has risen at a rate much faster than growth in gross national product (measured in constant prices). For the years 1908-56, omitting the depression years 1931-42, the *rate* of increase in timber sales from national forests has been remarkably constant— about 5.5 per cent annually—and deviations from a trend line showing this rate of increase have been small. In contrast, gross national product has risen at a rate of about 3 per cent annually. A constant *rate* of increase obviously means that the actual increase in volume was greater in recent than in early years; on a trend-line basis, this rate of increase has meant annual increases of 250 to 300 million board feet in recent years compared with an annual increase only one-tenth as large in the years around 1910. A continuation of the past rate of increase would lead to very large sales figures in a few years and probably cannot be maintained even though sales continue to increase steadily.

The rapid increase of timber sales from national forests is simply a measure of the fact that timber cut in the nation has gradually shifted to national forests away from private lands as the latter have been cut out and as the more remote national forest timber has come into greater demand. The share of total cut coming from national forests has risen more or less regularly, except for the depression years, from about 1 per cent around 1910 to about 15 per cent today. Total lumber production in the United States reached a peak before 1910, and in recent years, even with a vastly greater population and much higher levels of construction, the earlier peak has not been exceeded. Demand for pulpwood and some other timber products has risen steadily, but per capita use of all timber products is much lower than it was fifty years ago. This is a reflection not only of partial exhaustion of the once great areas of virgin timber, but of changing technology in wood use.

The greatly increased cut of national forest timber is the more striking when viewed against this total national picture, and the cut, even with present management practices, is still below the level of growth. On the basis of present management practices, allowable annual cut on the national forests is estimated at 9 billion board feet annually. The main reason timber is cut below this level is lack of access roads in some of the more remote areas. By more intensive forestry practices; by harvest of timber in areas where there is not now adequate demand, such as along the Rocky Mountains; by harvest of smaller trees for pulp, thus thinning certain stands to their advantage; by sale of certain varieties of trees, particularly hardwoods in the South for which present demand is weak; and by other practices, in perhaps ten years the total sustained yield cut of the national forests could be increased to 15 billion board feet annually, and perhaps to more. Since the *Timber Resource Review* lists 81.3 million acres of commercial forest lands within national forests in the United States and 3.4 million acres in Alaska, this would mean a net annual growth rate of slightly less than 200 board feet per acre.

Timber sales of 9 to 10 billion board feet annually from national forests may be achieved within the next five years; they may reach 15 billion board feet in twenty years or less.

While the volume of timber sold from the national forests was increasing greatly, revenues from the sale of that timber were rising even more rapidly. This is true not only when revenues are expressed in current prices, but also when they are cited in terms of a constant general price level. With few exceptions, timber is sold on a competitive bid basis. In the earlier years, when demand for national forest timber was weak, there was often no competition in its sale—the problem was to get any bidder interested—and this may still be true in some localities. The Forest Service appraises its timber and offers it for sale subject to a minimum appraised price. For many years prior to World War II average stumpage prices on national forests were remarkably steady. (Figure 9.) They were not less than $2.00

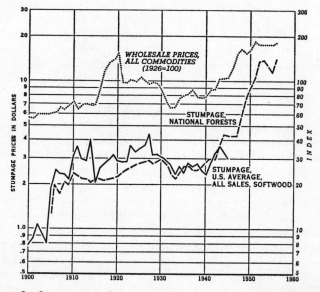

FIGURE 9. *Stumpage prices for national forests timber, 1905-56. All years are on a calendar year basis except for national forest stumpage prices, which are on a fiscal year basis.*

nor more than $3.00 per 1,000 board feet in any year from 1910 to 1942; there is virtually no trace in the prices received of the movements of the general price level, such as the inflation of World War I, the subsequent sharp deflation, the decline in prices in the early 1930's, and the like. Stumpage prices for national forest timber rose moderately, compared with average prices for all stumpage, in the

1910-30 period.[11] With large volumes of good-quality virgin timber still remaining for harvest, prices of stumpage reflected largely the advantages of good locations of the timber sold. Logs are heavy and costly to transport relative to their value, and hence accessible timber has a special value. But if an attempt is made to sell accessible timber at too high a price, sales are pushed to less accessible areas. The cost of stumpage has often been only a small fraction of the total cost of producing finished timber products, such as lumber and paper, and when lumber prices rise too much there are often substitutes whose use becomes economical. All of these factors operated to keep stumpage prices low and steady.

When World War II brought its great demand for timber products, and when the supply of good-quality, readily accessible private timber was reduced, stumpage prices for national forest timber rose rapidly. OPA price regulations did curtail prices during the war, but from 1947 to 1953 they tripled from slightly more than $4.00 per 1,000 board feet to a high of almost $14.00. The price rise of national forest timber is matched by the price rise of all other stumpage, especially high-quality timber. During the last fifteen years forestry in the United States, economically, has been on an entirely new plane. Previously stumpage prices had been so low, due to the large volume of virgin timber that needed merely harvesting, that to grow timber was uneconomic except in the most unusual situations. With present prices for stumpage, timber growing is profitable in many situations and locations.

Figure 8 shows a very great rise in the value of timber cut from the national forests. This rise is made up of three factors: (1) increase in the volume of timber sold; (2) increase in stumpage prices relative to all other prices; and (3) increase in the general price level. The influence of these three forces is shown separately in table 4, where the 1908-12 period is contrasted with 1951-55. In the forty-three years from the midpoint of one period to the other, total receipts increased 63.0 times. This was made up of: an increase in volume of stumpage sold, 10.47 times; an increase in stumpage prices relative to other prices, 2.35 times; and an increase in the general price level, 2.56 times. If the separate increases are multiplied, the total increase to 63.0 times the first level is obtained.

---

[11] Data on stumpage prices are not always fully representative of actual sales prices and all comparisons based on these data must be regarded as approximate. Stumpage prices for national forests are also influenced by the occurrence of salvage timber sales.

TABLE 4. *Increase in Receipts from National Forest Timber Sales, 1908-12 and 1951-55* [1]

Item	Annual average 1908-12	Annual average 1951-55	1951-55 as multiple of 1908-12
Volume of timber cut (million bd. ft.) ...	504	5,269	10.47
Average price per thousand bd. ft.[2]			
in current dollars	2.01	12.13	6.03
in 1947-49 dollars	4.62	10.89	2.35
Index of all wholesale prices			
(1947-49 = 100)	43.5	111.4	2.56
Total receipts from timber cut[3]			
in current dollars (million)	1,014	63,991	63.0
in 1947-49 dollars (million)	2,330	57,400	24.6

[1] Due to increased volume of stumpage sold, increased price of stumpage sold in constant dollars, and increased general price level.

[2] Calculated by dividing total receipts by total stumpage cut.

[3] Includes some minor receipts for forest products not sold on a stumpage basis.

This calculation shows clearly that the dominant factor in increased receipts has been increased volume of timber sales.

RECREATION [12]

The national forests have come to be one of the prime recreational areas of the nation and their use for this purpose is certain to grow greater with the years. "Recreation," as the term is used in this study, can apply to many kinds of human activity. The simplest may consist merely of looking at interesting scenery from an automobile, train, or plane. Then there is the occasional short-time use, such as the family picnic on Sunday. Or recreation may take the form of hunting and fishing, camping for a period of days, winter snow sports such as skiing, vacation-time living, and various activities. The recreation areas may be "developed" with good roads, parking places, fireplaces, picnic tables, sanitation facilities, ski lifts, and other man-made improvements, or they may be untouched. A special situation is the primitive or wilderness area, or other area in which no roads exist and in which commercial uses of most or all kinds are excluded. The various kinds of recreation may or may not compete with each other, depending on the physical situation and the extent of use; and the same factors may determine whether the various forms of recreation compete with other land uses.

[12] The specific data for this section are to be found in appendix table 4.

The volume of recreation provided by an area is not easily measured. The only practical yardstick is the number of persons who use an area and the length of time they use it; but this makes no allowance for differences in the quality of the recreational services obtainable. Most people derive greater enjoyment from one type of recreation than from another, and from one area than from another for the same type of recreation. There might even be general agreement among large numbers of people that one area is superior to another for a particular type of recreation. But there is no quantitative and accepted scale by which the value of different recreation types and areas may be judged. The output of recreation must therefore be measured entirely in terms of numbers of people and lengths of time, with no allowance for quality or value per unit of time.

Recreational use of an area may be measured in any one or a combination of three ways: (1) the number of admissions or entrances to an area, or the number of *visits;* (2) the total use made of the area, or the number of *visitor days;* and (3) the number of different individuals who use the area, or the number of *visitors.* These three measures are by no means identical. Under the first, each person who visits an area is counted as a visit, even though he may have used this same area or other areas other times during the same season. In practice, visits are usually counted or estimated as the number of people who enter a particular area. Thus an individual might be counted on each of successive days if he entered the recreational area each day. A visit is counted irrespective of how long it lasts—whether part of a day or a month. Visitor-days are simply numbers of visits multiplied by the number of days each visitor remains in the area. Parts of a day are ordinarily counted as whole days; thus a picnic party is counted as using an area for a day although its actual occupancy of the area may be limited to a few hours. Visitors are numbers of separate individuals and would always be less than numbers of visits. Some persons will use an area but once, and for these persons visitors and visits would be identical; others will use an area more than once, and for these persons visitors would be one-half, one-third, one-fourth, or some other smaller fraction of visits, depending on how many times the person visited the area. The relationship between visits and visitors will be different, depending on whether a single recreation area, a number of recreation areas of a particular type in a particular region, or all recreation areas in a state or other large area is the basis of consideration.

Each of these measures has usefulness in administration and in economic analysis. The total number of visits gives management personnel an idea as to the work load for those functions related to entrance, movement through the area, and departure from it, and of functions related to number of people within an area. It is also a measure of the total volume of recreation, somewhat akin to total paid admissions to athletic events, for the economic analyst. Visitor-days gives the land administrator an idea of the physical strain upon the recreational resources, and the economist an idea of total expenditures upon this type of recreation. The relation between numbers of visits and numbers of visitor-days reveals a great deal as to the character of the recreational use—whether it is predominantly one-day use, or whether it extends over several days, and this is an important fact for both administrator and analyst. The average stay of campers may be one day or it may be a week, and this has important meanings to the land manager as to the kinds of services these people need and the kinds of uses they are making of the recreation area. The number of visitors is important also, because it shows the numbers of individuals who are making use of the recreational areas. This is important to the land manager, as showing how general is the use of the resources he administers, and as providing a measure of the extent of his educational job; new visitors often require more guidance concerning fire prevention and resource use in general than do those who have used the area before. The number of visitors is important to the social analyst, because it shows how general among the total population is the use of the recreational resources in question; this may be critical in considerations of equitable financing of the cost of needed improvements and management.

A difficulty arises when these various measures of recreational use are confused—and they often have been confused—in use by the federal and local agencies and by the public. In practice, the most common data relate to numbers of visits, because it is easiest to count or estimate the numbers of people who enter an area. In this there should be no confusion. But the data for visits are often used as though they applied to visitors. In 1955 there were nearly 46 million *visits* to national forests and 50 million *visits* to the national park system for various types of recreation; but this does not mean that 96 million *persons* visited these areas. If all types of federal land and types of federal water development projects, state parks, local parks, and city parks are included, a total number of visits three or four or more times the total population is obtained, and yet the most elementary knowledge of recreational habits is sufficient to be sure that large numbers of people never take advantage of any of these areas. It is easy to treat data on numbers of visits as if they were data on numbers of visitors, and this has been done repeatedly in publications, articles, press releases, and speeches. But this represents a substantial confusion of ideas and of land uses, which becomes worse when large areas or several types of recreational areas are under consideration.

Doubtless, data on numbers of visits, and sometimes on numbers of visitor-days will continue to be collected by the administrative agencies responsible for different types of recreational areas. In addition, some attempt should be made to estimate the numbers of persons involved. This could well be done on a sample basis rather than by attempting to ascertain the use by all individuals. Recreational use of various types of federal, state, and local recreation areas, and probably private ones as well, should be considered. Some sort of ratios or coefficients could be estimated from which it would be possible to calculate the number of persons using any national forest, the number using one, two, three, or more national forests, the number using both national forests and national parks, the number using one or both of these and also state parks, and so on, for all possible combinations of recreational land use, given the present types of data as to total numbers of visits for each area. These surveys might well also consider such matters as location of the recreationists, their income class and occupational status, their reasons for using the recreational areas, and other related matters.

In the early days of the national forests recreational use was limited. Transportation was slow and most of the national forests were relatively remote from centers of population. In addition, the population was smaller, particularly in the West where most of the national forests are found; real incomes per capita were lower; and there was less leisure for the average person. Use was so small before World War I, in fact, that data on recreational use of the national forests are available only since 1924. In that year a total of about 4.5 million visits was recorded, of which about three-fourths were in improved recreational areas and the other one-fourth in unimproved areas. From 1925 through 1934 visits to national forests increased at a rate of about 5 per cent annually, as can be seen by trend line A on figure 10. It should be recalled that in this period the nation went from a state of fairly high prosperity to the depths of the worst depression of modern times. The relatively rapid increase in recreational use is thus the more impressive. In the period from 1935 through

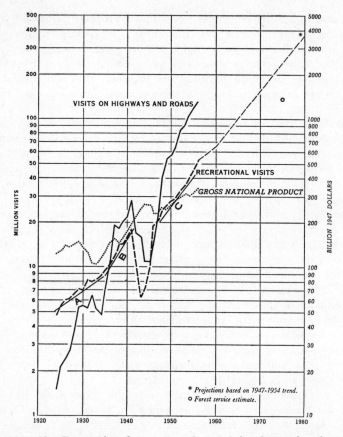

FIGURE 10. *Recreational use of and travel in the national forests, 1924-56 and projections for 1960 and 1980.*

1941 the rate of increase, as shown by trend line B, was about 11 per cent annually. In these years the nation went from severe depression to moderate prosperity. During World War II, with gasoline rationing, limited supplies of automobile tires, and with no new autos available, recreational use of the national forests declined sharply, falling nearly two-thirds in two years. Immediately after the war it rose again almost equally sharply. By 1946 total visits were back to a point slightly above that of 1941. From 1947 through 1954 the rate of increase, as shown by trend line C, has been about 9 per cent annually. This has been a period of sustained prosperity and high employment; the rate has been slightly less than before the war, when the whole economy was moving from depression to prosperity, but much above that of the later 1920's and early 1930's, when the economy was moving downward. If the war years 1942 through 1945 are omitted, and if 1946 is superimposed on 1941, the whole period from 1935 to 1954 forms one rather clear trend, with an average annual increase of about 10 per cent.

It seems clear that increased recreational use of national forests is encouraged by high national income and employment, but takes place even under unfavorable economic conditions. It is true that total population has been increasing, but further population increases seem certain for the future. The rapid and sustained growth in recreational use of national forests, especially during the later 1920's and 1930's, is the more remarkable when it is recalled that during these years several national parks were carved out of the national forests. While the areas of land involved were comparatively small, they had been popular recreationally; had they retained their national forest status, the increase in recreational use of national forests would have been greater than it was.

While the recreational use of national forests has increased, the percentage rate of increase has been constant and thus when a trend line is fitted to the data on semilogarithmic paper, as in figure 10, the result is a straight line. The remarkable thing about the data shown in figure 10 is that the same *percentage* rate of increase has been maintained from year to year over a comparatively long period. It will be recalled that the rate of increase in timber sold from the national forests followed the same constant pattern over an even longer period.

Assuming that the 1947-54 rate of increase in recreational use of national forests will continue in the future in periods of reasonable prosperity, the number of visits to national forests by 1960 would reach about 65 million, and by 1980, about 360 million. The latter figure may seem extreme,[13] yet it represents less than a sixfold increase in twenty years. Almost as great a percentage increase took place from 1924 to 1941 and, if the war had not intervened, about an equal percentage increase would have taken place by 1944. Even with the war, the increase from 1934 to 1954 was nearly fivefold.

[13] The Forest Service, in commenting on this point, states that its estimate of recreational visits for 1975 is 135 million visits, or about 56 per cent of the 240 million visits that a projection of the 1947-54 trend would indicate.

The same factors that have lead to increased recreational use in the past—an increasing population, a rising real income per capita, more leisure for the average person, and greater population mobility through improved transportation methods—all seem likely to continue in the future, and probably at a higher rather than at a lower rate. The persistence and comparative stability of a rough 10 per cent rate of increase for the entire period from 1924, when data first became available, to the most recent years—excluding only the abnormal war years, but including periods of sharp decline and upward surges in the economy—puts the burden of proof on those who argue that future increases will be at a slower rate. Perhaps a mathematical projection of 360 million visits will not be reached by 1980, but visits in the neighborhood of 250 to 300 million seem highly probable.

Before World War II the use of improved recreational facilities was roughly three-fourths of the total, but during and immediately after the war it declined to half or less of the total. During the 1930's the Forest Service was able to take advantage of the Civilian Conservation Corps, Public Works Administration, and Works Progress Administration programs to construct a comparatively large number of recreational facilities upon the national forests. But after the war funds for construction of facilities were sharply limited, and even funds for care and management of existing facilities have been short.

There are no data, so far as we know, showing what part of the total recreational use of the national forests is made by persons residing at various distances from the forests. But it would seem logical to expect that visitors from relatively distant places are greatly outnumbered by the hunter, fisher, camper, and picnicker living within 300 miles of the forests. This is borne out by data on the kinds of recreation enjoyed in all national forests during 1955.

	Visits (millions)	Per cent of total
General enjoyment of forest environment	12.44	27
Picnicking	10.88	24
Fishing	8.28	18
Hunting	4.06	9
Winter sports	2.77	6
Camping	2.72	6
Swimming	1.37	3
Hiking and riding	1.05	2

The other 5 per cent of use was divided between many miscellaneous activities.

The twelve most heavily used forests (measured by man-days' use) were as follows:

Forest	State	Visits (millions)	Man-days' use (millions)
Angeles	California	1.71	3.04
San Bernardino	California	1.27	2.44
Pike	Colorado	1.86	2.17
Pisgah	North Carolina	1.52	1.83
Inyo	California	0.91	1.75
Black Hills	South Dakota	1.73	1.64
Wasatch	Utah	1.63	1.59
Mt. Hood	Oregon	1.72	1.46
Eldorado	California	0.47	1.44
Snoqualmie	Washington	0.95	1.41
Sierra	California	0.30	1.23
Superior	Minnesota	0.41	1.20

These twelve forests contain only 7.6 per cent of the area of all national forests, but they account for 32 per cent of the recreational use of this type of federal land. Even within these forests recreational use was concentrated largely upon rather small areas.

It is notable that five out of the twelve most popular national forests are in California. While some of these forests have superior recreational qualities, their rank in public favor perhaps rests more upon the large urban population of California than it does on any inherently superior physical characteristics. The popularity of the Black Hills national forest, for example, is at least partly due to the fact that there are few comparable areas of publicly owned forested and mountain land within a relatively long distance.

Recreational use of national forests tends to be sharply limited seasonally. Most national forests are mountainous areas, and while they are used for fall hunting and, increasingly, for winter sports, most of the concentration takes place in the summer, often in a three-month season. The more southerly forests have a larger winter use. Recreational activity also tends to be heaviest on weekends and holidays. As a result of the great variations in use, facilities adequate to care for peak crowds will be unused most of the time. This is a problem more or less common to all recreational areas, although greater, perhaps, for national forests than for areas like city parks. If some of the public could be induced to use the national forests at off-peak days and seasons—in the middle of the week, the fall, and the spring, especially—they would find the recreational areas less crowded, and the recreational facilities would be more fully used.

Statistics on the average number of days that visitors spend within the national forests shed further light on the use made of the forests' recreational facilities. For all recreational uses in 1955 the average number of days spent within the forest was 1.36. For summer homes owned by individuals but located on tracts leased to them by the Forest Service, the average stay was 6.6 days; for organization camps owned by the organizations, the average stay was 5.4 days; for organization camps owned by the government, it was 3.6 days; and for wilderness areas, the average length of stay was 2.5 days. But these, comparatively, are the less popular recreational uses, and for every other use the average stay was less than 2 days. Use of the public camp and picnic areas was almost 40 per cent of total recreational use; here the average stay was 1.27 days. Since any fraction of a day's use is considered statistically as one day, it is apparent that the predominant use was confined to one day. The use of "other areas" was 34 per cent of the total, and here the average stay was 1.15 days. Use of winter sports areas was only 1.01 days on the average. Even the average use of resorts was only 1.07 days. It seems clear from these data that the typical visitor used the national forests for recreation for all or part of one day, or at most overnight, and that the visitor who stayed longer was distinctly in the minority.

Road travel on the national forest highway system has increased much more rapidly than recreational use as such. Until 1936 such visits numbered less than recreational visits, but in 1952 they were more than twice as many.

A different type of recreational use is made of the relatively remote back-country portions of some national forests, variously designated as primitive, wilderness, wild, or roadless. These terms have had special meaning at different times as to area, types of use permitted, regulations applicable, etc. In general, however, they are alike in their intent to imply exclusion of commercial developments of most types, and of most or all roads. There are presently some 14 million acres in some seventy-nine areas of these types in national forests.

For the most part, their value for commercial development would be low even in the absence of restrictions. Their real purpose is to preserve in a relatively unspoiled condition the qualities and values of the primitive areas as white man first found them. These areas are used by a limited number of persons who hike or, more commonly, use pack animals to get back into the country and enjoy its beauties. In 1955 there were 462,000 visitors to such areas, for a total of over 1 million man-days' use; this is 1 per cent and 2 per cent, respectively, of total national forest recreational use. The value of such areas cannot be measured by their use—in fact, heavy use would destroy their very purpose. It rests instead upon unique qualities which can be enjoyed by a relatively small number of people. Among the problems of multi-purpose management, which will be discussed later in this chapter, the primitive or wilderness areas present special difficulties. Some conservationists have expressed concern that these areas are not adequately protected by law against commercial encroachment.

WATERSHED UTILIZATION

One of the purposes recognized by the Congress in authorizing national forests was protection of watersheds. Some people believe that, at least in large areas, this is their most important use and that it will become even more important as time goes on. National forests often lie in high mountain country where total precipitation is greater and where the winter snows become the source of summer flows. Thus it is that in the eleven western states, where 21 per cent of the land area is in national forests, as much as 53 per cent of the total runoff in streams originates within these forests. They are the main source of water supply for some 1,800 towns and cities and for some 600 hydroelectric plants.

In watershed management, whether on national forests or elsewhere, there are two rather distinctly different phases which, for lack of more precise terminology, may be distinguished as the "preventative or maintenance" phase and the "manipulative or adaptive" phase. The object of preventative or maintenance watershed management is to prevent impairment of the watershed. Prevention of "wild" fires is usually a major part of preventative watershed management. While fire increasingly is coming to be recognized as a useful tool in forest and other land management, it must be controlled as to season and burning conditions. Reduction of erosion through control over roads, logging methods, and grazing are other types of preventative watershed management.

The Forest Service has done a good deal of preventative watershed management on the national forests. From the beginning it has regarded fire control as basic in national forest management. To reduce erosion hazard, it employs road construction specifications framed to avoid the accumulation of large volumes of water which may acquire considerable velocity and hence major cutting power; it often controls the gradient of roads, especially logging roads; and may prohibit the skidding of logs directly downhill where the log trails are in danger of causing serious erosion channels. Where skid roads or other areas are disturbed by logging it may see to it that reseeding is conducted.

The object of manipulative or adaptive watershed management is to modify the stream flow. Often the objective is to get more water, usually without more sediment, from the area; this is especially important in the arid and semi-arid West. Another objective might be to modify the seasonal character of the stream flow so as to obtain more water at times of low natural flow, and perhaps reduce the volume of flow at times of high flow or of flood. This type of watershed management is in its infancy. It may be possible at some future date to bring about changes in stream flow through modification of the vegetation on the watershed—by means of a reduced transpiration by the plants, reduced evaporation from the soil and from the plants, better snow pack and slower snow melt, or other processes. Some highly suggestive experimental work has, in fact, been done along these lines, but there are still many unanswered problems before watershed management of this type can be put into widespread practice. In most situations the physical effects of different possible manipulations of the vegetative cover are uncertain. Some possible measures might not increase stream flow in the ways desired and might lead to accelerated erosion and consequent later difficulties. Until the physical effects of different measures can be estimated with some confidence, it is obviously impossible to estimate the economic effects.

One type of manipulative or adaptive watershed management is through the use of physical structures. These structures may take the form of retention or detention dams on the stream channels, to hold back the flow from a peak period to a later, lower flow period.

Beaver have been used for this purpose on some watersheds. It may be possible to construct terraces or other waterways on the upper watersheds in a manner generally similar to the way the same kinds of structures are used on farm lands. However, the steep and rocky character of much national forest land severely limits the area to which such practices can be applied.

There is relatively little evidence that the total volume of water flowing off of national forests, its quality, or its seasonality of flow, have been materially modified before or during the years these lands were in national forest status. In some cases the lands had suffered damage from overgrazing, fire, or other causes before the areas came into national forests; in other cases the damage has been inflicted since. The preventative or maintenance type of watershed management has been generally effective in preventing a deterioration of natural watershed conditions and in helping to heal disturbed areas. However, marked changes have occurred in local areas and for smaller streams.

While the physical characteristics of stream flows arising on national forests have changed relatively little over the years, the importance of the water has increased greatly as a result of population growth and economic development. As water becomes more fully used, it becomes more valuable and more in demand; and that has occurred in many western locations. Much may be wasted in customary use and if water becomes scarcer, and thus more expensive, large savings might be made. Preservation of watershed characteristics is important, too. But it has not always been clear how much use of the land, solely to preserve watershed qualities, would differ from its use under good management for such purposes as grazing, forestry, and recreation.

MINERAL DEVELOPMENT

With few exceptions, the national forests have been open to development of minerals under the mining laws and the mineral leasing laws. In the early days of the West considerable mining activity took place upon lands now within national forests. However, since valuable mineral deposits nearly always passed into private ownership, relatively little actual mineral production has taken place on national forests as such.

In recent years, the mining laws have been subject to many abuses and have frequently been used as a subterfuge for obtaining control of land that would not be available under laws or regulations for the purposes sought. The Forest Service has estimated that only 15 per cent of all mining claims that went to patent, and only a very small fraction of those not patented, have been used for commercial mining operations. The others have been used for grazing, timber harvest (permitted after patent), summer homes, or for many other purposes.[14]

Since 1955 sand, gravel, and the other building materials have been removed from the operation of the mining laws. Oil and gas, coal, phosphate, potash, and other minerals are open for mineral development under the mineral leasing laws on national forests, subject to Forest Service approval and the co-ordination of this type of land use with others. So far any important mineral development has been quite localized.

MISCELLANEOUS USES

In addition to the major uses outlined above, the land in national forests is used also for relatively minor purposes of which right of way—for private roads, electric power lines, irrigation canals, etc.—is perhaps the most important. Other minor uses, such as leasing for resort, summer home, and commercial and industrial sites, or exchange with private lands, have been referred to in different context.

SUMMARY

1. The use of national forest land has increased greatly. Grazing, however, has decreased by about two-thirds from its peak, and actual mining operations have apparently not increased materially.[15] Since 1941, the prewar peak, timber cut has trebled, recreation has more than doubled, travel has trebled, and the value, but not the volume, of water has become much greater.

[14] The terms under which mining claims are made available are discussed in chapter four, pp. 226-28.
[15] Recently there has been an increase in mining for uranium. See also, for grazing districts, p. 95.

2. Past trends toward increased use seem almost sure to continue for some years, perhaps at an accelerated rate.

3. Multiple use of national forest land has been a conscious goal of administration, and the various uses of national forests have often occurred on the same areas.

4. Some conflicts and competition among uses in the achievement of this goal of multiple use have occurred in the past. With the probable greater total use of national forests in the future, these conflicts and this competition are sure to increase, thus making more difficult the attainment of the goals of multiple-purpose administration.

5. Decisions among alternative uses and alternative degrees of different uses have been necessary in the past and will be increasingly necessary and difficult in the future. The nature of the managerial processes and problems involved is the subject of chapter three.

Use Pattern on Grazing Districts, Other Public Domain,
Oregon & California Revested Lands, and Submerged Areas
of Outer Continental Shelf

The diverse types of federal land management units discussed in this section are alike in two broad ways. They fall, for the most part, under the jurisdiction of the Bureau of Land Management; and they consist of those portions of the original public domain remaining after such homogeneous units as the national forests and national parks had been established. They are considered in this place for a variety of reasons, among which are their size, which slightly exceeds the area of the national forests and is far larger than that of other types of federal land units; their revenues, which are greater than those of the national forests; and their character, which in many ways resembles the character of the national forests. Various proposals for governmental reorganization have stressed this latter point in suggesting administrative consolidation of these lands and the national forests.

The grazing districts were set up under the Taylor Grazing Act. The boundaries of the fifty-nine districts enclose 168 million acres of federal land as well as 97 million acres in other ownerships. For the most part, this land is covered with shrubs and grass and is physically best suited to grazing and mineral development. It contains comparatively little commercial forest, although several million acres, which are classified as woodland, support sparse stands of trees, mostly juniper. Cropland is rare, potentialities for recreation are not high, and watershed values are rather special ones.

Outside of grazing districts, the public domain includes several different physical types. Sheer desert covers extensive areas in southern Nevada, southeastern California, and southwestern Arizona. Elsewhere, extensive areas with extremely low forage-producing capacity can support only rather marginal livestock operations or are only occasionally usable. Some scattered tracts of better grazing land are located along the eastern edge of the grazing districts in New Mexico, Colorado, Wyoming, Montana, South Dakota, and North Dakota. Throughout the mountainous regions of the West other scattered tracts, many with commercial forest although sometimes of rather low grade, lie on the edges of the grazing districts and national forests. Scattered tracts also are to be found throughout most of the other states created out of the original public domain, the largest of which are in Minnesota and Arkansas.

The Oregon and California lands, and the Coos Bay Wagon Road Grant Lands which are ordinarily classified with them, are mountainous in character and are heavily forested with what today are highly valuable old-growth stands of timber, mostly Douglas fir. The unusual origin of these lands has already been traced in chapter one, but their history is further complicated by features which require some explanation here before their use pattern can fully be understood. The original grant, like most railroad grants, provided that alternate sections of land within a certain distance on either side of the railroad would be granted to the railroad, and further, that alternate sections in a still wider band would be available to the extent needed, to provide land in lieu of that already in private ownership. Actual title passed to the railroad company only as the lands were surveyed. As it turned out, so much of the valley lands in the Willamette Valley of Oregon along the railroad was in private ownership that the entire area of the "in lieu" lands was required to satisfy the grant. However, survey proceeded slowly, so that when the granted lands were revested to the United States, roughly half a million acres of land had not been made available to the railroad company. By this time national forests had been established in much of the mountainous area of Oregon, and all or nearly all of the unselected lands lay within the boundaries of national forests. The acts of 1916 and of 1937, and intervening acts, placed management of the O & C lands in the Department of the Interior, specifically rejecting proposals to place them under the Forest Service. These acts, however, failed to deal clearly with the unselected lands, with the result that a dispute over them arose.

The Forest Service claimed that the lands unselected by the railroad company at the time of revestment of the grant reverted to original public domain status and thus were part of the national forests created out of that public domain. The Department of the Interior claimed that the lands were actually part of the grant and were to be administered as such. It later appeared that for many years each agency thought it was administering these lands and was unaware that the other agency thought they were under its jurisdiction. Each made timber sales, allowed homestead entries, or took other action on these lands as though they were under its jurisdiction. This overlapping of claims became evident only about 1939. Until that time these lands, which lie some distance back from the valleys, were not in great demand for timber harvest or for other purposes.

From 1939 until 1954 the Forest Service managed the lands, which became known as the "controverted lands," under an agreement with the Department of the Interior; but revenues therefrom were placed in a special status or escrow account in the Treasury and the share due the counties was not paid to them. This issue was brought to a head by a suit instituted by some of the counties in which the lands lay, demanding that their share of the funds in escrow be paid to them under the terms of the O & C Act, which terms are more generous than those of the acts applicable to the national forests. A federal court ruled that the lands were in fact O & C lands, and that the revenues were to be disbursed accordingly. The issue was further resolved by Act of Congress in 1954 [16] which states in part that these lands "are declared to be revested Oregon and California railroad grant lands; and said lands shall continue to be administered as national forest lands by the Secretary of Agriculture subject to all laws, rules, and regulations applicable to the national forests." Thus these lands are part of the O & C grant so far as revenues are concerned, but part of the national forests so far as management is concerned. In this same act the Congress also considered the intermingled character of O & C and national forest lands, other than the controverted lands. It authorized and directed the two departments concerned to exchange lands within certain areas so as to block up the holdings of each.

This history of O & C lands is traced in some detail—although in far less detail than is needed to fully understand all the twists and

---

[16] 68 Stat. 270-272.

turns of their long and complicated legal and political history. The value of the lands is great, but the arrangement for their administration remains something of an anomaly. Although they contain some of the finest federal forests, the noncontroverted O & C lands are not under the jurisdiction of the Forest Service despite that agency's repeated attempts to have them placed there.

The submerged areas of the outer continental shelf have only recently been established formally in federal ownership. Beginning in the 1930's, some coastal states had issued oil and gas leases for underwater areas off their coasts. This action was later challenged by the federal government and a suit carried to the Supreme Court established federal title in the areas. Attempts to pass legislation turning these areas over to the states were unsuccessful until May 1953, when the Submerged Lands Act was passed which gave to the states all lands under navigable inland waters and seaward to a distance of three miles into the Pacific and Atlantic Oceans and up to three marine leagues into the Gulf of Mexico.[17] The Outer Continental Shelf Lands Act, passed in August 1953, provided for leasing of submerged areas seaward of these boundaries.[18] Although the act set no outer boundaries, in practice the outer boundary will depend upon the ability to drill in deep water. A few years ago drilling in even 50 feet of water was difficult; now the technical limit is perhaps 200 feet of water depth, and the economic limit may be less, depending on prospects for oil discovery. Calculations of the area of the outer continental shelf usually adopt a depth of 600 feet as maximum, but it will be some years before drilling at this depth is feasible. Within this area valuable deposits of oil and other minerals are known to exist and still larger deposits are believed probable. The addition of the submerged areas of the outer continental shelf to the federal "land"—if it is proper to designate as "land" something always covered with many feet of water—illustrates the dynamic effect of technology on the resource base of the country.

GRAZING [19]

Like the national forests, the lands now within grazing districts were grazed long before passage of the Taylor Grazing Act in 1934.

[17] 43 USC 1301-15.
[18] 43 USC 1331-43.
[19] Data for this section are found in appendix table 12.

The same factors that led to unregulated use of the forage on national forest areas, with consequent overuse, applied here also. But the situation was worse on the grazing district lands for at least two reasons. In the first place, these lands had often to act as a shock absorber when reductions in grazing were made on the national forests. Ranchers whose use of the national forests was reduced sought frequently to maintain their numbers of livestock by increased grazing on the public domain. Prior to passage of the Taylor Grazing Act the Forest Service was often faced with an impossible dilemma: if it reduced grazing on the national forests, grazing increased outside; if it hesitated to do this, its own areas deteriorated. In the second place, the lands now within grazing districts are areas of low precipitation and scanty vegetative cover. Moreover, on the whole there is a closer and more fragile balance between soil-forming or soil-holding and soil-destroying forces on these lands than on the national forests. Many areas now within grazing districts were not naturally in a state of equilibrium between soil-holding and soil-destroying forces when the white man occupied the West, but rather were eroding relatively rapidly. In many areas seriously accelerated erosion began many years ago, often leading to a succession of changes in the soil and moisture relationships. In these circumstances stopping erosion or restoring the vegetative cover is a difficult or impossible task, no matter what the type of management.

When the Taylor Grazing Act was passed and administration of the grazing districts began, use of these lands was largely legalized and regulated. In this respect the pattern of administration was similar to that adopted for the national forests some three or four decades earlier. Regulations for use of the grazing districts placed emphasis on the ownership of complementary or commensurate private lands or watering places, and on prior use of the public land in question. Specific rules largely eliminated the so-called "tramp" sheepman—the operator who owned little or no land and who migrated with his flocks from area to area, taking feed wherever he could find it. At that time drought and depression had already reduced livestock numbers throughout the range region and the ranges could in many cases be improved, or at least their use safely increased, by means of water developments in areas previously lacking them. The combined effect of these various forces tended toward an approximate balance of range use and forage-producing capacity without drastic reductions in livestock numbers, except where local situations made this necessary.

The Grazing Service, which preceded the Bureau of Land Management in administering the grazing districts, was fortunate in that it was not exposed to strong demands for major increases in livestock grazing during World War II, as the Forest Service had been in World, War I. The increase in grazing on national forests between 1912 and 1918 created many difficulties with which the Forest Service had to struggle for many years.

The number of livestock permitted to graze and the total grazing load on the grazing districts have been largely stabilized since about

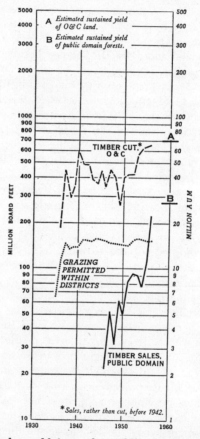

FIGURE 11. *Timber sold from the public domain and O & C lands, and permitted grazing within grazing districts, 1935-56.*

1937, when the area within grazing districts reached approximately its present level. (Figure 11.) [20] Total permitted number of livestock grazed has varied between 3.5 and 3.7 million animal units; because of economic conditions during and after the war, a fairly substantial shift out of sheep took place, but the numbers so reduced were largely replaced by increases in cattle grazed. Total grazing load by domestic livestock in most recent years has varied from 14 to 16 million animal-unit months a year. [21] In this respect, the grazing district lands are fairly typical of all grazing lands in private ownership in the West, where the grazing load, while varying with dry and wet years and with depression and prosperity, has remained relatively constant.

The Bureau of Land Management has developed a system of range inspection and range evaluation which permits systematic checks upon the progress the range is making under different stocking and management programs. Some reductions in numbers of livestock permitted and grazed have been made in recent years—relatively heavy ones in certain local areas. Offsetting these reductions, at least partially, will be some increases in range use made possible by a comparatively large range reseeding program and by improvements in the range resulting from general management and from programs initiated earlier. While there may be some net downward movement in livestock numbers grazed over the next few years, no major reduction now appears probable.

Outside of the grazing districts, some 18 million acres of public domain, consisting for the most part of relatively small and scattered tracts, or of low-grazing-capacity desert areas, are under lease. The total grazing load on these lands is some 2.5 million animal-unit

[20] The data presented in figure 11 relate to numbers permitted to graze; actual numbers grazed are slightly lower. In recent years, most cattle permits have been filled about to the limit; but some sheepmen, because of labor or other difficulties, have not run their full permitted number.

[21] An animal-unit month, used as a unit of measurement of grazing, does not represent an amount of feed which is always constant or equal in volume or nutritive value. While by definition it is enough feed to carry one animal unit for one month, this may vary from only a maintenance level to a growth or higher level ration. The volume of feed consumed by one animal unit also varies greatly between livestock of different ages, but it is customary to count all cattle above the age of weaned calves as equivalent to animal units and to count five sheep as equal to an animal unit with no allowance for unweaned lambs. The nutritive requirement of a ewe with suckling lamb is far higher than that for a yearling unbred ewe, for instance. Even if the volume of feed and nutritive values were constant, its value might differ greatly depending on the location of the grass and the market, just as the values of other feeds and other commodities vary between locations and over time.

months a year. With few exceptions, these lands had been fully used prior to the passage of the Taylor Grazing Act, and for the most part the leases legalized and regulated, to an extent, the uses which had grown up.[22]

WILDLIFE IN GRAZING DISTRICTS

The grazing district and other public domain lands have some value for wildlife purposes, especially seasonally. Forage used by wildlife is roughly 10 per cent of the total on grazing districts, compared with 45 per cent on national forests. Although the extent of this use on the grazing districts is less, it is often crucial at certain seasons and hence may be critical to a wildlife program in the area. The grazing districts and intermingled private land are especially important as a home for antelope. In general, the various federal agencies and state officials have co-operated in developing a game management and harvest program in the various areas. State officials have the right to establish hunting conditions, but since the land which provides the feed for the game is in large measure federal land, the two groups of officials work out programs jointly in many areas.

TIMBER HARVEST[23]

Timber harvest and other forestry programs on the lands discussed in this section fall into three distinctive parts, based to an extent upon geographic and physical factors and to an extent upon differences in legal history. They are (1) the Oregon & California revested lands of western Oregon, (2) the public domain forested lands in the United States, and (3) the forested public domain in Alaska.

The total area of the O & C lands is about 2.5 million acres, of which 0.5 million acres, previously considered controverted lands, are under Forest Service administration. (See pages 82-84.) The currently available inventory data indicate a timber volume of about 50 billion board feet on the noncontroverted lands; but this inventory is somewhat out of date—in part because standards of commercially usable timber have changed greatly over the past few years—and an up-to-date inventory will probably show a volume of 60 billion board feet. On

---

[22] The fees charged for grazing livestock in grazing districts and in the national forest are discussed in chapter four, pp. 220-23.

[23] Data for this section are found in appendix tables 13 and 14.

this basis, the previously controverted lands have about 10 billion board feet of timber. The currently estimated sustained yield of the noncontroverted lands is 660 million board feet annually; that of the previously controverted lands is about 120 million board feet. These figures will be raised by completion of the inventories now under way. In addition, a vigorous program of reforestation of areas now not satisfactorily restocking, estimated at from 100,000 to 200,000 acres, would increase the total growth of these lands and thus in time make possible an increase of perhaps 140 million board feet in the allowable annual cut. These estimates would indicate an ultimate sustained yield cut from the entire O & C area of at least 1 billion board feet annually, equalling a net annual growth of 400 board feet per acre.

The cut of timber from O & C lands (including controverted) has varied considerably from year to year, depending in large part on the demand for lumber and the consequent activity of the lumber mills. (See figure 11.) An irregular upward trend in cut is evident, however. The cut of about 700 million feet in 1955 and 1956, from 2.5 million acres of land, is a very much heavier rate of timber harvest than was found for all national forests, although not heavier than that found in national forest areas adjacent to O & C lands.

Management of O & C timber presents much the same problems as management of nearby national forest timber, except that the intermingling of federal and privately owned lands is usually aggravated. As with national forests, the chief obstacle to a higher cut on the O & C lands has been the scarcity of access roads. For many years funds were lacking to build any roads so that the only roads built were those contracted for as part of timber sales. In recent years appropriations for road construction have been available, but not for a long enough time nor in sufficient amount to build all the roads needed. Funds also have been lacking for reseeding or replanting trees on an adequate scale. It is significant that the O & C counties of western Oregon have not only urged a larger program of reforestation on improperly stocking lands, but have offered to have it paid for out of funds which otherwise would accrue to them.

The complex intermingled landownership situation on the O & C lands has created many difficult management problems. Fire control and insect and disease control measures, as well as road construction and use, must obviously be correlated with activities of the intermingled owners.

A special feature of O & C lands which has materially affected their administration has been the revenue-sharing arrangement with the counties in which the land lies. (Specific data on this will be presented in chapter five.) The lands had been on the tax rolls of the counties when owned by the railroad company. After they returned to federal ownership various plans of revenue-sharing were incorporated into law, with the general objective of compensating the counties in full for the revenues they had lost. But timber sales were so low that these various arrangements failed to yield the counties the amount of revenue they had previously enjoyed. Tax arrearages were paid by the federal government to the counties at various times, and in the 1937 Act a new revenue-sharing arrangement, whereby the counties received 50 per cent of the revenues, was put into effect. In addition, another 25 per cent of the revenues was used to liquidate the Treasury account from which the tax arrearages and purchase cost of the lands had been paid. When that account was repaid in early 1952, the counties then received the 25 per cent of the revenues which had previously gone into it. However, since the 1953 fiscal year the sums appropriated for road construction have been deducted from this 25 per cent fund, and only the remainder paid to the counties. The cost of reforestation may also be deducted from the 25 per cent fund. In recent years, as will be shown later, the counties have received considerably more revenues from these lands than the lands' tax equivalent. The existence of this unusually favorable arrangement for the counties, in contrast to the national forest arrangement whereby the counties receive 25 per cent of the revenues from timber sales and other sources, has been a constant source of friction, comment, and political maneuvering by the counties to prevent a transfer of the O & C lands into national forest status.

The price of stumpage from O & C lands shows a rise in recent years somewhat similar to that found on national forests, but much more extreme.[24] The average price of all stumpage sold from the O & C lands varied between $2.00 and $3.00 per 1,000 board feet in nearly all years up to fiscal 1942, in which year it averaged $2.81. The average price by fiscal year doubled in 1947, again in 1950, and nearly doubled again in 1951, with the 1956 price now nearly ten times that of the

[24] Average stumpage prices per 1,000 board feet: (Prices are based on sales, rather than cut, because sales more accurately reflect timber values at that time. Prices are for sales from noncontroverted lands.)

1943	$3.80	1948	$10.45	1953	$22.81
1944	3.46	1949	11.04	1954	18.73
1945	4.22	1950	12.16	1955	28.45
1946	4.35	1951	21.65	1956	37.63
1947	6.88	1952	25.05		

price in 1943. The average for the years 1952-56 was $26.53 per 1,000 board feet. This represents a rise nearly twice as great as was found for all timber sold from national forests. This striking rise in average prices understates the true extent of the rise for stumpage of the same quality, equally well located. Due to changes in timber utilization practices in the lumber industry, the average timber sold in the later years included some logs of a quality that would not have been harvested in earlier years, and often it included timber taken from areas where comparatively expensive roads had to be built—roads which it might not have paid to build earlier. The price rise of stumpage from the O & C lands was brought about by the same factors that underlay the price rise of national forest stumpage—depletion of privately owned old-growth stands, rising prices in general, and increasing demand for timber during and after the war. And there was an additional factor: during these years southwestern Oregon attracted the location of large-scale lumber manufacture.

Until fairly recently it was believed that no merchantable timber was left on the public domain—that all of it had been transferred to private ownership or had been included in national forests. However, a considerable volume of timber—something like 20 billion feet of saw timber and 80 billion feet of timber of less than saw-timber size of the woodland type—now exists on the public domain exclusive of Alaska. The saw timber consists for the most part of relatively small tracts, often of light stands per acre, and sometimes of less valuable species. But with the exhaustion of better and more accessible stands in many areas, and with new methods of logging which make profitable the harvesting of smaller, lighter, and more remote stands, these timber resources have come into active demand.

For many years there was no authority to sell green timber from the public domain, even if it were overmature and in need of cutting. During World War II, however, this authority was granted, and in 1947 permanent legislation was adopted under which timber sales have climbed from 32 million board feet in 1948 to 223 million feet in 1956. While this is a small volume of timber compared with O & C sales, and more particularly with national forest sales, it is not negligible and is often of considerable importance locally and to some types of lumbermen.

It has been estimated that the sustained-yield cut of these lands under present management is about 210 million board feet annually and that it can be increased considerably, to 300 million feet annually by 1980. Access roads are a problem, for timber sales from such land generally cannot be large enough to warrant the operator building much road. Sales are usually conditioned by access from other roads. A shortage of personnel to make and supervise these sales has also been an inhibiting force.

The forest situation on public domain in Alaska is very different. In southern Alaska excellent stands of high-quality timber are included within national forests, and climatic conditions render fire hazard almost negligible. In recent years a beginning has been made, through a few relatively large undertakings, to harvest these timber stands for pulp and other products. Most of the country in interior and northern Alaska was originally covered by forests consisting largely of spruce and of trees which never grew large or made good-quality lumber. However, these forests were a major asset in the early exploitation of the country. Unfortunately, they are highly susceptible to fire during the relatively short summer season. Nearly all of the more accessible areas have burned once or several times. As a result, accessible trees for even such humble uses as firewood and Christmas trees are scarce in the vicinity of many towns. In recent years fire protection has been extended to the more accessible areas and gradually to those more remote. In the latter case it is based on airplane detection and suppression. Men and equipment are flown in to the endangered area. This effort has been handicapped by wholly inadequate funds, but has been notably successful within the scope of the funds available. In addition, timber is now sold and cut under law and constructive forestry practices, in contrast to the situation which existed for many years. At present annual timber sales from public domain in Alaska are still small, in the magnitude of 20 million board feet. Conceivably, at some future time the spruce forests of Alaska may become an economic source of pulpwood and the birch forests the basis of a woodworking industry. Forest management in Alaska in one sense is like the management of the national forests in the States several decades ago; it does not produce as much revenue as it costs, the adverse ratio running roughly 5 to 1.

RECREATION ON PUBLIC DOMAIN AND O & C LANDS

Virtually no data are available as to the recreational use of the public domain and O & C lands. So far as the public domain is concerned, the lands are often so intermingled with other lands that it would be difficult to distinguish on which land the use occurred.

By far the greater part of the general public prefers wooded areas with water for its recreation. Judged by this standard, comparatively little of the public domain, in or outside of grazing districts, is good recreational area. For those who like desert scenery and climate and the broad sweep of open spaces, much of the public domain is superior. Areas of this type are not ordinarily used intensively; but in recent years there has been a sharply rising trend of demand for desert land for winter vacation use or for part-time homes. Some measure of this use is found in the leasing of small tracts, mentioned on page 109. Near some of the cities and other relatively densely populated areas of the West there are tracts of public domain which have some recreational value and are used.

There is also some hunting for deer, antelope, elk, and a few other game animals, and for various game birds; in some areas there is a little trout fishing; and occasionally campers use the land. But, in general, the public domain does not have the qualities which attract large-scale use and, by and large, it is no more conveniently located with respect to most users than are national forest areas which are deemed more attractive. For all of these reasons, recreational use of the public domain in the States is probably low and likely to remain so.

A considerable amount of recreational use occurs on the public domain in Alaska. Some of the better sites have been withdrawn for this purpose. Public Law 507, 84th Congress, 2nd Session, authorizes the construction of campgrounds and other recreational sites on public domain in Alaska. This legislation contemplates that the Territory of Alaska will take over the operation of these campgrounds later, but no legislation to this end has yet been passed by the Territory.

The O & C areas contain some excellent recreational areas, some quite close to centers of population. The 1937 Act specifically provides that O & C lands shall be administered to provide recreation as one of the uses. However, until recently no funds had been appropriated for construction or operation of recreational facilities. Without some minimum improvements, such as sanitary facilities and safe water supply, areas cannot safely be opened to recreation. In the exchange of O & C and national forest lands authorized by the legislation which settled the controverted land issue, the Bureau of Land Management acquired several areas with developed recreational facilities, which will now be maintained and operated if funds are provided. Presumably the Forest Service will develop similar facilities on the lands it acquired by the exchange.

The grazing district and other public domain lands have important watershed values. As a broad and perhaps over-simplified generalization, it may be said that in the West the national forests have the water and the grazing districts have the silt. In many areas the higher mountains, which are predominantly in national forests and private ownership, receive relatively high precipitation and as a consequence provide the bulk of the runoff. Areas at lower elevation, mostly in grazing districts and in private ownership, receive much less precipitation, and a much smaller proportion of it enters stream channels as runoff. On the other hand, these lands were often contributing considerable silt to streams even when white men entered the West—the Missouri River was not called the Big Muddy for nothing, and the stories about the silt in the Colorado River are legion. Overgrazing and other unwise use growing out of a lack of control and management by anyone on these lands, destroyed the precarious balance between soil formation and soil loss in many areas, and greatly accelerated erosion has occurred in many streams. There are several watersheds in the West where 80 per cent of the runoff comes from areas which contribute but 20 per cent or less of the silt, and where only 20 per cent of the runoff brings down 80 per cent of the silt. As an example, the Rio Puerco, a tributary of the Rio Grande, contributes only 6 per cent of the total stream flow entering the Elephant Butte reservoir, but brings 52 per cent of the silt.

In many valleys on the grazing districts and intermingled private lands, especially small ones bordering small streams, the soil was originally a deep alluvium brought down by water from the surrounding hills and held in place by grass and other vegetative cover. The ground-water table was often rather near the surface in such areas, and frequently there were perennial flowing streams. With deterioration of the watershed and weakening of the valley grass cover, floods gradually cut channels deep into the alluvium. This greatly changed the ground-water situation and hence the plant cover, and the channels, once started, grew and fed upon the forces they set in motion. It is extremely difficult to cure such a situation once it has begun, irrespective of the use of the land and of the structures placed on it, and irrespective of cost.

Since the passage of the Taylor Grazing Act a good deal has been done to improve the watershed situation on the grazing districts, but by no means enough. Stabilization of livestock numbers at levels the forage will support, and proper seasonal use of grazing, have helped greatly. In addition, special conservation programs of various kinds have been undertaken in limited areas, up to the extent of the available funds. Siltation from such lands, regardless of their ownership, can seriously affect downstream reservoirs. Remedial measures have important values for the land to which applied, but they also have values, sometimes greater ones, for downstream areas.

MINERAL PRODUCTION ON PUBLIC DOMAIN AND ACQUIRED LANDS[25]

The grazing districts and other land have had important mineral values. But, as with the national forests, lands containing minerals to which the mining laws apply—the metals, generally—are usually taken into private ownership via the mining laws; hence there is little production of these minerals from the public lands as such. When previously unimportant minerals suddenly become important, as with uranium in recent years, the mining laws are applied on relatively large areas of public domain having, or suspected of having, the minerals sought. Today, with most obvious surface outcroppings already exploited, the mineral deposits to which the laws apply are harder to find. The importance of the grazing district land for further mineral production is therefore largely dependent upon new methods of discovering minerals. New technical methods for locating deeper-lying deposits are being applied, although further technical advances are needed and ways to apply the mining laws to these deeper deposits are urgently needed.

As in the case of the national forests, the mining laws have frequently been used to obtain uses of land unavailable to the applicant under the relevant laws. The mining laws have often conflicted with land use for recreation, timber harvest, and right-of-way purposes.[26]

The grazing districts and other public domain land created, like the national forests, out of the original public domain are open for leasing under the Mineral Leasing Act of 1920. Since the grazing district lands are in greatest demand for this type of mineral development, the Bureau of Land Management handles the issuance of leases upon all types of federal land. The Mineral Leasing Act applies particularly to oil and gas, coal, potash, phosphate, and other less important minerals.

---

[25] The specific data for this section are to be found in appendix tables 15 to 20.
[26] See chapter four, pp. 226-28, for an account of the operation of the mining laws.

The total number of oil and gas leases upon the public domain has risen from less than 5,000 in 1942 to slightly over 100,000 in 1956. (Figure 12.) This is an extremely rapid and, on the whole, constant rate of increase—in the rough magnitude of 35 per cent annually. However, the number of leases upon which oil and gas had been discovered and which were producing is very much smaller—about 700 in 1942, increasing to nearly 4,000 by 1956. By 1956 a substantial part of all public domain which might be expected to have future possibilities for oil and gas was under lease.[27]

The acreage leased for oil and gas has shown a trend rather closely paralleling that of the number of leases. Total area increased from less than 3 million acres in 1943 to over 70 million acres in 1955 and 1956. On the other hand, the acreage of producing leases has been small, rising from about 250,000 in the 1941-44 period to slightly over 2 million by 1954-56.

By far the greater part of all these leases are noncompetitive. They are issued to the first applicant, who pays a modest filing fee and a rental amounting to $1.00 per acre for the first five-year period and $2.50 per acre for the second five-year period. If oil and gas are discovered on a lease, the rental becomes $1.00 per acre annually until royalty payments, at the rate of $12\frac{1}{2}$ per cent of the value of production, replace the rental. It is only when an area of land not previously open to leasing is found to be within a producing field that competitive sale of leases is possible.[28]

Oil and gas lessees assume no obligation to drill or even to explore for oil. The rate at which they explore or drill is also a matter of their discretion, as is the rate of exploitation of the discovered fields (subject to general federal and state laws as to oil conservation). The degree of discretion permitted an oil and gas lessee is much greater than that permitted the lessee or user of federal land for timber harvest, grazing, or recreation. However, in his drilling and production from wells he must conform to certain regulations and supervision.

Noncompetitive leases are seldom issued direct to explorers for oil and gas. Much of the public domain is leased, through brokers, to persons unconnected with the industry who hold them for speculative purposes.

By the end of 1955 the total number of wells drilled at any time

[27] "Public domain," as used here, is almost synonymous with original public domain not specifically reserved from oil and gas development. That is, it includes original public domain within national forests and some other types of federal land management units, as well as within the grazing districts and other present public domain.

[28] See chapter four, pp. 223-26, for a more detailed account of oil and gas leasing.

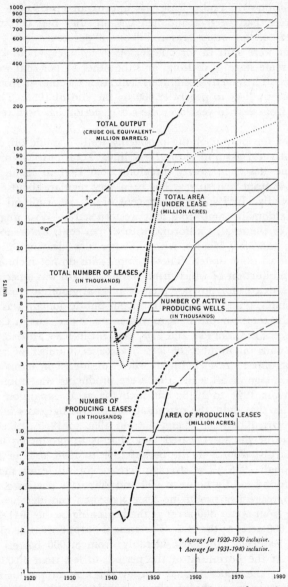

FIGURE 12. *Numbers of leases, acreage leased, number of producing wells, and crude oil output from the public domain, 1941-56 and projections for 1960 and 1980.*

on public domain under lease was approximately 23,000. Of these, 41 per cent had been abandoned because they had become dry or exhausted, or for other reasons; about 6 per cent were productive wells, but were shut in for one reason or another; about 2 per cent were in some stage of drilling; and the other 51 per cent were active producers. These active producers had risen in number from slightly over 4,000 in 1941 to nearly 12,000 by the end of 1955. The rate of increase from year to year over the entire period has been remarkably uniform.

Most of the output of the producing wells is crude oil, but there is some natural gas and natural gasoline. Total output, in crude oil equivalent, has risen nearly threefold from 1941 to 1955. The rate of increase from year to year has been very regular, about 8 or 9 per cent annually. In 1952, 97½ per cent of all the crude oil produced on public domain came from four western states—Wyoming, with 42 per cent of the total; California, with 27 per cent; Colorado, with 15 per cent; and New Mexico, with 13½ per cent—leaving only 2½ per cent from all other states. These comparisons do not include natural gas, the production of which from public domain was especially large in New Mexico, nor do they include natural gasoline. In these four leading states, crude oil production from public domain was 57½ per cent of the total for the state in Wyoming, 7 per cent in California, 46½ per cent in Colorado, and 21½ per cent in New Mexico.

These data on number of leases, acreages, number of wells, and output become more meaningful when considered in terms of ratios. The percentage of all leases that were producing was from 14 to 17 for the years 1941 to 1948; but with the great expansion in leases issued after that date, the percentage of producing leases fell sharply and has varied between 3 and 4 from 1952 to 1955. Likewise, the percentage of the total leased area that is in producing leases has fallen sharply, from 8 in the period 1942 to 1948, to 3 or less from 1951 through 1956. The average acreage for all leases shows little trend, varying mostly between 600 and 800 acres per lease. But the average acreage per producing lease has risen considerably, roughly doubling from about 300 acres at the beginning of the 1941-55 period to about 600 acres at the end. The annual output of crude oil equivalent per lease has fallen considerably, from 80,000 barrels or more annually at the beginning of the period, to less than 50,000 barrels annually at the end. Annual output per acre in producing leases has fallen even more sharply, from considerably over 200 barrels at the beginning of the period to well under 100 at the end.

The explanation for these latter trends is to be found in the number of producing wells. The number of active wells per producing lease has declined somewhat, and the number per 1,000 acres of producing leases has fallen to one-third or less over the 1941-55 period. On the other hand, the annual output per producing well on public domain has stayed remarkably steady over the entire period at about 13,500 barrels per well per year, or 37 barrels per well per day. There is a slight upward trend in output per well for all oil wells in the United States. The average daily output per well in 1953 was 13 barrels. In the western states where oil and gas from public domain is most important, average daily production from all wells is about the same as from wells on public domain.

A consideration of these data leads to the following conclusions:

1. The rate of exploration of oil and gas leases on public domain has declined considerably over the 1941-55 period. There are probably two explanations for this lag in exploration: (a) an increasing proportion of all the leases may best be described as "fluffy" speculation, the purpose of which was as much to profit from some purchaser's gullibility as from any possibility of ultimate oil exploration; and (b) the low rental charges on these lands lead genuine oil developers to withhold exploration on public domain and to push it on private lands whenever there is any real choice in the matter.

2. Even when drilling takes place and is successful, full development of the leases has been postponed or delayed, again partly because the low rental rates make this sort of reserve in the ground relatively cheap to carry. The extent to which development has been delayed on the newer producing leases can be estimated, if it is realized that most wells on the earlier producing leases have continued in operation on those leases. Thus, if there were over 4,000 active wells on 256,000 acres of producing leases in 1941, a major part of these wells are still active on the same leases. By the net addition of about 7,300 active wells between 1941 and 1955, some 1 million acres of leases were brought into production and development. Intensity of development on the older leases with over 16 wells per 1,000 acres, or about 60 acres per well, is in sharp contrast with the intensity of development on the more recent leases where there are less than 4 wells per 1,000 acres, or 261 acres per well. Thus the average rate of exploitation of all leases brought into production since 1941 is about one-fourth that of the average in 1941.

Projections of possible or probable oil production from public domain comparable with the projections on timber sales from national forests, O & C, and public domain, seem desirable, but the difficulties are great. While additional oil fields or pools are likely to be discovered, no one can now confidently assert where or how many they will be. Several elements are involved in projections of oil (or petroleum equivalent) from public domain and errors may enter at each point.

We have assumed that by 1960 the total area under lease will have risen to 90 million acres. This is somewhat more than 20 per cent above the acreage under lease in mid-1956, but it involves a slower rate of expansion than has prevailed for the past several years. It is assumed further that the percentage of all leased land that is included in producing leases will have risen slightly to 3.2. This assumption is based upon the expectation that drilling will continue on the comparatively large areas leased in recent years, and thus the ratio will be partly restored to its earlier levels. On the basis of these two assumptions there would be 2,880,000 acres in producing leases in 1960. It is further assumed that the number of active wells per 1,000 acres of producing leases will rise slightly to 7 wells per 1,000 acres, because it will be profitable to exploit these leases somewhat more rapidly than at present. On this basis, there would be 20,160 active producing wells on public domain in 1960. A further assumption is made of a continued stable annual output per producing well of 13,500 barrels. This would then mean a total production of 272 million barrels of crude oil equivalent from the public domain lands by 1960. Such a projection is exactly in line with a simple extension of the trend in output from 1950 through 1955, and only a little above the trend in output for the longer period 1941-55.

For 1980 a similar projection process is possible. It has been assumed that the area under lease would rise to 150 million acres, and that the percentage of this in producing leases would rise somewhat further to 4.0. While this latter figure is above the ratio of the years since 1950, it is only half of the ratio that prevailed for several years before 1948. On the basis of these two assumptions, there would be 6 million acres in producing leases by 1980. It is further assumed that the number of active wells per 1,000 acres of producing leases will rise still further, to 10; while this is also higher than in recent years, it is only half of the ratio that prevailed for several earlier years. On this basis, there would be 60,000 active wells on public domain in 1980; on the further assumption of a constant output per well of 13,500 barrels annually, this would mean a total output of crude oil equivalent of 810 million barrels in 1980. This output is almost exactly in line with the trend in output for the 1941-55 period, and substantially below the trend for the 1950-55 period.

A substantial part of the public domain leased for oil and gas development is used for other purposes, especially grazing. This is true even when the land is actually producing oil and gas, although there are sometimes conflicts in use between petroleum production and grazing. Use of heavy ground equipment for exploration purposes may lead to accelerated erosion from these lands. Where the land is leased, but is neither explored nor developed, often the user of the surface resources is unaware of the existence of an oil and gas lease on the same land.

Public domain is also leased for minerals other than oil and gas—notably for coal, potash, phosphate, and sodium. While the areas leased are not large compared with the total area of public domain, and the rentals and royalties are much smaller than from oil and gas leases, this is an important use of land in local situations. In the case of potash, a major part of the total supply of the United States lies on federal land, and a major part of the total production comes from leases on such land. As with oil and gas leases, a substantial part of the areas have surface uses, especially grazing. In at least one case, land leased for potash is also leased for oil and gas development. The minerals are found, or are believed to exist, on the same area but at different depths.

The acquired lands are subject to leasing for different types of mineral development under laws similar to those in effect for public domain. Leasing of these lands began in 1947 and is still small compared with that of the public domain; but it is growing at a rapid rate. Full data for the acquired lands are not readily available, but it appears that the same general relationships as to proportion of leased area under actual development prevail here as on the public domain.

SUBMERGED AREAS—A NEW AND SPECIAL RESOURCE AREA[29]

The total area of the submerged lands of the outer continental shelf is in one sense unknown. While the area out to any assumed depth can be estimated with considerable accuracy, the selection of a depth depends upon one's estimate of the physical and economic limitations

---

[29] The specific data for this section are to be found in appendix tables 21 and 22.

on underwater exploration and development. The conventional estimate of total area goes out to the line of about 600 feet of water depth based on a geologic definition. But this is far beyond the limit of practical operations today. The distance to this depth is mostly 5 to 10 miles along the Pacific Coast, 25 to 100 miles along the Atlantic Coast, and 100 to 125 miles along the Gulf Coast. Within this depth limit there is something of the order of 200 to 250 million acres. The Alaskan coast offers further but still largely unexplored potentialities.

The Geological Survey has estimated, on the basis of oil and gas occurrence in the coastal plain adjoining the submerged areas, that the areas off the Gulf Coast may contain 13 billion barrels of oil and 65 trillion cubic feet of natural gas. Converting the gas to a crude oil equivalent on the basis of 6,000 cubic feet per barrel, the reserve has roughly 24 billion barrels of oil equivalent. These estimates may be very conservative. They include that part of the water area which has been transferred to the states, but the greater part of the potential area is federally owned. How much of this may be economically exploited is unknown today.

The submerged areas were surveyed by the Bureau of Land Management and divided into blocks. A block off the Louisiana coast contains 5,000 acres, conforming to the practice of that state in surveying; off the Texas coast, a block is 5,760 acres, or 3 miles square. This latter unit will probably be used elsewhere and generally in the future. The leases issued have mostly been for blocks, although in some cases half or even quarter blocks have been leased as units. The latter course has been followed primarily where the boundary of the coastal waters led to less than full blocks, or when holders of earlier leases were interested in bidding on smaller areas in order to round out their holdings.

When the Outer Continental Shelf Lands Act was passed in 1953, those who held leases that had been issued by the states and which met the requirements of the act were given an opportunity to continue their leases under federal ownership. Although 401 leaseholders filed under these provisions, the number of leases eventually accepted was reduced, primarily through the elimination of leases which proved to be on state rather than federal land. On June 30, 1956, only 367 of these so-called "state" leases remained. Some were in production when transferred to federal status and others have developed since.

Under Section 8 of the Act new leases could be issued on a competitive sale basis. Major sales were held in the fall of 1954 and in the summer of 1955, at which time 109 and 121 leases, respectively, were sold. These leases are subject to a royalty of one-sixth of production compared with the one-eighth exacted on public domain lands and common in the industry for private lands. The minimum bonus bid accepted was $15.00 per acre. The average bonus paid per acre was $303 in the first sale and $269 in the second sale. For the average lease this meant a bid in total of $1,280,000 and $890,000 respectively.

There was, however, great variation in the amount of the bonus bid, as can be seen from table 5. The median bid per acre was roughly $170 in fiscal 1955 and roughly $70.00 in fiscal 1956, substantially below the arithmetic average in each year because of a relatively few very high bids. More than 10 per cent of the high bidders bid a bonus of over $1,000 per acre, and about 1 or 2 per cent bid above $2,000 per acre. The range from the lowest to the highest bids is over one hundred times; and the range which includes the middle 50 per cent (interquartile range) is about one and one-half times the mean for each year. By any test, these are statistical data with high variability.

TABLE 5. *Number of Leases Issued on Outer Continental Shelf, with Specified Bonus Bids per Acre, 1955 and 1956*

Bonus bid per acre	Number of leases issued in fiscal 1955	Number of leases issued in fiscal 1956
Less than $20 [1]	12	16
$ 20 - $ 49	13	36
50 - 109	18	22
110 - 169	11	7
170 - 229	9	3
230 - 349	9	5
350 - 469	6	5
470 - 589	8	6
590 - 749	8	2
750 - 849	4	1
850 - 1049	1	2
1050 - 1249	8	2
1250 - 1849	1	12
1850 and more	1	2
Total	109	121

[1] Minimum acceptable bid $15.00 per acre.

The amount of the bonus that may rationally be bid depends on a number of factors.[30] There is the risk of a dry hole, or of not striking oil in paying quantities. There are differences in the costs of exploration, development, and oil production from the lease, and in availability of marketing facilities and allowances, even if it can safely be assumed that oil will be struck. There are also differences in the yield of the lease, even within those wells that are commercially profitable to operate. It is evident that, on balance, these various factors must combine in a way that is attractive to many oil companies in order to induce them to pay the comparatively large bonuses actually paid.

At the same time, it must be recognized that the bonus is in the nature of a residual item in calculation, and that comparatively small differences in other items in the calculation can produce very large differences in the amount of the bonus. For instance, suppose it be assumed that each well on a lease will produce 25,000 barrels annually for twenty years, or a half million barrels per well in total. At prevailing royalty rates for these leases, this would mean a total royalty of about $167,000 per well at present prices. If there were only three active wells per 1,000 acres, there could be fifteen active wells per lease, or a total royalty payment of $2.5 million over twenty years. These calculations are purely hypothetical, and in practice total royalty payments may be much higher. However, they serve to show that bonus payments of $1 million may be much less than the total royalty payments under a lease. Drilling and other costs may be even larger. Comparatively small differences in estimates of any of these constituent factors might greatly change the amount of bonus that could be bid.

By the end of fiscal year 1956 there were 367 leases from the former state group, of which 130 were producing, and 230 leases issued since passage of the Act, of which all but 8 had not had sufficient time to come into production. In total, less than one-fourth of the number and of the acreage for all leases was in production, but these proportions were far above those on the public domain. Although the number of wells drilled to date is still comparatively small in relation to the area under lease, it is evident that development is actively under way, as the following figures show:

[30] For an interesting account of oil production problems of the submerged areas, including an analysis of profitability prospects, see Richard Austin Smith, "Troubled Oil on Troubled Waters," *Fortune*, December, 1956.

	Number of wells at end of calendar year		
	1954	1955	1956
Wells abandoned	103	175	261
Wells actively producing	71	146	227
Wells shut in	59	93	130
Wells in process	27	41	76
Total wells	260	455	694

During 1955 and 1956, a substantial number of wells were drilled and tested. In fiscal year 1955, 148 wells were started. From them 59 oil wells and 31 gas wells came into production. The total daily output of the oil wells was 22,336 barrels, or 378 barrels per well. Gas wells produced 258,969 million cubic feet, or 8,354 million feet per well per day; on a petroleum equivalent basis this is more than three times the output of the average oil well. In fiscal 1956, 230 wells were started and 98 oil wells and 25 gas wells were brought in. Production from each oil well was almost exactly the same as that brought in in 1955. Production from the gas wells was somewhat lower than in the previous year. In each year nearly as many dry wells as producers·were brought in. The average output per well per day is roughly ten times what it is on the public domain and about thirty-five times the average for the whole United States.

The output of petroleum equivalent for both oil and gas wells is about 165,000 barrels annually in each year per lease producing at the end of the year, and almost as great per well producing at midyear. The royalty per lease producing at the end of the year averaged over $40,000 annually—a rate of about $11.00 per acre of producing lease at such date—and the rental per acre of nonproducing lease averaged about $3.00 annually. On the other hand, there was only one-fourth of an active well per every 1,000 acres of leased land in production, and even including shut-in wells the fraction is less than one-half. Compared with oil and gas leases upon the public domain, and indeed almost anywhere in the United States, this is a very light rate of drilling per unit of area, but a very high rate of output per well and per acre of producing lease.

Projections of future oil and gas production from the submerged areas are particularly difficult to make in view of the short experience with these areas and the fact that much of the most promising area has not yet been extensively drilled. There are serious technical diffi-culties to overcome in exploration, development, and production of these potential areas, especially those in deeper water and farther from shore. There are also serious economic questions as to the profitability of development, even where it is technically feasible. On the other hand, the high bonuses paid for these leases, the higher annual rentals for nonproducing leases, and other factors will all operate to push development here much faster than it has been pushed on the public domain. The following projections must be considered as extremely rough.

It is assumed that by 1960 the total area leased will be 5 million acres, of which 3 million will be in production. It is assumed that the drilling on producing leases will be stepped up to 2 wells per 1,000 acres, which is about four times the present rate, but still far below even the present low rate on public domain. On the other hand, it is assumed that production per active well will fall from the present annual rate of over 150,000 barrels, to 50,000 barrels. This is still about four times the output per active well on public domain. Thus, with one-third as many wells per 1,000 acres, but four times the output per well, a production only moderately larger per 1,000 acres than on public domain is assumed. We believe these to be conservative estimates; they result in a 1960 production of 300 million barrels of petroleum equivalent.

A similar process can be followed to project production for 1980. The total area under lease is assumed to be 8 million acres, of which 5 million are assumed to be producing. The number of wells per 1,000 acres is now assumed to be 3, and output per well assumed as before; this gives a 1980 production of 750 million barrels of petroleum equivalent.

In addition to oil and gas leases, five sulfur leases on the submerged lands have been issued, but these are not yet in production. When looking to the future, however, it should be borne in mind that not only sulfur, but quite possibly other minerals will be exploited from these areas within the next twenty-five years or so, although what these minerals may be is still to be discovered.

MISCELLANEOUS USES[31]

During the disposal era of federal land history about two-thirds of the original public domain was released to states and individuals. The flood tide of disposal ran from about 1850 to about 1920, after which, with the best lands taken, disposal dropped off sharply even though

[31] The specific data for this section are to be found in appendix tables 23 and 24.

the unreserved public domain was still open to entry. With the passage of the Taylor Grazing Act in 1934, the public domain was closed to disposal in a way it had not been for nearly 150 years.[32] While it was still possible to acquire title to public domain in various ways, indiscriminate disposal stopped. During World War II disposals slowed down to almost nothing, but since, they have risen again, in part because of reclamation homesteads and in part because of homesteading in Alaska.

When land is subject to disposal the management job becomes more complicated. The agency and its personnel are uncertain as to whether to make investments and carry out management practices which, primarily, will have long-run benefits. This is especially true for forest management, the results of which can be achieved only if the land remains under good management for many years. Disposal of land also requires the time of agency personnel that might otherwise be devoted to continuing management. Difficult problems are apt to arise, many of which stem from land pricing policies imposed by law.

The process of public land disposal usually begins with an individual filing an application. In practice today, a substantial proportion of the applications are stimulated by a land broker or other promoter and are made by persons who hope to reap a quick financial reward. Following receipt of the application the land is classified. The first basis of classification is the land's suitability for continued efficient and satisfactory federal management, or for its disposal. Sometimes suitability for the purpose sought is also considered. Many of the applications are rejected, but in such cases applicants have the right of appeal, which a few of them exercise.

For some types of applications—public sale and small tract applications, for example—disposal may go forward promptly. For other types, after the entry is allowed the applicant must over a period of some years perform certain requirements such as residence, improvement, irrigation, and the like. This is especially true of homestead and desert land entries.

Since World War II the number of homestead entries allowed has varied mostly between 400 and 600 annually. Essentially all of these, nowadays, go through to completion, although there is some delay between allowance and final entry. For the sixteen years covered by

---

[32] Peffer, E. Louise, *The Closing of the Public Domain*, Stanford: Stanford University Press, 1951.

appendix table 24, more homesteads went to final entry than were allowed, owing to the large number that had been allowed before 1941. The reclamation homesteads since the war have generally involved a substantial subsidy or gift; the winner in one of the drawings for such homesteads would be foolish not to complete his entry if he could. About one-third of all homesteads since the war have been of this type. Another third or more have been in Alaska, where until very recently a veteran with two years' military service could get a 160-acre homestead on the basis of seven months' residence, erection of a minimum habitable dwelling, and without cultivation or clearing of land. During the sixteen-year period 1,306,000 acres of land have been disposed of via the homestead route.

Desert land entries require irrigation and improvement of a portion of the area before final proof and title may be obtained. This law has been widely criticized because it readily lends itself to fraud and misrepresentation. Its use had declined almost to the vanishing point by 1950, but in recent years it has been applied to the exploitation of ground water in desert areas. Large numbers of applications (over 7,500 in 1950-54 inclusive) have been filed, usually as a result of promotional activities. If all had been allowed, these applications would have required about 6 million acre-feet of water annually and shortly would have exhausted the limited ground-water stocks. Applications have been allowed in areas where a continuing supply of water, sufficient to irrigate, seems reasonably certain and when rights to water can be secured under state law. For the sixteen years covered by appendix table 24, only one-third of the filings have been completed. Even allowing for the fact that some of these entries may be awaiting eventual completion, it is apparent that many filings never will be completed.

The consolidation of federal land holdings into manageable units must involve some disposal. Under the Taylor Grazing Act, isolated tracts of public domain not exceeding 1,520 acres in size, or rough and mountainous but not necessarily isolated tracts not exceeding 760 acres, may be sold at public auction. Nearly a million acres were disposed of at public auction between 1940 and 1956—much of it on the initiative of the Bureau of Land Management. Prices for the land varied between $3.00 and $5.00 per acre, although some tracts were sold at much higher prices. Much more land remains for disposal; in fact, it would be desirable to dispose of somewhere between 3 and 5 million acres of the area that was in federal ownership when the Taylor Grazing Act was passed. Perhaps as much as one-third of the total could be sold in this way by an Administration determined to dispose of as much public domain as possible. However, many of the present users of this land would rather hold it under some form of lease or permit than incur the costs of ownership, and there would surely be strong opposition to large-scale disposals.

The Small Tract Act is important as a means of getting small areas of land into private hands under lease or by sale, primarily for residence, recreation, or other site purposes. It has been used chiefly in the desert areas of California, Nevada, and Arizona for winter recreation dwellings; in various mountain and seashore locations, largely for recreation or retirement homes; and in Alaska. The area of land involved has been small, however, because of the limited area in each entry. A far larger area is under lease than has been sold; leases in effect rose from 15,000 in 1950 to 33,000 in 1954. But even the latter number applies to a comparatively small area—not over 165,000 acres, or less than 0.1 per cent of the public domain area in the states to which the law applies.

Authority to exchange land is important to the federal land managing agencies as a means of simplifying the land patterns they administer. The kinds of land exchanged may differ widely and be managed by varying government agencies, but without exception all land exchange agreements, including those involving the national forests, are subject to approval of the Bureau of Land Management.

In practice, land exchange is not as effective a method of consolidating federal land as it might seem. It is often overlooked, for instance, that many a private landowner gains from the present intermingled landownership pattern: through ownership of adjacent private lands, he may be in a position to use public land fully and unrestrictedly at less cost than ownership would entail. If his tract of timber abuts on public timberland, he may have a major advantage in buying the public timber; or if there is a watering hole on his private lands, he may essentially have a monopoly over the surrounding public range land.

Moreover, there is another obstacle to land exchanges. When a landowner trades land, he is buying land with the value of the land he sells. Naturally, then, he will agree to an exchange only when he believes the exchange will benefit him; and the federal agency will agree to an exchange only when it believes the exchange will improve its position, or at least not impair it. Under the law, the value of the lands the government acquires cannot be less than the value of the land it gives. There are situations when each party is richer as a result of a trade of land for land, because the tracts of land may differ in physical character, and they certainly differ in location. (Some exchanges, for instance, are initiated by individuals who wish to secure tracts of federal land that are unavailable under any other law.) But there are many more situations where it is hard to see how both parties to the exchange can gain.

Exchanges of land in grazing districts and other public domain numbered close to 2,000, involving an area of 2.6 million acres, over the sixteen years 1941-56. Some of the exchanges were made with individuals, other were made with states. Some of the latter were on an equal area basis, others were on an equal value basis. The total area received and the total area given in the exchanges with state lands were almost exactly equal, but individual exchanges often varied greatly. Presumably these exchanges aided in simplifying the land pattern but, taken as a whole, they amounted to only 1½ per cent of the total area of land in grazing districts and other public domain.

Legal authority governing the exchange of either national forest land or national forest timber for private land specifies that the land to be acquired must lie within established national forest unit boundaries or within other areas specified by law. From 1941 through 1956 over 1,000 such exchanges were made whereby over 3 million acres were added to the national forests and about 700,000 acres were transferred to private owners. The difference in acreage is due in large part to the trading of national forest timber for private land. This type of exchange has aroused a good deal of criticism and now, as a matter of administrative policy, has been abandoned, although legally it is still possible.

A modest disposal and exchange program is an important part of managing the grazing district and other lands considered in this section. Some of these lands are in active demand for residential, industrial, and other purposes; in the past five years there has been an amazing movement into the western deserts, where nearly all the land is federally owned. Small tract leases and sales, sales of isolated tracts that cannot efficiently be managed by the federal agency, exchanges both within national forests and elsewhere, and some other types of disposal seem to be essential in the expanding economy of the future. But desert land and homestead disposals are subject to more question. In view of present and prospective surpluses, it is difficult to see the rationality of adding to the agricultural productive plant of the nation. Disposals of these types are in demand largely because of the nominal prices at which the land is made available.

(This matter will be considered further in chapter four.) Examination of the homestead and desert land laws and how they operate leads to the conclusion that considerable adjustment is needed, at least as they relate to land disposal.

The public domain and other public lands are used for many other purposes—rights of way, roads of various types and purposes, electric power or telephone lines, oil or gas pipelines, irrigation and drainage canals, and a host of others—each of which is important, but usually is concerned with only small areas of land. Sometimes, as in the case of a power line, the land can continue to be used for grazing or other purposes.

Generally speaking, requests for use of land for these purposes are granted subject to inquiry to verify facts, and subject to general provisions; but sometimes special provisions are added to prevent erosion or other loss of resources arising out of a right-of-way use. In some situations the government has a direct interest, for itself or for the purchaser of its products, in the use of the road or gas pipeline constructed on the right of way. For instance, purchasers of O & C timber may wish to use roads constructed by other private timber operators across O & C lands. Without the right to use such roads, operators other than the builder of the road may find it impossible to buy the timber and market it economically. The builder of the road obviously should be paid for use of the road he has built, and its use by others should not interfere with his own needs for the road. The ways in which the federal agencies have used authority to grant or refuse rights of way across federal lands as a means of implementing various federal programs are considered in chapter four.

SUMMARY

1. The grazing districts, other public domain, Oregon & California revested lands, and the submerged areas of the outer continental shelf contain a wide variety of physical land types and use possibilities, and as a result present a great variety of problems.

2. The grazing use of the grazing districts has been relatively stable for nearly twenty years, and is expected to remain so in the future. This is in sharp contrast to the situation on the national forests.

3. The O & C lands are managed primarily, if not exclusively, for timber production.

4. The recreational uses and possibilities of these varied lands are

largely unknown, but seem much less than those of the national forests.

5. The watersheds of most of these lands are characterized by relatively heavy movements of silt and low water yields, part of which is due to past mismanagement, but part is inherent in their climate.

6. Although metal production from these lands is comparatively unimportant, largely because the more productive metal-yielding lands go into private ownership, the output of oil and gas and other leasable minerals has risen steadily and rapidly, and bids fair to continue to do so.

7. The submerged areas of the outer continental shelf are a new and unique federal resource area whose possibilities are yet largely unknown. Large bonuses paid for leases there, and other reasons, lead to an expectation of major oil and gas production.

8. Much of the land described in this section is open to disposal. This creates many difficult management problems.

9. The lands differ in physical types, or at least in the combinations of physical types, from national forest lands. But, basically, the problems of their management are similar to those applying to the national forests; each, in different ways, is capable of multiple uses.

Use Pattern on National Parks, National Monuments, and Other Areas Administered by the National Park Service

The National Park System is composed of areas noted for their inspiring scenery or for their historical, prehistorical, and scientific interest. The largest and perhaps the most important units in the system are national parks, of which there are twenty-eight, with a total area of about 12.5 million acres of federal land.[33] They range in size from less than 1,000 to over 2.25 million acres, but twenty-two of the twenty-eight extend between 30,000 and 1 million acres. National parks may be created only by an act of Congress, and modification of their boundaries or their abolishment also requires an act.

The eighty-four national monuments included in the National Park System cover nearly 9 million acres of federal land, of which more than two-thirds is to be found in three monuments: Katmai and Glacier Bay, in Alaska; and Death Valley, in California. Of the other monuments, forty-seven occupy less than 1,000 acres each, and one covers

[33] The number of parks and monuments shown is as of June 30, 1955.

less than an acre. National monuments may be created by Presidential proclamation, and in fact sixty-seven of them were so created. In these cases the monuments may be abolished or their boundaries modified, also by Presidential proclamation.

In addition to the national parks and monuments, the National Park System includes fifty-eight areas that are primarily of national historical interest—military, memorial, historical, and battlefield parks; battlefield and historical sites; memorials; and cemeteries. The total area of federal land in this rather miscellaneous category is about 116,000 acres; several of the units cover less than an acre of ground. The group includes many structures that are highly popular and rich in history, for example the Lincoln Memorial, the Lincoln Museum, the House Where Lincoln Died, the Jefferson Memorial, and the Washington Monument, in Washington, D. C.; and the home of Franklin D. Roosevelt in New York State.

The National Park Service also administers the National Capital Parks in the District of Columbia and surrounding areas; five national parkways, three of which are in the general Washington area; four national recreation areas in the West, each of which includes reservoir area created by a major dam built by the Bureau of Reclamation; and various other miscellaneous areas.

Our concern is chiefly with the national parks and monuments. These include comparatively large areas of land—areas with at least some physical similarities to land in other federal land managing units, and that are valued less for their major structures or historical background than for the recreational qualities they have to offer.

PURPOSE AND HISTORY OF NATIONAL PARKS AND MONUMENTS

The dominant purpose of the national parks and monuments is to provide recreation at its highest inspirational level. Selected primarily for their magnificent scenic features, these lands are not intended to provide play areas and amusement of a character to be found in municipal parks.

The area of national parks and monuments has increased rather steadily over the years. Many of the units added had already been in federal ownership, but in different form—sometimes as part of the national forests. Other units have included private lands given to the federal government or purchased by it from individuals. Among the national parks formed largely out of national forest or other federal land since 1910 are Glacier, Rocky Mountain, Lassen Volcanic, Mount McKinley, Grand Canyon, Zion, Bryce Canyon, Grand Teton, Carlsbad, Olympic, Hot Springs, and Kings Canyon. Those formed largely out of other land during the same period include Big Bend, Great Smoky Mountains, Shenandoah, Mammoth Cave, Isle Royal, and Everglades.

COMMERCIAL USES OF NATIONAL PARKS AND MONUMENTS

With limited exceptions, the national parks and monuments are not open to grazing, timber harvest, mineral development, or the other types of commercial use considered in connection with the national forests, grazing districts, and other areas. The exceptions occur in a few areas, and arise from a variety of circumstances; previous use of the land may have been permitted to continue after it was set aside as a national park or monument; or the use is so limited that it does not interfere with the primary purpose of the area; or war or some other emergency may have brought about certain uses.

However, a different type of commercial operation exists within many of the areas. Private individuals and corporations have been encouraged to construct hotels, motels, stores, restaurants, gasoline filling stations, and other works necessary to provide the many services demanded by the millions of visitors to the national parks and monuments. Such facilities conceivably could have been built by the federal government, and operated either direct or by lessee. But appropriations for this kind of activity have seldom been available, and usually it has been necessary to seek the investment of private capital. Where, in a few areas, structures or improvements have been built with federal funds, the operations of the concessionaires are under lease or agreement with the federal government.

RECREATIONAL USE OF NATIONAL PARKS AND MONUMENTS [34]

Statistics on the use of the national parks and monuments are kept in terms of visits, rather than visitors. While in general they are based on actual counts of persons entering an area, and thus possibly

[34] Data for this section are found in appendix table 36.

are more accurate than data on the use of the national forests, they suffer from the same characteristics and deficiencies as do the national forest data. (See pages 69-71.) There are other problems also. The constituent units of the National Park System vary as to the purpose for their existence and the type of recreation they provide. Statistics on total visits therefore include, in addition to the visits to national parks and monuments, the visits to various historical areas—buildings, memorials, battlefields, cemeteries, etc. as well as general recreational areas and parkways. For the purposes of this study, in which interest focuses upon the rural public lands, statistics on visits to national parks and monuments have been separated from those dealing with visits to other units of the National Park System.[35]

When comparing the statistics for a series of years it must be remembered that they refer to varying areas of land and varying numbers of parks. The number of national parks and monuments has increased greatly, and the area more or less proportionately, over the decades. However, the effect of this expansion upon the numbers of visits is not as great as might be imagined. At the time of inclusion of most areas within the National Park System, the number of visits was often relatively small. Hence, no immediate major discrepancy was introduced into the data by the addition of another park. Over the longer time period, it is true that the total number of visits to the National Park System would be lower, and that to the national forests somewhat higher, if the lands had remained in forest rather than in park status. However, the data on recreational visits as shown in the following pages, while not statistically perfect, do present an essentially correct picture of the use of these lands.

The use of national parks and monuments and the recreational use of the national forests show both similar and differing characteristics. For each type of area there has been a relatively long period of rapidly rising use from the earliest years for which data were available up through 1941. During World War II the use of each declined greatly; since the war the use of each has swiftly increased. These are the major movements, and similar for each type of area. The differences are most marked in the rate of increased use. Visits to the national parks and monuments during the period from 1910 to 1941

---

[35] Later, when dealing with revenues and expenditures in chapter five, it is not possible to separate the statistics on national parks and monuments from those concerned with other units of the National Park System.

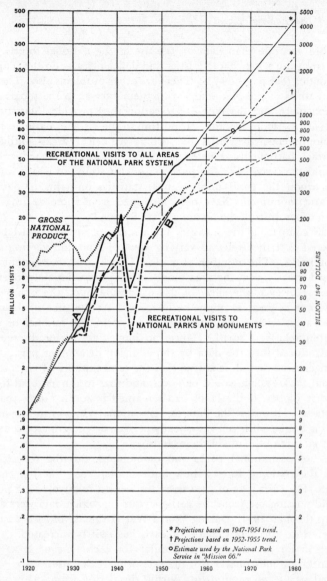

FIGURE 13. *Visits to national parks and monuments, and to other areas of the national park system, 1920-56 and two levels of projection to 1980. Trend line A approximates the annual rate of increase in park use for the period 1920 through 1941 while B represents the somewhat slower rate of increase since 1946.*

increased steadily at a relatively uniform rate, as can be seen from figure 13, although there were some year-to-year variations. Unlike the national forests, and despite setbacks in 1932 and 1933, use of the national parks and monuments continued to rise, though slowly, during the severe depression of the early 1930's. After this period both areas rose quite rapidly as the whole economy recovered, and both continued at a lesser but steady rate until 1941. For the 1920-41 period the average rate of increased use of national parks and monuments, as shown by trend line A, was about 11 per cent annually. For the whole period up to the war, therefore, use of the national parks and monuments increased somewhat faster than did the use of the forests. These were the years when Americans were "discovering" the national parks.

Wartime travel restrictions, the draft, and curtailed vacations caused the recreational use of both national forests and national parks to decline by about two-thirds—the parks slightly more than the forests.

As one looks at the whole 1910-55 period (omitting the war years), there are some signs of a declining rate of growth, but they are far from conclusive. The rate was higher from 1910 to 1920 than later, but if the extreme depression years are excluded, there is no sign of a diminution in rate of growth from 1920 to 1941; the rate from 1947 to 1954 is somewhat lower than before the war, at about 8 per cent annually, and the years from 1952 to 1955 are at a still lower rate.

As with figure 10, which shows rates of growth in recreational use of the national forests, it should be borne in mind that the uniformity in growth shown in figure 13 is in terms of *percentage* rate, not of absolute figures annually. The scale of the chart has been selected with this in mind. Equal percentage rates of growth are measured by equal distances vertically.

Projections of past trends of use into the future yield some interesting results. If the trend of the 1947-54 period is extended, the following use picture results:

	Millions of visits in		
	1960	1966	1980
To national parks and monuments	45	75	250
To all areas under Park Service jurisdiction	80	135	440

If, on the other hand, the lower rate of use indicated by the most recent, and too brief period 1952-55 is extended, the following use picture results:

	Millions of visits in		
	1960	1966	1980
To national parks and monuments	32	40	65
To all areas under Park Service jurisdiction	60	78	135

These projections may seem extreme, even fantastic, when measured against the comparable use figures for 1955—about 27 million visits to national parks and monuments and about 50 million to all areas. But those who challenge such projections, which admittedly are merely based on past trends, should ponder carefully the historical record: for the entire length of time the rate of increase has been *greater* than that even of the 1947-54 period. In 1920, when visits to the national parks and monuments totalled only slightly more than 1 million, few persons could have foreseen that in twenty-one years they would have reached 12 million; and again in 1935, when use was about 5.5 million visits, few persons would have foreseen that by 1955 it would have reached 27 million. Considering the economic and social trends in this country—more people, much higher per capita income, more leisure for the average person, and greater mobility of population—there is every reason to believe that the use of the national parks, monuments, and other units of the system will increase enormously in the decades ahead; the only question can be: Just what is "enormously"?

The National Park Service has prepared a program for the next ten years.[36] Based upon estimates of use of different parks and other areas, the Service's plan is geared to a total use for the entire system of 80 million visits by 1966. This is a modest increase in view of the past record. True, it would apply if the very recent flattening out in growth rate (of the 1952-55 period) continues. Should the rate for the 1947-54 period continue, however, use will far exceed the Park Service estimate.

TRAVEL OF VISITORS TO NATIONAL PARKS

It is generally believed that visitors to the national parks and monuments are in a somewhat different category from visitors to the national forests. As we have seen earlier, the latter are often local

[36] National Park Service, *Our Heritage, A Plan for Its Protection and Use,* 1956.

picnickers, fishermen, hunters, or campers, whose homes are within 300 miles of the forest. While some of the visits to the national parks and monuments are of this type, many of them are undertaken as part of more extensive journeys. The remoteness of many of the national parks is one good reason.

This is well illustrated by the data shown in table 6. To reach even Shenandoah and Yosemite, which are closer to large metropolitan areas than are most national parks, a majority of visitors had to drive more than 100 miles, and many more than 300 miles. Even for these

TABLE 6. *Use of Five Major National Parks*

Item	Grand Canyon	Glacier	Yosemite	Crater Lake	Shenandoah
Per cent of total visitors arriving by auto	92.4	96.7	97.0	[1]	[1]
Average miles traveled on entire trip [2]	[3] 4,192	3,683	1,904	[1]	968
Per cent of visitors whose homes by airline one way were: [4]					
Up to 100 miles	0.5	3.0	18.0	[1]	25.0
100 to 300 miles	2.6	20.0	28.2	[1]	38.4
300 to 500 miles	22.9	20.5	29.0	[1]	20.2
500 to 1,000 miles	19.3	19.4	5.0	[1]	12.8
1,000 to 1,500 miles	19.1	18.9	2.5	[1]	2.3
1,500 to 2,000 miles	20.5	12.2	7.7	[1]	0.3
2,000 to 2,500 miles	13.4	5.7	3.5	[1]	0.6
Over 2,500 miles	1.7	0.3	6.2	[1]	0.4
Average expenditures per party, entire trip [2]	$508	[5] $373	[6] $243	[7] $271	[8] $125
Average expenditure per person per day while in park [2][9]	$10.90	$4.12	[1]	$5.48	[1]
Per cent of visitors who stayed overnight in park [3]	[10]	46.6	64.0	17.0	48.2
Average persons per car [2]	[3] 3.3	3.2	3.3	3.5	3.34
Days spent on entire trip [2]	[3] 22.5	21.1	10.6	14.1	5.51
Days spent in state [2]	[3] 4.0	4.6	[1]	2.0	1.38
Days spent in park [2]	[3] 1.3	1.8	[11] 3.1	[11] 1.2	[1]
Per cent of visitors for whom the principal reason for the trip was visit to park	19.9	31.1	56.0	63.4	62.3
Per cent of visitors who had previously visited this park	[1]	[1]	[1]	[1]	52.8

Footnotes on following page.

¹ Data unavailable.

² Automobile travelers only.

³ South Rim only.

⁴ These are very rough estimates made by the present authors from data given in publications as to state (for Yosemite, for California, county also) of origin of visitors. Assumptions as to residence of visitors within their home states were made, based roughly on population distribution.

⁵ Not reported; calculated by multiplying average daily expenditure per person in Montana ($5.52) times number of persons per car (3.2) times number of days per trip (21.1). No information as to items of expense included.

⁶ Calculated by multiplying average expenditure per person for trip ($73.69) times average number persons per party (3.3).

⁷ Calculated by multiplying average expenditure per person per day ($5.48) times average number of persons per car (3.5) times average days per vacation (14.1).

⁸ Calculated by multiplying average expenditure per person per day ($6.79) times average number of persons per vehicle (3.34) times average days spent away from home (5.51).

⁹ For Grand Canyon, includes park and vicinity; calculated by dividing reported expenditure per visitor by average number of days per visitor spent in park.

¹⁰ Not reported; apparently nearly 100 per cent of visitors would stay in park if facilities were available. Considerable numbers depart each day at height of season because of lack of accommodation.

¹¹ Those staying in park overnight.

Sources: Grand Canyon: Arizona Highway Department, U.S. Bureau of Public
Roads, and National Park Service, *Grand Canyon Travel Survey;* data are
for 1954.

Glacier: Montana State Highway Commission, U.S. Bureau of Public
Roads, and National Park Service, *Glacier National Park Tourist Survey;*
data are for 1951.

Yosemite: California Division of Highways, and U.S. Bureau of Public
Roads, National Park Service, *Yosemite National Park Travel Survey;* data
are for 1953.

Crater Lake: National Park Service, *Vacation Survey, Rogue River Basin;*
data are for 1950.

Shenandoah: Virginia Department of Highways, U.S. Bureau of Public
Roads, and National Park Service, *Shenandoah National Park Tourist
Survey;* data are for 1952.

two parks, the average visitor had spent 5.5 and 10.6 days, respectively, on the trip which took him into the park; and he and his party spent on the average $125 and $243, respectively, on the entire trip. For such parks as Grand Canyon and Glacier, whose fame is international, the picture is more extreme. Comparatively few visitors to these parks came from a distance of less than 500 miles, and a good many came from over 2,000 miles. The average visitor spent 22.5 and 21.1 days, respectively, on his journey to the park; and he and the members of his party spent on the average $508 and $373, respectively, for the trip of which the visit to the park was a part.

It is obvious that visits to these parks are major travel. Other data indicate that for a considerable proportion of the visitors, enjoyment of the park is the major purpose of their travel, while for others it is an important purpose. A considerable but unknown proportion of the visitors to each park also visited other parks on the same trip; and many, but an unknown proportion, camped in, passed through, or otherwise enjoyed national forests. It is also obvious that visits of this kind are primarily vacation in character, rather than week-end or single holiday. So far as duration of the visits is concerned, however, the time spent within the parks is on the average short, though twice as long as the average stay of recreationists in the national forests. In Yosemite it is 3 days; in the other national parks, 2 days.

A continuation of present rates, or even of present absolute amounts, of increase in visits to national parks will intensify the management problems of the parks. The number of visits the National Park System can accommodate without serious impairment of basic values is not rigidly fixed, but depends on many factors. One of them is a fairly even distribution of the increased use among the various parks. Another factor is a seasonal or uneven distribution of the increased use. Some popular western parks attract many thousands of visitors daily in the summer, and none at all in the winter. This is especially true of the more remote parks in high mountain country where snow often closes the roads. In other areas, such as Yosemite, where winter sports are a major attraction, week-end visitation is at a high peak, with far fewer people using the areas on working days. If off-seasonal enjoyment can be made attractive to more people, total use can be increased considerably with present facilities or with modest expansions, without serious crowding.

The fact that present recreational use is concentrated on small areas, shows that there is some opportunity, through building more roads and other facilities, to distribute the use over a larger area. However, the most popular features of many parks are themselves concentrated in relatively small areas. The extent and nature of facilities and park personnel will also greatly influence the number of visitors that can be accommodated comfortably, without serious injury to park resources at any point.

Side by side with these problems, which deal with amount of use, are others which turn upon type of use. Some visitors require no overnight accommodations because they simply drive through the parks; some wish to camp in their own tents, staying perhaps in the one spot for the whole of their vacation; some want simple, inexpensive tents or cabins; others prefer better accommodation; and some look for the best in hotel service, and are prepared to pay for it. Some want the native values of the parks in as near their virgin condition as possible; others would like golf courses, night clubs and all the accompaniments of urban life. The widely varied interests among the visitors impose difficult administrative burdens because often the wants of one group can only be met by sacrificing the interests of another group; and sometimes the wants of several groups must rank second to protection of the parks themselves.

WATERSHEDS AND WILDLIFE

In the management of the national parks and monuments for their primary purpose—recreation at its highest level—substantial values also accrue for watershed protection and for the protection and management of wildlife. No special watershed programs as such are undertaken. But by keeping fire out of the national parks as far as possible, and by reducing erosion losses and hazards, the natural conditions of watersheds are maintained.

As for wildlife, its abundance constitutes one of the main attractions of many national parks. In Yellowstone, for instance, one may see black bears, grizzly bears, buffalo, elk, moose, deer, and many smaller animals and varieties of birds. The number and variety of game native to the various park areas differ considerably, but an attempt has been made to preserve and protect the game. In some instances this presents problems; sometimes it has been necessary to undertake special protective programs for certain kinds of game animals, and this in turn has required suppression of other kinds. The problem posed by certain types of wildlife in areas where thousands of tourists come is not simple, either. Some tourists insist on trying to feed or pet the black bears, which are great beggars and often very tame appearing; but they are, after all, wild animals, and sometimes they revert to actions which are perfectly natural to them, but which damage the foolish tourist.

SUMMARY

1. The chief use of these areas is for recreation.

2. Use has been growing steadily and rapidly, at a rate of about 11 per cent annually for many years and at a rate of perhaps 8 per cent annually during the past few years. Although there are some signs of a slowing down in rate of growth, they are not certain as yet.

3. If the growth rate from 1947 to 1954 is extended, total use figures reach very large figures in a few more years—by 1960, about 60 per cent above 1955; and by 1980, nearly ten times 1955. The lowest growth rate, from 1952 through 1955, results in lower projections.

4. The chief management problems of these lands grow out of the guidance and assistance of sightseers, and out of the reconciliation of different interests among the various sightseeing groups.

5. Uses other than recreation are unimportant or secondary.

Use Pattern on Wildlife Refuges [37]

A number of areas of diverse physical types are included among the wildlife refuges. The first refuge was established in 1903, but until 1929 additions were made on an individual basis, e.g., the Upper Mississippi Wildlife Refuge in 1924 and the Bear River Wildlife Refuge in 1928. It was only in 1929 that refuges as a system became firmly established by law.

Several types of areas are managed for wildlife purposes by the Fish and Wildlife Service.[38] First, there are the areas managed primarily or solely for wildlife; some of these were originally public domain, others were purchased from private owners. These are the areas of our primary interest. Secondly, there are areas jointly administered by the Fish and Wildlife Service and the Bureau of Land

---

[37] Data for this section are found in appendix tables 43-46. In addition, House Committee Report No. 1941, *Preservation of National Wildlife Refuges,* 84th Congress, 2nd Session, presents much information on the nature and use of these areas.

[38] As in other sections, the discussion of the Fish and Wildlife Service relates to the period before July 1, 1956.

Management. Chief among these are game ranges. The acreages and most of the uses of the latter are included in the section dealing with lands managed by that agency (pages 81-112). Thirdly, there are areas, either originally public domain or purchased, managed primarily by another agency for its purposes, but also managed by the Fish and Wildlife Service for wildlife purposes. Reclamation withdrawals, Coast Guard areas, Corps of Engineers areas, and areas under the Tennessee Valley Authority fall into this category. Fourthly, there are privately owned lands used for wildlife purposes under various leases or easements to protect the wildlife values.

In the above four categories there are nearly 7 million acres in the continental United States,[39] about 8 million acres in Alaska, and about 2.5 million acres of federally owned lands managed by the states, under various co-operative agreements, for wildlife purposes.

A considerable part of the present area of wildlife refuges was in its natural state swamp or overflow land on which forestry and agriculture had never been practiced or had been found impractical. This is true of most of the waterfowl areas. In many areas dams and other structures have increased control over water conditions. Some of the upland areas were once in farming, but generally in very poor farming. Much of this type of land was acquired in the 1930's under the submarginal land purchase program. On most of these areas agriculture and forestry would not be practical. Some of them, however, are suspected to have mineral values, and some are so located as to be in demand for highways and other right-of-way purposes.

The primary purpose of the wildlife refuges is to provide, on annual or seasonal basis, a suitable habitat for various kinds of wildlife. Every year some 20 million migratory waterfowl use the refuges. Their length of stay may vary from a few days to several weeks. In general, the refuges have been established at key points along the great migratory waterfowl flyways, where the birds have need of resting- and feeding-grounds and where such grounds otherwise are not likely to be available. Besides these migrants the refuges harbor other birds that remain there throughout the year.

Big game on refuges is relatively limited. Sometimes it is incidental to other purposes of the refuges; sometimes it is preserved as key species. The numbers of bison and bighorn sheep are large compared

[39] Appendix table 1 shows about 4 million acres; this area is essentially equivalent to the first listed category.

with total numbers in the country; for other species, the numbers on the refuges are comparatively much smaller.

People use the refuges partly for hunting and fishing, partly for the study of wildlife, which may include photography, and partly simply for recreational purposes. In 1955, 6 per cent of the users came to hunt, 38 per cent to fish, and 56 per cent for other purposes. Much of the wildlife area is not open to hunting, which reduces this use. The total number of visitor-days in that year was nearly 7 million. If it is assumed that the average visitor spent less than two days per visit, this would perhaps be the equivalent of 4 or 5 million visits. Use of the refuges for this purpose is thus roughly 10 per cent of the use of the national forests and roughly 15 per cent of the national parks and monuments for the same general purposes. However, the area of refuges is very much smaller than that of either of the other two land types. Refuges cover less than one-third the area of national parks and monuments and hence, on an equal area basis, receive roughly half as many visitors. And they cover about one-fortieth the area of the national forests, which, on an equal area basis, gives them nearly four times as much recreational use as the forests. Moreover, recreational use of the refuges is growing fast, having roughly doubled in the five years from 1951 to 1955. This is a faster rate of increase than either of the other two types of land area can show in the same time. There seems every reason to expect a continued rapid rate of increase in the human use of wildlife refuges.

In addition to these primary uses, the wildlife refuges do have some secondary or incidental uses. In several instances farmers are encouraged to grow crops on a sharecropping basis. The government's share of the crop is not harvested, but is available for wildlife, particularly waterfowl, as feed. In this way the wildlife get feed at no cash cost to the government, and their depredations on the crops of neighboring farmers are reduced. Some small revenues are also obtained from the lease of either crop or pasture land, and larger revenues, but still small, are obtained from sale of hay or the privilege of cutting it, and from grazing. Some small sales of timber are made. All of these uses are on a minor scale, and revenue from them is subordinate to wildlife needs.

The refuges are also in demand for various right-of-way purposes. In most cases those for power lines, telephone lines, and other similar purposes do not interfere seriously with wildlife needs. Highway construction takes up comparatively large areas and generally interferes seriously with management of the areas for wildlife purposes. Hence, attempts to build highways have been resisted by supporters of the refuges.

Another demand upon the wildlife refuges has been for mineral development, especially oil and gas development. A few such leases were issued prior to 1953, followed by comparatively many more in the following two years.[40] If a wildlife refuge happens to be within a producing oil and gas field the federal government would lose considerable revenues by refusing development for this purpose. Many supporters of wildlife refuges would concede that under these circumstances mineral development should be allowed. Directional drilling and other means can keep interference with wildlife purposes to a minimum. However, most of the demand thus far has been of the speculative type common to the public domain, and thus has engendered much opposition. Revenues in excess of $1 million annually have been received in the past few years from oil and gas royalties.

Conflicts and Competition in Use, Actual and Potential

Competition among various types of land use and land users, and actual conflict in land use, have occurred innumerable times in the past on each of the major types of federal land. Competition may occur between almost any pair of major land uses—forestry and grazing, forestry and recreation, forestry and mineral development, grazing and recreation, grazing and mineral development, recreation and mineral development, and so forth.

Competition may also occur between different kinds of use within a broad type of use—between different types of recreational use, for instance. Hunting, camping, sightseeing, enjoyment of wilderness areas, commercial entertainment, and many other activities fall under the broad classification, "recreation." There may even be conflict as to the manner in which a particular kind of use is to be enjoyed.

It should be clear that competition and conflict in the use of resources of the federal land grow out of public demand for these resources rather than from anything inherent in the resources them-

---

[40] House Committee Report No. 1941, *op. cit.*

selves. The American Indian who used these same resources did not encounter the same conflicts in their use because he was unable to utilize the resources in many of the ways we do today. Even as late as 1870 or 1880 there was little conflict in use of the resources in most of the western states; some conflict occurred among ranchers for use of forage, occasional conflicts arose among miners or prospectors, and some disputes were involved with water rights. But most of the conflicts have arisen or become intensified in more recent years. In large measure they reflect the economic expansion of the country. With a growing economy resources not previously used intensively have come into demand.

There seems every reason to believe that the use of public lands, and hence the competition and conflicts in their use, will increase in the decades ahead. A substantial population increase in each next decade seems fairly certain. We may not be sure of the size of that increase, especially for the more distant decades, but no one would now argue that a large population increase will not occur. There is almost equal agreement that a substantial rise in real per capita income will occur in each decade for many decades into the future. Again, we may be unsure of its exact extent, but few informed persons would contend that major increases in per capita real income will not occur. Both of these factors, and the economic and social phenomena associated with them, will mean greater demand for resources of nearly all kinds—greater demand in order to produce more, and greater demand for consumption arising out of higher incomes. This increased demand will fall with greater relative force on the federal lands. Only a few decades ago most of the lands were submarginal for use under the circumstances of that time. Today most such lands are in heavy demand. We have seen, for example, the extent to which timber sold from the national forests has increased in recent years while total timber cut in the nation was increasing far less. The increase in area under oil and gas lease is almost surely greater on the federal lands than for all private lands. The earlier sections of this chapter have presented projections of future use or output of the federal lands, and in nearly every case the projection is for greatly increased use.

As the extent of competition and conflict among uses increases with demand, the problems of administration, especially of multiple-use administration, will become greater. The nature of the management problem is considered in the two following chapters.

Need for Better Data on Uses of Federal Land

The foregoing sections of this chapter have dealt with the major uses of the various types of federal land. Consideration of these uses points to the need for better data, especially in the future, if the management problems of the lands are to be properly understood and provided for.

First of all, there is a need for better annual summarization of existing data than is now available. The summarization of the future should be undertaken not only agency by agency, or type of land by type of land, but should also include an over-all picture of all federal lands. While today an agency's annual report of its operations provides a part of this picture, these reports generally suffer from over-concentration on the year of report with inadequate consideration of past trends and emerging future problems.

An over-all summary of all the federal lands, however, would provide much more than this; it would annually present the facts somewhat along the lines followed throughout this chapter and in chapter five dealing with revenues and expenditures. Such a summary should bring together the available statistics, interpret them as well as possible, and outline emerging trends and problems. There is also a need for summaries of all agencies by states; this would be particularly helpful to the officials and the people of each of the western states. Such summaries might be prepared by the various land managing agencies acting together, or by the Bureau of the Budget, or even by one of the Congressional committees most directly interested. (Suggestions toward this end are made in chapter six.) For some years Congressman Walter Horan, working only with his staff, did something akin to this for a single aspect of federal land management— range reseeding, range improvement, and range management. He had found a co-ordinated, consolidated picture of this one aspect impossible to obtain, except by putting it together himself from the data supplied by the various agencies.

Another need is for more information yearly on the area of land associated with each federal land use. The data on numbers of recreational visits, or on volume of timber cut, or on numbers of livestock grazed, do not indicate the area of land included. Although it may be difficult for some agencies to estimate the area of land involved for some uses, the best possible estimates undoubtedly would be helpful. It is possible that the area of land used for various purposes changes less from year to year than does the amount of the use—that is, some of the changes in amount of use may be reflected in changes in intensity of use. But if this is true, it is important, and should be known.

Yet another major need is for data on water relationships on federal land—how much water the soil stores, for how long, and how much is used up by vegetation. Considerable data, but much less than most hydrologists consider necessary, are available on precipitation, runoff, and stream flow. But quantitative data on a comprehensive scale about water-soil-vegetation relationships are lacking, thus putting severe limits on economic analysis.

Improved analysis of data is required also to give a more accurate picture of the conflicts, actual or potential, in use each year. Some administrators may feel that the existence of such conflicts reflects adversely upon the administration of his agency. The fact is, however, that these conflicts spring out of the public's growing use of the land for the many purposes for which it is suitable. An explicit facing of conflicts, actual and potential, without at the same time magnifying their scale or seriousness, would lead to a better public understanding of the problems of federal land management. A first step would be to formulate definitions and methods of measurement of conflicts. As already has been suggested, such an analysis should by all means be consolidated for all the federal lands, partly in order to give a comprehensive picture, and partly because the resolution of conflicts in land use on one type of federal land may well involve other types of federal land.

The greatest need for more data on use of federal lands is with respect to recreation which, as we have seen, will surely increase greatly in the coming decades. Data need to be more complete and more consistent. As pointed out earlier in this chapter, some data are now assembled on a *visits* basis: each person who visits an area is counted each separate time he visits the area. Other data are on a *visitor-day* basis: the number of visitors is multiplied by the number of days spent in the area, usually with each part of a day counted as a whole day. The latter measure is useful to indicate the total recreational burden upon the resource and upon the administrative setup. But the number of visits is also a useful measure; data have been collected on this basis for many years, and a consistent statistical series should not be abandoned lightly. More important, the number of visits will be useful some day for estimating the number of visitors.

There are almost no data now available on the number of recreational *visitors* to the various types of federal land. It is essential that the various federal agencies begin to tackle this problem energetically in the near future. What is needed is some sort of discount ratio by which data on numbers of visits could be reduced to numbers of visitors. Clearly, it would be too much to ask every recreational user of federal land to account for every other area he has used during the year. Equally usable ratios could be obtained on a sample basis. The estimates should deal not only with all types of federal land, but with various types of federal water recreational areas also, and with state and local recreational areas. To illustrate: in 1955 some 50 million visits were made to the entire national park system. Does this figure represent 50 million persons, or 25 million, or 10 million? In the same year 40 million visits were made to the national forests. Do these visits represent 40 million, 20 million, or 10 million persons? Whatever the number of persons on each type of federal land, how many of these persons used more than one type of land, and what lands were they?

More than a mere estimate of the total numbers of persons using each and all types of federal land is necessary. Information is also needed as to the residence of the people in relation to the federal land area visited, their general income bracket, their occupation, the family composition of those using the lands, and other items that will round out the picture of the population using the federal lands.

Information of the foregoing types is an indispensable part of reaching wise decisions in the management of the federal lands. If use of the various types of federal land is widely dispersed among the total population, then the propriety of their rather intensive development, largely at federal expense, is much greater than if the use is highly localized as to area and restricted as to classes of population. One would not expect many persons to use some types of federal land, especially the more remote national parks, every year, although some may use them several times over a period of years. If recreational use of these areas is restricted to certain classes of the population, the question may well be raised as to the desirability of charging more for the use. On the other hand, if the use of certain national forest areas is predominantly local, question might be raised as to the wisdom of moderately large federal expenditures for what is essentially a local activity. These are but illustrative of the types of policy problems that arise in the administration of federal lands.

The important matter is to obtain the necessary facts upon which wise policy decisions may be based. The types of data needed should be obtained for each type of federal land; but they will miss their greatest potential usefulness unless they are also assembled and analyzed on an over-all basis for all types of federal land as a group.

CHAPTER THREE

Policy Formation

and Decision Making

THE COMPETITIVE MARKET WHICH ALLOCATES
privately owned resources between uses and users has
generally been rejected for federal land resources. Instead, by administrative actions of various kinds, the major kind of use must be
decided and the resources allocated to particular users. All of this
requires a governmental organization and procedures adequate to deal
with the problems. Thus, even a study that emphasizes the economic
side of federal land management must take fully into account the
way in which policies are formed and decisions made. A heavy and
growing use of the same or of closely intermixed tracts of federal land
for the major purposes and their variations, such as has been described in chapter two, has inevitably led to occasional conflict of
one use with another, and to competition between individual users.
With the increased use of the federal lands which clearly lies ahead,
we can expect an even greater degree of competition between uses
and users. The machinery for dealing with thes problems of federal
land management has developed over the years. Often it is cumbersome; always intricate in the interrelationship of its parts. Nevertheless, it has sufficed for many years to resolve many problems, not always
perfectly; and a clear understanding of the processes by which it
operates is more than ever necessary when we contemplate the future
of federal land management.

In chapter six, where we consider various alternative forms of future federal land management, the strengths and the weaknesses of the present structure should be borne in mind. The purpose here is to describe the application of these general governmental processes to the particular circumstances and problems of federal land management. This chapter cannot be viewed as a contribution to knowledge of the functioning of the federal government in general.[1] It merely attempts to outline the environment in which the necessary administrative decisions must be made, and to indicate something of the various forces that are a part of this environment. The specialized studies that have been made in this field are drawn on freely.[2]

Before considering the various elements that contribute to policy formation and decision making on matters to do with the federal lands, it may be useful to define some of the words employed. In so

[1] Some of the major books in this field are as follows:

Appleby, Paul H. *Big Democracy*. New York: Alfred A. Knopf, 1945.

———. *Morality and Administration in Democratic Government*. Baton Rouge: Louisiana State University Press, 1952.

———. *Policy and Administration*. University: University of Alabama Press, 1949.

Bailey, Stephen K. *Congress Makes a Law*. New York: Columbia University Press, 1950.

Bentley, Arthur F. *The Process of Government—A Study of Social Pressures*. Chicago: University of Chicago Press, 1908.

Burns, James M. *Congress on Trial: The Legislative Process and the Administrative State*. New York: Harper & Bros., 1949.

Friedrich, Carl J. *Constitutional Government and Democracy*. Boston: Little, Brown & Co., 1941.

Gross, B. M. *The Legislative Struggle, a Study in Social Combat*. New York: McGraw-Hill Book Co., 1953.

Herring, Pendleton. *The Politics of Democracy—American Parties in Action*. New York: W. W. Norton Co., 1940.

Lippmann, Walter. *The Phantom Public*. New York: Harcourt, Brace & Co., 1925.

Riddick, Floyd M. *The United States Congress Organization and Procedure*. Manassas, Va.: National Capitol Publishers, 1949.

Simon, Herbert A. *Administrative Behavior—A Study of Decision-making Processes in Administrative Organization*. New York: Macmillan Co., 1947.

Truman, David B. *The Governmental Process—Political Interests and Public Opinion*. New York: Alfred A. Knopf, 1951.

[2] In addition to the more general works cited above and on p. 16, see the following:

Frank, Bernard. *Our National Forests*. Norman: University of Oklahoma Press, 1955.

McKinley, Charles. *Uncle Sam in the Pacific Northwest*. Berkeley: University of California Press, 1952.

Loveridge, Earl W. "The Administration of National Forests," *Trees* (U. S. Department of Agriculture Yearbook), 1949.

Kaufman, Herbert. "The Field Man in Administration." Unpublished report prepared for the Institute of Public Administration, 1952.

doing, the interrelationships of the processes to be described may perhaps be clear at the outset. "Policy" is a settled course adopted and followed. A "program" connotes a more detailed plan of procedure, ordinarily to achieve the objectives of a policy. A "decision" is a judgment or conclusion reached after consideration of a matter at issue, on the basis of which action will ordinarily follow. A program at one level of government may become a policy at another. A decision made by an official in the development of a detailed program to implement an adopted policy, and the program too, becomes policy to subordinate officials to guide their actions.

Public Participation in Federal Land Management

The citizens of this country influence federal land management considerably, more by their actions than by their words. Their significant action is the use they make of the land and its resources; this direct act on their part forces various actions upon the land administrator and creates situations which the whole machinery of the federal government must consider.

The amount of use made of the federal lands is large and growing. The approximately 100 million recreational visits to federal land very likely include 25 million people, or roughly 15 per cent of the total population today; in 1920 less than 3 per cent of the people were involved. Other types of use do not involve as large numbers of people as recreation does, but still there are substantial numbers, and sometimes interest is greater. There are 100,000 mineral leases in effect, representing an unknown but substantial number of people; the 65,000 grazing permits and licenses probably include 40,000 or more livestock operators; several thousand persons purchase timber or get it under free-use provisions, and thousands more men work for these timber harvesters; finally, large but unknown numbers of people are directly concerned because a major source of their water supply originates on federal land.

The trend in nearly all of these uses is upward, as was shown in detail in chapter two. Growth rates of the order of 10 per cent annually are found for several of the more important uses of federal land. This is greatly in excess of the rate of population growth or of increase in gross national product in this country; in modern society comparatively few industries or social phenomena show growth rates this large. Many officials of federal land managing agencies have had to cope with a mounting tide of recreationists seeking to use the lands under their jurisdiction, or with a demand for larger timber sales than it is possible to make with limited staffs. These public demands have forced adaptation of administrative programs at every level, and they have been basic to the increased budget requests presented to the Congress and to the requests for new legislation. The new major era in federal land history, described in chapter one, is characterized by the increased use of the federal lands, with its larger numbers of citizens concerned.

In spite of this large and growing use, most people in the United States know or care little about the federal lands. Many people do not use the lands because they live in areas where use would be difficult, or because they lack the income to travel to the lands, or because they simply lack interest. Few of these nonusers are informed on or interested in federal lands. Even among users there are many who take the lands and facilities they use for granted, without concern as to their management. There are probably users of national forests and national parks who do not know the difference between them, the names and departmental origin of the administering agencies, and other relatively elementary facts about federal lands. The land managing agencies often must cope with users too ignorant to make proper and safe use of the lands. In the complex economy and society of today, it is perhaps neither surprising nor cause for criticism that so many people are uninformed about the federal lands. But it is a major fact to be considered in federal land management.

Yet upon occasion many of the normally uninterested public can be roused to take action, especially when the issues can be simplified and dramatized and they can be made to feel that their personal interests are jeopardized. When aroused, they can be politically highly effective. This has been proved several times in federal land history.

Some unusually well-informed, unusually able, or very energetic individuals are able to exert influence on federal land management by direct contact with the Executive or Legislative branches of the federal government. Generally, however, they and others interested in the lands have found it most effective to work through associations of various kinds. Associations, the growth of which has been one of the outstanding social phenomena of the last fifty years, can exert a direct or indirect influence, even though the purpose for which they exist may be far broader than that of influencing federal land admin-

istration. The motivation for individuals, whether working alone or
through associations, may be idealism, profit, or pleasure.

A number of organized groups have been influential in federal land
management in the past, and are likely to continue so in the future.

The organized groups interested in federal land management have
some of the characteristics and problems common to all organized
groups: an active minority in the lead, with an inactive and largely
voiceless majority of followers who often provide the funds and the
bulk necessary to make the organization effective; usually a paid staff,
sometimes small, which has its own interests and often influences the
affairs of the association in its own directions; programs of varying
content, but often including attempts to influence government action
in ways favorable to the group by means of contacts with the Executive and Congressional branches at all levels; and working relationships, sometimes amounting to alliances, with other organized groups.

Among the various organized groups there is a continuum from a
few whose primary purpose is concern with federal land management,
through a much larger number whose interest in this matter is considerable but not dominant, to the great majority of associations
which are interested in federal lands only when they have been
aroused to some particular issue by other groups with whom they
have working relationships on other matters. Those groups whose
interests in federal lands is at least considerable may be grouped as
follows:[3]

I. Groups whose major interest in federal lands is in forestry or
   timber harvest; these can in turn be grouped as follows:
   A. Professional associations, similar to those in other professional
      fields. Chief among those in this group is the Society of Ameri-
      can Foresters, founded in 1900 and now with about 11,000
      members. Others include the Association of Consulting Forest-
      ers and the Forest Products Research Society.

[3] For a detailed account of associations and groups with interests bearing on the
federal lands, see: Erle Kauffman (ed.), *The Conservation Yearbook, 1956.* Washington, D. C.: Cornwell, Inc. Also, *Directory of Organizations and Officials Concerned with Protection of Wildlife and Other Natural Resources,* Washington,
D. C.: National Wildlife Federation, 1956.

B. Semiprofessional, general-public associations, with a less professional and more popular membership than the foregoing. Chief member of this group is the oldest forestry association, the American Forestry Association, founded in 1875 and with a present membership of about 25,000. There are also the Forest Conservation Society, the American Tree Association, and a number of state or regional associations similar to, but independent of, the American Forestry Association.

C. Industry-sponsored associations. These include a wide variety; their major interests are generally the economic and governmental programs that affect their members, but some of them have direct interest in federal lands. The latter associations include American Forest Products Industries, Inc., American Paper and Pulp Association, American Pulpwood Association, Forest Industries Council, National Lumber Manufacturers Association, and a number of regional associations, of which the Western Forestry and Conservation Association, the California Redwood Association, Pacific Northwest Forest Industries, West Coast Lumbermen's Association, and Western Forest Industries Association are the most important.

D. One endowed research foundation, the Charles Lathrop Pack Forestry Foundation, is primarily concerned with forest problems.

II. Groups whose major interest is grazing of livestock, on federal lands or elsewhere. These have the following subgroups:

A. The major professional association concerned with grazing is the American Society of Range Management; founded in 1948, its membership today is about equally divided between ranchers and technicians, many of whom are employed by the federal agencies.

B. There is no semiprofessional, general-public counterpart in the grazing field of the American Forestry Association in the forestry field.

C. Industry-sponsored associations fall into two main categories: those primarily concerned with sheep production, and those primarily concerned with cattle. On the national level, these are the National Wool Growers Association and the American National Livestock Association, respectively. Each has counterparts, often affiliated with the national association, in most of the western states.

D. The only endowed research foundation concerned with grazing is the Grasslands Research Foundation.

III. Associations primarily concerned with mineral development on the federal lands divide more or less definitely into those whose interest is primarily in petroleum and other leasable minerals, and those whose interest is the hard metals, obtainable under the mining law. Although there are professional societies in both fields, these have not, in general, taken much direct interest in federal land management. There is no semiprofessional, general-public interest group comparable to the American Forestry Association. The American Mining Congress, on the national level, has taken a major interest in federal lands; state and local mining associations, some associated with the national and some independent, even hostile, exist in all western states. One of their chief interests is the mining law as applied to federal lands. There are several regional associations interested in oil development on federal lands; the best known ones are the Rocky Mountain Oil and Gas Association, Independent Petroleum Association of America, Mid-Continent Oil and Gas Association, Western Oil and Gas Association, Independent Petroleum Association, New Mexico Oil and Gas Association, National Stripper Well Association, and National Royalty Association. There is no endowed research foundation particularly concerned with this field.

IV. There are a large number and variety of associations in the recreation, conservation, and general resource-use field. None is strictly professional in character, but most are semiprofessional, general-public in their appeal. Included among the latter are the American Institute of Park Executives, founded in 1898, with a present membership of about 1,500; American Nature Association, founded in 1922, with a membership of about 60,000; American Planning and Civic Association, founded in 1904; Friends of the Land, formed in 1940; Izaak Walton League of America, founded in 1922; National Audubon Society, founded in 1905 and believed to be the largest national conservation association; National Conference on State Parks, founded in 1921; National Parks Association, founded in 1919; National Wildlife Federation; Nature Conservancy; Natural Resources Council of America; Outdoor Writers Association of America, Inc.; Save-the-Redwoods League; and the Wilderness Society. There is one organization, similar to the foregoing but largely industry sponsored—the Wildlife

Management Institute. There are several endowed research and educational foundations interested in natural resources, including federal land management. In addition, there are a number of associations of regional or state scope, some of which are perhaps more influential than the national organizations. These include the Federation of Outdoor Clubs, the Federation of Western Outdoor Clubs, the Sierra Club, and others.

These associations and interest groups more or less directly concerned with federal land management can sometimes enlist the support of other groups whose concern with federal lands would ordinarily be slight. Upon occasion the general farm organizations, such as the American Farm Bureau Federation, the National Grange, and the Farmers Union, especially in the West, have been drawn into federal land management matters; the same is true of the major general labor unions, of general business organizations such as chambers of commerce, general clubs such as the General Federation of Women's Clubs, conservation groups such as the National Association of Soil Conservation Districts, and many others. The issue must appear as a major one and must often be simplified, and the general co-operation of the specialized association must be employed to the full if these associations of more general interests are to become directly and importantly concerned with an issue of federal land management.

A mere listing of the major associations interested in federal land management suggests their great numbers and wide variety. A careful appraisal of their operations would obviously lead us far astray here. The objectives and interests of the various associations are usually stated in such general terms that it is hard to ascertain the precise differences between them. In some instances, personalized leadership or localized interests account for the multiplicity of organizations. Accurate data on their memberships are even lacking, at least for some. Total membership in all of the associations listed above probably is 500,000 and may be much higher (even allowing for a common tendency to overstate membership). There is some overlapping of membership among associations of generally similar character.

These associations have been effective in influencing federal land management in the past. Their influence has been exerted in support of, or more frequently in opposition to, legislative proposals. They have also tried to influence administrative action at every level from the President down to the district ranger. No land managing official at any level dares ignore the existence of these interest groups, for they are likely to block his proposals if they seem harmful. At other times these associations may be helpful in securing needed legislation or administrative reforms or popular support for an agency's program. On the whole, however, their actions, like those of many parts of the government process, tend to be negative more often and more forcefully than they are positive. The professional societies have influenced federal land management more through indirect measures than directly; establishment of a common body of professional knowledge and interchange of ideas through annual meetings and periodicals has had a profound influence on federal land management.

A few illustrations of the actions of some of these associations may suggest their importance in federal land management. The American Forestry Association was a major influence in establishment of the first Forest Reserves and in the creation and early operations of the Forest Service; for a recent example, it was influential in the passage of the amendment to the mining laws in 1955. The Society of American Foresters has been a major force in the development of forestry as a profession; for many years this effectively meant the development of the Forest Service as a professional group, with the public stature that this implies. It has been a major source of support for the Forest Service for many years, on many issues. The influence of the livestock associations on grazing administration has been felt many times, most notably in recent years, in the operations of the Bureau of Land Management. The mining associations have successfully withstood every proposal to modify the mining laws until 1955, and have repeatedly been concerned with administrative actions on particular mining claims. No change can be made in the mineral leasing law without at least the sufferance of the oil and gas associations; and they have opposed or supported administrative actions, sometimes quite minor or technical ones, whose effect they thought harmful to the interests of their members. The general resource and conservation associations have been in large measure responsible for the general climate of public opinion which regards parks, conservation, forests, and a number of related resources or activities as inherently good and not to be disturbed for political reasons.

The influence of these various associations on federal land management will continue in the future to be significant, if not controlling, as it has been in the past.

There are some rather easily discernible differences between the industry groups, on the one hand, and the general conservation or resource groups on the other. The industry groups have a definite economic purpose and can often operate to the demonstrable economic advantage of their members; they can usually enlist the support of a large enough share of their potential membership to be effective and to have sufficient funds to carry on as organizations. By devoting rather continuous and direct attention to the matters affecting their members, they can often guide or influence both legislative and administrative action in ways favorable to their members. Their major weakness is the difficulty they have in enlisting widespread public support, or in combatting such support when enlisted by other groups. The general conservation or resource groups find themselves in a very different position. Their appeal is not economic, but idealistic; they often have difficulty in building a large membership, especially one that is large compared with their potential interest group, and many such associations have had serious financial difficulties. They are less effective in continuous and detailed scrutiny of federal land management, but can sometimes arouse a great deal of popular support for a dramatized issue. They thrive best on "emergencies" and "crises," and sometimes seem to sleep when times are quiet. These conservation groups, and the professional groups also, frequently find it difficult to arrive at a consensus on policy issues. A common professional background will not usually overcome a divergent economic interest.

As nearly as one can judge, political strength of the timber harvest, grazing, mineral development, and recreation- conservation- general-resource interest groups is nearly balanced today. Each group is able to stop legislation or new administrative action that it finds highly objectionable, but at the same time no group is able to push through legislation or new administrative action that it wants but that one or more of the other major groups oppose. Where events have proved otherwise, the associations' success has hinged not only on the intensity of their interest but on the degree to which they have been able to interest the general and usually indifferent public. In such cases the issue has been simplified for public judgment and has been one which touches with some impact on the public's value system. When these criteria are met the public will respond in considerable numbers. In a closely balanced political contest rather small minorities can often be decisive, as they were in some states in 1954 and 1956.

THE ROLE OF ADVISORY BOARDS OF LAND USERS

Advisory boards of federal land users or others with an interest in federal lands are widely used by the federal land managing agencies at all levels of organization. These boards may serve an important function in providing the federal official with a channel for disseminating information and as a source of support for his agency's program in that area; they may also serve as a means for interest groups to convey ideas and viewpoints to the administrator.

At the local level, the Forest Service uses many small livestock advisory groups on the national forests; the Bureau of Land Management has advisory boards made up of livestock men and a wildlife representative for all of its grazing districts, and the same agency uses advisory boards of mixed interests for the O & C lands.

Advisory boards may also be used at the intermediate and Washington levels in agency organization. The higher the level in the bureaucratic chain at which the advisory board is used, the more formal are likely to be its operations. At the lower levels, particularly, the members may operate as individuals, giving the federal official the benefit of their localized knowledge and experience, and providing him with some indication of the public reaction to various agency programs or procedures. At the higher levels, members of such groups are more likely to act as spokesmen for their interest group even though they have been asked to serve in an individual capacity.

Officials of the federal land managing agencies at both local and intermediate levels can use their relationships with the public and with advisory boards to further their own, as contrasted with their agency's, interests. Some local support is always for an agency and its program, but some is also for its man—it is often virtually impossible to tell which is which, partly because, under many conditions, the two are in complete harmony. But they may not always be so.

Although the advisory board is an excellent administrative technique, its efficient functioning requires time and forethought on the part of the administrator. Moreover, such boards may exceed their advisory role and attempt direct administrative action; this must always be guarded against. At the other extreme, some boards may be useless because not consulted on significant matters.[4]

THE ROLE OF STATE AND LOCAL GOVERNMENT

Units of state and local government are also part of the public of federal land management. Employees of these governmental units

[4] Clawson, Marion, *Uncle Sam's Acres,* New York: Dodd, Mead & Co., 1951, pp. 368-76.

often have a similar or common professional background with employees of the federal agencies, and yet their position as employees of state and local government gives them a different perspective on many resource management problems. Interchanges of ideas on an informal professional basis may be highly influential in the long run, both as to the management of the federal lands and as to the conduct of state and local government.

There are many joint problems of resource management, especially in areas where federal lands are sizable. Fire control is the most obvious and most urgent of these common resource management problems. Forest and range fires are no respecters of property lines; and fires cannot be fought successfully and efficiently on an emergency or ad hoc basis. A well planned, carefully co-ordinated organization for fire fighting is needed, the costs of which, and provision of parts of it, should ordinarily be borne in proportion to the responsibilities of the respective agencies; but the operations must very often be joint. State agencies have a major interest in the programs of fire control adopted by the federal agencies, and vice versa; out of this necessary working together common approaches to a variety of resource management problems can be developed.

To a lesser extent, insect and disease control, especially on forest lands, and weed control, especially on grazing lands, pose management problems of a serious nature which require joint action for their successful solution.

State agencies are often interested in federal land disposal programs. While land disposal is not, strictly speaking, land management, the two are very closely interrelated. In most western states there are state land boards or commissioners established to manage, sell, and lease state lands. These agencies are often much interested in federal land disposal and management policies and programs, and try to influence them directly. State foresters and state fish and game boards or departments are also interested in obtaining federal land at times. However, in the latter case the state government's most direct point of contact with federal land management is through game management and harvest. State officials establish rules for game harvest, yet the game graze upon federal lands during part of the year. Federal officials have an interest in seeing that the game harvest is large enough to prevent the animals from overgrazing the federal lands. In several western states a more or less formal procedure exists whereby state and federal officials jointly work out game management plans, including game harvest. Associations of state foresters and of state fish and

game commissioners can be effective instruments for state-federal
co-operation.

Officials of states and counties are often greatly interested in federal
land management insofar as it affects the revenues received by their
respective units of government from the federal lands. This aspect of
the federal lands will be considered more fully in chapter five. In the
West there is an organization of state land commissioners and an
organization of county officials in the areas of major federal land
ownership. The O & C counties of western Oregon also have an organization. These various state and local officials constitute a very special
and yet important part of the public interested in federal land
management.

The Legislative Process

The processes fundamental to any governmental operation—legislation and appropriation—are in many ways interdependent. While
the first supplies authorization for activities, and the second supplies
funds deemed necessary to undertake them, the terms under which
funds are made available are, for instance, often in themselves tanta-
mount to legislation. However, in analysis of federal land management it is useful to distinguish between the processes. Each involves
the Legislative and Executive branches of the federal government;
and either may on occasion involve the Judiciary as well.

It is the intention here to present very briefly the framework of the
legislative process in order that, in later pages of this chapter, it may
more readily be perceived how the legislative process bears upon
decision making in connection with the federal lands.

In the legislative battles it is easier to defeat change than to make
a change. There are innumerable obstacles to the passage of federal
land legislation, even when there is no opposition at all. The legislative process is often a time-consuming one, and federal land legislation
must compete for the time and attention of the legislators against
legislation in many other and possibly more important fields. There
may be extensive time lags at every stage, from the introduction of
the bill, to its referral to committee, through action by the latter
(including getting reports from the agencies of the Executive Branch
that may be interested), to action by the parent house when the bill
is reported, and through the whole process in the other house. Even

when there is no opposition a bill may not run this course in the two years of a Congress, in which case the next Congress starts all over. Many bills are not introduced until well into the life of a Congress and this further reduces the time available for their passage.

SPECIALIZED INTEREST OF CONGRESSMEN

Most congressmen are elected primarily on the basis of local issues; their constituents regard the congressman as representative of their interests, not as a man from their area representing the national interest. Hence, while each congressman is likely to be guided, but not controlled, by the leadership of his party in the Congress and by the President if he is of the President's party, he knows that he must fight his own battles in his district or state, and that he can expect little effective help from the leaders of his party.

Even the ablest congressman cannot be well informed on more than a small proportion of the measures upon which he is called to vote. Moreover, he and his constituents are likely to have little interest in the majority of the items in this long and complex list of matters. Under these circumstances, in order to vote at all congressmen often must follow the lead of other congressmen in whom they have confidence. At its worst this process is mere log-rolling, or trading of votes without regard for the merits of the issues. At its best it is a means for specialization among congressmen, and results in a more careful consideration of issues than would otherwise be possible.

THE COMMITTEE STRUCTURE

Most legislative matters affecting the federal lands come before the committees on Interior and Insular Affairs or the Agriculture committees, in the House and Senate.

Composition. For many years a substantial proportion of the representatives from the eleven western states, in which most of the federal lands lie, have sought membership on the House Committee on Interior and Insular Affairs. In recent years the single congressman from Nevada and from Wyoming has each obtained representation on the committee; and at least one of the two representatives from Montana, Utah, Idaho, Arizona, and New Mexico is likely to be serving on it. If the two members from these last states are from differ-

ent political parties and have different philosophies about the federal
lands, they may both be on the committee. In addition, one or more
members from the larger delegations in Colorado, Washington,
Oregon, and California may be represented. In the 83rd Congress,
the committee had twenty-seven members, not counting the delegates
from Alaska, Hawaii, and Puerto Rico. The eight intermountain
states have only sixteen congressmen in total. The three Pacific Coast
states have only forty, most of them from urban areas and quite
uninterested in federal lands.

Considering the location of the congressmen and the interests of
their constituents, the maximum number of interested congressmen
from the West for the Interior and Insular Affairs Committee is about
twenty. A more realistic estimate is fifteen, but even this represents
a degree of concentration on this one committee which limits the
region's direct representation on other aspects of federal business.

The remainder of the committee has to be drawn from elsewhere.
Some members have come from states bordering on the region, such
as South Dakota and Texas. But some must come from quite different
regions, including the South and the East, where there is little political
pressure on their actions with regard to the federal lands. In such
cases the congressmen may sometimes have acted more in the general
public interest than their western colleagues, although there have
often been instances of complete indifference.

In the Senate Interior and Insular Affairs Committee the situation
is similar, but somewhat more extreme. Of the fifteen committee
members in the 83rd Congress, ten came from the eleven western
states, and of those states only Arizona was not represented. Since
senators are on two or three committees, this concentration on the
Interior and Insular Affairs Committee does not bring about the
degree of underrepresentation of the region on other committees that
it does in the House.

The House and Senate Agriculture committees are perhaps as
sharply specialized, in terms of the interests of their members, as are
the respective committees on Interior and Insular Affairs, but the
basis of selection is different. Members of the Committee on Agriculture are selected because they come from districts or states where
agriculture is highly important, and because as individuals they are
known to be friendly to the interests of agriculture. Of the thirty
members on the House committee of the 83rd Congress, only two
came from the eleven western states, and these were from areas where
federal lands were comparatively unimportant. Of the fifteen-member

Senate committee of the same Congress, only two came from the West. With their primary interest in commercial agriculture, rather than in federal lands, these committees are in a position similar to that of the nonwestern members of the House Committee on Interior and Insular Affairs—their interest in what they have to do may be lower, but the pressure on them for group-interest action is less.

In stressing the fact that the representatives and senators having most to do with legislation on federal lands come predominantly from the West, it would be a mistake to leave the impression that the pressures of interest groups on these men are wholly from one or a few groups. It is true that in the West the grazing and mining interests are stronger politically, compared with recreation and conservation groups, than they are elsewhere in the nation. In an earlier era —say prior to 1930—western members of the Congress often had few interest groups among their constituents other than grazing, mining, and lumbering. But today in the West there is a substantial interest in other aspects of federal land management, including that sort of general and rather vague conservation philosophy which has long been relatively strong elsewhere in the country.

Functions. The subject matter of the two committees on Agriculture includes "Forestry in general, and forest reserves other than those created from the public domain." The committees on Interior and Insular Affairs include the following items relating to federal land, as we have used the term:

"1. Public lands generally, including entry, easements, and grazing thereon.
2. Mineral resources of the public lands.
3. Forfeiture of land grants and alien ownership, including alien ownership of mineral lands.
4. Forest reserves and national parks created from the public domain.
5. Military parks and battlefields, and national cemeteries.
6. Preservation of prehistoric ruins and objects of interest on the public domain."

"10. Mining interests generally.
11. Mineral land laws and claims and entries thereunder."

"14. Petroleum conservation on the public lands and conservation of the radium supply in the United States."

The dividing line for jurisdiction of the two committees for national forests is not clear. In practice, bills have been drawn by members of the committees on Interior and Insular Affairs in such a way as to facilitate if not require reference to those committees; and doubtless the same has been true of bills drawn by members of the committees on Agriculture and by the Executive branch for introduction by those members. The fact that two committees, of completely different membership in the House and of largely different membership in the Senate, consider legislation relating to different types of federal land introduces a measure of divergence at the legislative level. A single committee would have a measure of co-ordinating power which is now absent. As will be noted later, the situation is different when it involves appropriations.

A recent innovation. A new note in Congressional consideration of federal land management matters was struck in the 84th Congress with the organization of a new subcommittee of the Committee on Government Operations in the House—the Public Works and Resources Subcommittee. Its ten-man membership had a background largely different from that of the House Committee on Interior and Insular Affairs; only one member came from west of the Mississippi River, and he from an area not particularly concerned with federal lands.

This new subcommittee, together with the Subcommittee on the Legislative Oversight Function of the Senate Committee on Interior and Insular Affairs, held extensive joint hearings on various matters of federal land management, as well as on other matters, but it has not so far functioned in a legislative way. The committee issued a report[5] and also a supplementary staff report. These reports got into such matters as consolidation of federal agencies managing forest lands, access roads, personnel, budgeting, and other management affairs. It remains to be seen how influential and how long continued this different approach will be.

PASSAGE OF FEDERAL LAND LEGISLATION

The difficulties associated with getting federal land legislation passed are not unique to this class of legislation. Nevertheless, they greatly affect the volume and content of the federal land bills that are passed. In each session there are a number of private bills—bills

---

[5] *Federal Timber Sale Policies,* House Report No 2960, 84th Congress, 2nd Session. Union Calendar No. 1212.

relating to a specific, individual case—and items of legislation of relative unimportance that are brought to the floor of the Congress under various arrangements requiring unanimous consent. The majority of bills dealing with the federal lands fall into this category. They can be passed in this way, and passed speedily, but one or a few members can prevent their passage by merely raising an objection, without necessarily supporting this objection in any way, nor even revealing his or their identity. The necessity of obtaining unanimous agreement severely restricts the committee action to matters on which agreement can be reached and restricts the content of the bills accordingly. While this procedure possibly is adequate for dealing with unimportant items, it quickly reaches its limit. There are alternatives under which bills can be brought up for general floor debate, but they may be difficult to apply to land legislation. Pressure of other business and sometimes the attitudes of the Rules Committee in the House or of the top leadership in the Senate often prevent consideration of a bill in this way; even more serious, it may be hard to get interested and informed floor debate and voting upon a measure. For the largest and most controversial matters it is possible to get interest, if not informed action. The bill in 1953, turning to the states the submerged coastal lands, is a case in point. But there is a class of bill, and even more a class of potential legislation, that is too important to be intelligently acted upon under a unanimous-consent procedure, and yet is not sufficiently general in its interest to secure adequate consideration under general debate. This situation is easily understandable in view of the volume and complexity of the work of the Congress, but a reasonably complete description of federal land management today must take it into account. Because the situation does exist, a few men in the whole legislative process are in a key position, and the action of the Congress is often an affirmation of the decision of these key men.

POLITICAL STRENGTH EXERTED ON FEDERAL LAND LEGISLATION

Generally speaking, federal land legislation has not been a matter of sharply partisan political action. On all major legislation there has been both support and opposition from different members of each major political party. Some federal land legislation has been advocated by a majority of one party or the other, and opposed by a majority of the other, but in general such partisan divisions have been less sharp than differences between individual members. The proposals of the Executive Branch have generally been supported by a majority of the members of the same party, but not invariably so, and also opposed by several if not by a majority of the opposition party, but again not invariably so. Regional and economic interests have in general been more influential in determining congressional attitudes than have political party lines.

With the political strength of the four main interest groups concerned with federal land management nearly balanced, legislation cannot readily be passed. Reconciliation of competing interests is necessary at some point in the legislative process, or else nothing is likely to be forthcoming.

As we have seen, a single determined opponent may be able to stop a bill. In so doing, he will naturally incur the displeasure if not dislike of the proponents of the measure, and this may react adversely upon other measures which he may wish at some stage to advance. Opposition is more likely to take the form of stalling. This is particularly easy for the chairman of a committee; he may simply delay calling hearings or taking other steps, without refusing to do so. It is also easy for an agency of the Executive Branch; it may delay reporting on proposed legislation, always with some good excuse for the delay. In view of the unavoidable difficulties of getting consideration for federal land legislation, and the limited time available, these delaying tactics may be sufficient to make action impossible during a particular Congress, or even at any time. If the opposition takes the form of objecting to unanimous consent, and if this happens in two Congresses, even the sponsors of a bill may decide it is hopeless and abandon it.

The Budget-Appropriation-Allocation Process[6]

The formal division of powers in the Congress is between legislation, which sets forth what an agency may do under a particular law, and appropriations, which provide the money with which to do it. The dividing line cannot be a neat one. The terms of the authorizing

---

[6] For a general reference describing this process in more detail, see Arthur Smithies, *Budgeting Process in the United States*, New York: McGraw-Hill Book Co., 1955.

legislation may be such that the appropriation process has little discretion left in it. On the other hand, the amount of money appropriated and the conditions established for its expenditure may be such as to greatly modify if not repeal a piece of legislation.[7] Many students of government have decried the attachment of detailed specific conditions to the use of appropriations, regarding it as an improper extension of the powers of the Appropriation Committees. But it is also true that some federal agencies have operated in ways not intended by the Congress, and that detailed control over their appropriations is one device the Congress has found effective in getting agencies to conform to its wishes, or at least to the wishes of the Appropriation Committee.

Whether the appropriation method is the most desirable means of deciding policy issues is debatable, but it is nevertheless true that some of the most important legislative policy affecting federal lands has been part of appropriation acts. The most notable is the Act of 1897 which provides the basic authority for national forest administration and management. From the creation of the forest reserves under the Act of 1891 until 1897, no authority existed for sale of timber or other use of the areas, and considerable opposition arose over the locking-up of these lands and resources. Broad legislation to correct the situation, which has served as the basis for national forest management since then, was added to the appropriation act. A more recent example is the change in method of financing road construction on O & C lands, also added as a rider to an appropriation act.

The budget-appropriation-allocation process involves both the Executive and Legislative branches, and within the former it involves several levels of administration. On a formal level, a budget is prepared within the Executive Branch, submitted to the Congress by the President, and passes in the form of an appropriation by the Congress, to be allocated and spent by the Executive agencies. But there is much informal give and take in this process. A substantial amount of the thought and effort of top agency personnel is required in the making of a budget; it is not a routine or mechanical matter but includes policy and tactical decisions of the highest order. As an example of one way in which an agency handles its appropriation requests, the procedure followed by the Forest Service is outlined on pages 160-65.

[7] McKinley, Charles, "Federal Administrative Pathology and the Separation of Powers," *Public Administration Review*, Vol. XI, No. 1, 1951.

PREPARATION OF A BUDGET

Formal preparation of a budget begins some fifteen to eighteen months before the beginning of the fiscal year to which the final appropriation will apply. However, the basic resource management planning on which the budget request is to be based may have started long before that. Between January and June the Bureau of the Budget, usually after consultation with the President, requests the departments and bureaus to submit their estimates of probable requirements for funds in the year in question; and provides them with general guides and assumptions on which to base their requests.

The departments and bureaus, relying in part on information obtained from their field offices, will then prepare their requests for ceiling allowances. Concurrently, the Bureau of the Budget makes its own preliminary estimates for the year in question. In so doing, it takes into consideration not only program needs, as far as it knows them, but also probable revenues and expenditures in total and the economic situation in general.

In June, a full twelve months before the beginning of the fiscal year to which the planning applies, the Bureau of the Budget assembles the requests from the departments and bureaus and compares them with its own tentative analysis. At this time conferences with the President on broad policy and strategy issues will be held and budget ceilings decided. The Bureau of the Budget regards a ceiling as a reasonable total sum of money for the agency and program in question, given other requests by other agencies, the revenue situation, and other national considerations. The Bureau of the Budget does not guarantee that the agency will be allowed the full ceiling as a budget request; neither does it preclude requests over the ceilings. In practice, however, the ceiling allowance certainly sets the level of the budget request that will ultimately be approved, and frequently it virtually determines it.

Ceiling allowances may be made directly to bureaus and even to programs within them, or they may be made, at least in part, to departments for their allocation to bureaus. In any event, the federal land managing agencies are given ceiling budget allowances about the end of June. During the next two and one-half months, they must prepare detailed budget estimates; for the relatively small bureau these are likely to run to 100 pages or more, with much of the statement taking the form of detailed and administratively technical tables. The numbers of persons in each job class and grade must be listed with their salaries, and other estimates often in as much detail. In addition, general narrative or explanatory statements must be written to explain why the amounts requested are needed, what it is proposed will be done with them if the request is granted, and what the results are expected to be. In recent years emphasis has been placed on work loads and a "performance" budget to explain why funds are needed, what can be expected, and to put the whole in as quantitative terms as possible.

These detailed budget requests are due at the Bureau of the Budget by September 15. Following a brief period of study by the Budget staff, the requests for each agency are considered at a hearing conducted by the Budget Bureau. In the Bureau of the Budget, the detailed review of the requests of the different federal land managing agencies is made by the same men, or by a few men in the same division, and the requests of the different agencies are reviewed by various officials in a more or less comparative fashion before recommendations are made to the highest level of the Bureau of the Budget for its final decision. A measure of co-ordination among agencies is achieved in this way.

The Bureau of the Budget ordinarily reaches its decision on the detailed requests about December 1; if it does not approve all that is requested, the agencies must quickly revise their requests to the amounts and items approved. In early January the President's Budget is forwarded by him to the Congress. In recent years it has included with its appendix over 1,600 closely printed pages, mostly of statistical tabulations, plus about 100 pages of message. Obviously, no individual could read or understand all of it, even if he tried. Much is understandable only if one has a fairly close knowledge of the budget history and situation for a particular agency. In this detailed budget, the items relating to the federal lands are obviously but a small part.

CONGRESSIONAL CONSIDERATION

Congress handles appropriations, as it does legislation, through committees. Committee consideration of the President's Budget is likely to begin in the House during February and March, and in the Senate during April and May. Generally speaking, the Appropriation Committee of each house has a broader basis of representation, both geographically and by interests, than does the legislative committee. The major work on budget requests is done by subcommittees, some members of which are likely to have had long experience with the requests of particular agencies, and thus to be familiar with their situations and problems. Since 1954 the same subcommittee considers the requests for all federal land managing agencies, in spite of the fact that the agencies themselves are in different departments. Thus a degree of co-ordination is now provided at this level.

The subcommittee normally holds hearings at which first the Secretary of the department or his representative is heard, then the bureau heads or their representatives, and finally individuals from the general public or representing various groups.

In general, its examination of the budget request is somewhat similar to that of the Bureau of the Budget: it seeks to discover the appropriateness of the particular lines of activity, their legal basis, the need for them, the need for funds to carry them out efficiently, the general efficiency and competence of the agency, and related matters. As with the Bureau of the Budget, emphasis is placed on experience in earlier years, and special attention is paid to deviations from previous patterns. On the basis of this evidence, the subcommittee prepares a report and submits it to the whole committee, which generally accepts the recommendations of its subcommittee. In the House, appropriation bills are considered under limited debate; for the land management agencies, debate is often brief, and usually there are no attempts at amendment.

In the Senate the same process is repeated, with attention ordinarily focused on those items reduced by the House. There is more likely to be floor debate and perhaps changes than in the House, but usually the recommendations of the Senate committee are followed. Differences between the two bodies are ironed out in conference, and the final act usually involves a compromise. The action of the Congress on appropriation requests, like that of the Bureau of the Budget, is more commonly negative than positive, in the sense that the agency proposals which were accepted by the Bureau of the Budget are likely to be further trimmed, and only occasionally does the Congress make proposals of its own (except those included in budget reductions).

FUND ALLOCATION AND EXPENDITURE

The appropriations are supposed to be made before June 30 in order to provide funds for the new fiscal year. Sometimes they have been late, in which case the agencies are authorized to carry on under some sort of resolution for continuing operations. Once an appropriation is passed, funds are allocated to the agencies by the Bureau of the Budget, and cash deposited to the account of the agency with the Treasury. The agencies obligate funds for salaries of permanent personnel immediately, and for other purposes as soon as a firm decision is made to incur the expenditure. The obligations are often estimates; the precise cost being unknown. Obligations must be made immediately, and appropriations may not be over-obligated. At the same time, there is heavy pressure on the agencies to obligate the full amount of the appropriations; if they do not, the agencies lose the funds in question for the year in question, thus reducing the accomplishment possible that year. In addition, their failure to use available funds is likely to be used as an argument by the Bureau of the Budget and the Congress in cutting appropriations for succeeding years.

Agencies are required by the Bureau of the Budget to estimate the amount of the appropriation which they expect to spend in each quarter of the fiscal year, although these expenditures need not be uniformly distributed through the year. Such estimates may be changed during the year and even during the current quarter until within thirty days of its end. The purpose is to prevent unnecessary and excessive expenditures toward the end of the fiscal year which would otherwise revert as unspent funds. However, this process does introduce a further complexity into the expenditure of funds.

Actual expenditures of cash by agencies are made to pay the amounts obligated. Payrolls for personal services are paid regularly through the year, and when the year is over the obligations are fully liquidated for them. For other types of expenditures, bills are paid when presented and there is likely to be a greater lag between obligation and outlay of cash. If a program contains much construction activity, or if its level is rising from year to year, there may be a considerable discrepancy between obligations and actual expenditures in each year. The obligations may be liquidated, from the appropriations for a given year, for as long as two years after the close of the fiscal year to which each applies. For agencies on a relatively steady budget, and where personal services are a major item, obligations and expenditures each year are closely similar.

At any given time a bureau is concerned with appropriations for several fiscal years. At least one, and during part of the year two, appropriations are in the budget request stage, either with the Bureau of the Budget or with the Congress. Funds are always being obligated and spent out of the appropriations for the current year; and expenditures of cash are being made to liquidate obligations of appropriations for the year preceding, and usually for the one preceding that. Budget making, obligation, and expenditure are thus a continuous process.

The budget-appropriation-allocation process described above has evolved to meet the needs of all aspects of government, not simply those of land management. Its evolution is not finished; rather, changes are constantly being made to improve the process. Considering the vast complexity of the federal budget today, it is inevitable that some shortcomings in procedure should exist; and considering the increased values of the federal lands today, it is also inevitable that some of these shortcomings should seriously impede management of the lands. The defects can be itemized as follows:

1. The basic philosophy of the process is wrong, in that resource management is placed in the same category as general government services. Good resource management creates wealth and directly contributes to the national economy and the national treasury. Up to some level of expenditures, more spent on management of federal lands results in greater national income in physical goods, and greater income to the government. Even though the primary goal of federal land management is not necessarily one of maximizing revenue to the government, but rather of making the greatest contribution to the welfare of the people, larger revenues may up to a point still be possible and consistent with this goal. To maximize public welfare may well mean pushing the level of expenditure and investment beyond the point of maximum cash revenue to the government. Expenditures in the past, however, have seldom been sufficient to permit revenues to reach even this point. If spending $1 million more on federal land management results in a net revenue to the Treasury of more than $1 million as well as other advantages, it is surely uneconomic to refrain from spending this money; even in time of war the goods which produce the extra revenue also may well contribute to the war effort. General governmental activities can, it is true, indirectly be wealth producing, but in these cases the time span is longer: good education and good nutrition for children result in added productivity one or more decades later. Some part of federal land management is of this indirect wealth-producing kind, but a great deal of it is directly productive in the short run.

In view of these differences, the kinds of budgetary questions asked of an agency might well be, not "Why do you need this much money?" but, rather, "At what level of expenditure for these general purposes will the net revenue to the federal Treasury be the greatest? At what level will values other than those expressed in cash returns be the greatest?"

2. The whole process puts too much emphasis on the previous year, and is too slow to respond to changes. While, undoubtedly, attempts are made to study the needs of the programs presented, pressures of the budget schedule routine prevent satisfactory appraisal. Consequently there is little direct examination of each budget in relation to need; the assumption is that what was arrived at last year was correct for that year, and that all that is now needed is a look at the changes from last year. But, in fact, budgets can get seriously out of line with needs, and when they do, the process tends to perpetuate the situation rather than correct it. When basic conditions of federal land management change drastically, as they have in the past fifteen years, budgets lag behind seriously.

3. The process is also open to criticism because it provides little systematic review, at any level, of past operations. There is a common feeling of relief that what is past is past and a disinclination to exhume any corpses. At no point is there a careful economic and policy review of the effect of various programs at various levels, or a review of over-all efficiency in attainment of goals. To a degree, some of the land managing bureaus do carry out this type of program evaluation, but it is conducted internally rather than as part of the appropriation process.[8]

4. Several serious issues arise out of the timing of appropriations in relation to the needs of federal land management.

First, estimates must be prepared so far in advance that realistic detailed estimates simply cannot be made. Supplemental appropriations can in part meet this problem, but they too are slow—usually several months elapse between preparation of estimates and appropriation of money—and in any event there is considerable opposition to them in Congress and elsewhere.

Second, the fiscal year begins at the wrong time for resource management. July 1 is ordinarily the height of the field season, the time of greatest activity of all kinds. It is exactly the wrong time either

[8] An exception is the Forest Service's budget analysis undertaken in 1949 at the request of the Bureau of the Budget. See pp. 162-65.

to accelerate or to brake a program. The effects are especially bad for insect and disease control, fire control, reseeding programs, road building, and other activities closely tied to seasonal weather. If the appropriation is late, as it sometimes has been, the difficulties are vastly greater. At best, activities may carry on, but in a cloud of uncertainty as to their level. When the appropriation is finally passed it may appear that a more rapid rate of operations would have been appropriate, or the available funds may be so nearly spent as to cripple activities for the rest of the year.

Third, these difficulties are compounded because there can be no carryover of unspent funds from one fiscal year to the next. The accompanying obligation to spend the full amount of the year's funds has already been pointed out. In consequence, the federal administrator finds himself between the devil and the deep blue sea: he must wind up on June 30 as nearly broke as possible, but not "in the red." Whenever the tempo of federal land management activities is speeded up or slowed down in a new fiscal year, as compared with an old one, July 1 may loom up as a point of discontinuity—a divide between two watersheds. One arrangement which, more than any other, would help bring economy into federal land management, is permission to carry over from one year to the next a modest sum—say 15 per cent of the appropriation. This arrangement would still enable the Bureau of the Budget and the Congress to keep control over the agency's activities—it could operate only for about two months on the carry-over—but at the same time it would provide a modest working balance, similar to the minimum daily balance in an individual's bank checking account. Contract authorization for periods longer than one year, and in advance of actual appropriation of cash, is one recourse granted to an agency. This is particularly helpful for road construction, the growing of seedling trees, and other activities which cannot possibly be completed in a single year. But at best this procedure is not a complete substitute for cash, and in practice its use has been restricted.

The fourth issue related to bad timing is the inflexibility of the budget-appropriation-allocation process to meet unexpected and unforeseeable situations. In emergencies such as disease or insect outbreaks or timber blowdown, quick and decisive action will often go far to lessen the loss. If fire-killed timber can be sold and logged promptly, losses in value are much less than if logging is delayed; but this requires money to cruise timber, make sales, build roads, etc., immediately. It is obvious that the process does not provide such funds. While limited authority exists enabling the agency to use other funds for certain types of emergency, notably fire control, this does not meet all situations.

The unexpected situation is not always an emergency; it may be an unusual opportunity which should be taken advantage of in any efficient operation. For instance, certain species of trees and grass produce seed abundantly in some years and sparsely in others; a well-run organization should be in a position to harvest or buy seed in years of abundant crops and store it for use when needed. In this matter of inflexibility the federal land managing agencies suffer badly in comparison with the best managed large private companies, which, through emergency meetings of their boards of directors, can adjust to a new situation in a matter of days. This was true for road building in western Oregon in the spring of 1952, to facilitate harvest of windthrown timber before it was badly damaged by beetles. The windthrow for the most part occurred in December; by May, when the weather was most favorable for road construction, the lumber companies were building roads. But the federal agencies could begin activity only in July, and then only on a small scale until the following July, when a new budget and appropriation had been prepared and carried through all the channels.

5. Budgets contain much irrelevant detail, which takes time to prepare and review, and which diverts attention from important issues. Tabulations showing numbers of persons, average salary, and other items for each kind of job and grade are one of the most useless and elaborate bits of detail. Similarly, the listings of items of equipment proposed for purchase are also of dubious value. The Bureau of the Budget and the Appropriation Committees do not make their decisions on the basis of these details, although they devote much of their attention to them. Moreover, to the extent these estimates are binding upon future expenditure of funds, they increase the rigidity of the whole process.

6. The present process of budget making and appropriation tends to substitute the judgment of the Bureau of the Budget and the Congressional Committee for that of the operating bureau. The restrictions have been imposed in an effort to correct observed weaknesses of agency operation, such as excessive staffing, use of funds for purposes not intended, and, especially at the end of the fiscal year, excessive purchase of equipment. But it is doubtful if they have resulted in major net benefits in these directions, and they certainly

have encumbered the operations of an agency able and willing to do a good job.

On the whole, the budget-appropriation-allocation process provides too little incentive for economy and efficiency in operations, and too little incentive for attainment of maximum desirable revenues from the federal lands. An agency's greatest rewards derive from compliance with the system rather than actual performance. The emphasis throughout is on costs, not revenues, even though today revenues exceed costs. These shortcomings are serious; but one should also preserve some balance of viewpoint. The system has managed to work well for many years, in the sense that the federal lands are administered on a level of professional competence and idealism equal to that of any other public program. Improvements are possible, and desirable; but ". . . in my effort to stress the need for further improvement I may conceal my opinion that it is not far short of miraculous that the process works as well as it does." [9]

BUDGET MAKING IN THE FOREST SERVICE

The Forest Service follows more formal and elaborate methods of budget making than do the other federal land managing agencies. Although the broad pattern of all the agencies' budget-making procedures is similar, the methods followed by the Forest Service are believed by that agency, and by many independent observers as well, to be superior. Hence, a brief examination of them seems warranted.

The budget is part of the whole structure for organizing the work of administering the national forests. Thus, it has value far beyond that of its restricted purpose. The essence of the Forest Service's organization is job-load analysis.[10] Five separate steps are involved:

(1) defining the objective of each particular job;
(2) breaking the job down into component parts;
(3) determining and establishing standards of quality, quantity, frequency, methods, and other practices needed to do the job as it should be done;
(4) determining the unit-time requirements for each job as it should be done; and

[9] Smithies, *op. cit.*, p. xiv.
[10] Loveridge, Earl W., *op. cit.*

(5) grouping the separate jobs into the months in which they can be done, as controlled by the work requirements, the climatic conditions, available time, and other factors.

By using this procedure, it is possible to estimate total man-hours required for various tasks, programs, or policies; and from this to calculate numbers of employees, amounts of equipment and supplies, and total funds required. This method of procedure is used in the Forest Service as a basis of planning programs, as a means of developing budgets for them, for the allocation of available funds to the various units, and as a basis of supervision over work and accomplishment.

This type of job analysis, and the management methods built upon it, has many advantages. In the first place, as applied by the Forest Service, it requires the co-operation of the entire organization, from the top man down to the field officer. Co-operation enters into the formulation of the standards of work particularly, but also into the other parts of the process. Through job analysis, a common goal and a common approach to that goal are arrived at by the different levels in the organization. In the second place, the process makes formal and conscious the estimates, procedures, assumptions, objectives, and other aspects of the agency's program that might otherwise not be thought out so carefully. The procedure of reducing thoughts and ideas to writing and subjecting them to the criticism of fellow workers tends to develop more careful thought. Thirdly, this process enables others, inside the agency or outside, to check every stage along the line. If there are differences of opinion, then this formal process usually permits more exact definition of the points at which such differences arise. Lastly, this type of job analysis gives a specific and objective basis for budgets, their allocation, and the necessary supervision of work. Although estimates and judgments enter, the scope of arbitrariness and subjectivity is narrowed.

While this method of job analysis is desirable and its use as a tool, if well handled, leads to better administration, it is not perfect. It has some shortcomings or weaknesses that often are not recognized. In the first place, the job standards themselves are by no means fixed or fully objective in their origin; many of necessity are based on judgment, or are even subjective in origin. What constitutes an acceptable standard of fire control in a given area? It may easily be possible to point out that excessive burning will result in no harvestable timber growth, or so little as to be unprofitable; but there are many degrees of better fire control among which it may be hard to prove that a particular degree is optimum. What constitutes an adequate degree of camp ground supervision? What is the optimum degree of timber cruising, or of range supervision? On all of these and many other questions it is necessary to make judgments; and even good judgments are not completely objective measurements.

In the second place, the unit job requirements cannot be wholly objective, because they must include a judgment as to the degree of thoroughness with which a job is to be done.

Thirdly, and most important, this type of analysis is made at one level of intensity of management only. One most desirable level of work standard is established, one most desirable degree of thoroughness of doing the job, and so on. This level of intensity is based on judgment and generally reflects the experience, ability, and personal competence of the persons making the judgments. However, there is no direct examination of the effects of either more or less intensive management. This characteristic is particularly serious when used for budgeting and for financial planning and management generally.

The Forest Service made a particularly detailed analysis of its budget in 1949.[11] This study examines some basic problems that ordinarily are not so closely scrutinized. It was made in response to questions raised by the Bureau of the Budget concerning the protection and management part of the budget for national forest administration. The questions raised by the Bureau of the Budget were analyzed by the Forest Service under four headings, as follows:

1. The Bureau of the Budget had queried whether the increase in this appropriation during the preceding fifteen years, when account was taken of other contributing appropriations, had reached a level where recurrent operating expenses on the national forests were getting out of line with values, tangible and intangible.

The Forest Service, in reply, presented figures by five-year intervals from 1932 through 1947, and also for 1948. Expenditures were divided between an operating and a capital budget, and estimates were made of nonmonetary returns received by the public from the forests, as well as cash income. Estimates were also made of the increased value of the timber added by growth. Recreational values were based upon an estimated fair market value, and water values upon unit values for stream flow used for various purposes. The latter may be criti-

[11] U. S. Department of Agriculture, *National Forest Protection and Management,* "P & M" Budget Study [processed], July, 1949.

cized as providing a measure of water value rather than of watershed management as such. More than three-fourths of the estimated receipts were in the form of recreation and water, which are provided nearly free to users; another 15 per cent were in the form of increased values of timber stands, leaving less than 10 per cent as cash receipts. On the basis of these estimates, it was concluded that annual costs had decreased in relation to estimated receipts, that the latter had risen in relation to national income, and that fire control costs had fallen in relation to other costs. From these relationships, the Forest Service concluded that the financial level of the national forests had not been getting out of line with values, tangible and intangible.

2. The Bureau of the Budget had queried whether, from the standpoint of the protection and management appropriation, the national forest system would be self-supporting and whether it was logical that some reasonable relationship between operating costs and revenues might be established.

In answering this question, the Forest Service divided the total area of the national forests into commercial forest land, which was 44 per cent of the total, and various classes of noncommercial forest or nonforested land. The commercial forested lands were credited with 80 per cent of receipts in recent years and 90 per cent in 1948. It was further pointed out that in 1948, out of a total of 153 national forests, there were some fifty-two national forests in which receipts exceeded "P & M" expenditures, and of these, receipts from twenty forests exceeded total expenditures. It was further pointed out that in many areas there was little demand for timber, but a need to protect it from fire; that in some areas, especially lands that had been purchased, the forest cover had been largely destroyed and must be rebuilt; and that in other areas there were large areas of slow-growing trees. It is especially interesting to note that the 1949 estimates of 1956 timber harvest, made for this study, were 6 billion board feet bringing a total price of $32.5 million. It will be shown in chapter five that actual sales in 1956 were slightly over 7 billion board feet for a total revenue in excess of $100 million. This section of the report is summed up by a statement that receipts from the commercial forest lands of the national forests were carrying all the legitimate costs normally borne by owners of private forest properties, and in addition were yielding a net surplus.

3. The Bureau of the Budget had queried the extent to which increases in the "P & M" appropriation during the past few years had been needed to handle an increasing volume of use, revenue-

producing or free, and whether the "P & M" appropriation had reached a point where it was out of line with the values involved.

In reply, the Forest Service classified its expenditures into three main groups: (1) operating costs, or those related to the use of products, privileges, and services of the national forests; (2) protection expenditures, particularly fire protection, insect and rodent control, and certain watershed management activities; and (3) production development expenditures, especially for reforestation, revegetation, and timber stand improvement. It was pointed out that expenditures in the first category might vary according to the volume of activity of all kinds, but that those in the second category would remain more or less fixed from year to year. From an analysis of the budget data presented, the Forest Service concluded that expenditures in the first category had not increased out of line with volume of business and revenues. While there had been some increase in expenditures in the second category, it was felt that these were justified by the greater fire risks due to more people using the forest and to more slash from the increased level of timber harvest, and that the added protection provided had been fully offset, and more, by the reduced fire loss because of the added protection. At the time this study was made, there had been no significant increase in expenditures in the third category.

4. The Bureau of the Budget had suggested that the study should seek to establish a general policy or other basis on which future estimates of appropriations for "P & M" might be predicated.

The Forest Service took the position that it was most unlikely that adequate staffing and other financial requirements based on the scientific principle of a measured work load could approach the level of the annual returns from national forest resources. The report referred to a survey of private land management and the management of other public lands, made by the Forest Service, from which the Service had concluded that its costs were reasonable in comparison with those incurred by others. The report concludes by estimating a necessary appropriation for fiscal 1950 of $53 million for "P & M" funds. This compares with $27 million actually appropriated for these purposes in 1950, and with $30 million in 1955.

The "P & M" budget study is a serious attempt to answer important questions; the Bureau of the Budget deserves much praise for asking the questions, and the Forest Service equal praise for attempting to answer them carefully. This type of analysis is uncommon, but greatly needed in federal land management.

However, the study can be criticized for several defects inherent in its character.

1. It was undertaken once, not annually. Other somewhat similar studies had been made in earlier years, and partial studies based somewhat upon this study have been made at intervals since 1949; but no regular system has been set up to undertake such a study on an annual basis.

2. The results of the study have not been made widely available. Thus, they have had little opportunity to influence the thinking of others; neither have they been exposed to the scrutiny and criticism which lead to refinement and improvement.

3. The study was perhaps more defensive than constructive in nature. This may have been due, in part at least, to the fact that the Bureau of the Budget had, in effect, asked the Forest Service to justify its expenditures and the budget requests it was making. The tone of the report is defensive in many places. In several respects a good case could have been made for larger appropriations, whereas the report sought chiefly to defend the appropriations actually available.

4. The study was limited to protection and management items and did not include investment expenditures. Yet in many instances it is hard to differentiate between operation and investment, and certainly the two are closely interrelated. A full consideration of expenditures on national forests should include investment as well as operation expenses.

5. From the economist's viewpoint, the report's most serious shortcoming is that it was made at only one level of intensity of management. The relation between more or less expenditure and the results possible from either, both in monetary and other terms, were not considered explicitly and quantitatively. The existing intensity of management was defended, but the effect of other levels of intensity was not adequately explored.

The Decision Making Process

Within the framework that has been outlined in the preceding sections of this chapter, the federal land managing agencies operate in broadly similar ways. In each there is a hierarchy of staff and decision making levels, and in each this hierarchy works from the local or field office, through the intermediate or regional office, to the headquarters in Washington, where the chain of authority again moves upward to the department level and thence to the President and to Congress.

In any large organization which operates over a large area, the practical alternatives of administrative organization lie between the extremes of functional and geographic approaches. As a group, the federal land management agencies trend strongly toward the geographic basis for their organization and operation. The ranger districts, national forests, national parks, grazing districts, wildlife refuges, regions, and other geographic units are a major basis of their organization. In each of these areas an official in charge has a large measure of discretion in administration of all aspects of his agency's program in that area. But all, or nearly all, such geographically oriented officials have subordinate to them various functional specialists, as needed. This is generally known as a line and staff organization; a direct line of authority, from top to bottom, by areas, with specialized staff at each or most levels to assist and guide the line officer.

The emphasis on area as a basis of organization in the federal land managing agencies has several explanations. In the first place, most of the agencies operate over all or many of the states, and often in Alaska and the other territories as well. Such widely dispersed operations would require some geographical specialization even if the major basis of organization were entirely functional. Another reason is the frequent necessity to reach a decision locally and act upon it quickly. Fire control is the extreme and dramatic case; it must be undertaken by a man on the ground, who can make immediate decisions and throw all the resources of his organization behind the fire control effort. Slowness of communications, especially in the more remote areas in the early days, may well have been a factor in the early Forest Service emphasis on local responsibility and action.

But beyond these reasons, organization primarily on an area basis is closely related to the philosophy of multiple use. The essence of multiple-use management of federal lands is conscious planning and conscious choice among uses so as to minimize conflicts and maximize total output. This is far more likely to be achieved if there is one man in charge of a particular area, who has the responsibility for fitting various uses together. He has the responsibility for co-ordinated action, but is exposed to various specialized interest groups and pressures. He is more likely to consider all aspects of resource use in his area than would a series of specialists, each dedicated to his own specific program.

AT THE LOCAL LEVEL

The local office in the Forest Service is the ranger district, in the charge of a ranger. There are 753 such offices in the national forests, and perhaps three-quarters of all land administration in the Forest Service is done at this level. In the Park Service the local office is primarily the park or monument superintendent; while there are rangers within each of the larger areas, they are not generally line officers exercising most of the functions of their agency for a specified area. In the Bureau of Land Management the local office is the grazing district or forest district, each under a manager. There are 65 such offices. Since the total area the managers administer is roughly equal to that administered by the Forest Service, it is obvious that the area per office is more than ten times as large, on the average, as the area in the Forest Service local office. This is partly a measure of differences in resources, partly a measure of intensity of management. In the Fish and Wildlife Service the local office is the refuge manager, who carries out for his area essentially all of the functions of his agency in land management. Not only does the size of the area administered by local offices vary from agency to agency, and within agencies, but the volume of work also varies, as does the extent of the authority and responsibility. In spite of some differences, however, there are characteristics which they share in common.

1. By definition, local offices are at the lowest bureaucratic or organizational level, and nearest to the land administered, where, with a few rather specialized exceptions, essentially all functions of the agency are exercised. Because the local officer has as a primary duty the integration of various uses of land on the area he administers, he must primarily be concerned with the interrelationships of various types of use. Above all, he needs facts about the resources under his direction, and this requires forest surveys, grazing surveys, and other types of fact gathering. The local office is the place where the most detailed and most intimate knowledge of the resources must be assembled, must exist at any time, and must be translated into action.

2. More than any other, the local office represents the agency to the public, and the public to higher officials in the agency.

This position as bridge between agency and public creates many of the local man's problems, and sometimes internal conflicts. His agency has established one set of goals and standards, often based on its general public support and on its legislative history and Congressional relationships; the local people may have an entirely different set of goals and standards, stemming either from a different conception of the nature of the resources or from different motives and objectives. The local officer is put in the difficult spot of resolving the conflicts, if possible, while carrying out his agency's policies and at the same time remaining acceptable to the local people.

It is at the local level that the various interest groups are often most effective. While they are unlikely to be formally organized, as they are at a state or national level, they may be all the more powerful because of the face-to-face nature of their contacts with the federal employee. Many of the individuals are the local officer's friends. They can exert substantial pressures on him to conform to their standards and their objectives. There is a real danger of his identification of interests with those of local people; a federal agency is always exposed to serious centrifugal forces which operate to lead its men away from its central core of ideas and convictions.

At the same time, the local federal employee can be too rigid in his adherence to agency policy; part of his job is to make necessary adaptations of procedures, within the limit of his authority, to local needs.

A major job of the agency is to keep its goals and standards foremost in the thinking of its local employees. The standards it uses in selection of men, the training it gives them in technical matters, the indoctrination given into agency goals and methods, the amount and kind of current information provided from upper levels to the local employee, and above all the transfer of men from one local area to another, all serve to keep local employees from straying too far from the central path established by the agency.

3. Local offices originate most of the factual data used by the agency in its work. And, indeed, since the difference between "facts" and "ideas" is often far from clear-cut, they also supply many of the ideas on resource management. Men at the higher levels can personally see no more than a sample of conditions on the ground, and their thinking must inevitably be guided in very large part by what their local men or their intermediate-office men tell them.

4. Personnel of the local offices take many actions, in a final way, and accept responsibility for them. The decisions involved are usually the simpler or more repetitive ones; nevertheless the need for action

is constant, and often—as in the case of fire control—of the greatest urgency.

5. The local offices are the points of entry for most of the professional men in the federal land managing agencies. This has been especially true for the Forest Service—most of its recruits begin in local offices; vacancies at higher levels are almost always filled by promotion from within, and few recruits are added at upper levels. But, to a large extent, it has also been true for the other agencies. Absorption of agency techniques and ideas can start even before permanent employment. Many men get their first on-the-ground training during summer employment while still college students. If most of the men in an agency have shared a common experience, there is a strong unifying force which may go far toward offsetting the normal centrifugal tendencies in any agency. The varied experience gained as men are shifted from area to area, in their progress up the bureaucratic ladder, is invaluable to their service with an agency.

Factors influencing decisions in local offices. In making decisions, several factors influence the local officer.

1. The nature of the resources themselves, their technical, physical, and economic suitability for different purposes. If a particular spot has high inherent qualities for recreational use, but rather mediocre timber-producing qualities, this fact will influence the local officer in his decisions. If grazing in a particular area is incompatible with tree reproduction, and if the area has high value for timber production, this, too, will influence the local officer in his decisions. While the inventory or fact-gathering type of survey is important to these decisions, more than this is needed if the local officer is to do a good job. For each local area within his jurisdiction, he should know the effect upon the land of different amounts of use for each purpose— different rates of livestock grazing, different intensities of timber harvest or of recreational use, and the like. Far more research of this kind is needed than is now available to the local officer, whose decisions can have far-reaching effects.

2. The public attitude or interest in the use of the resources. If there is active demand for a particular use of an area, this influences the local officer; on the other hand, if there is virtually no interest in some use of some resource, this is equally influential. The strongly upward trend in most uses of most federal land has an important bearing on this matter. The local official needs to know what the trend has been in his area, and this is usually available from the records in his office. But local officials may not be in a good position

to correlate the trend in their area with other social and economic data, such as growth of population, income, and leisure in their service area. Above all, they may find it difficult to estimate future demand for the lands they administer, for different purposes. Yet it is future demand that is often critical in formulating plans for future action, or even for present action, in resource management. More localized economic and social studies would surely be helpful to local land managers. Although the local official knows how many people are using the area under his management, he often does not know exactly why they are using it, or what they expect from it. This is especially true for recreational use. Resource use often depends as much on what the customer wants as it does on what the resource is capable of. Surveys among users might develop facts and ideas helpful to the local administrator.

3. The objectives, policies, procedures, directives, and similar matters from within the agency itself. The local officer is one unit in a much larger organization. Under the best circumstances, the objectives and policies of the higher levels of the agency are a reflection of broader interest groups than the local official experiences locally. These broader interest groups make their influence felt upon the federal land managing agencies, but at higher levels than the local official. The agency may simply be bringing to bear upon him the wider influences which it experiences, but he does not. Under other circumstances, however, agency policies and objectives may grow out of entrenched bureaucracy and outmoded experience. Even if it is argued that in such cases top agency policy and objectives are wrong, a good case can be made for having local officers follow them; if local officers establish their own policies, objectives, and standards, then the agency is no longer national even if it is federal, but is, rather, a collection of localized groups. Thus, local officials must follow agency policies and objectives rather closely.

4. The officer's own interests, training, background, and philosophy. No two men, looking at the same physical situation, under the same conditions of public attitudes, and within the same agency framework of rules and regulations, will see a particular situation in exactly the same way. One man, for example, may think that a particular area, while not the best recreational spot in the world, is, in view of the expressed interest of some group, better suited for recreational than for grazing or forestry use; another man may regard the same area as so inferior for recreation, and the expressed recreational interest in it so weak, that it had best be used for something else. In spite

of their divergence of opinion, if two officers' training and background for their jobs have been similar, they will usually choose to follow essentially the same broad course of action in essentially similar situations. The training and experience of most men in the federal land managing agencies is sufficiently similar to provide a substantial integrating force within each agency. A large percentage of the men have had prior training as foresters or range managers, and in many schools these types of training are closely similar. Of those with other professional backgrounds, many of the elements of their training are also similar.

5. Limitations of the jobs. The amount and kind of work performed by a local officer is to a large extent determined by the manpower and funds available to him. He may want to sell some merchantable timber for which there is an active demand, but if he has not the staff or the time to cruise and sell it, the sale cannot be made. The fire control problem may be so great, in relation to his resources, that he has no time for the range surveys he may wish to make. It can be argued that limitations of time and money merely impose priorities, and in one sense this is true; but urgency and importance are not necessarily synonymous, and if the priorities exhaust *all* the available time, they have become limitations.

Actions by local officers. The scope of local activity varies from agency to agency, and even from place to place and from time to time within an agency. Forest rangers are usually permitted to sell timber up to a value of $2,000 in a single sale; Bureau of Land Management grazing district managers and forest district managers may sell up to 10 million board feet in a single sale (which would ordinarily be worth far more than $2,000). BLM grazing district managers may issue licenses and permits to graze domestic livestock, specifying the number to be grazed, the season, the area, and any other range practices deemed necessary. All local officers must control fires within their jurisdictions. And they are usually permitted to make minor improvements on structures or works in their areas, and even construct minor new ones.

One important activity of the local officer is the development of plans for his area. This planning may be formal, following carefully developed procedures, or it may be informal; the plans may be for different periods of time; and the use of the plans may differ. Planning of this kind has been most formalized in the Forest Service. There it becomes the basis of the agency's entire program in each district, guides the local officer, and provides other levels with a measure of his performance. The plans are written and usually cover five or more years ahead. Each new plan is built upon the former ones, and each man's activities are built upon his predecessor's. Written plans are especially important when men are moved rather frequently.

Within considerable limits, the local officer has control over the use of his own time and that of his subordinates. In the Forest Service the plans generally allot the over-all time of the available staff for the year ahead, and these are supplemented by similar monthly plans. But such plans must be flexible to meet weather, fire, and many other situations, and the timing of work from day to day and from hour to hour must obviously rest with the local officer. A generally similar situation exists in the other agencies.

A large part of the time and energy of the local officer is taken up with the performance of tasks his superiors specifically direct him to do. Nevertheless, the chain of authority leaves him considerable latitude. Although, for example, he cannot make the decision for selling a tract of timber, he may recommend that it be sold; later he may be directed to cruise and appraise it and to supervise the operations of the timber buyer.

Generally speaking, the local officer must accept as given the budget, or allocation of manpower and funds, made available to him. He may help prepare budget data, but his influence beyond this point is negligible.

For all practical purposes, the local official has no direct influence on legislation. Indirectly, however, his actions may be extremely important, especially in the long run—the young camper of today may be the congressman of tomorrow. Public attitudes toward the federal land managing agencies are formed in large part by the public's experience with local officers and the fact that today these attitudes are so favorable is eloquent testimony to the character of the job the local officials have done in the past.

To a large extent, the actions of the local officer are controlled by the laws and by the regulations and policy and procedure statements of his agency. They are also controlled by the plans which he himself may have in part prepared. The agency applies these various controls through the media of inspections, audits, and other supervisory devices. Inspections are particularly important. Periodically, an official from the regional or Washington office spends some time in the administrative area of the local officer. Records are checked, plans re-examined, and actual inspections of resource use on the ground are made. Deviations from established procedure, failure to meet obvious needs, inefficiencies, and other shortcomings are noted, if any exist. By discussion between the inspector and the local official, differences of viewpoint are identified and often reconciled. The inspection is not only a means of assuring consistent action at lower levels; it is also a training device, not less so for the inspector than for the man on the ground.

Examinations undertaken as a result of public appeals from the actions of local officers provide a further, though rather limited, means of checking on the work of the local officer. But appeals in themselves are not adequate for this purpose, for they are not always forthcoming when laws and regulations have been violated.

AT THE INTERMEDIATE LEVEL

In each federal land managing agency there are one or two organizational layers between the local and the Washington offices. Various kinds of offices fit this general description. The Forest Service and Bureau of Land Management have two levels of offices intermediate between local and Washington offices. In the Forest Service, 128 forest supervisors' offices oversee the ranger district offices and 10 regional offices (including one in Alaska) supervise the supervisor offices. The Bureau of Land Management has 12 state offices which supervise the local forest and grazing district offices, and 4 area administrators (including one in Alaska) over the state offices. In the Park Service and Fish and Wildlife Service there is but one layer between local offices and the Washington office. In the Park Service there are 5 regional offices exercising supervision over park superintendents and others. In the Fish and Wildlife Service there are 5 regional offices (including one in Alaska) performing essentially similar functions.[12]

Perhaps the greatest differences in administrative organization of the different land managing agencies lie in these "intermediate" offices. The area included in each, the boundaries of their areas, their responsibilities, their relation to units below and above them in the administrative line, their names, and many other features differ greatly.

---

[12] This discussion deals with the Fish and Wildlife Service as it was prior to July 1, 1956; later the commercial fisheries part was split off, without much direct effect on land management.

For a detailed understanding of each agency, the character and operations of its particular offices must be studied carefully.

In spite of considerable differences, a few common features characterize these intermediate offices.

1. A major part of their work is to guide and supervise subsidiary offices. The emphasis, in fact, is much more upon supervision, and less upon direct action, than in lower offices.

One type of supervisory activity is the correction of deviant actions at lower levels, and sometimes disciplinary action against the employees involved. The indirect methods of insuring action at lower levels consistent with agency policy and objectives, described earlier, are very powerful; but at times they will not be effective. A local officer may misunderstand agency policy, misinterpret facts of the local situation, or for other reasons he may take an action which is clearly wrong, or one which may be interpreted as being wrong.

One of the best and most generally used techniques of supervising local offices is the conference of field men. Such conferences can be primarily training in character, as when a new program or new method is adopted; or they can be in the nature of review and reappraisal of existing programs and methods. Personnel from intermediate offices may convey information and instructions to local officials; but the latter may also pass information and ideas upward on the bureaucratic ladder.

2. The intermediate offices carry on nearly all of the operations which were too difficult, too specialized, or too important for policy, to have been done in the local office. All but the smallest of the timber sales are made in the forest supervisors' offices, or in the regional forest offices, for instance. Decisions are made here as to where to build major improvements, such as roads, and much of the construction is performed, or contracted for, out of these offices. Timber sales by intermediate offices usually are made on the basis of factual data provided by the local office, or gathered by specialists operating out of a higher office, and the sale made at this level is supervised by personnel from the local office.

3. They exercise many of the administrative functions that are too infrequent or complex to be handled efficiently at the local office level. Personnel actions (except the hiring of emergency crews for fire fighting), detailed budgeting of funds and accounting of expenditures, payrolling (but on the basis of time records kept in the local offices), purchases and repair of major equipment, purchase and stocking of most supplies, and many other functions of this kind will be

performed at the intermediate office level, primarily for the benefit of local offices. Performance of these administrative functions is generally cheaper here than if done in the local offices; it also is a mechanism of supervision.

4. They have functional experts of more experience and specialized training, who can both help the local offices do their job and advise the head of the intermediate office on his decisions. For instance, it is possible for the Forest Service to have one or a few wildlife specialists, or recreation specialists, at the regional headquarters to help on all problems falling within the field of their special knowledge, whereas in one ranger district there is not enough work of this kind to occupy fully such an experienced and trained man. In the fairly large areas covered by most intermediate offices the variety and complexity of technical and administrative problems may be great; highly competent, mature specialists are needed. The specialists themselves have often had experience in the local offices.

5. The intermediate officers seek to balance resource administration and development in one unit or area with that in others. They have a wider view and perspective than the local officer, and they are expected to apply this wider perspective to the operations in the various local offices under their jurisdiction. The intermediate offices are the first major mechanism in each agency to co-ordinate the program between local areas. They go far toward insuring relatively uniform operations in their areas by their agency's local offices, and operations of roughly equal intensity in relation to the resource capabilities and needs.

6. They are ordinarily the first level of formal or informal appeal from the action of local officers. The rancher who thinks the Forest Service ranger has reduced his grazing preference unduly, goes first to the Forest Supervisor, and then, if not satisfied, to the Regional Forester. Appeals of this nature are a useful administrative device for supervisors at these levels, and also a valuable public relations tool.

7. They have a major concern with the public relations of their agency in their respective areas. This concern is much broader than the local officer's responsibility of answering questions and trying generally to promote good will. The intermediate office is more concerned with how the work of its agency in its area relates to the work of other federal and state agencies, and to that of various private groups. It is more concerned with the general economic, social, and political climate of its area, and of the relationship of its agency's work to it, than are the local officers typically. At this level organized pressures begin

to be more frequent, and informal personal pressures less so, than at
the local offices. The men in charge of these intermediate offices look
outward from their agency to a greater extent than do the men in the
local offices.

Influences and limitations. Officers in intermediate offices are subject to the same general influences and limitations that circumscribe
local officers, but men in intermediate offices usually do more toward
modifying those forces somewhat. The intermediate officer is likely
to have a greater hand in framing the budget request, and perhaps
even in defending it. When an appropriation is made, he may have
some slight latitude in allocation of the available funds, either by
function or by area or both. The views and arguments of the men in
charge of these various areas will be influential, but his will be the
deciding voice. He can have a larger hand in the framing of regulations, policy statements, and similar administrative tools, and thus to
some extent mold the framework within which he has to operate. His
is more generally the job of trying to influence public opinion along
lines considered desirable by his agency, and thus to affect in some degree the environment in which he has to operate. He is more likely to
have a relationship to the governor of the state in which he works,
or to key legislators, and to members of the Congress. These are all
perfectly proper aspects of his job, although in some instances they
may have been performed improperly.

Administrators at intermediate levels are chosen with regard to their
ability to do the job required, including the public relations activities
just referred to. Men not skillful in this, or not acceptable to their
public, are likely at this level to be diverted into various technical
specialist roles, and out of the direct line of administration and public
contact.

AT THE WASHINGTON AGENCY LEVEL

Each of the agencies maintains a top or main office in Washington.
Heading the Washington office of the agency is a chief or director and
his associate and assistant heads. There are also certain administrative functions and officers—fiscal, budget, accounting, personnel, information, and the like—and various subject-matter specialists in such
fields as timber management, fire control, range management, engineering, and the like.

In considering the functions of the Washington offices, it should be recalled that for none of them is land management the only job. For the Bureau of Land Management and the National Park Service, land management is the dominant concern, with only minor attention to cadastral surveys and land records, and to recreation planning outside of national parks, respectively. The Forest Service has three major functions: land management, research, and co-operative work with the states and private forest owners, especially on fire control. The Fish and Wildlife Service has important functions in research, enforcement of game laws and treaties, and in co-operation with the states on their programs, as well as management of wildlife refuges. The chief functions of the Geological Survey are in water measurement and study, topographical and other mapping, and general geological studies; but its Conservation Division does have major responsibility in supervision of mineral leases on original public domain and on acquired land, as well as other duties. An agency must consider its total program, but the discussion which follows is directed principally to the land management part of the agencies' functions.

The characteristics and the functions of the Washington office of the federal land managing agencies are as follows:

1. The primary job of the Washington office is to formulate agency policies and objectives. These must fall within applicable law and Administration policy and objectives, but in the long run the bureaus have much to do with the latter. The nature and scope of legislation depend to a large extent on the facts and ideas that the bureaus develop. The facts about the federal lands and their uses, and many of the ideas about federal land management, come from the lower levels of an organization, up through the various levels and ranks to the top office. The men there, with their broader viewpoints and experience, are usually able to contribute materially to agency policy and objectives out of their own knowledge and ideas.

Ideally, there is an interplay of facts and ideas among all levels of an organization. But the Washington office has the job of crystallizing the various ideas into a whole, and putting them into definite form. This process may be deliberate and direct or it may occasionally be indirect; it is nonetheless effective in establishing an agency's policies and objectives.

2. The main office directs, guides, and supervises the activities of its entire organization. To the top officials falls the responsibility for maintaining uniformity and consistency throughout the organization in the manner that the provisions of law, regulations, and agency policy are carried out.

The direct and indirect controls used at the lower levels are used here as well. In fact, the nature of these controls is often formed in the Washington office. Inspection is a major tool of supervision. On occasion the office may take corrective and even disciplinary action on lower levels in the organization.

3. It is particularly concerned with the balance of activities between different functions and different regions or areas. The top office must make judgments as to the relative importance of different types of work in different regions, and must strive to obtain a program which is properly distributed between regions.

4. The main office is particularly concerned with appropriations, and with the processes by which appropriations are obtained for the agency.[13] The amount of time of the top people devoted directly to this activity may not be particularly large. Specialists in the Washington office may perform most of the detailed work on appropriation matters; but indirectly, the top personnel of an agency may spend a lot of time on appropriation matters. There are major issues of strategy to be resolved, and even more time may be devoted to working with various interest groups with the aim of obtaining support for appropriations.

In the budgeting and appropriation process the agency head, with the help of his staff, must make many decisions. The first decision concerns the size of the ceiling request. An estimate of the minimum amount needed to administer efficiently the lands under the agency's jurisdiction is not easily determined since lands may be administered with different degrees of intensity. Furthermore, there may be reasons of strategy for requesting a ceiling of either more or less than this amount; on the one hand to anticipate the usual scale-down, on the other to guard against accusations of unreasonable (even if defensible) planning. Sometimes an agency head may in fact have little discretion because of Bureau of the Budget or departmental restrictions and instructions.

Once a ceiling amount is set by the Bureau of the Budget, another range of decision making ensues. Now it must be decided which specific budget needs will go under the ceiling requests, and which will be over. Urgency or priority of need, while important, may not be the only consideration. Some activity which might otherwise receive high priority may be passed over because there is reason to be-

[13] For the more general aspects of budget-appropriation-allocation process, see pp. 150-60.

lieve either the Bureau of the Budget or the Congress will look upon it coolly or with disfavor. Unless the agency officials ask for what they sincerely believe most needed, their prospects of ever getting adequate appropriations for these purposes are very small, but if they use some of their limited ceiling amounts to ask for something they fear will be refused by the Bureau of the Budget or Congress, they are to the same extent circumscribing other important activities.

Once the agency has made a detailed submission to the Bureau of the Budget, its main problems from then on are strategy to obtain the maximum amount of the request, rather than decisions about the content of the request. However, the latter are not excluded even here. The Bureau of the Budget or an Appropriation Committee may decide upon a reduction of a certain percentage or a certain sum, leaving the reduction in specific items to the affected agency. If that occurs, the agency head and his staff have the same general problems of choice on program importance vs. expediency or appeal, for each item.

The administrator has the responsibility of explaining, supporting, and defending his budget to the Bureau of the Budget, and to each Appropriation Committee. This may occur on a formal level, at hearings; it may also be on an informal basis, in the individual congressman's office. He may also seek to rally to his support interested parties and his general supporters, or he may merely inform his supporters, at the latter's request, of the essential facts.

The agency head may be in a difficult position. On the one hand, the action of his department and of the Bureau of the Budget in approving the appropriation request which has gone to the Congress, and in refusing to approve other requests which he has made, constitutes a policy decision by the Executive Branch which he is expected to support. On the other hand, if this requested sum is insufficient to provide the kind of management of the federal lands which he believes is necessary, and which important interest groups demand, he is almost sure to be blamed later. If he keeps quiet, or does not make known his position with sufficient clarity and emphasis, he will be criticized; if he speaks up in criticism of his department and of the Administration, he may be disciplined by them. At no place in the whole government and appropriation process is the line between proper and improper political activity more difficult to draw.

The final stage of the appropriation process is the allocation to functions and to areas of the appropriation as is passes the Congress. Sometimes the agency has no choice, because the Congress has specified the purposes for which and the areas where the money is to be used. In any case, the agency's own budget request is a major guide. The appropriation was made on the basis of the budget submission, and expenditures are expected to follow the same pattern. The terms of the Appropriation Act are legally binding upon an agency and may not be violated except at risk of punishment to the responsible officials. The Appropriation Committee reports are more in the nature of advice to the agency. Even though there may be no legal barrier to shifting some funds to other uses or areas, the agency that did so might jeopardize its future appropriations. However, in many instances less is appropriated than was requested, but some discretion is left to the agency as to the use of available funds. In this case, decision making again enters.

The top official of a land managing agency has the duty of translating into specific budget requests the general policy objectives of his agency. Action on appropriations and budget requests is far more significant in establishing policy than any amount of talk.

5. The Washington office of each land managing agency represents its agency in numerous negotiations or relations with other agencies in its department or in other departments. A substantial part of the time of the administrator and his staff is taken up in this way. Much of this activity is defensive. Other agencies may wish to undertake programs which would have a harmful side effect upon the land managing agency. There are also bureaucratic raids to be fought off. Various proposals by private groups, members of the Congress, or other agencies may seem similarly dangerous. On the positive side, an agency may try to obtain support or consent for some part of its own program. Of special importance is the effort to obtain new legislation to make possible some desired program or extension of program. This calls for work not only with the Congressional committees, but also with the Bureau of the Budget, often with other federal agencies, and usually with various private groups.

In such negotiations and in many of its other activities, the Washington office looks out and away from its agency, perhaps as much as it does inside. The activities of offices at lower levels are by no means confined to purely internal matters, but the degree of the outward look increases at the upper levels.

The top office is concerned with public relations in the broadest sense. It must consider this aspect of the work not only from the national viewpoint, but also from that of its regional and local offices. A special phase of public relations work is the mollification of critics, whether in government or outside—the meeting of the man with a "gripe.". One of the mechanisms for ascertaining public opinion, and for influencing it, is the public hearing, conducted by the bureau or department.

6. The agency heads of the federal land managing bureaus may serve as part of a policy-making team within their respective departments, if the Secretary so chooses. Practice in this regard has been highly variable, ranging from situations in which these officials were not consulted in the least in the making of department policy, even within their respective fields, to situations in which they were fully involved in policy making.

7. They act upon formal and informal appeals from all levels within their organization. The review of appeals at this level provides something of a check upon the work of the lower offices, but by no means a complete one.

8. The headquarters office may act directly upon some of the agency's most important and difficult problems for which authority to act has not been delegated to lower levels. For instance, the approval of a forest co-operative agreement under which substantial quantities of public and private timber are committed for long periods of time to a particular management program may be reserved for the Washington office. The establishment of a new grazing district or the establishment of a primitive area may also be reserved for action at the Washington level. In general, the reserved decisions are those which are so inherently difficult, or unusual, or so fraught with political controversy, that the Washington office feels that only it is capable of acting and accepting the responsibility.

The recruitment, training, indoctrination, transfer, and other personnel policies stem from actions at the Washington level. The recruitment and training policies of these agencies and their emphasis on a "career service" have been in large measure responsible for the indirect controls, or attitude conditioning, by which common goals, policies, and objectives are held at all levels in the agency. While this has been a conscious policy by all the agencies, it is something in which the Forest Service pioneered.

AT THE DEPARTMENT LEVEL

The Secretary of Agriculture and the Secretary of the Interior are responsible for the direction, supervision, and guidance of the land managing bureaus. Many of the legal authorizations for land management are in their hands. In the chain of decision making the Secretary is a major link; and on many crucial issues he is the final authority. At this level, however, responsibility broadens far beyond the management of the public lands. The problems of administering large and complex farm programs, in Agriculture, and the problems concerned with the territories and island possessions, water and power development, minerals and fuels, Indians, and other responsibilities, in Interior, occupy the larger part of the Secretary's time.

A Secretary must personally delegate most of the activities attaching to his office, for they are too numerous for any one man to carry. He retains the responsibility for the actions taken, however. Much of the detailed load handled at the Secretarial level is taken over by the Assistant Secretary in charge of such matters, and also by some of the staff agencies. The bulk of authority he delegates to the line agencies and bureaus, which operate under his direction.

The Secretary of a department is a political figure, part of the President's top staff or "team"; as such, he is concerned with Administration policy and program as a whole, as well as with that of his department. It is his duty to outline his proposed programs to the President, and try to obtain support for them, but also to keep his programs in line with the over-all program of the Administration. This may require him at times to take actions which, if considered solely from the viewpoint of the resources alone, would not be the best. For instance, a land managing agency may wish to build some roads into and across the lands it administers, to provide access for various purposes to certain resources. From a resource-administering viewpoint, such roads may be not only necessary but urgent. But the Administration may wish to limit federal expenditure to some level in order to balance the budget, or may forbid civilian construction because of the more urgent needs for military construction, and thus decide not to build the roads at a particular time. Though the Secretary may argue against such action within Administration circles, he may nevertheless accede to it as part of a larger program.

For some agencies, there has been greater continuity of agency heads than of Secretaries. When this is the case, the Secretary is handicapped by being less well informed on the broad program of the agency than is the bureau head, and less well informed, also, on the sources of support and opposition to the program. Agencies generally have well-established group interest support, both within and outside of the Congress, which may hamper his taking action contrary to the agency's wishes. While theoretically the Secretary's control over the land managing bureaus is nearly complete, in practice it may be far less; but it is also true that in the latter situation the agency is never sure when the Secretary may move to exert his power, even in the face of outside opposition.

The Secretary exercises his control over the bureaus under him in several ways. First of all, there are the departmental regulations, which translate the general language of laws into more specific and detailed instructions and procedures. These are the guiding lines for work of most officials within the agencies. While regulations are usually drafted within the bureaus, they are approved by the Secretary. In the second place, the Secretary issues a series of delegation orders which state specifically what bureaus may and may not do. In the third place, he exercises his control over bureaus by means of his actual appointments to key positions and his control over appointments to the higher positions. By selecting or approving men in whose judgment and ability he has confidence, he can largely control the actions taken.

In time of a changing national Administration, the judgment of the new Secretary is a major force in the way an agency continues to function. If the new Administration's policies with respect to the federal lands differ from those of the old, he may decide to replace top agency personnel with others whom he believes capable of putting the new policies into effect. In so doing, he may in some cases introduce much-needed vitality, but at the same time he runs the risk of losing experienced assistance. Administration of the public lands has become more complex and more specialized with the growing use of the lands, and it is becoming increasingly difficult to find people outside of the agencies concerned who are capable of directing their administration. This situation is not altogether desirable; it does make the public more dependent on a professional managerial class than was once the case. But it is a situation that will surely grow more evident as the pressures for use of the federal land grow and as their reconciliation becomes more difficult.

The Secretary is ordinarily the last or highest step in the line of administrative appeals, and as in the case of the lower levels of administration, appeals provide a valuable mechanism for supervision of the work of lower units.

The fact that the Secretary, in such fields as personnel, fiscal, and legal matters, is necessarily dependent upon his specialized staff has the effect of putting a considerable number of persons between him and the bureau head, although on a strictly line basis the latter is directly under the Secretary. Much of the work of this staff is negative, in the sense that these people can forbid a specific proposed action because it does not conform to regulations, law, or policy, but cannot approve all phases of the proposed action. The Secretarial staff ordinarily remains more nearly anonymous than can either the Secretary or the bureau head. There are thus several hurdles that proposed actions, especially proposed new types of actions, of a bureau must clear before they can have Secretarial approval.

The Secretary and the Assistant Secretaries are almost wholly dependent upon the bureaus and their own staffs for facts regarding the operation of the bureaus. They may visit areas of controversy in order to better understand the issues involved, but they have no time for independent study and fact gathering. Often in the past the Secretary, or responsible citizens, or both, have been concerned that not all pertinent facts in controversial situations have been available, or have not been properly presented. This is not to accuse the bureau and other officials of bias or misrepresentation, but perhaps they did not see the problem as broadly, or with as many ramifications, as the Secretary would have liked.

This is one reason why both Agriculture and Interior at one time or another have established groups such as the Office of Land Use Co-ordination and the Program Review Staff, and also river basin committees. The former have served to provide technical personnel in the Secretary's office, to review the programs and proposals of the land managing bureaus, as well as to perform other functions. They have often reviewed the items the Secretary has to sign, and have served as a means of considering the complaints directed against the bureaus. The river basin committees have been staffed mostly by representatives of the agencies, but were in all cases established by Secretarial order. These committees have prepared programs for the entire river basin, and their attention has included matters other than federal land management. They have served to assemble facts and make analyses; but it is generally agreed that they have not served to resolve policy issues or to formulate comprehensive and balanced programs.

Some Secretaries have taken a major role in the preparation and defense of budget requests. They have presented their department's request for ceiling to the Bureau of the Budget and urged with vigor the grant of larger allowances. They have taken an active personal hand in division of the ceiling among bureaus, even conducting abbreviated but purposeful budget reviews with the bureau heads to guide them in their decisions. And in the defense of the budget before the Congress, both in the formal hearings and with members of the Congress privately, they have taken an active hand. With others, participation in these matters has been less active.

Finally, the Secretary may personally approve certain types of land management actions and personally sign the effectuating documents. There was a time in the Department of the Interior, for instance, when all mineral leases of certain types were signed personally by the Secretary. Generally speaking, however, federal administration is not as centralized at the top today as it once was. Still, there may be actions of such importance or so full of political implications that a Secretary would and should wish personally to review and approve them. Since the Secretary must take the political consequences of the actions of his department, he may feel that only his personal action is sufficient in a particular situation.

AT THE PRESIDENTIAL LEVEL

The President, as the chief federal elective officer in the Executive Branch, has the ultimate decision making power of that branch in the management of federal lands, along with all other fields of federal activity. Also, as the political head of the party in power he largely formulates and implements his party's policy.

But, as in the case of the Secretary of a department, though in infinitely greater degree, the increase in authority is attended by a decrease in specialized interest and knowledge. Federal land management is only one of the President's concerns in the natural resource field, which in turn is but one of his domestic concerns; and foreign affairs in recent decades have often overshadowed domestic affairs in the demands they have made for the time and attention of the President. Many years ago public land matters were major, often critical, matters for the personal concern of the President. In the last fifty to seventy-five years public lands for the most part have been eclipsed by other matters, although they were of large concern to Theodore Roosevelt in the early years of the present century, and more recently were of personal interest and of some importance to Franklin Roosevelt. The submerged lands, at least, were of direct Presidential concern in both the Truman and Eisenhower administrations. While some problems of the public lands still can be of considerable interest to Presidents, it is generally true that they have received, and in the nature of things can expect to receive, only incidental attention from the President.

The President exercises his authority over the federal lands in several ways. First, he appoints the Secretaries of Agriculture and Interior, and the Assistant Secretaries concerned with land management matters. The various interest groups concerned with federal land will try to influence his appointments to these positions. The types of men he selects, and their previous experience and attitudes, largely set the tone of the top executive decision making on the federal lands. Second, he confers with these men at intervals regarding federal land management. Third, his broad budget decisions may exert a major control over the federal lands; sheer availability of funds goes far in determining the nature and extent of public use. Fourth, the President has a major control over federal lands by his action on legislation—many bills are sponsored by the Executive Branch in his name, and he may veto those which are not.

The President, even more than the Secretary, must delegate authority, and even more than the Secretary, he is dependent upon subordinates for facts and analyses. In the federal land management field, the President works mainly through three channels: the Bureau of the Budget, the Civil Service Commission, and various Presidential assistants.

The Bureau of the Budget exercises two main functions: review of the budget requests, and review of proposed legislation. In its review of budget requests, it is concerned first of all with the conformity of specific budget requests to whatever broad budgetary policies the President may have laid down. It also examines the specific budget requests, to make sure that the amounts requested are reasonable in view of the ends sought, that the work is efficiently carried out, and that excess staffing is avoided. Such examination, no matter how skillfully done, cannot go much beneath the surface of requests, for the Bureau of the Budget has normally had but a few men to review the budget for each department. Great emphasis is placed upon experience in previous years, and in deviations from previous requests.

The Bureau of the Budget also reviews proposed legislation carefully. This applies both to the proposals which originate in the Executive Branch, and to those which originate in the Congress. In the field of federal land management, most legislation in recent years has fallen in the former class. In the course of the review all interested federal agencies are advised of the proposals, and have an opportunity to comment upon them. The Budget Bureau examines them in relation to earlier legislation, and to general legislative principles accepted by the President. If something new is proposed, or if there are major and irreconcilable differences among the departments, the President personally may be asked to decide. The land managing agencies, like other federal bureaus, may work directly with members of the Congress and with interest groups in drafting or in formulating legislative proposals. But the official reports of the Executive Branch on pending legislation are supposed to clear with the Bureau of the Budget, and for the land managing agencies invariably do so.

The Bureau of the Budget, in the name of the President, exercises great power over federal land administration. This power is often anonymous; in many instances it is not clear to the Congress or to the public that it was the Bureau of the Budget which took a particular action or made a particular decision, and the individuals in the Bureau of the Budget responsible for the action or decision are almost never identified to the Congress and to the public. This anonymity enables the Bureau of the Budget to operate with less direct pressure from interest groups; responsibility for its decisions is shifted to the Secretaries and bureau heads who must carry out its decisions. The actions of the Bureau of the Budget are more generally negative than positive. Its decisions are upon budgets or proposed legislation that originated elsewhere; it says what can or cannot be done; but it rarely says to any agency, this or that should be done. Moreover, while negatively it can usually act effectively, it usually cannot make its affirmative decisions stick in the face of opposition or other pressures. Its function is review, not administration as such, and it would shortly come in for much criticism if it started telling the agencies what they should do, for this would make the Bureau of the Budget into a line agency, taking it out of its role of staff agency. But this exclusive concern with the review function is likely to engender skepticism or even antagonism to new ideas and actions.

The Civil Service Commission establishes general standards and qualifications for jobs and persons, specifies what kinds of personnel actions the agencies may and may not take, post-audits their personnel actions, and in general serves to review and supervise their personnel work. It, too, has considerable effect on federal land management, although not as much, in general, as the Bureau of the Budget; and its personnel are also generally anonymous as far as the Congress and the public are concerned.

Matters which in a day of simpler government would have gone directly to the President are today commonly referred first of all to one of the Presidential Assistants. If there is a major difference of opinion between two departments over a piece of legislation which the Bureau of the Budget cannot resolve, this is likely to be taken first to the Presidential Assistant, who will try by conferences and other devices to resolve the differences or at least to define them. If he fails, it will have to go to the President personally.

The President, both in his capacity as head of the Executive Branch and as head of his political party, exercises great influence over the Congress if he chooses to use it. This applies to all phases of government business, and not simply to land management matters. Thus, what the President decides to do about new land legislation or about budget for land administration will depend in large part on what he thinks the Congress will approve, and on the degree to which he is willing to throw his influence and power behind a specific program which the Congress may be reluctant to accept. A popular President can often put over almost any specific program which does not have major popular opposition, but he cannot put over every such program. His influence is effective in inverse ratio to the frequency with which he uses it.

AT THE CONGRESSIONAL LEVEL[14]

The power of the Congress in the legislative field is co-ordinate with that of the President in the Executive Branch. The relations between the two branches may range from close co-operation to active opposition.

There is a basic difference between the President and the Congress which applies to all of government, not simply to federal land matters: the President is one man, the Congress is a moderately large body of men. The President may have a difficult time reaching a decision in a particular matter, but at least there is but one mind to be made up. Any group, especially one of diverse backgrounds, is likely to have more trouble in reaching a decision on a difficult matter. There may

[14] The previous discussions about the budget-appropriation-allocation and the legislative processes should be borne in mind here also.

be several alternatives, and no clear consensus for any of them. A group may come to an action which is not satisfactory to any member of it, and yet is less unsatisfactory than any alternative. A group is more likely than an individual to take inconsistent and even contradictory actions. The federal government is so complex today that many members of the Congress cannot hope to be well informed on most of the issues they deal with, because they have given their major attention to other matters.

Congress, like the President, is concerned with the whole range of federal government. Like the President, its concern over public land problems has diminished over the decades. It is difficult to get the Congress to take much interest in public land management today. While any President must take some responsibility for public land management, however uninterested he may be in it, some members of the Congress can remain completely unaware of the federal land problems. Considering the multiplicity and complexity of government programs these days, and the desire and need for congressmen to specialize, this is neither surprising nor a basis for criticism. But it is a fact that must be considered in examining how decisions are made for public land management.

Congress operates chiefly through committees. The make-up of the Interior and Insular Affairs and the Appropriations committees in the two Houses has previously been described (pages 145-47). It is in committee that specific and detailed attention is given to particular problems of legislation or of appropriations. Individual members of committees, and especially chairmen, are exposed to much pressure from various interest groups during consideration of important and controversial bills. The committee often acts upon the recommendation of the subcommittee, which was largely dominated by one or a few men; and the Congress often acts upon the recommendation of its committee. Thus, in any specific field, action is commonly largely determined by a relatively few persons within the Congress.

This is the way the Congress has devised for dealing with the complexity of modern government, and few students would suggest anything else, though many have suggested improvements in the functioning of the committee system. There is a continuously changing balance of power and of personal interrelationships. What is true today may not be true tomorrow, even in the same Congress; what is true on one issue may not be true of another; and what is true in one Congress may change materially in later ones.

Congress exerts its power on federal land management (as on most other federal problems) chiefly in four ways:

1. By action on appropriations. Congress acts upon the President's budget. It is unlikely to go above it, by substituting its own proposals for the President's, especially in the House, although this has happened in recent years for federal land managing agencies; but it frequently goes below his proposals, substituting its judgments for his. The Congress has, and accepts, the responsibility for decisions upon appropriation matters.

2. By other legislation. Laws may be relatively general, laying down broad policies and general courses of action, and leaving considerable freedom of action to the administrator; or they may be highly detailed and specific, with little room for the application of administrative judgment. Laws may deal with either general or specific situations. Laws relating to federal lands fall in both categories, but there is an immense body of detailed and specific land law. In recent years at least, the Congress has acted on federal land legislation much more by accepting, rejecting, or modifying the legislative proposals of the Executive Branch, than by originating legislation itself.

3. By special investigations. Congress may authorize one of its regular committees, or a special committee, to investigate a particular problem or activity. There have been many Congressional investigations or studies of federal land management. The purposes of the investigations have varied, from that of attempting to ascertain the basis of complaints by the public, to that of getting facts on which to base new legislation. While some committees have had funds for a sizable staff, and the authority to subpoena witnesses, giving them the means to make an independent study, others have lacked these aids and have been forced to rely largely upon witnesses who ask to be heard. Public hearings may bring to light a large body of facts. Often, however, their primary purpose is to arouse public sentiment for or against a particular idea or proposal, with the interest groups rallying to present information and viewpoints. While such hearings are often carefully planned in advance, they frequently turn up information or ideas previously unknown. There has been a good deal of criticism of the Congressional hearing as often biased in purpose and unfair or inefficient in method; but properly handled, the hearing is one of the most effective tools for ascertaining facts, discovering and molding public opinion, and providing the impetus for new legislation.

4. By contacts of individual congressmen with the land managing agencies. Such contacts are usually in the interest of a constituent on a particular matter, rather than on general issues or policy. However, this is often one of the most effective means the Congress has of intervening in the decision making process as applied to federal lands. If a constituent wants to obtain a tract of federal land, its use, or its products, under some arrangement which the congressman regards as reasonable but the federal agency does not, there is opportunity for an exchange of views, perhaps for the conversion of one person or group to another viewpoint.

An arm of the Congress is the General Accounting Office, which has the duty of supervising the accounting and other activities of the federal agencies, to insure that expenditures have been made within the law, and that their activities otherwise conform to Congressional policy or to good management. Aside from specific action of the General Accounting Office, its very existence serves as a continuous reminder to the agencies that they should operate in a manner which will be approved by it.

Congress strongly affects the decision making process in federal land management, in what the federal officials think it may do as well as in what it does.

Congress accepts the responsibility for its own decisions, but it cannot accept the responsibility for the final actions in federal land management, because those are so largely in the hands of the Executive Branch. It does set some of the major terms of reference—largely the laws and the appropriations, but even on these it acts to a considerable degree within the framework of the suggestions made by the Executive Branch.

The Congress sometimes takes the view that it has provided a sound framework for actual administration, and that good results are largely a logical consequence of its framework, and bad ones due to disregard of its suggestions and strictures. On the other hand, the Executive Branch sometimes feels that it has to labor under such unsatisfactory conditions that it cannot produce good results; or that the good results it does achieve are due to its efforts and not to those of the Congress. There is obviously plenty of room for argument as to who did what. When over-all results are generally satisfactory—as they have mostly been for federal land management—it would appear that each branch has done its job at least tolerably well, wherever may lie the most glory.

Summary and Interpretation

In summarizing this chapter certain conclusions require re-emphasis.

1. The federal lands have many and varied publics. There is a certain general public interest, which is gradually being stimulated by the ever-increasing use of the lands. There is also a set of far more specialized interests. The latter falls into four main groups: timber harvest and forestry, grazing, mineral development, and recreation-conservation-general resources. Each of these groups, whether professional, semi-professional, industrial, or public in character, strives in different ways to influence the management of the federal lands. It appears that the four groups have each roughly equal strength today, so that any one may be able to prevent action to which it strongly objects, but none is able to push through legislative or administrative action that others strongly disapprove of. State and local governments, through their resource-managing agencies, also exercise an influence on federal land management.

2. The two major processes by which the federal lands are managed are the legislative and the budget-appropriation-allocation processes. Each involves both the Legislative Branch and the Executive Branch. The specialized nature of the interests of the typical congressman greatly influences both processes, but especially the legislative one. A majority of the active members of the Interior and Insular Affairs Committee in each House are from the West; the Appropriation committees have a broader geographic base, and the Agriculture committees (which handle some of the national forest legislation) are specialized as to their interest in agriculture, not as to their interest in federal lands. There are many serious flaws in the budget-appropriation-allocation process as applied to federal lands.

3. The decision making process as applied to federal land management is rather widely diffused through the federal government. The number of persons involved is partly due to the relatively great extent of the federal lands and to their widespread geographic location. It is also partly due to the complexity of the land management job, and to the size and complexity of modern government itself. Although the field man may make what appears to be the final decision, a host of other officials are looking over his shoulder and participating, either directly or indirectly, in major land management decisions. As a result, it may be difficult to judge who in the chain of responsibility is responsible for action or inaction.

4. Most of the decision making points in the chain of responsi-

bility and authority have more negative than positive strength. There are a number of persons whose position enables them to reject a proposed course of action; few if any of these persons can of their own initiative approve a course of action and make their approval stick. A new idea or proposal must run a long gauntlet of critics or reviewers, any one of whom may be able to kill it, but none of whom can give it safe conduct to its destination.

5. Men in the chain of decision making must be concerned with what they think others in this chain will accept and approve. At its best, this means conformity with regulations, statements of policy, and procedures established by the agency—governing documents which, ideally, men at each level have had a hand in formulating. But even where there is a common body of guiding principle and a consensus as to its meaning, the interpretations of the men at the upper levels of the decision making chain, rather than those of men at the lower levels, govern or control. By and large, men in the lower ranks of the federal land managing agencies have tried to take actions which they thought were wise and sound, and have not yielded to temptation to take actions which they thought would be popular. The top leadership of these agencies have encouraged independent thinking and action.

6. On the whole, federal land management has been forward-looking. The tendency toward inertia which is a natural result of the points made in the two preceding paragraphs—which, after all, are common to the governmental system as a whole—has been counteracted by idealism. It may well be questioned, however, if the public should always rely on a high level of idealism to safeguard its interests.

We live in an age of big government; the sheer size and diversity of government operations necessitate rules and procedures, and tend toward decision by rote rather than by initiative. The federal government has been designed, especially at the top, to provide a series of checks and balances to prevent unwise or excessive use of power by any branch or group. Our Founding Fathers feared government power more than they saw the need for it. Many good things can be said in favor of this situation—a certain stability of government operations is achieved; ill-considered actions are less likely to take place; there is less likely to be action in the interest of certain special-interest groups, and so on.

But the question may also be raised: is this system of government operations basically compatible with efficient progressive management of federal lands in a dynamic economy? If resources are to be used fully and effectively, there will be the need for relatively quick decisions, by someone who can carry them out and accept the responsibility for doing so. Decisions in the future should be based less upon routine and precedent and more upon the nature of the resource and the demands for its use. There should be more emphasis on constructive decisions, and less upon negative ones. The role that the federal lands must play in the future will grow, and the nature of the decision making process may have to change with the changing role.

Even though their goals may be different, some aspects of federal land management are rather directly comparable with private business. Investment or expenditure for current operations up to the point where added revenue just covers added cost, while at the same time nonrevenue-yielding functions are improved or at least not worsened, is as sound for federal as for private lands. Some of the lessons learned from experience on private lands may well have great value for public lands. On the whole, the management of private lands is vastly simpler, with fewer stages in the decision making process, than is the management of federal lands of the same value.

CHAPTER FOUR

Pricing Processes

and Investments

on Federal Land

THE USE OF LAND AND ITS PRODUCTS IS IN PART
determined by the prices charged; the latter are in
part conditioned by the potential uses of the land and its products.
The nature of the decisions that must be made is strongly affected by
the methods by which prices are determined. And the amount of
revenues received from the lands is partially an outgrowth of the
prices charged. There is thus a considerable interrelationship between this and the preceding chapters, and between this and the
chapter on revenues which immediately follows.

Price Making and Investment in a Truly Competitive Economy

Economists long ago set up a market model for the purpose of
showing how the truly competitive market operates to establish prices
and to guide investment. In such a market some persons offer goods
and others buy them until a price is reached at which supply and
demand are equal—a price which just .clears the market. It is always
assumed that the number of buyers and of sellers is great enough to

prevent any one individual from having a significant effect upon the market. It is also assumed that the buyers and sellers operate singly, not in combination. Other qualifications and limitations are also assigned. Such a market may never have existed, but as an economic abstraction it has great analytical usefulness and sometimes it fits actual markets reasonably well.

It does not fit the method by which the federal lands and their products have been disposed of. Such a market could not have been established, even if the nation had desired to do so. While not the only seller of land, timber, and related resources, the federal government is the major large supplier in many markets and is in a position to influence the market.

The buyer's side of the equation is also different from the traditional competitive market, for there are few buyers able or willing to buy federal land or its products. The number of ranchers well able to use a particular grazing area does not often exceed two or three, and may only be one. The same situation often exists with respect to operators of sawmills within economic hauling distance for the logs from a particular tract of federal timber. Locational factors and spatial relationships thus limit the number of potential buyers. Even when several buyers are interested, each one may give as much consideration to the probable actions of the others in this or in future sales as he does to the characteristics of the product and its value.

Price Making in an Economy of Limited Competition

In recent years several economists have developed a body of theory of "monopolistic" or "imperfect" competition to deal with the market situation which is not fully competitive in the older sense, and yet is not completely monopolistic.[1] The essential characteristic of such markets is that the number of buyers or of sellers or both is small enough that each has to consider the effect of his actions upon the whole market and the price. While such conditions are often associated with large-scale industry and business, they may also apply to small-scale business if operating in a small local market.

---

[1] Robinson, Joan, *Economics of Imperfect Competition*, London: Macmillan Co., Ltd., 1933, and E. H. Chamberlin, *The Theory of Monopolistic Competition*, Cambridge: Harvard University Press, 1933.

The major automobile firms, or even rival gas stations across the street from each other in a small town, may fit this description. Each knows or suspects that if he cuts prices in an attempt to get more business, his rival or rivals will promptly meet his price cut. Competition may still be severe in all areas but price, taking the form of high-pressure selling, advertising, and attempts to create a distinctive product, and thus attract a special group of consumers to this product, and the like. The businessman in such a situation is supposed to be influenced not by price alone, but by his marginal revenue; if he cuts prices, this not only lowers the price on the additional units of products sold but on his whole volume of sales, so that relatively small cuts may have serious effects on income.

By the use of this system, relatively careful calculations of expected income and expense are possible, and the businessman can and does operate according to such calculations. In so doing, he takes into account not only the present market price, but what the market price may be if he expands his output, or if competitors expand theirs, simultaneously or independently. There are the same, or perhaps greater, uncertainties about the future, but the system permits price making and investment to follow rules that are based on reasonably definite calculations.

Even this modification of the competitive market is not fully applicable to disposal of federal land and its products. Neither the situation involving a few sellers competing for the purchases of a large number of buyers nor that of one or a very few purchasers buying from a large number of sellers (the tobacco companies buying tobacco from many thousands of farmers is a good example of the latter), fits well the case of the federal government selling land or its products. There is now but a single seller of these particular lands or products, although there may or may not be individual sellers of more or less similar products in the same area. There may be a single buyer, several potential buyers, or a number of potential users or buyers so large as to be, for practical purposes, considered unlimited. When a federal agency is trying to interest a forestry concern in establishing a sawmill or pulp plant in an area where none exists, or in using species not commonly used, the first situation—that of a single buyer—exists. Where, as is more normal, several established lumber mills may be interested in a particular tract of timber, the second situation exists. And where thousands of persons are using recreational facilities, the third, unlimited, situation exists.

If it were desired to operate federal lands so as to produce the maximum revenue (although this is not, in fact, the basis of their management), then in the case of a single buyer for federal lands or their products, the situation would be one of monopolists or quasi-monopolists dealing with each other, as for example in the case of wage bargaining between the automobile makers and the labor unions. Economists have pointed out that in these circumstances price is in one sense indeterminate—the outcome depends on the relative bargaining strength of the two contestants, and this in turn depends on many other factors. As a practical matter in such circumstances, the federal agency is often in a weak bargaining position, even should it strive to operate as a monopolist.

A situation like the foregoing is found only where development of a particular resource in an area has not yet begun, or where it has not yet been profitable to exploit a type of resource. The Forest Service was obliged to coax the first pulp mill into Alaska. Special inducements may be necessary to persuade the first lumber mill to use subalpine types of timber in Oregon. In these circumstances, regardless of the profit motive, the federal government would gain from any productive use of a resource that otherwise was going to waste, even though it would not get high prices for its product.

A more common situation for timber harvest, grazing, and even mineral leasing, is the presence of two or more potential buyers, but still only a few, as against the single seller, the government. In this case, each buyer considers the possible actions of his competitors. At one extreme there may be agreement or collusion among the possible rivals—an open or a tacit agreement that one bids in one area or at one time, another in another area or at another time, etc. At the other extreme there may be the most intense rivalry, sometimes with intense emotionalism, between the possible buyers. The latter cases have arisen with respect to allotment of grazing privileges. The situation in general has many of the characteristics of a poker game: each person in the "game" considers not only his "hand" or position, but the possible "hands" or positions of all other players in the game. When the oil companies bid for areas of submerged land on the outer continental shelf, or when lumbermen bid for tracts of national forest or O & C timber, speculation about and consideration of possible rival bids may be as important as estimates of the value of the oil or timber to the particular bidder. An examination of the individual bids submitted in such cases will sometimes show very wide gaps between the highest and the next highest bids, for instance, and discussions with some of the bidders will show that miscalculation of probable competition is often a reason for the gaps.[2]

Later sections of this chapter will consider actual timber sales problems and show how this situation involving a limited number of bidders often works out.

Competitive Market Rejected for Federal Lands

Without explicit consideration of its technical character, the purely competitive market has been largely rejected as a basis for the sale of federal land, its products, and its uses. In no case does the choice between major uses of federal land rest on sale by competitive prices; and only in the case of most timber sales and some mineral leasing does the choice between applicants rest on competitive sale.

Competitive sale of the original public domain was tried early in our history, partly as a means of raising revenue for the new nation.[3] But little of the public domain was disposed of in this fashion, one reason being that the states were also selling much land and, perhaps more important, the concept of selling the land on the frontier at the greatest possible price was repugnant to the whole social value system of the frontier. The pioneer contending with Indians, carrying on a subsistence type of agriculture with very little cash income, was neither able nor willing to pay much for land himself, nor did he want nonresident purchasers to be allowed to buy land. Competitive sales were discouraged by the settlers and, in some instances, there was actual interference.

The political strength of the frontier was exercised to the end that pre-emption, or the prior right of the squatter to buy land as against the outside bidder, came to be recognized in the early nineteenth century. During this same period the idea of competitive sale of land was gradually abandoned and a system of low, fixed prices for land was established instead. These prices seldom if ever changed and gradually became lower in comparison with rising price levels and land values. Still later, through homestead and other laws, the idea of "free" land was accepted.

---

[2] This general approach has been explored in detail by J. Von Neumann and O. Morgenstern in *Theory of Games and Economic Behavior*, Princeton: Princeton University Press, 1944. A student familiar with theory and methodology in this field might find some rewarding examples in timber sales by federal agencies.

[3] See any of the standard books in this field, by Clawson, Dana, Hibbard, Robbins, and others, as cited on p. 16.

The federal mining laws of 1866 and 1872 legalized the appropriation of public domain for mining purposes. Those laws have always been primarily concerned with rights between individuals and with rights of individuals as against the federal government. There has been little or no concern shown for the rights of the general public as represented by the federal government, or for the rights of other land users, to land embraced in mining claims.

The result of a century or more during which the terms to obtain public domain land or its products were increasingly liberalized, was an attitude that the public domain was common property, available to the first comer with little regard for the general public. The idea that these resources should be sold and at competitive prices ran counter to the trends of the disposal policy and had virtually no support. The first real change in this policy was the Forest Reserve Act of 1897, which provided legal authority for management of the forest reserves. It authorized the Secretary of the Interior, in whose department the forest reserves still were, to sell such dead, matured, or large growth of trees as in his judgment was compatible with the utilization of the forest, at not less than its appraised price, and after advertisement. At the same time it permitted the continued free use of resources for many purposes. The mining law was explicitly made applicable to these areas.

The act contained no mention of grazing nor explicit authority to charge fees for grazing or other uses of the reserves. The authority to control grazing on the forest reserves was challenged successfully in the courts until as late as the period of 1908-11. For many years the authority to charge grazing and other fees was disputed.[4] Yet, the principle of selling timber at not less than appraised price and on competitive bid seems to have been accepted from the passage of the act of 1897, possibly because so much good timber in various ownerships outside of these areas was available at reasonable prices.

The Forest Service has tried to establish grazing fees on a level comparable to those on other grazing land. While it was able to increase the fees greatly above the nominal levels of the early years, various compromises were made and it is doubtful if the fees today are on a fully competitive level.

The Taylor Grazing Act, passed in 1934, merely called for reason-

---

[4] For a brief account of this history, and references as to details, see Marion Clawson, *The Western Range Livestock Industry*, New York: McGraw-Hill Book Co., 1950.

able fees without explicitly defining "reasonable." In the hearings on the act, however, Secretary Ickes and others from the Department of the Interior had made it very clear that the level of administration of the grazing lands was to be low, and that fees, although not to be regarded as revenue producing, would cover the cost of administration. This position was taken in part as a means of convincing the Congress that administration of these lands should be in the Department of the Interior rather than in the Forest Service. Another protracted struggle over grazing fees ensued, with the result that fees on grazing districts today are somewhat higher than they were previously, but they still are somewhat lower than those on national forests even when differences in character of forage are taken into account.

When the Mineral Leasing Act was passed in 1920, it provided a somewhat intermediate position on the matter of the level of prices: competitive sale of leases in areas where mineral deposits had been proven, royalties at about commercial levels, but noncompetitive leasing at nominal rentals and on most generous terms elsewhere.

Recreational users of the public domain have never paid anything for such use. In the national forests recreational use was free until recent years and still is free in most areas. In the national parks users have been admitted free or for the payment of a nominal entrance charge.

This brief review of federal land history serves to show why the idea of competitive sale of federal land, its resources, and its uses was early and generally abandoned, and how, in the few instances it has since been adopted, the idea has often been resisted and often, too, found unacceptable in the social standards of the day and place. "A large part of these federally-owned resources are and must be allocated among private enterprisers by administrative decision and not by competition." [5]

PRICING BY ADMINISTRATIVE DECISION

Establishment of prices for products from federal land is in part an economic process, and in part a political one. In the sense that it is economic, considerations of maximum price and maximum receipts are dominant in the same way that they would be for private

[5] Kelso, M. M., "Current Issues in Federal Land Management in the Western United States," *Journal of Farm Economics*, XXIX (1947), No. 4, Part II.

landowners. In the sense that it is political, the prices are fixed, in whole or in part, by governmental and primarily by political processes, and the objective is not maximum price but something else—usually assistance to certain types of federal land users. The word "political" has for many a derogatory connotation, but it is a fact that prices fixed in this way may be far more in the public interest than those determined by strictly economic processes.

Congress, often acting upon the recommendations of the President, has established bases other than highest price for the administration of most uses of the federal land. Generally speaking, the administrator has been left a large measure of discretion to determine which uses shall have priority on particular pieces of land, how intensive the use shall be or under just what conditions it shall be carried on, and even who the individual user shall be.

That the allocation takes place on a basis other than competitive price does not mean that the process is arbitrary or improper; it simply means that other criteria have been established and used. And there are some advantages in the process. Greater attention can be given to the commercially less valuable, but perhaps socially more desirable, uses of the federal land. Water is an extremely important product of much federal land, yet no charge is made for it; indeed, it is difficult to see how a charge could be made for that part of the total water yield that might be credited to good watershed management. While recreation might be made to yield some revenue to federal lands, in many areas this would be difficult, and most people would argue that it is undesirable to place this use in competition with many other uses. Other examples might be cited.

Another advantage lies in the opportunity the process affords to practice multiple-use administration. This can be done to a far greater degree than if the market were purely competitive.[6] In that case the uses that do not yield a commercial return would be pushed aside, as might the less-than-dominant commercial use: many forest operations would not develop the grazing resource as fully as might be, and many ranchers would neglect the forestry possibilities.

---

[6] The essence of multiple use is not simply the occurrence of two or more uses of the same land at the same time, but the carefully planned articulation of various uses so that each interferes as little as possible with the other. The techniques of multiple-use management have been excluded from the scope of this book, but their development and use are possible only because the laws have given the administrator an opportunity to exercise some discretion. See Kelso, *ibid.*, for development of this idea.

Lastly, this economic-political process permits more concern for the more vulnerable groups than would a process based on competitive prices. The small rancher might find it very hard to match the bid of the largest ranchers in competition for grazing use, for instance.

But the advantages of decision making on bases other than competitive prices exact their price. In the first place, the very fluidity of the process puts a major strain on the whole administrative structure. Instead of merely awarding the use of land or its products to the highest bidder, the administrator has to devise other criteria, defend their rationality, apply them under difficult situations, and resist the pressures of the unsuccessful applicant. Although an administrator is not entirely immune from pressures when decisions are made on the basis of price alone, a dissatisfied applicant can argue with much greater force against a public official than he can against an open bid which he is unwilling to match or top.

The use of methods other than those of highest price inevitably increases the complexity of government processes—the "red tape" which every citizen and every critic of government deplores. The methods by which criteria are established and their application, at every stage, call for more involved governmental procedures. In particular, appeals procedures must be established and used, even at the cost of much time, delay, and complexity, as a safeguard against arbitrary, capricious, or unfair actions by administrative officers. Finally, decision making of this kind is an open invitation for political pressures.

It should also be obvious that a process of decision making that is not based on highest competitive price must result in a lower revenue to the federal government from the federal lands. The difference may be great or small, depending on the criteria used and how they are applied. However, it should not be assumed that competitive bidding alone will always insure the maximum price and revenue. As has been pointed out, the effective market is so "thin" for many products from federal land that competitive bidding under no restrictions would produce a low price. There is always the danger of collusion among potential buyers. For this reason, most federal agencies for most sales on a supposedly competitive basis insist on some minimum price at which the bids must begin, the minimum price being established by an appraisal process. The competitive price often is much above the appraised price. Nevertheless, it is not unlikely that in the absence of such precautions competitive bidding in the past would have produced less revenue than has been obtained, because in so many situations effective competition was lacking. With the rising trend in use of federal land, this will not be as likely in the future.

Pricing of Products and Services from Federal Land

The desired goal of federal land management—maximization of the national welfare—must include considerations far broader than revenues and costs. At the same time, even with this borne strongly in mind, the latter are an important part of management; other factors being equal, a large revenue is preferable to a small one. A study of sales arrangements for specific products and services can reveal many of the problems inherent in the administrative process by which the federal lands are managed. If maximum revenue is not achieved, are the shortcomings of the administrative process balanced by advantages in the public interest?

TIMBER SALES BY COMPETITIVE BID [7]

With exceptions noted later, timber is sold from federal land on the basis of competitive bid. However, there are many steps involved, most of which require discretion on the part of the administrator.

Timber inventory. A timber sale must be based on some sort of timber inventory, an estimate of annual growth and safe annual cut, and a sales plan. If the maximum allowable cut is to be made annually, this requires an accurate and up-to-date inventory, by species, age class, size class, condition of the timber stand, and other relevant items. Timber utilization practices have changed so much in recent years that new inventories and new methods of calculating sustained yield have been required. Most of the federal forest lands contained mature old-growth timber when brought under management. Until these old trees have been harvested and young ones allowed to grow up in their place, there will be no significant net growth. However,

---

[7] Data on methods of timber sale, pp. 204-17, draw heavily on material published in *Federal Timber Sales Policies,* supplementary staff report, Public Works and Resources Subcommittee of the Committee on Government Operations, House of Representatives (to accompany House Report No. 2960, 84th Congress, 2nd Session), November 2, 1956.

under the sustained yield concept, harvest must not proceed so fast as to create a situation in which there is as yet no second-growth stand mature enough for harvest when all the old growth has been cut.

Timber inventories made for the purpose of calculating growth and yield on a national or regional basis need not be as detailed as those which are made to serve as a basis for timber management and sale plans. Inventories of the first type exist for the whole country but with different degrees of accuracy. Those of the second type are often deficient or out of date. As a result, in many areas the forest managers cannot be sure that they are putting up for sale all the timber that can safely be sold; nor can they be sure that they are not selling more than the annual growth. There is need for accurate inventories by working circles on national forests, and by sustained-yield forest units on the O & C lands.

Timber sale plans also vary in their degree of detail and specificity. A general timber sale plan is ordinarily part of a timber inventory; it shows the average annual volume of different species and types of trees that may be sold. On the basis of this the federal agency may seek to interest buyers if there is no active competition for timber in the area.

Size of sale. A basic policy issue is the size of the timber sale. If the volume of timber included in a single sale is large, then obviously only the largest timber processors can buy, for the smaller ones will lack both capital for large purchases and the sawmill capacity to handle a large volume within a reasonable length of time. On the other hand, if only small sales are made these may not appeal to the larger operators, and if sufficient timber is available from other sources they may hesitate to bid. A great deal depends on the general competitive situation in the area and on the relative supply of timber. Small sales are usually necessary for certain types of salvage and relogging operations.

The timber industry on the west coast generally considers sales of a million board feet or less as very small and even sales up to 5 million feet as small. A sale of from 5 million to 10 million feet is considered medium, and one of 10 million to 25 million feet is large; sales of over 25 million feet are very large. The federal agencies selling timber differ in the volume of timber they usually offer in an individual sale. During one eighteen-month period in 1954 and 1955 the Bureau of Land Management made 360 sales of less than 5 million board feet, 43 sales of 5 million to 10 million board feet, and 6 sales of over 10 million board feet, from the O & C area. Even as a proportion of the volume of timber sold, sales of less than 5 million board feet were more than half of the total. In the same period, Forest Service sales from the Willamette National Forest in Oregon consisted of 47 sales of less than 5 million board feet, 8 sales of 5 to 10 million board feet, and 13 sales of 10 million board feet or more. The latter included two-thirds of all timber sold. For its Region 6, which includes western Washington as well as Oregon, the Forest Service in the same period made 53 sales of 10 million to 25 million board feet, 16 sales of 25 million to 50 million board feet, and 3 sales of over 50 million board feet. Thus the Forest Service sales tend to run much larger, at least in this region, than do those of the Bureau of Land Management. (The Bureau of Indian Affairs in this same region has made one sale as large as 640 million board feet of timber.)

The record of competition in the sales made over this same period shows that for the Willamette National Forest, competition was lacking in only 13 per cent of the sales of less than 5 million board feet, but in 25 per cent of the larger sales. For all of Region 6 of the Forest Service, competition was lacking in 24 per cent of the sales of 10 million to 25 million board feet, 62 per cent of the sales of 25 million to 50 million board feet, and in each of the three sales which involved 50 million board feet. These figures strongly suggest that the larger the sale, at least above 10 million board feet, the less the competition. But one must be careful in drawing such a conclusion; it may well be that sales of any size will draw no competition in some of the large-scale areas because only one processing plant may exist in each area.[8]

The specific relationships for the Pacific Northwest would probably not hold elsewhere where the volume of timber per acre is not as high or the average logging operation is not as large. But there clearly seems to be some optimum size of sale in each situation; smaller sales will not attract the larger and often more efficient plants because they are not worthwhile, but sales much above the optimum exclude much of the potential competition. Aside from the question of getting the best price for the timber from federal lands—a matter which is considered in more detail later—the size of the timber sale has a significant effect upon the structure of the timber processing industry in areas where federal timber is a major part of the total supply. If sales are large, this will tend to force smaller operators out of business, and

---

[8] For the same eighteen-month period, there was actually somewhat greater competition in sales of 10 million board feet and more from O & C lands, than from smaller sales. All of the larger sales, although these were comparatively few, brought more than one bid; but in 15 per cent of the smaller sales only single bids were entered.

thus in time result in a larger average size of operation in the area.

Timber cruise and scale. The sale of timber requires relatively accurate information about the timber to be sold. If the inventory is recent, in sufficient detail, and applies to the same area of land as that for which the sale is proposed, then the data in the inventory may be sufficient. More commonly, timber inventory data will not meet these standards and a special timber cruise is necessary. The thoroughness of the cruise depends upon the value of the timber, and upon whether the timber is to be measured again after cut.

At best, a cruise is only an estimate of timber volume. It must be based on average timber utilization standards for the area, and these change in time as lower grades of logs become more usable. The amount of timber that a particular firm harvests, or its saw yield, may vary considerably from the volume estimated by the cruise. Such a divergence would not prove, though it may suggest, that the cruise was inaccurate. A major difficulty in producing accurate cruises is the necessity for allowing for log defect or rot, which may not be fully evident until the tree is cut down or sawed. Another difficulty has to do with labor: properly trained men are hard to come by and retain within the limits of the prescribed salary scale.

After the timber is cut the logs may be measured or "scaled." At this time, allowance for rot and defect can be made more accurately, since the poorest logs have already been eliminated; moreover, the dimensions of the logs can be measured rather than estimated. Given equal personal competence, scale should be much more accurate than cruise, but it is still only an estimate. Actual output of lumber may still vary from scale, depending on skill at the sawmill and on the accuracy with which rot and defect have been allowed for.

In the O & C area the Bureau of Land Management sells timber on a cruise basis. The Forest Service here and elsewhere uses cruise as the basis for timber sales, but nearly always bases settlement or payment on scale. Considerable criticism has been voiced as to the accuracy of the cruises of each agency. This is more serious in the case of the Bureau of Land Management, because the cruise is the final basis of payment.

Timber appraisal. The laws applicable to most federal timber sales require that the timber be sold at not less than the appraised price; hence an appraisal must be made. The appraisal also provides possible buyers with estimates of value of the timber which may supplement the data on volume and grade of logs, and thus assist them in arriving at a bid.

To calculate the value of the timber, the appraiser ordinarily starts by determining what the value of the timber would be at the first point in the logging and manufacturing process where a recognized market for the product exists. In some areas this may be for logs at a central point; in the Pacific Northwest the Forest Service bases its appraisals on log prices along the Columbia River or at other recognized log markets. Where there is no market for logs as such, or where it is believed that log prices may not fully reflect competitive values, the timber appraisal must begin with lumber values, which must include estimates of lumber output from logs and lumber prices at the mill. From whatever point the timber appraisal process begins, costs of cutting, yarding, and hauling logs and of necessary road construction must be deducted from the market price to get a residual timber value. In so doing, it is necessary for the appraiser to estimate a logging plan or "show" for the timber to be sold. This plan must be one which, in his judgment, is practical and at the lowest cost for the average operator, but which will also meet whatever conditions the agency imposes for conservation of trees and soil. The successful bidder for the timber is not required to follow this plan if he can devise a cheaper one that will also meet agency requirements.

After the residual value at the stump is calculated, the division of this residual into a stumpage price and into an allowance for profit, risk, and perhaps for interest or other costs omitted in the calculations, still must be made. For the O & C lands, the Bureau of Land Management makes a 50-50 split of this residual—50 per cent for the stumpage as such, 50 per cent to the buyer as margin for risk and profit. The Forest Service does not have a single formula, but splits the residual according to its estimate of risk and profit margin necessary to induce buyers to harvest the particular tract of timber. A uniform splitting of the residual has been criticized; it means that high-value timber that can be cheaply harvested offers a greater profit and risk allowance than low-value, high-harvesting-cost timber, which is exactly backwards from what would seem to be required. The Forest Service system, while open to the criticism that it does not provide enough objective standards for establishment of margin, is much more realistic in this regard.

A moment's reflection on the above process will suggest many reasons why a particular bidder may be able to bid more than the appraised price for a particular lot of timber. The volume and grade of the timber may be underestimated in the cruise; a more efficient logging "show" than was used in the appraisal may be possible; road costs may have been overestimated; perhaps the bidder is able to forego some part of the risk and profit allowance. Moreover, the usual appraisal process allows for depreciation and other capital costs of sawmills and other items; this is proper, for over the long run such costs must be met. However, this is not necessarily true for a particular lot of timber, where the operator has to meet only his variable or operating costs. For all of these reasons, bidders often can bid far above appraisals for timber; and, as will be shown below, they often do.

Sales methods. The sale itself may be by oral or sealed bid. If, over a series of sales, there is active competition in a locality and the volume of timber sold is not too large, enough bids will develop to bring in an approximation of the timber's full value, regardless of the sales method used, although this is not necessarily true of individual sales.

Where there is less competition or when the size of the sale is comparatively large, the method of sale can have a considerable effect on the purchase price. When timber is sold on oral bid a single bidder need offer no more than the appraised price; but when the bid is sealed the applicant is likely to bid above the appraised price against unknown competition.

Forest Service regulations permit sales by either method but provide that where competition is likely oral bidding is to be preferred. In the Pacific Northwest the Forest Service sells commercial timber entirely by oral bidding. In other localities where little competitive interest exists, written bids are used. The Bureau of Land Management sells O & C timber by both methods, except, under certain conditions—when the sale is part of a road use agreement with the owner of intermingled timber, he may specify oral bidding. Timber from public domain is sold by sealed bid.

The consequences of using one or the other method of bidding can be illustrated by data for all sales made by the Bureau of Land Management from O & C lands from July 1954 to December 1955, and for all sales from the Willamette National Forest during the same period.

For the O & C sales, when more than one bid was received oral bids brought 77 per cent and sealed bids 74 per cent above appraised price. On the other hand, where there was only one bid, oral sales brought only 1.5 per cent above appraised price, while sealed bids brought 27 per cent. In twenty-five of the latter sales, all but four were within $10,000 of the appraised price and nine were within $1,000.

For each of thirteen sales of varying size from the Willamette

National Forest during this period, all of which were by oral bidding, there was but a single bid, and in no case was it more than the appraised price. Thus, although in form the sale was competitive, it was in fact essentially, though not deliberately, a negotiated sale.

In fifty-five other sales from the same forest during the same period, also all by oral bidding but involving two or more bids, an average of 40 per cent above appraised price was received. There was great variation in the extent of the increase above appraised price, from as little as 1 per cent to several instances of more than 100 per cent. In general, the more bidders, the greater was the spread between the sale price and appraised value. The fact that there would be only one bidder was perhaps not known with certainty until the sale was actually held. If competition had actually developed, higher prices would have been paid. These were not negotiated sales in the sense of agreement between the seller and the buyer.

Size of sale and price. The earlier general discussion of the relation between size of sales and price can be illustrated with some data on the relation between sales price and appraised value, by size of sale. Sales from the O & C lands from July 1954 to December 1955 using oral bidding and involving two or more bidders, brought timber prices that averaged 81 per cent and 80 per cent above the appraisal when tracts of less than 5 million and from 5 to 10 million board feet were sold. Sales of over 10 million board feet averaged 56 per cent higher than the appraised value. When sealed bids were used the comparable figures were 72 per cent and 82 per cent for the smaller sales and 62 per cent for the larger. These data indicate that sales of over 10 million board feet bring a relatively smaller price; however, there were too few such sales to be sure this is true generally. For sales up to 10 million board feet, no significant difference seems to occur.

Sales involving two or more bidders for timber from the Willamette National Forest averaged 54 per cent and 77 per cent higher than the appraisal on sales of 5 million and 5 to 10 million board feet, but 22 per cent greater on the sales of over 10 million board feet. The number of such sales from this one forest exceeded that of sales made from all the O & C lands, and hence may be significant. For all sales made by the Forest Service in its Region 6, sales prices were 53 per cent, 39 per cent, and zero per cent above appraised price for sales of 10 to 25 million, 25 to 50 million, and over 50 million board feet, respectively; however, these figures include single-bidder as well as multi-bidder sales and hence are not precisely comparable with the previous percentages based on multi-bid sales only.

Large timber sales seem to have a double effect on price: there are fewer bids made, hence more single bidder sales; and even when there are two or more bidders the sales price is smaller in relation to appraised price than for small sales.

In considering timber sales with limited numbers of bidders, the possibility of collusion among potential bidders should not be ruled out. "Gentlemen's agreements" were said by the General Accounting Office to exist in and before 1953.[9] In at least one case, suit was brought by one lumberman against another, alleging breach of contract, one term of which was refraining from bidding for O & C timber. The GAO alleged that personnel of the two agencies "stated that they are generally aware that agreements exist between certain operators" to restrict bidding. However, in 1955 each agency denied the existence of such agreements in Oregon, at least.

If sales of 10 million board feet or more of timber from the Willamette National Forest in the July 1954-December 1955 period had brought the same percentage above appraised value that sales smaller than this actually yielded, total revenue from all sales from this forest in this period would have been 21 per cent higher than they actually were. If this percentage is applied to the roughly $100 million timber sales from national forests today, a large sum is obtained. This possibly represents the maximum additional revenue available from national forest timber sales, by adjustment of sale volume and in other ways. In practice, far less than this increase might be realizable because demand in some areas is too weak to permit higher prices for stumpage. Some increase in revenue does seem possible, however.

Criticisms of timber appraisals. Timber appraisals methods and results have received sharp criticism. It is understandable that under some circumstances buyers are willing and able to pay more than the appraised price for timber, yet when large numbers of sales over comparatively long periods of time average 70 per cent above appraised price, the accuracy of the appraisals is open to question. In individual cases, prices up to twice or three times the appraisals have been paid.

It seems utterly fantastic that the large increases over appraised price in multi-bid sales could have been based, for such a long period, on other than the true value of the timber. The weight of evidence suggests that the appraised price established by the agencies

[9] U. S. General Accounting Office, Office of Investigations, "Report of Investigation of the Sale of Government-owned Timber by the Forest Service, Department of Agriculture, and the Bureau of Land Management, Department of the Interior," I-17338 (mimeographed), March, 1953.

is materially less than the fair market value. As long as these base prices remain so conservative, large increases [in bids over appraisals] will continue. In addition, firms which purchase timber at the appraised price, either at noncompetitive sales or under renegotiation of long-term contracts, may receive substantial benefits.[10]

The low appraisals seem to result from errors in cruises and calculated costs of harvest and transport, and particularly in the method of splitting the residual between stumpage and profit and risk. There is evidence to suggest that the gap between appraisals and bid prices has widened in recent years.

In view of the tendency to bid at or only slightly above appraisals on many timber sales, the question may be raised: Why advertise the amount of the appraisal?

Revealing the appraised price in the advertisement of sale often serves to rob the sale of its genuinely competitive character. On one-bid sales the appraised price is virtually the negotiated price, especially in oral bidding. Even with sealed bids, the appraised price often determines the sale price if a bidder can be confident there will be no competition. Bids would more nearly conform to a competitive price if the bidder did not know what the appraisal is.

On the other hand, it can be argued that the more information the bidders have about the timber, the more likely they will be to pay what the timber is actually worth to them. The advertisement of sale contains the volume and grade of log by species. The appraised price serves a purpose if it reveals something of the relative accessibility of the timber. Offering a tract of timber for sale requires a considerable amount of work by federal personnel that would be largely lost if the only bid had to be rejected because it was lower than the appraisal.

One way to attack one-bid sales is to offer timber in volumes that permit more processors to bid and to reject in more cases all the bids (or the only bid) if they are unreasonably low. More realistic appraisals would also help. However, no maneuver is likely to produce many or high bids where demand is weak; and the federal agency wants mature timber harvested in order to permit new growth and to salvage what may otherwise be lost. Perhaps the solution to the problem lies in acquainting equally well both the agency and all possible bidders with the potential competitive interest in particular lots of timber, and to plan sales to take advantage of such competitive interest as does exist.

[10] *Federal Timber Sales Policies, op. cit.,* pp. 156-57.

Other terms of timber sale. Timber sales involve a number of terms other than price. There is the matter of a down payment for the timber at the time of sale. Through the decades a system has grown up under which the purchaser, in effect, is given credit to finance his timber purchases. After he makes the down payment at the time of purchase, he pays only as the timber is cut. The payments are arranged so that he has always paid for somewhat more timber than he has yet harvested, up to the end of the contract. This is necessary to provide a margin of error against the possibility of cuts larger than estimated, and to assure that the purchaser will complete the contract. The amount of down payment for national forest timber sales is determined by the officers in charge of the sale; it is not a constant percentage, nor one varying directly with size of timber sale. The Bureau of Land Management requires a down payment on O & C sales that varies according to the size of the sale from 20 per cent for the first $1,000 of sale price to 3 per cent of the estimated value of the contract for sales of over $1 million.

Longer contracts for timber sale generally provide for renegotiation. The Bureau of Land Management provides for reappraisals in contracts extending over two years, but the reappraised price cannot be less than the contract price. In practice, this means that the government rather than the timber purchaser will initiate the renegotiation. On Forest Service sales reappraisals are made for all sales of five years or longer, and may be to a price lower than the contract price. Shorter contracts may specify reappraisals at shorter intervals. Since renegotiations of contracts involve use of appraised prices, with no opportunity for competitive bidding, the method of appraisal and the relation of appraised to sales prices become especially important in this situation.

Marketing and processing areas. The Forest Service and Bureau of Land Management have legal authority to establish various types of areas within which timber from lands under their jurisdiction must be processed. Under the 1937 O & C Act, the O & C lands have been divided into twelve master units. A marketing area has been established for each, within which the timber sold must undergo the primary stage of processing (manufacture of rough green lumber, or its equivalent). Sales are competitive. There is no restriction on processors' bidding and no restriction on establishment of new processing plants. In addition, the law provides that co-operative agreements may be made with private landowners under which the co-operator has the privilege of buying government timber at the appraised price without competitive bid. In return, he agrees to operate his lands on a sustained yield basis. The Bureau entered into negotiations for several such co-operative agreements, one of which in 1948 progressed to the stage of public hearing. However, full agreement between landowner and agency was never reached, public opposition developed, and eventually the whole idea was abandoned. Since then co-operative agreements have not been revived by the Bureau.

The 1944 Sustained Yield Act extends similar authority for national forest lands, the public domain, and Indian lands. Under the act an agency can create federal units which in many respects are similar to the marketing areas established by the Bureau of Land Management for the O & C lands. The timber sold from designated areas must be processed within certain defined areas. Within these there is no restriction on bidding by timber processors and no limitation on the establishment of additional processing plants. The Forest Service has established five federal units to date.[11]

This same act also provided for co-operative agreements similar to those provided for under the O & C Act. The Forest Service has entered into one such agreement with the Simpson Logging Company. It applies to part of the Olympic National Forest and runs for a hundred years. The agreement provides for purchase of national forest timber by the company at appraised prices and without bid. In return, the company agrees to operate specified areas of land in accordance with agreed-upon plans for sustained yield management. The validity of timber appraisal methods under these conditions is crucial.

USE OF RIGHTS OF WAY AS A MEANS OF
IMPLEMENTING TIMBER SALES POLICY

In areas of intermingled forest landownership where public roads do not extend into the federal forest lands, roads to haul out federal and private timber are likely to cross lands of both ownerships. In mountainous areas the efficiency of one route to tap timber may exclude all others from consideration. Ideally, such a road would carry the logs downhill continuously from point of harvest to point

----

[11] Units are located near Grays Harbor, Washington, including part of the Olympic National Forest; Lakeview, Oregon, including part of the Fremont National Forest; Flagstaff, Arizona, including part of the Coconino National Forest; Vallecitos, New Mexico, involving part of the Carson National Forest; and Big Valley, California, involving part of the Modoc National Forest.

of processing, avoiding adverse grades and hence high hauling costs. A road of the width and curvatures suited to modern logging trucks is costly to build, but when built it is likely to be capable of handling all the timber harvested in a watershed. Moreover, with the appraisal process used for government timber, whatever the building cost of the road system, the value of the stumpage is reduced thereby.

All of these facts suggest an obvious solution: one road system to serve all forest lands within a watershed, to be located where the logs would naturally come down. In many situations it can be shown that this is by far the cheapest way to harvest the timber, and that it results in much higher total values to all the timber than any other arrangement. While there are technical problems involved in joint use of a single road system, they have been solved by private forest operators who have built roads jointly. The economic problems—particularly who pays for the road and how costs are calculated and shared—offer difficulty, but these too can be solved.

One method is to amortize the cost of the road as quickly as possible and make no further charge except for maintenance; thus, each user has an equity in the road to the extent of the cost he has helped amortize. If the rate of timber harvest from different forest ownerships varies, amortization must be proportionate to ultimate volume of timber to move over the road. A different arrangement may be for one party to bear the cost of building the road, with other users paying what is essentially a rental charge. This method has been urged in the O & C area, where some operators would like to retain major control over the roads they have built or plan to build, and in so doing obtain larger payments. Whatever the method, whether amortization or rental, it is entirely possible to devise a formula that would result in equal charges.

The single road system for federal and private timber does, however, pose difficulty of another kind. If the federal government builds the road, presumably it could bear the risk that the charge made to a private operator might be inadequate to cover appropriate costs should the operator fail to use the road for all his logs. But if the private timber owner builds the road he is likely to request assurance, prior to setting his charges, that all the federal timber will come out over his road. Assurance of this nature might well interfere with the marketing of the federal timber. While the operator's road may be the most economic way to haul out the timber, it may not be the only way. A road charge based on such an assurance might seriously affect the competitive position of potential timber purchasers.

On the O & C lands, under certain conditions, the Bureau of Land Management requires the right to cross private lands as a condition to granting federal right of way.

> Where a road system is adequate or can economically be made adequate to accommodate the normal requirements of timber haulers, the granting of rights-of-way across federal lands will be conditioned upon grants to the government with adequate provision for just compensation. Where a road cannot be made adequate to handle the normal requirements of both parties, the government will not request rights. In entering into a right-of-way agreement the government will seek to reduce all the terms and the costs to specific statements and fixed figures. Provision is made for arbitration of disagreements by the road owner and the purchaser of government timber. Provision is also made for short-term permits.[12]

The regulations to carry out this policy were adopted in 1950, and somewhat modified in 1955.[13] The regulations have been criticized, particularly by timber owners who are unwilling to share the use of roads they have built with other potential buyers of government timber. On the other hand, they have been strongly supported by lumbermen dependent on federal timber. The problems of negotiating agreements would have been less difficult had the Bureau been equipped with funds to buy rights of way and roads on a large scale, and had it vigorously used its power of eminent domain to do so. These reciprocal road use agreements permit only those who enter the agreement with the government to use the roads. Thus, third parties in the same area whose lands are not included in these agreements are denied a ready access to market.

The situation on national forests is different. The Forest Service and the Department of Agriculture have taken the position that under the Forest Management Act of 1897 they lack the authority to deny a right of way to anyone requesting it. This view has been challenged on legal as well as on other grounds. Since rights of way are available on application, the Forest Service has no bargaining strength against a private timber owner who refuses to grant the right to use a road system constructed on national forest and on his land. Nevertheless, the Forest Service has sought reciprocal road use agreements, and has obtained some.

---

[12] *Federal Timber Sales Policies, op. cit.,* p. 16.
[13] Since 1950, more than 1,200 miles of logging roads have been made available to the use of buyers of O & C timber through 416 such reciprocal road use agreements.

Timber is ordinarily not put up for sale unless access to it by any purchaser can be guaranteed. The Forest Service has reported:

> In Oregon and Washington adequate rights-of-way have not yet been obtained to about 20 per cent of the commercial timber on the national forests. In most working circles sufficient access has been obtained to permit cutting at close to full allowable rates. Heretofore it has been possible to use effectively all available funds for timber sales administration by adjusting our sale program away from areas with unsolved access problems in other portions of the working circle. Opportunities to make such sale program adjustments are now getting scarce. We estimate that in Oregon and Washington approximately 150 million board-feet of the gap between actual and allowable annual cutting rates is involved in right-of-way difficulties.[14]

Each of these agencies has the right to condemn land or roads to provide access to federal timber. However, each has used this authority sparingly. Partly this is because funds have not been available to build all the roads needed. Partly, the agencies may have feared to arouse antagonism to their access-road programs, with possible adverse effects on appropriations. Certainly, condemnation procedures used in some areas would have to be used in others, and this, with limited funds and manpower, would be difficult. The stubborn situations have, in effect, been put aside for the present, but they will have to be met sometime.

OTHER METHODS OF TIMBER SALE

Although by far the overwhelming volume of timber from federal lands is sold competitively there are at least four other types of timber disposal from federal lands:

Free use of certain forest products is allowed. Such items as Christmas trees, firewood, mine props, fence posts, and lumber for home use may be taken without cost. Free-use permits are much larger in number than commercial timber sales, and the administrative work in handling them is unavoidably considerable, but the volume of timber taken today is low.

Noncompetitive sales are made where the volume is small and little or no competition is probable. Such sales are particularly effective

[14] *Federal Timber Sales Policies, op. cit.,* p. 17.

for salvage operations where the value of the timber is unlikely to be high and harvesting costs may be large; and where the main objective is not revenue but better forestry. Even in these cases the administrator may make an informal check to determine what interest there may be, and what value is ascribed to the timber. Sales up to $2,500 in value may be made from the public domain, up to 100,000 board feet from O & C lands, and up to $2,000 from national forests, without competitive bid. Such sales, if wisely handled, are quite important to certain local groups, and can be a major tool in getting better forestry. Their numbers are relatively large, but the volume is small. Liberalization of existing laws might well result in even larger sales of this type.

Exchange of stumpage on national forests for private land added to national forests constitutes a form of timber sale. Such exchanges include varying amounts of timber on both the offered and the selected lands. In these exchanges the value of the timber sold is based on appraisal only. The volume of timber involved in such exchanges has never been large compared with the volume of commercial sales, and they are now prohibited by the Secretary of Agriculture.[15]

Some timber is cut in trespass actions on federal lands. Federal land managers take a cold view of protestations of innocence in trespass, because this is nearly always the claim. But where trespass is inadvertent—perhaps through misapprehension of legal boundary lines—the trespasser should pay more than the market price of the timber; if he does not, there is no incentive to greater care in the future, and soon the federal agency is selling, at the option of the trespasser, more of its timber than is consistent with good forestry. Willful trespassers should obviously pay far more, and if persistent may be prosecuted for criminal trespass. Trespass actions, civil and criminal, are ordinarily brought under state law governing trespass, which varies greatly from state to state. In Oregon, for instance, innocent trespassers pay double the market rate for stumpage cut, and willful trespassers pay three times the rate. While the scale of trespass timber cutting from federal land today is nothing like as large as it once was, it is serious enough. Unless trespass is closely guarded against and vigorously prosecuted when found, the entire system of federal land administration could in time break down. The volume of timber going through trespass cutting is relatively small, but the administrative effort which goes into trespass detection and prosecution has to be relatively large.

---

[15] The numbers and acreages of such exchanges are shown in appendix table 24.

CONDITIONS OF LIVESTOCK GRAZING

In the case of grazing, neither the decision between grazing and other uses nor the decision between individual applicants is made on the basis of highest prices that can or will be paid. Grazing is recognized as a proper and important use of most federal lands, explicitly so in the case of the Taylor Grazing Act for the grazing districts, and more generally and broadly so in the basic national forest legislation; but it is specifically excluded as a use of national parks. The eligibility of various types of ranchers is also set forth in the Taylor Grazing Act as far as the grazing districts are concerned, and in the regulations applicable to such lands and to the national forests it is indicated in considerable detail.

A basic factor in the use of federal lands for grazing is "commensurability," or the rancher's ownership or control of sufficient private lands to care properly for his livestock in the seasons they are not on the federal land. The use of the public and private land, usually of different physical types, is thus explicitly tied together. The Forest Service has also used "dependency" as a measure of grazing use on national forests. As the term implies, this is the extent to which the rancher is dependent upon the national forest land for grazing at certain seasons. A rancher may have commensurate land that can provide feed at other seasons for the livestock he seeks to run on the national forest, but he would not be dependent if there were other good sources of grazing at the same season.

On the grazing districts, major use has been made of priority—the use of the same range prior to the passage of the Taylor Grazing Act or to the establishment of the grazing district. To be in the first priority class a rancher must have used that particular area of range for two consecutive or three nonconsecutive years in the five years before establishment of the particular grazing district.

The Forest Service has maintained minimum limits below which ranchers would not have their numbers reduced as long as other ranchers in the same area have larger permits. It has also limited the numbers of livestock that a rancher may run on a particular national forest. There are no size limits of any kind on the grazing districts.

These and other less important criteria for use of the federal lands have been applied to the allocation of grazing privileges on national forests and grazing districts. Once these criteria have been applied and the users of the range chosen, the latter tend to continue their use of the federal lands except as the need for adjustments in livestock numbers or season of grazing use is necessary to protect the range. At one time the Forest Service made reductions in grazing of established users for "distribution"—that is, to provide grazing privileges to new operators who otherwise would not have them. In recent years very few if any such cuts have been made.

Neither the choice between uses nor that between users is determined on the basis of highest payment. Competitive bidding for grazing privileges has sometimes been suggested but has never been seriously considered.[16] Ranchers are strongly opposed to it. It is doubtful that it would produce desirable results since the number of possible users of the range is limited in some areas by the few tracts suitable to a rancher's needs, especially considering the seasonal factor.

GRAZING FEES

Although grazing privileges are allocated on bases other than competitive pricing, they are none the less valuable, and a fee for grazing must be established. Establishment of grazing fees has had a long and often bitterly contested history on both the national forests and the grazing districts. After some years of fees at more or less nominal levels, and after the legality of grazing fees had been established, the Forest Service began action during World War I to raise grazing fees commensurate with the commercial value of the forage. To put the fees on a more meaningful economic basis and to meet the objections of the livestockmen, an elaborate study was made in the early 1920's. Data were collected on rentals of hundreds of privately owned tracts of range land, and a system of comparison between these and the national forest lands was developed. Following much negotiation and some adjustments, a new system of fees was inaugurated in 1931. Under this system, grazing fees each year are adjusted in proportion to changes in the livestock prices of the previous year. The actual fee in each area is based on a careful range appraisal. The average grazing fee per animal-unit month, for cattle and sheep combined, was about 10 cents in 1933, and then moved steadily upward as livestock prices

---

[16] Competitive bidding has been used for Indian Reservation tribal lands, the leasing of which is partly carried out by federal employees, but always subject to the approval of the tribal council. But even here the competitive bid idea has often been modified in practice.

rose, to a peak of nearly 70 cents in 1952. Since then it has declined somewhat.[17]

Livestockmen would probably argue that national forest grazing fees are as high as the forage is worth. The Forest Service has said that they are not. It seems unlikely that the full value of this grazing can be more than double the present fees.

The history of grazing fees on the grazing districts has been in many ways similar to that of fees on the national forests although the events came much later. The Taylor Grazing Act had merely specified that "reasonable" fees should be charged. In testifying on the act, however, Secretary Ickes and other Department of the Interior officials had stated that the fees would not be used to produce revenue but only to meet cost of administration. This cost would be low because the type of administration contemplated was at a relatively low level of intensity. Such statements were made in part in response to questions of western senators and representatives, whose livestockmen constituents, operating under depression conditions, wanted low fees. But Secretary Ickes was also trying to persuade the Congress to put the administration of these areas in his department, rather than in the Forest Service.

When districts were established under the act, no fee was charged for the first year. Then a relatively nominal fee—5 cents per head per month for cattle and 1 cent per head per month for sheep—was charged, and it was the same in all areas. When initiated, these fees were about one third as high as those charged for grazing on national forests, which in general were somewhat more valuable.

It shortly became apparent that the act could not be administered for the costs promised, and efforts were made to get larger appropriations. For a time the use of Civilian Conservation Corps and other special programs helped to offset the short appropriations. But the Appropriation Committees, especially in the House, increasingly questioned the larger appropriation requests and the low fees. At the same time, certain western senators opposed any increase in fees and objected also to some of the administrative actions of the Grazing Service. Three incompatible movements existed: the effort of the Grazing Service to get higher appropriations; the insistence of the House Appropriation Committee to make increased grazing fees a condition of higher appropriations; and the opposition of western

---

[17] The average fee paid each year for grazing privileges on national forest lands is shown in appendix table 2.

senators to increased fees. Matters came to a head in 1946 when the appropriations of the Grazing Service were severely cut to the level supported by the fees. That agency was soon merged with the General Land Office.

The Taylor Grazing Act was amended in 1947 to state more clearly the principle that grazing fees were to be based on the cost of administration. At the same time, agreement was reached with leading livestock interests that the intensity of administration should be increased somewhat, especially at the local level, and that fees should be raised to 8 cents per head per month for cattle and 1.6 cents per head per month for sheep. In addition, the total fee was divided into two parts, a range improvement fee and a grazing fee. The division of the grazing fee was also changed. The states and counties in which the land lay, which had been receiving 25 per cent of the total fee, now received no part of the range improvement fee and only 12½ per cent of the grazing fee. The remainder went to the federal Treasury.

Meantime, livestock prices had advanced greatly and national forest grazing fees with them, so that grazing district fees were relatively even lower than they had been in the middle 1930's. With rising general prices and salaries, the new grazing fees proved to be insufficient to cover the costs of administration at the level planned. Differences of opinion arose in the Congress as to how the costs of administration were to be calculated. The fee was increased again in 1951, to 12 cents per month per head of cattle and 2.4 cents per head of sheep. This provided sufficient revenues, and the Congress was willing to make the necessary appropriations to provide the level of administration agreed upon. More men were then available for management in the districts than at any previous time.

In 1955 the total fee was raised again. It now varies within limits in proportion to changes in livestock prices, much as does the grazing fee on national forests, but it is still the same on all grazing districts. Grazing fees on national forests meantime have fallen as livestock prices have declined, so that the relationship between fees on grazing districts and fees in national forests is roughly what it was in the middle 1930's.

The forage available on grazing districts is less valuable than that on national forests.[18] Had the formula applicable to the latter been applied to grazing districts, the resulting fee would almost surely be lower than the average for national forests, although probably higher

[18] The significance of animal unit months as a medium of value is given in chapter two, p. 87.

than the fee now in effect on grazing districts. However, the discrepancy would be less marked today than in the 1947-52 period, when livestock prices were high and rising.

Low grazing fees on grazing districts have for long been criticized by those interested in recreation and conservation in general. However, taken in comparison with the increases in revenues possible from other resources of the federal lands—from timber sales and mineral leasing, for example—the amounts are not large. Grazing district fees and rentals on nondistrict lands have yielded an average yearly revenue of $1,766,000 in the past ten years, reaching a high in 1956 of $2,386,000. The most generous estimate of maximum total grazing fees and rentals would perhaps quadruple the present fees and thus would yield an additional revenue of $5 million.

PRICING OF MINERAL LEASES[19]

The Mineral Leasing Act of 1920, as amended, applies to the leasing of various minerals on public domain and acquired lands, primarily oil and gas, potash, phosphate, coal, and a few other minerals.[20] The terms under which these minerals are available to lessees differ considerably, depending on whether the area is one of known mineral occurrence or is a strictly unproven "wildcat" area.

Where a mineral deposit is known to exist, and, in the case of oil and gas, where the geological structure of the area is known and is one that is likely to contain oil or gas, leases are awarded on the basis of competitive bid. The tract is put up for bid with the provision that the lessee shall pay a fixed known royalty rate—usually $12\frac{1}{2}$ per cent for oil and gas, but it may be as high as 25 per cent. The bidders compete for the tract with offers to pay an initial bonus which may vary from less than a dollar to many thousands of dollars per acre. The bonus is paid only once, but the royalty continues as long as oil or gas is found in paying quantities.

The arrangements for the submerged areas of the outer continental shelf are similar except that all areas, whether proven or not, are put up for competitive bid. The minimum acceptable bonus bid is $15.00

[19] See chapter two, pp. 95-101 and pp. 101-6, for discussion relating to the extent of leasing and oil production, including leasing of submerged areas of the outer continental shelf.

[20] Acquired lands came under the act in 1947.

per acre, and the royalty rate is 16⅔ per cent rather than 12½ per cent.

The arrangement for other minerals subject to leasing is similar to that for oil and gas, except that the royalty rate may vary according to the richness of the deposit and other factors. Some rate of expenditure by the lessee for development of the area under lease, and a minimum rental, are also usually required. In the case of coal, a lease is not issued unless it seems clear that there is a good local market for coal not supplied by mines already in operation.

When the competitive bidding procedure is used for oil and gas, the resulting payment to the federal government is probably about as large as it would be if the land were privately owned. However, the cases where this procedure can be used are relatively rare. Noncompetitive oil and gas lease applications can be filed for any federal land not explicitly closed to such leasing. The Secretary of the Interior has the power to refuse to lease land for this purpose to anyone, and in practice sometimes refuses to lease land when it can be shown that it will interfere with other uses. However, if he leases the land at all, he is required by law to lease it to the first applicant. Such leases are issued for five years or for so long as oil is produced in paying quantities, and are subject to renewal for another five-year term without requirement for exploration. In practice, all lands which now, or at any future date, may have value for oil and gas development, are leased long before the area is a proven geologic structure and hence available for competitive leasing. Much public domain has been leased where the prospects for oil seem so unlikely that the only purpose appears to be the disposal of leases to gullible persons. It is only when a tract of land previously unavailable for leasing has oil discovered near it and is then opened for leasing, that competitive provisions come into operation.

The Secretary of the Interior has authority to fix the rentals on nonproducing leases; however, he may not charge a rental for the second and third years of the five-year lease. In practice, the lease rate is 50 cents per acre for the first year, nothing for the second and third years, and 25 cents per acre annually for the fourth and fifth years, or a total of $1.00 for the five years. Leases may be renewed for a second five-year period at a rental of 50 cents per acre per year. This schedule of rentals was established in 1940, when the rental rate was lowered from a total of $1.50 for the five years. In spite of the general rise in prices since 1940, there has been no revision of the rental rate, and in most areas it is far below what is paid for privately owned land. The difference between what is paid as rental for federal and for private land is often not as great in the very early stage of speculative interest in a locality (when most federal land is leased) as it would be later but still prior to actual exploratory well drilling.

The low rental for oil and gas leases on federal land has sometimes been defended as an aid to oil and gas development, but of this there is some doubt. The lessee is under no obligation to drill or otherwise explore the lease, and in fact most leases are held for some years and finally dropped without exploration. The actual driller must buy the lease from the lessee, paying the cost plus, generally, an overriding royalty which largely absorbs the profit potential of the low rental. The government has foregone its revenue, not to help the actual oil developer but to benefit the lessee who, in turn, is likely to pay a lease broker a good share of his profit. The lease broker is the real beneficiary of the low rental rates. Low rentals may very well be the cause of the lag in the development of all leases, and even the development of proven leases, in recent as compared with prewar years.

Except for the low rental feature, returns from oil and gas leasing and from other mineral leasing on the federal lands approximate those from private lands. At present, more than two-thirds of the receipts from the Mineral Leasing Act come from royalties. However, if the rental rate on the nearly 71 million acres of nonproducing leases in 1956 had been $5.00 per acre for the first five-year period and $12.50 for the second five-year period, and if the same acreage had been leased, total revenues from rentals of nonproducing leases would have been about $95 million, some $75 million higher than they actually were.[21]

Even if it is argued that raising the rentals would have cut the acreage leased by half—a highly speculative assumption in view of the substantial sums paid for leasing some of the submerged areas of the outer continental shelf—total rental revenues would still have increased by $25 million to $30 million.[22] In any event, if acreage now leased solely for "fluffy" speculation were lower, this would in itself result in a net gain, to the Bureau of Land Management through savings in the processing of useless paper, and to the general public through reduction of nonproductive activities.

Assuming that encouragement of oil and gas exploration on the

[21]Data on these revenues are shown in appendix table 15.

[22] Compare these estimated increases in revenue with similar increases that might be possible from timber sales at maximum prices ($20 million) and from grazing receipts at maximum levels ($5 million).

public domain is desired, it would seem reasonably simple to devise a rental system that would provide incentive, based on similar, or even higher, rates than those suggested above, but allowing for a substantial rebate to the lessee if he expended in well drilling or other exploration funds equal to or greater than his lease payments. Such arrangement has been made in at least one case in Alaska, but on the basis of existing rather than increased rentals. The Secretary of the Interior has special powers for mineral leasing in Alaska; however, it would seem to be possible for him to do the same thing for public domain in the States; if necessary, the law might be amended. Such an arrangement would make leasing without serious intent of exploration costly, and hence would drastically reduce it; at the same time, costs to the actual oil developer would not be raised, but on the contrary might be lowered.

It should be remembered that the federal land managing agencies have never provided assistance to mineral lessees comparable to that provided to some other types of federal land users. Well drilling and other activities on leases are subject to supervision, but this is scarcely special help in the exploitation of the lease. Various federal agencies conduct research and provide information on different aspects of oil development, production, and marketing; but these aids are available for private as well as for federal land. The special expenditures to benefit recreationists, the investments to improve grazing capacity, encourage reforestation, or reduce erosion, have no parallel in benefits to oil and gas lessees, despite the high regard with which the Mineral Leasing Act is held and the large revenues it has returned to the federal government.

TERMS AND PRICES APPLICABLE TO THE MINING LAW

For the mining law minerals—the metals, for the most part—a different set of laws applies. Anyone may enter federal land, except national parks and other areas closed by law or administrative action to mining, and seek for minerals. He may "stake out" a claim, or claims, each of which may be about 20 acres in size. He may continue to search for minerals with the exclusive right to do so as long as he diligently continues his search. If he finds minerals he is permitted to hold the claim indefinitely, as long as he does the annual assessment work to the amount of $100 annually per claim. The figure of $100 was established in 1872 when it represented a far larger outlay of work and funds than it does today. Even this requirement has been waived by the Congress in a series of special acts over the past twenty-five years. He is entitled to use such forest products from the claim as may be necessary in the development of his mineral operations, and the grazing to the extent it is used by animals for his own use, e.g., a milk cow. He is not entitled to sell forest and other surface products from an unpatented claim.

The holder of an unpatented but valid mining claim on which a discovery has been made may secure patent to it. To do so, he must have the claim surveyed, prove that he has spent $500 in improvements on the claim, and comply with other legal provisions. In practice, the matter of discovery of minerals is usually not brought into question until a patent is sought for the claim. The law and the court decisions require that the discovery be sufficient to warrant an ordinarily prudent man investing further of his time and money in an effort to develop a commercial mine. They do *not* require that commercially profitable mining operations be possible at that time, or even at a future date.

If all the legal requirements are met, issuance of a patent is mandatory on the government. The Secretary of the Interior and his subordinate officers may not take into consideration the usefulness of the land for other purposes, the value of the timber, or any other such facts. When patent is issued, the owner gets full title to the land, including any surface resources; payment is $5.00 per acre if a lode claim is involved, $2.50 per acre if it is a placer claim—prices which also were established in 1872. In recent years a claim has often been allowed to land with stands of timber valued at several hundred dollars per acre.

It is evident that the government does not get as much from its disposition of mining claims as private landowners would expect from sales of similar land, nor even as much, in many cases, as the surface resources of the land are worth.

The mining laws were originally enacted to favor and encourage the miner in order to obtain development of minerals. Their extremely generous terms are the root cause of most of the administrative difficulties arising out of the mining laws. They encourage many people to stretch the already rather elastic provisions of the laws to unreasonable lengths in an effort to obtain land for much less than its full value. The arguments between the federal agencies and mining claimants revolve around such items as the validity of the alleged discovery, whether the land has been properly surveyed, whether the requisite improvements have been made, whether proper notice has been given about the patenting in order to permit possible rival claimants to come forward, and so on; but usually the real basis of argument is the effort to apply the law where in fact it does not apply.

The act of 1955[23] which prohibits, for claims filed after its passage, the use of unpatented mining claims for purposes other than mining, provides some alleviation of the abuses of the mining laws and, besides, removes from their operation sand, gravel, and other building materials. But the act does not affect claims already filed, nor does it affect land use after patent is issued. If the land within mining claims were to be patented only on payment of a reasonable appraised price for the surface resources instead of the present arbitrary and out-of-date prices fixed by law, most of the argument over applicability of the law would disappear because the potential nonmining profits would also disappear.

PAYMENTS FOR WATERSHED MANAGEMENT

Only limited payments are made for the water which flows off federal land and no payments are made for watershed management as such. Hydroelectric plants on federal lands, under license from the Federal Power Commission, pay for water through payments based on horsepower capacity and on kilowatt hours of power generated. They also pay annual fees for occupancy of the federal land. However, these payments are essentially for stream flow, not for watershed management.

In general, water in the western states is appropriable under state law, and irrigation districts and others have appropriated most of the stream flows, sometimes adding storage and stream regulating mechanisms as well. In the southern and eastern states, water is generally controlled under a different type of state law embracing the old English riparian doctrine. Under this doctrine anyone owning land bordering on a stream or lake may use the water as he wishes, as long as neither its quality nor its quantity is impaired. Except as noted above, in almost no case does the owner of watershed land, whether federal government or private individual, receive payment for the stream flow which originates on his land. While he might be sued by some downstream landowner if he deliberately lowers the

[23] 30 USC 612.

quality of the water or changes its seasonal flow characteristics, in practice he can carry out a wide variety of protective land uses and measures without incurring legal sanctions, and, also, without reimbursement for improved value of stream flow.

All of this means that there is no financial incentive to good watershed management as such. There are, however, major public benefits. Sometimes measures undertaken for good grazing or forestry management are also good watershed management, but this is not necessarily so. Often additional measures could well be undertaken which would increase the total water flow, improve its seasonal distribution, or improve its quality, but only at the expense of some direct return from the land. In these cases, the federal government might decide to undertake the necessary measures. Some cities have acquired land for municipal watershed purposes, in order to have greater control over the areas, and have borne the expense of watershed ownership, management, and control because of the benefits they obtained. This kind of public service is clearly beyond the scope of the private landowner.

CHARGES FOR RECREATION ON FEDERAL LAND

Recreation from the federal lands is available under varying terms, depending on the type of land and the type of recreation enjoyed. On the grazing districts recreational use has always been free; and on the national forests it is for the most part free. Hiking and riding, for instance, in no case involve fees and, except in certain areas, camping, picnicking, hunting, and fishing, are also freely come by. So far as hunting and fishing are concerned, a special fee is charged in some areas in co-operation with the states in which the areas lie. Licenses to hunt or fish, regardless of whether the land so employed is federal or state managed, are always a state rather than a federal preserve. Fifty-seven of the larger and more heavily used recreation areas in the national forests are under permit to concessionaires, who charge moderate fees for the use of camping or picnicking facilities and are required to provide adequate sanitation and maintenance standards on the areas. Of nearly 46 million recreational visits to all national forest areas in 1955, 1 million were made to these charge areas. In addition, occupancy fees are charged for recreational residences, organization camps, resorts, and in some cases for winter sports.

In most of the national parks an entrance fee, varying from $1.00

to $10.00 per car, is charged. The total fees are only a small fraction of the costs of administering the national parks and, in general, their scale is based on historical and arbitrary decisions. High fees have been avoided, but the fees are higher in parks maintaining a long distance of improved roads and a relatively large amount of interpretational and other tourist service.

Total revenues from charges for recreation on federal land are well under $10 million annually at present, with total visits running well above 100 million.

It has always been a public policy, with strong popular support, that public recreation areas, whether federal, state, or local, should provide for those who cannot afford private recreation; thus, maximum or competitive revenue from the public recreation areas has never been attempted. At the same time it must be recognized that the enormously increased demands of the future are unlikely to be met without increasing expense, involving perhaps higher taxes if free or low-cost availability is to be maintained.

PRICES FOR LAND SOLD AND LEASED

When the federal government disposes of land or permits its use for rights of way, many highly variable and inconsistent provisions come into effect which depend on the particular law under which the land is obtained. At one extreme are the Homestead Act, Desert Land Act, and various other laws through which the applicant can obtain the land virtually free or on payment of a nominal filing fee, or can secure it for a flat sum per acre. Where the latter is true, the sum paid usually was fixed by law in the nineteenth century. In part, the large volume of applications for federal land—often filed under laws not applicable to the type of land sought—is due to these low prices. Isolated tracts of public domain are sold by competitive bid under Section 14 of the Taylor Grazing Act, but with a minimum appraised price. In this case, the owner of adjoining land has a preference right to buy the land if he meets any alternative bid or if he is willing to pay three times the appraised price for the land, whichever is lower. Land made available under the Small Tract Act is usually priced below the competitive market. In the case of rights of way, the charges are sometimes competitive with, and sometimes lower than, comparable charges for private lands.

Price Making Forces

Once timber or a competitive oil and gas lease has been put up for bid, it is assumed that essentially competitive forces govern the bids of the rival applicants, and that the choice between them will be made on the basis of their bids. This assumption may not always be true, since collusion or "gentlemen's agreements" may limit bidding for timber, or various types of imperfectly competitive markets may affect bidding for oil and gas leases. However, such imperfections are not now considered. Attention is focused on the price making forces when there is no competitive bidding, or upon the forces which attempt to influence administrators' decisions before the competitive bidding process, as such, actually begins.

When prices of the uses or products from federal land are specifically fixed by law, that is, are noncompetitive, the process is chiefly political. The legislators, the officials of the Executive Branch who advised them or consented to the legislation, and the various interest groups which supported or opposed the legislation, in most cases had in mind more than the collection of maximum revenue; their intent was to foster a certain kind of use of the lands, or to aid a certain type of federal land user. Although the issue is primarily political, ideas of economics may have influenced the participants; often—as would seem to be the case with noncompetitive oil and gas leasing—their actions may not have had the effect intended. Most prices of federal land or its products that are fixed in legislation were established long ago, often in the last century. Presumably they were not excessive then, and, with the passage of time and rise of land uses, they are certainly relatively far lower now—usually much lower than similar commercial prices. There are long lags between legislative action and changing times, in this field at least, especially since the public land laws involved are no longer of major national interest.

In situations where some measure of administrative discretion is possible, either in the charges that can be levied for the land or its products, or in the terms on which they are put up for competitive bid, many pressures are exerted on the federal administrators. Those wanting the land or its products will naturally submit all the facts, data, and arguments possible in an effort to obtain the most favorable terms. The lumberman who wants to buy a specific tract of timber under favorable terms, or the rancher who would like to have his grazing allotment increased, has a heavy stake in the final decisions that will be made. If first, individual, and more or less factual approaches are unsuccessful, applicants will often enlist the support of interest groups, urging them to take general positions applicable to individual cases. Upon occasion, though this is rare, raw political pressure may be exerted through members of the Congress or other influential persons.

These pressures are almost wholly in the direction of lower prices for federal land and its products. Often industries, of which the applicants are a part, will join in the pressure to lower prices. Ranchers who use the federal range lands, for instance, have consistently sought low grazing fees on national forests and grazing districts, and they have tried, with considerable success, to enlist the support of the national livestock associations, western congressmen, and the public in general. This situation is not limited to grazing fees; it applies also to the terms on which grazing privileges are granted, and is at least as marked in the case of rentals of nonproducing oil and gas leases. Such actions are entirely normal in a democratic society, and they are perfectly proper if kept on a reasonable plane of fact presentation and argument.

It might be argued that it is irrational for an industry to support lower prices or fees on federal land. Low grazing fees, for instance, do not benefit the whole livestock industry, but only those who graze on federal land, and they are less than half the industry. It might even be argued that low land costs give these ranchers an unwarranted competitive advantage over other livestock producers. More probably, the full advantage of lower grazing fees on federal land is capitalized into the private land used in conjunction therewith so that only the original owner of the land benefited. Similar arguments could be advanced in the case of oil and gas leases. As we have seen, low rentals on nonproducing oil and gas leases provide no help to the actual oil developer. The fact remains, however, that the various industry groups have almost without exception supported low prices for use of federal land, whether this action has been rational or not.

On the other side, there are few pressures leading to higher charges for federal land, its uses, and its products. Some interest groups will often oppose other interest groups on legislation or administrative action they believe to be unfavorable, and often this opposition will be effective. But they will rarely take action on issues concerned with prices or charges for the use of federal land or its products. The recreationists and livestockmen have not criticized rentals on oil and gas leases or prices for timber; nor have the lumbermen and oilmen criticized grazing fees or recreational use charges. As a result there have been no effective counter pressures from interest groups against individual group pressure favoring low prices or fees.

Some years ago the issue of a Congressional public land hearing in the West was the transfer of a certain unit of national forest to grazing district status. It had been proposed by local livestock interests. At the hearing every other interest group of the area (mining, recreation, fish and game, general business, and social clubs) opposed the proposal vigorously—so vigorously that the congressmen were persuaded the change should not be made. Whatever the rationality of the attitude of these local people, and whatever their motivation, it is significant that considerable numbers of the leading people in the area took an active public position on a land management issue; but the issue was not one that challenged the principle of low grazing fees. Had the proposal been to raise grazing fees on the national forest, it is highly doubtful if a single voice would have been heard in its favor, despite the fact that, in such a case, the county would receive 25 per cent of the increased fees.

Within government, pressures for higher prices and higher fees on federal land do, it is true, exist. But they are exerted only occasionally, not continuously, and hence not often effectively. Perhaps in part this may be because in these cases political influence is not sought as persistently as it is when industry and interest groups oppose higher prices and fees.

The Bureau of the Budget and Appropriation Committees of the Congress may urge a federal agency to make higher charges and collect more from the sale or lease of the lands and their products. But these are only annual pressures and are usually very general in nature. Agencies are not often compelled to carry out the programs proposed. On the other hand, the downward pressures on prices and charges are continuous, specific, and directed to particular points of decision. To a degree, the administrator cannot help being affected by them.

The federal agencies administering federal lands attempt to carry out not only the letter but the spirit of the law, as they understand it. On the whole their achievements are notable; in the circumstances, the wonder is that they do so well, not that they do not do better.

Use of Revenue from Federal Lands

The use of revenue from federal lands is closely related to the pricing of products from the land. The laws relating to use of these revenues [24] operate in different ways for funds of different source. This is important in considering the effect of the whole revenue-sharing process on appropriations and hence upon administration that is discussed in chapter five.

As we have seen, when the public domain was first established one objective of its disposal was to raise revenue for the new nation. This policy did not raise substantial sums; most of the money that was obtained went into the general Treasury in the same way as revenue from tariffs or from other sources. A fraction, however, was used to aid the new states in providing roads and schools, and to aid the new settlers on public land in getting established.

When Ohio, the first public domain state, was admitted to the Union in 1802, it was provided that 3 per cent of the net proceeds from sale of public domain in the state was to be granted the new state for roads construction, and that 5 per cent of the net proceeds was to be spent by the federal government for the construction of roads through and leading to the state. In return, Ohio agreed to exempt from taxation all land sold by the federal government for five years from date of sale. Also, the Northwest Ordinance, passed in 1785, had provided for reservation of one section out of each thirty-six-section township for the support of common schools.

When Louisiana was admitted to the Union in 1811, and Indiana in 1816, their admission acts provided that 5 per cent of the funds received from sale of public domain was to go to the states for the construction of roads, levees, and canals. Thereafter, this provision for payment to states of 5 per cent of the revenues from sale of public land became general, and has continued to the present. Five per cent of receipts from timber and miscellaneous sales from the public domain is also paid to the states.

RECLAMATION FUND

The first major change in the use of revenues from public domain came with the passage of the Reclamation Act of 1902. Irrigation had gone forward under private financing and construction from the time the Mormon pioneers entered Salt Lake Valley in 1847. But by the last years of the nineteenth century, the more easily developed projects had been undertaken and a cry went up for a government

[24] Summarized in Appendix A.

program of irrigation development. The first response was the passage of the Carey Act in 1894 which offered to give as much as 1 million acres to each western state, if reclaimed by irrigation. Although some good projects were built under this act, in general the states lacked the technical capacity and financial means to construct them efficiently. Many projects undertaken under this act were essentially failures. Even before the Carey Act had proved fully its limitations, demand arose for a federal irrigation program. There was much opposition to this in parts of the country other than the West. The question was asked: Why should taxes raised from all the people be spent to benefit one area, and by so doing increase the competition of farmers in other areas?

The political compromise which enabled the federal reclamation program to go forward provided that it should be financed out of revenues received from the sale of public domain lands in the western states to which the act was applicable. It was expected that these revenues would be sufficient to finance a substantial program of irrigation development. That program encountered serious difficulties in the twenty years following its initiation, largely because construction costs were so greatly underestimated.[25] However, from the time the act was passed until the present, 95 per cent of the revenues from sale of public lands has gone into this fund. This same division applies to receipts from timber sold from public domain. Later, additional funds were directed toward the Reclamation Fund. This was the first large-scale earmarking of funds from a resource for the development of resources; the difficulty has been that funds have come from one type of resource and have been used for another. Until 1928 the reclamation program was financed almost exclusively out of the Reclamation Fund, which also received repayments from irrigation contracts and revenues from power sales. In 1928 Hoover Dam was authorized, to be built from general appropriations.

USE OF NATIONAL FOREST RECEIPTS

When, in 1905, the forest reserves were transferred to the Department of Agriculture, Pinchot persuaded the Congress to allow the Forest Service to expend its receipts. These funds were to be available

---

[25] *Federal Reclamation by Irrigation*, Senate Document No. 92, 68th Congress, 1st Session. This is generally known as the "Fact-Finders' Report."

without the necessity of appropriation, for as long as five years after receipt. Under the appropriation act for fiscal 1907, 10 per cent of the receipts was given to the states for the benefit of roads and schools in the counties in which the forests were located. Revenues from the forests reached nearly $1 million in 1907—much higher than the Congress had expected. Consequently, it revoked the authority to spend receipts without reappropriation. It is interesting to note that at this time Pinchot presented revenue and expenditure estimates which indicated the national forests would be self-supporting by 1911.[26] He was about forty years too early in this estimate.

In May 1908 an act was adopted which changed the counties' share of national forest receipts from 10 per cent to 25 per cent; this is the share that has been paid ever since. The debates in Congress on this measure make it reasonably clear that the payments were in lieu of taxes on these lands.[27] Some members of the Congress objected to the payments on grounds that the revenue belonged to all the people of the United States, and that the states and counties in which the land lay could not claim a loss in taxes since the land had never been on the tax roll. Those who favored the payments maintained that the western states and counties in which all the national forests then lay needed all the revenues they could get to support even the minimum government services; that had the public domain not been withdrawn from entry for establishment of the national forests the lands would, at least in part, have been on the tax rolls; and that the states and counties performed certain governmental services on these lands, and thus should be reimbursed for the expense involved. In the end, this latter view prevailed. Explicit debate took place on the share of the receipts going to the counties; it was felt that 10 per cent was too small, but that 25 per cent was fair as a tax substitute. The funds were made available for roads and schools.

In addition, 10 per cent of national forest receipts are available for use by the Forest Service for roads and trails in the national forests. The remainder goes into the Treasury as a miscellaneous receipt.

In addition to cash receipts from sale of timber, the Forest Service can require the purchaser of timber to dispose of slash and brush or to put up funds which will permit the Forest Service to do the job itself. For other activities, particularly site improvement after the timber has been cut, the timber purchaser may be required to deposit

[26] Peffer, E. Louise, *The Closing of the Public Domain*, Stanford: Stanford University Press, 1951, pp. 92-93.
[27] *Congressional Record*, May 8, 1908, p. 5924, and May 11, 1908. pp. 6058-59.

funds in addition to the cost of timber to permit the Forest Service to remove undesirable trees and growth from the cut-over area and to reforest the area. The Forest Service may use these K-V (Knutson-Vandenberg Act) funds without the necessity of the appropriation process. This arrangement makes it possible for forested land from which trees have been harvested to be kept in productive condition. It is one of the few arrangements by which funds derived from the federal lands are spent back upon them for their improvement without loss of time or money en route.

USE OF REVENUES FROM MINERAL LEASING

When the Mineral Leasing Act was passed in 1920, it followed some of the precedents of the national forest distribution of receipts, but introduced some new ideas and new proportions. The Congress desired to aid not only local government, but also irrigation development, for by the time the act passed the Reclamation Fund had been in serious trouble for several years.

The Mineral Leasing Act provided that 37½ per cent of the receipts from mineral leases should go to the states in which the land lay, for construction of roads and support of schools. Thus a larger percentage than that of national forest receipts was made available, and the money went to the states instead of to the counties. At the same time, the Mineral Leasing Act provided that 52½ per cent of the revenues should go into the Reclamation Fund. This has amounted to a substantial sum over the years. Out of total receipts, only 10 per cent has gone into the Treasury as a miscellaneous receipt. Apparently the idea was held that the sum involved would approximate the cost of administration and that, in effect, all the net revenue should be returned to the states from which it originated.[28]

USE OF RECEIPTS PROVIDED BY TAYLOR GRAZING ACT

When the Taylor Grazing Act was passed in 1934, it provided still a different scheme for distribution of the receipts. Of the total, 50 per cent was to be paid to the counties in which the lands were located,

[28] The act creating the Federal Power Commission, passed only a few months after the Mineral Leasing Act, gave the states 37½ per cent of the receipts from license fees under the act, and provided that 50 per cent should go into the Reclamation Fund. See Peffer, *op. cit.*, pp. 131-32.

for such use as the counties decided. In practice, in all the states of the West these funds were turned over to grazing district advisory boards for use in making range improvements, and most of them were expended by the Grazing Service or Bureau of Land Management under co-operative agreement with the district boards; hence, the funds were actually used for range improvement. Twenty-five per cent of the fees was to be used directly by the federal agencies for range improvements; the remaining 25 per cent was to be paid into the Treasury as a miscellaneous receipt.

When, in 1947, the act was amended as part of the process of putting grazing fees on a cost-of-administration basis, the arrangement was changed for the grazing districts but not for the leased grazing land outside of districts. In the districts a separate range improvement fee was provided for; of the grazing fee proper, only 12½ per cent was to be paid to the counties (which continued to use this smaller sum as they had previously used the larger sums), and 87½ per cent was put into the Treasury as a miscellaneous receipt. The sums so derived are expected to pay the costs of grazing administration.

O & C AND COOS BAY RECEIPT DISTRIBUTION

For the Oregon and California revested lands and for the Coos Bay Wagon Road Grant lands still other formulas are used. When these lands were taken back into federal ownership in 1916 and in 1919, respectively, they had been on the tax rolls of the counties in which they lay for many years, at least to the extent that patents or certificates for patents had been issued. The counties, some of them thinly populated, had thus been receiving from the lands some revenues which they were anxious not to lose. The law provided that the counties were to receive tax equivalents from the lands, but limited to a share of revenues. This from time to time made it necessary for the federal government to appropriate funds to make good the tax deficiencies, a situation which continued from 1919 to 1937, when the O & C sustained yield act was passed.

Under this act, the basis of payments was changed for the O & C lands, but not for the Coos Bay Lands, which have continued on a tax equivalent basis. The act provided that the counties would receive 50 per cent of the revenues from the O & C lands in lieu of taxes.[29]

---

[29] In recent years these payments have been far more than taxes would have been. See chapter five, pp. 324-29.

It also provided that 25 per cent of the revenues would go into a special fund in the Treasury to repay past advances of taxes and the cost to the federal government of paying the railroad for the land; after these advances had been paid, the additional 25 per cent would go to the counties. When in 1952 all conditions had been met, another, possibly temporary, change was made: the appropriation act for fiscal 1953 called for a substantial appropriation for construction of timber access roads with the provision that the cost of these roads should be deducted from the "third 25 per cent" which otherwise would have gone to the counties. This change in the law took the form of a rider to the appropriation act, and as such was subject to a point of order. Had even a single member of either House spoken against it, it would have been stricken, without debate or vote. Its continuation unchallenged in subsequent appropriation acts rests upon the consent of the Oregon members of the Congress, which in turn is dependent on the consent of the Oregon counties. This is obviously legislation by the lowest possible level of consent; at any time in the future that the counties wish to overturn this method of distributing revenues, they can do so. At present, however, the counties get 50 per cent of the revenues plus whatever may be left over from the 25 per cent funds after deducting the costs of road construction, tree planting, and possibly other items.

Throughout, 25 per cent of the funds from O & C lands have been available for administration and management of these lands, if appropriated for this purpose. In addition appropriations can also be made out of general tax revenues. In practice, appropriations have never fully utilized the 25 per cent funds, but have averaged about half the sums involved.

MISCELLANEOUS REVENUE-SHARING ARRANGEMENTS

In addition to the major revenue-sharing arrangements discussed thus far, there are many that are less important. Of these, only three will be mentioned: (1) with minor exceptions, revenues from national parks and monuments go into the Treasury as miscellaneous receipts, and only in a few limited cases is anything paid to states or counties or is any part available for expenditure by the agency; (2) 25 per cent of the receipts from wildlife refuges are paid to the counties, in a manner similar to payments from the national forests, with the remainder largely available for expenditure by the Fish and Wildlife

Service for refuge management; and (3) 25 per cent of the gross receipts from the land utilization project lands now administered by the Forest Service are paid to counties for roads and schools.

The foregoing discussion of specific receipt distribution programs emphasizes the variations among them. They "just growed." Some highly inconsistent situations exist in some places in southern Oregon. There, national forest, O & C, and public domain lands are so intermingled that were three trees, located within an area the size of a large living room, to be cut, the three sharply different methods of revenue use described above would be brought into effect. The state would receive 5 per cent of the receipts from the sale of the tree on public domain and the counties nothing; the counties would get 25 per cent of the receipts from the sale of the tree on national forest, and the state nothing; and from the tree on O & C lands, the state would get nothing, and the county 50 per cent, or 75 per cent if it chose to forego building of roads.

The diverse arrangements this example illustrates were not based on careful economic analysis. Laws were passed providing for a particular distribution of revenue, with no real idea as to the amount of revenue that would be forthcoming. The most extreme recent instance of this is the O & C Act of 1937. The act provided revenue sharing instead of tax equivalent largely because the federal agencies believed this would lead to less revenue to the counties and because the Congress and others objected to the appropriation of general funds to cover tax deficiencies. In practice, however, the counties have received and are now receiving far more from their 50 per cent of revenues than tax equivalent, and ultimately, should they so decide, can receive even more. Neither were the various revenue-sharing arrangements made with an eye to the needs of the counties and states. Some units of local government in southern Oregon have received far more revenues from the federal land than they needed; other units have received far less, though they have expended funds to benefit the federal lands. There seems to be no relation between revenue received and equitable tax payments.

In only exceptional cases are receipts from the federal lands invested or "plowed back" on them. For instance, on the national forests the 10 per cent available for roads and trails, and the K-V funds, fall into this category; on grazing districts the range improvement fee can also qualify. Apart from these, almost all revenues from the federal lands go into the Treasury and must be reappropriated in order to be available for federal land management and improvement.

On the other hand, a substantial part of the total present revenue from federal lands goes into the Reclamation Fund, to assist in a program not directly related to the federal lands. As can be seen in appendix table 29, in both fiscal 1955 and 1956 payments into this fund from federal lands averaged about $36 million annually. This approximates the amount spent on road construction on these lands for each of the two years. The rationale of continued financial aid from the federal lands to the Reclamation Fund is not clear. The scale of the reclamation program since 1928 has been too large to be supported by the fund alone; substantial appropriations from general funds have also been made. There is no reason to believe that reclamation appropriations would have differed had there been no reclamation fund. On the other hand, this substantial use of revenue from federal lands obscures the revenue-expenditure picture for the lands.

LACK OF PRESSURES FOR MORE REVENUE

Earlier in this chapter the point was made that most pressures on the Congress and the federal land administrators have been in the direction of lower prices and fees for use of federal land and its products. Since the states and counties share in the revenues from federal land in the different ways described above, it might be expected that they would try to exert a counter-influence directed toward higher prices and fees. In practice, it has not generally been the case. Local governmental units have sometimes urged federal agencies to extract larger revenues from particular areas of federal land. But their urgings have not been backed by public support for higher prices or fees to be paid by local people.

Possibly the benefits of higher revenues from the federal land are themselves too diffused to stimulate effective pressure. The use of the grazing fees from grazing districts, described above, may serve as an illustration. When the Taylor Grazing Act was passed some people thought that it would more or less put the grazing district lands on the tax rolls, as far as local government was concerned. In practice, however, because of the influence of the western livestock interests, local governments receive no revenues for general government purposes; instead all the revenues are spent in improving the federal land, with consequent improvement of the local livestock industry and of the local economy as a whole.

Of the three major forms of taxes on land or on income from land —real estate taxes, taxes based on a share of net income, and taxes based on a share of gross income—the latter most resembles the federal government's situation with regard to revenue sharing. Only extremely profitable businesses can survive when gross income tax is levied, even when it is on a small percentage basis. The greatest net profits are obtained when an additional dollar of expenditure will return just an additional dollar of income; but when a gross profits tax is levied far more than a dollar of return is necessary. The units of local government get a cut out of gross revenue, whether there is a net revenue or not. Moreover, as we have seen, their share is not small. When the counties get 25 per cent of gross revenue, a net revenue above expenses is possible only if gross revenues are 1.33 times or more operating costs. If more intensive management or investment for some other purpose is contemplated, a net return to the federal government is possible only if gross returns exceed costs by a wide margin. Those businessmen who complain about the stifling effects of the federal income tax should try revenue sharing with states and counties.

To the extent that the appropriation process considers revenues at all, revenue sharing has an adverse effect upon appropriations. It is particularly marked in the case of appropriations for capital improvements or investment, which are considered in the following section. But the current administrative or resource management appropriation is also affected. If, for instance, another $1.00 or another $1 million, is appropriated for national forest management, and as a result revenues are increased, the federal Treasury has lost money unless a return of at least $1.33 or $1.33 million, as the case may be, is obtained. This is true because the counties get 25 per cent of the revenues. In the case of a private business, real estate and (net) income taxes are a part of the cost of remaining in business, and must be met. But they do not necessarily increase because the gross income of the business rises. The owner or manager of a business can afford to spend $1.00 as long as it returns $1.05, or even $1.01, because his net income will rise thereby. He may be forced to share his increment of net income with the federal government, and his real estate taxes may in time rise as he uses his land more intensively; but he does not have to share his increment of gross income. If private business were forced to bring in $1.33 for each $1.00 spent, the level of business activity would be far lower than it is today.

While a comparison of anticipated revenues from a given level of planned expenditures is not a major factor in the decisions that govern appropriations for federal land management, considerations of this nature do have some effect. If the federal lands were to be administered on a basis comparable to industry, the relation between expenditure and receipts could become much more important. The prospects of the larger role that federal lands may play in the total economy of the country have been indicated in chapter two. Looked at from a private business point of view, more intensive land management offers profit. But as long as receipts from federal lands are shared with the states and counties, there will be a serious obstacle to proper resource administration on an intensive basis.

Revenue sharing is not entirely to the advantage of the states and counties concerned. Funds obtained in this way are likely to be irregular both as to timing and sum, and may bear little relation to revenue needs. Tax rates on private property are higher where the need for revenue in relation to taxable property is high, and lower where the need is less. Some states and counties may need a larger proportion of income from land than the federal law provides; others may not require as much. The more or less accidental rate of oil discovery on federal lands, for example, should not have a major effect on local governmental finance. Chapter five will show that total payments from the federal government to all states and all counties, out of receipts from federal lands, are probably as high as would be the yield from taxes. Possibly they are even higher. The chief difficulty is that they are not distributed as taxes would be, either geographically or through time.

Another point should be considered. Benefits to local government from the federal lands are by no means limited to the revenues they receive. In many parts of the West a considerable part of the local economy has its resource base on the federal lands, and income is produced as a result. It is this income which supports the value of private property and thus the taxes on that property. The value of a rancher's private land is greatly enhanced by the federal range on which he also runs his cattle; thus, indirectly, the local government taxes the federal land. Its harvest of national forest timber to a large extent helps a lumber company. Tourists who are drawn to national parks create the basis for a local tourist industry on which taxes may be levied.

Investment on Federal Land[30]

Investment is needed if federal lands are to be most productive. Structures and roads must be built and maintained; equipment is needed to prevent fire and fight it; range and forest reseeding, brush removal, and tree pruning must be undertaken as part of changes in vegetative cover; and terraces, dams, and other works must be constructed as part of changes in the surface of the land itself. The variety and scope of investment is broad and varies greatly between different types of land and different areas.

Sometimes no clear line can be drawn between investment, broadly as the term is used here, and management in the day-to-day sense. Investment should be closely correlated with management; it should be designed to facilitate and promote good management. The latter in turn should provide the criteria and the bases for deciding the kinds and amounts of investment needed.

Investments on federal land require funds and, since investment of private funds through timber sales and other ways is relatively minor, these come chiefly from the appropriation process. The difficulties involved in this process are perhaps even more serious in their effects upon investments than they are for normal operations, because investments are likely to vary from year to year far more than do operation costs.

Confusion between the nature of investment and the nature of expenditure is another problem. Investments, if soundly made, have a flow of results extending over many years; but they are often considered as though they contribute nothing of value beyond the years in which the expenditure occurs. In recent years some attempt has been made in the federal budget to differentiate between construction and current management items, but even this has been incomplete.

---

[30] Complete data on investment in federal rural lands are lacking. The Subcommittee on Public Works and Resources of the Committee on Government Operations, House of Representatives, in the 84th Congress asked federal agencies to report current investment in real estate. When a summary report of this inquiry is published it may contain a comprehensive figure.

A more serious matter is the fact that investment does not always involve construction. Pruning young trees to produce higher quality saw logs some thirty years from now is surely an investment, but it involves no construction, no heavy machinery, and is almost wholly hand labor. Admittedly, it would be difficult to separate clearly investment from current operations because of the extent to which the two intermingle. Nevertheless, from an economic viewpoint the distinction is valid.

The optimum level of investment in the federal lands is not easily measured. On the one hand, investment in federal lands should ordinarily proceed at least to the point it would on similar lands, that is, where prospective gains from investment exceed prospective costs by at least as large a margin as would be possible from alternative investments. On the other hand, many of the benefits or gains from federal land management are nonmonetary, and therefore difficult to assess in relation to cost. However, consideration of these non-monetary benefits will usually lead to a greater investment than would be rational on purely monetary grounds. In any situation a careful analysis of available facts and a weighing of advantages and costs are necessary to achieve the ideal investment program—one which is both sound economically and acceptable in broad social terms to that part of the public most concerned with federal lands and most influential in their management.

No such analysis takes place in the appropriation process anywhere along the line. Even within the land managing agencies there is generally no careful economic analysis of investment costs and results such as a well-run private business would make. Analyses of this type have not been required by those making final decisions on appropriations and perhaps, even if they had, they would have had little effect on decisions. Since most federal land investments require a considerable period of years to bear fruit and amortize, it is admittedly difficult to make accurate projections. However, private business faces this problem also.

ROLE OF ROADS IN FEDERAL TIMBER MANAGEMENT

An adequate system of permanent roads is basic to continuous and intensive forestry. The road system facilitates both fire control and insect and disease control by making early detection possible and control programs easier to apply. It permits salvaging operations. In some forest types it is possible to predict from the general thriftiness of the trees which ones will fall victim to certain insects and diseases, and to remove these trees while yet healthy. Many of the damaged or killed trees can be salvaged without major loss in value if the salvage is prompt enough. Under some circumstances the gains from such salvage operations will pay the road-building costs. Permanent roads also permit economic thinning and other stand-improvement cuttings, thus adding to the rate of growth of the remaining trees.

Entirely apart from their contribution to intensive forestry, permanent roads, adequate to get out the logs, are necessary to the timber harvest. For each of the reasons enumerated earlier in this chapter, inadequate roads may be costly in the end even though initially requiring less investment.

An adequate permanent road system also permits multipurpose management of the forest area. Hunting, fishing and other recreational activities are greatly facilitated when public use of federal and state highway systems running through the national forests is augmented by public use of roads built primarily for forest management.

The importance of permanent roads in the federal forest lands has been increasingly recognized in recent years, and more money has been appropriated to build them. From fiscal 1947 through 1956 approximately $140 million has been available on national forests (not including forest highways) and $11 million on O & C lands.[31] In addition, substantial mileages have been built under terms of timber sale contracts. However, the sums by no means have been sufficient. It is doubtful if any of the various estimates of road needs on federal lands have been sufficiently comprehensive and forward-looking. It has been estimated that 22,640 miles of timber access roads will ultimately be needed in the national forests of Oregon. Of this, 4,802 miles have already been built to satisfactory standards, 3,360 miles have been built but must be repaired or rebuilt, and 14,478 miles are still nonexistent.[32] If, as a rough estimate, it is assumed that the average cost per mile of building these roads is $40,000, a total investment at present price levels of about $900 million will ultimately be required, more than two-thirds of which is yet to be made. It has been estimated that from $300 million to $400 million should be spent over a twenty-

---

[31] See appendix tables 10 and 31.
[32] Business Executives' Research Committee sponsored by Lewis and Clark College and Reed College, Portland, Oregon, *The Forest Products Industry of Oregon*, September, 1956, Part 2.

year period on the public forests of the Douglas fir region.[33] This would build 10,000 miles of primary access roads. An additional $35 million would be needed for 1,500 miles of lateral spurs and major branch roads, but these could be financed out of timber sales. Senator Wayne Morse, of Oregon, introduced a bill in the 84th Congress,[34] calling for the expenditure of $50 million annually for twelve years—a total of $600 million.[35]

It seems wholly probable that more than a billion dollars must be spent on road and trail construction of all kinds (except forest highways) over the next twenty years or so. On this basis, the approximately $160 million spent in the nine years following World War II does not look so large.

INVESTMENT ON GRAZING LAND

Investment on grazing land may be made for the purpose of increasing its grazing capacity, preventing erosion, and retarding runoff, or for a combination of these purposes. If solely to increase grazing capacity, the increased amount and value of that capacity and the permanence of the treatment can be judged against the cost. Range reseeding, often to crested wheat grass, has become common on both private and federal land in some parts of the West. Given at least average rainfall, if proper reseeding methods are followed on well-selected sites, range reseeding is as successful as dryland grain seeding. The value of the forage depends not only on its quantity and palatability, but also on how the grazing fits into the seasonal pattern and need for forage. In many cases the costs of reseeding are higher than the value of the forage, but the substantial federal subsidies available to private owners, amounting to roughly half of the cost, often make reseeding financially feasible.

If the major purpose of the range reseeding or soil erosion control

[33] Supplementary Staff Report to House Report No. 2960, 84th Congress, 2nd Session. Statement of Ed Stamm of the Crown Zellerbach Co.

[34] S. 3420.

[35] From fiscal 1947 through 1956 approximately $109 million has been available for building roads, trails, and parkways in the national park system (see appendix table 41). The National Park Service "Mission 66" report calls for the expenditure of $160 million in ten years for roads and trails in national parks and monuments, and for an equal sum for parkways. See National Park Service, *Mission 66 for the National Park System*, January, 1956 [processed], pp. 83, 88.

measures is to prevent siltation of streams, reservoirs, and other off-site areas, economic evaluation of the measures is more difficult. In many instances evaluation of the physical effects of the structures is difficult, and there may be far from unanimous agreement among experts as to the results of various measures. The problem is also complicated by the fact that the investment takes place on one tract of land and the benefits accrue to other areas, which may be in different ownership. Because it is interested in total benefits wherever they may occur, the federal government may undertake erosion control when a private landowner would not. Even so, beneficiaries should bear their fair share of costs.

Although the possible expenditures on grazing lands would almost surely be less than on forests for all federal lands, substantial sums for range programs are involved. On the grazing districts, a total investment of something like $150 million to $200 million in the next twenty years would seem to be reasonable for range improvement, reseeding, soil erosion control, and related programs. In 1951 the Bureau of Land Management proposed a program of range rebuilding in the West.[36] It included revegetation of 22 million acres, water spreading on 2.4 million acres, construction of 40,000 water conservation and erosion control dams, and other features. Its estimated total cost was $400 million to $500 million, part of which would come from private sources. Possibly as much as half of this program could be carried out if federal investment were in the range of $150 million to $200 million. The Forest Service has estimated that four million acres in the national forests need reseeding, and other range improvements are also needed.[37]

INVESTMENT ON NATIONAL FORESTS

The Forest Service keeps an investment account for the national forests, showing annual expenditures for investment out of appropriations and receipts.[38] Some items, such as equipment, are depreciated by groups rather than by individual items of equipment. Other items,

[36] Bureau of Land Management, U. S. Department of the Interior, *Rebuilding the Federal Range*, 1951.

[37] U. S. Department of Agriculture, *National Forest Protection and Management*, *"P & M" Budget Study* [processed], July, 1949.

[38] Data for the years since 1941, showing accumulated net values at the end of each fiscal year, are given in appendix table 8.

such as a building which has blown down or a road to be abandoned, are written off when no longer useful. The additions to the investment account are not limited to those made from appropriations and receipts, but include site-betterment investments from K-V funds, investments made directly by timber purchasers, and roads built under timber sale contracts. The additions also include transfers from other agencies, such as occurred when the submarginal lands were transferred to the Forest Service from the Soil Conservation Service.

Total net investment as of 1941 was $444 million, of which 47 per cent was for roads and trails, 19 per cent for land acquisition, and the remainder for a number of items. By 1956 net investment was up to $750 million, 59 per cent of which was for roads. Of the $306 million increase in net investment in these fifteen years, roads account for $239 million or 78 per cent of the total. Over $200 million of this increase in roads and trails has taken place since 1950—88 per cent as much in six years as in the fifteen-year total period. Approximately half of this increase in net investment for roads and trails since 1950 came from direct appropriations and the 10 per cent fund for roads and trails taken from receipts. The remainder, plus an amount equal to depreciation and write-offs, came from timber sales. This increase in value of roads due to timber sales is also a receipt to the national forests—one which does not show up as a cash receipt and hence is not shared with the counties or deposited in the Treasury. The mileage of roads and trails increased from about 105,500 miles in 1950 to about 213,000 miles in 1955.

The net investment in timber stand improvement shows a large relative increase, $15 million in the past few years. The net investment in other items shows only a modest rise over the fifteen-year period. From 1940 to 1950 net investment as reported remained fairly constant, new investment from appropriated funds and other sources being more or less offset by depreciation and write-offs.

This type of account is good and should be available for all types of federal land. At the same time it has serious deficiencies as an over-all capital account, even for the type of land to which it applies.

Its coverage is only partial: it includes nothing for land unless the land was purchased, and nothing for the value of stumpage or trees growing on the land. In 1953 there were 766 billion board feet of saw timber on national forests.[39] At present the average price of all timber sold from national forests is about $15.00 per 1,000 board feet.

[39] Forest Service, U. S. Department of Agriculture, *Timber Resource Review* (preliminary review draft subject to revision), September, 1955, chapter I, p. 49.

It would be improper to apply this price to the total volume of timber, which could not all be liquidated promptly at this price even were this desirable. Considering the time before marketing will take place, an average price one-third this high, or $5.00 per 1,000 board feet, is a more reasonable present price to apply to the total standing volume. On this basis, the standing saw timber is worth $3.8 billion, with no allowance for the value of anything smaller than saw timber. The value of the 160 million acres of land in national forests, with no allowance for timber values, must average several dollars per acre. While making generous allowance for the roughness of these estimates, it is apparent that the sum of the two excluded items is far higher than the present net value of past cash investments, which are reported at about $750 million.

Another deficiency of the investment account kept by the Forest Service is that it is in terms of prices paid after adjustment for changes in amount or condition of the property, but not after changes in price level. In other words, no allowance is made for the fact that an investment item may today be worth more than it cost. Lands which were purchased for the most part during the mid-1930's for $90 million could surely not be bought for that figure today. A timber access road, whether financed out of appropriations or by timber sale, may now have a value far in excess of its cost. Against this deficiency may be set an advantage: in the account useless investments have been written off in their entirety, so that there is a minimum of clutter.

INTERRELATIONS OF MANAGEMENT AND INVESTMENT

It is clear from the foregoing that land management methods are often closely related to investment on federal lands, and vice versa. Just how closely may be seen from the following examples.

A timber buyer normally can build spur roads more cheaply than the government. And they will be built to suit his harvesting operations. In the case of feeder and main roads, which are far more expensive, the situation may be different. Should the timber buyer build these he must buy a very large lot of timber in one purchase, which automatically reduces the number of potential buyers from the market and also may sharply reduce the net price the government gets for its timber. Data presented earlier in this chapter provide some quantitative measure of the extent to which this is true. It is obvious that, whether government or timber buyer builds, the cost of the road must be deducted from the value of the lumber in order to estimate the value of the timber that comes out over the road. Thus there can be no net saving to the government in arranging for a privately built road unless the timber purchaser is able to build an equally good road for less money. Effects on the county must also be considered. If the government builds the road, and hence the timber is sold for more money, the county's share is commensurately large; if the buyer of the timber builds the road, and hence pays less cash to the government, the county's share is smaller.

In many areas it is necessary to reserve seed trees when the timber is cut. Regulations for timber sale ordinarily provide that the officer making the timber sale may reserve such seed trees as in his judgment are necessary to insure a new stand of timber. In the Douglas fir areas it was once the usual practice to reserve three seed trees per acre. At current stumpage prices these may easily be worth $300. However, when these trees are due for harvesting it is often difficult to interest a logger in them, and he certainly will pay less for them than he would at the time he was logging in the area. An alternative is to cut the trees completely, anticipating that seed from surrounding forested areas will reseed the tract but, in the event this does not happen, being prepared to restock the area by seeding from a helicopter or by replanting with young trees. The former method costs possibly $10.00 per acre, the latter roughly $30.00. To remove all trees rather than to leave seed trees is good business if appropriations are available for prompt reseeding or replanting of the area; but if considerable delays are experienced, it may be good business to resort to the more costly method of leaving seed trees in order to lose fewer years in adequately restocking the land. Thus the wisdom of specific management practices depends upon the availability of appropriations for investment.

In the case of certain rights of way for telephone or electric power lines and where timber or other products have been harvested, it has been common practice to require the applicant to reseed the disturbed areas as a means of reducing erosion hazard or restoring the productivity of the area. There may be no basis of compulsion if the purchaser chooses to default on his bargain. If he has been made to post bond, the cost can be recovered but the proceeds must be deposited in the federal Treasury. The necessary work cannot be done unless an adequate appropriation is available. It was in part to meet this situation on national forest lands that the K-V funds, described previously, were established. The situation is even more extreme if a trespasser is apprehended for damage and is forced to pay perhaps double or triple the value of the resources he has taken. In such a case the Treasury may be ahead, but the land is behind, unless or until the necessary appropriations are made available.

Grazing administration offers another example of the close connection between investment and management. If part of an unfenced range is overgrazed, the only practical remedy may be to reduce stocking over the entire area, unless funds are available for water development in the less used parts or for fencing to prevent stock from using the overgrazed parts.

EFFECT OF REVENUE SHARING ON INVESTMENT

Revenue sharing with states and counties is also a sharing of appropriations for investments. Let us assume, for instance, that the Congress appropriates $1 million to build roads in a forested area, and that as a result of greater accessibility and more competition the timber in that area can now be sold for $1.2 million more than it could in the absence of the roads. Without the appropriation, the timber could have been sold and the roads built by the timber purchaser. While a profit of 20 per cent would strike most private businesses as attractive, the federal government in such a case would lose money as a result of having built the roads. Even in the national forests, 25 per cent of the timber receipts would go to the county in which the timber was located. Thus the county would receive $300,000 of the $1.2 million added income, leaving only $900,000 as a return to the federal government from its investment of $1 million. From the O & C area, if the provision for financing the cost of roads out of the counties' share of receipts were not in effect, the government would receive only 25 per cent of total revenues—$300,000 out of the added revenue of $1.2 million, thus leading to a loss of $700,000. Under these circumstances, the federal Treasury is ahead if the roads are built by timber purchasers; but this has the adverse effects noted previously. In some cases the increased competition with a road may raise timber prices enough to offset the sharing of revenue with the counties; but this will often not be true.

Everything but the most extremely profitable investments, by ordinary private standards, is thus made financially unprofitable to the federal government. This inhibits the making of appropriations for this purpose. The combined effect of these various forces and situations is a general and serious under-investment on federal lands.

Under-investment has had serious consequences in the past, but is likely to have even more serious effects in the future as the federal lands are called upon to play an increasingly large role in the national economy.

Summary and Interpretation of Pricing and Investment

1. A wide variety of pricing arrangements exists for the products of federal land. In part, these differences stem from a desire on the one hand to encourage certain types of land use or land users, and on the other to use the market-price forces; but one cannot avoid the conclusion that in some instances the differences are no longer rational. The competitive market is in no instance used as a basis for determining major use of land, and only for sales of timber and competitive mineral leases is it used as the basis of choosing among rival applicants.

2. Many pressures are exerted on the pricing process and on those responsible for it. These pressures may come when legislation is under consideration, or later when administrative action is undertaken. Their overwhelming weight is in the direction of lower-than-market prices for the products of the federal land; pressures for relatively high prices are diffused and dispersed, and hence not effective; pressures for lower prices are constant, persistent, and focused—the wonder is that they are not more effective than they are.

3. The pricing of products from federal land is partly economic and partly political. That is, considerations other than maximum revenue often are dominant, and as a matter of public policy products or uses of federal land are made available to some groups at less than a maximum price.

4. Prices and revenues from the federal lands are lower than they should be. Since this implies a judgment, it is necessary to state further by what standard they are judged too low. When any factor of production is priced below a reasonable market price, or marginal productivity value, this leads to its misuse in an economic sense. If some persons are able to use resources at less than full value, when in the nature of things others cannot be equally accommodated, a measure of unfairness is involved. Availability of resources at less than full market price involves difficult administrative problems. By each of these measures, the revenues from federal land, in total, are too low, although this may not apply to certain uses and certain areas.

5. The investment on federal lands is too low for their maximum economic productivity and social usefulness. The appropriation process by which the amount of investment is decided works to make investment lower than sound private business would countenance. Low revenues work in the same direction, by making investments appear less profitable than they really are. Although profitability of investment is not the major determinant of investment on federal land, it does have some influence, and should have more. The system of revenue sharing with states and counties also operates to keep investment too low, because a substantial part of the added income from investment must be shared with local government.

6. The whole process of pricing and investment works badly. This is especially true when considered on a strictly economic basis, but it is also true, though less easily demonstrable, when social or general welfare aspects of federal land use are considered. In particular, the whole process operates to keep an important segment of total resources at less than optimum productivity.

7. A serious side effect of the system of pricing and investment makes administration of the federal lands more difficult. The administrators are called upon to make many decisions, often under considerable pressure, between land uses and between applicants. They must face pressures for lower prices of the products of federal land with almost no countervailing pressures to aid them. The importance of making some resources available at less than market prices, and of aiding certain types of federal land users, may more than balance the difficulties, although this should not be accepted as proven. But the inevitable consequence is a more cumbersome and slower-moving administrative system, with more "red tape," more opportunity for appeals, and less decisive administration generally. Moreover, great opportunities for favoritism exist; that they have been taken advantage of so infrequently testifies to the integrity and high standards of federal land administrators.

CHAPTER FIVE

Revenues and Expenditures

FOR SOME FEDERAL LAND USES, NOTABLY REC-
reation and watershed management, revenues and
expenditures offer unsuitable measures. Yet for those uses that can
be expressed in monetary terms, financial measures provide a common
denominator useful to analysis. In this chapter specific attention is
directed to revenues and expenditures because they are important
though not dominant features of federal land management.

It should be a matter of national concern that the expenditures for
current management and capital investment on the federal lands are
at an appropriate level, so that to the extent that it is economic the
full productivity of the resources is realized. The demands of all types
for federal land are rising; the ability of the lands to satisfy demands
will depend in considerable part upon the amount of investment that
is made in them. The relation between receipts and expenditures is
also closely tied to the matter of efficiency and economy of government
administration, and is thus of general concern.

Before examining receipts and expenditures as they apply to the
various types of federal land we are studying, some conceptual and
definitional matters must be considered.

Levels of Economic Analysis

Receipts or revenues from federal land are not income in the strictly
economic sense of the word. They are *cash:* they are more than annual
income to the extent that they include money received from the sale

of capital assets, and less than annual income to the extent that they exclude increasing value of assets managed.[1] But as a practical matter, nearly all of the cash receipts, except from the sale of land, are income. Receipts from timber sales are income if the timber is managed under a sustained-yield program and sales are less than or equal to the sustained annual yield. Mineral leasing revenues are in one sense the sale of assets since they are derived from the sale of a nonrenewable resource. The bonus paid for a mineral lease might be construed to represent the sale of a capital asset, but a rental receipt from a mineral lease would be income. The royalties accruing to private owners are considered income under usual accounting practices and for income tax purposes, but a depletion allowance exempts a portion of these receipts from taxation.

On the other side of the account, not all the cash expenditures each year are annual costs, in a useful economic sense of that term. They often contain funds for capital outlays, especially for roads and buildings. Some of the money spent for this purpose can be shown separately, but in many cases it is difficult to separate what has been spent for management from what has been spent for capital improvement, partly because the two types of expenditure are often closely interwoven. The expenditures by the land managing agencies also generally include some money for activities not strictly related to the management of the lands. Surveys of various kinds, general information gathering of all sorts, and other comparatively small items are included here, although it is usually possible to identify and exclude the major research expenditures. Cash expenditures also exclude charges that private enterprises would consider as operating costs—charges for annual depreciation and for interest on past investments. The amount spent annually for improvements in recent years has generally been above the level of the depreciation charge on earlier investment expenditures; hence, cash expenditures have not been lower than annual operating costs.

In this study no attempt has been made to put cash receipt and cash expenditure data on a basis of annual income and annual operating cost. To do so with precision would have been difficult in view of the nature of the data available, and in some cases the lack of it. Instead, the discussion is entirely in terms of "receipts" or "revenues" rather than "income," and of "expenditures" rather than "costs." The

---

[1] If an accrual system of bookkeeping is used, an accounting of any net changes in inventory is required before income can be determined. The federal government, however, uses a cash rather than an accrual system.

expenditure data are not actual expenditures, since these are not precisely known until two years after the fiscal year to which they apply has closed. They are "obligations." The difference between the two is not great although obligations tend to be larger than expenditures because most agencies tend to obligate a little above actual expenditures to insure that sufficient funds have been set aside to cover all contingencies.

There is another complication to the presentation of adequate data on land receipts and expenditures. Appropriations are made to agencies, whereas our concern is with land. As far as possible, in what follows, discussion and analysis are in terms of a land area, not of an agency. Activities of the agencies which do not relate to the lands are excluded. In this some inconsistency is unavoidable, but it is believed that on the whole substantial accuracy has been achieved. The general overhead administrative costs of each of the four major land managing agencies have been prorated roughly among the activities of the agency, and only those chargeable to land have been included among the expenditure data on land. However, for the Bureau of Land Management and the National Park Service, which have few functions other than land management, all costs of the agency have been included.

This is the most direct level of economic analysis of federal land receipts and expenditures. In addition there are at least three other less direct levels at which they may be considered. Even if an accounting system were established to reflect the true income and cost situation on the federal lands, an appraisal of the economic efficiency of these lands in contrast to state and private lands would be in error unless the contribution that the lands make to the economic life of the nation and to the community in which they are located is recognized, and unless federal expenditures on private land are shown as a charge against that land or similar expenditures on federal lands are deducted before comparisons are made.

The federal government makes substantial subsidies through grants-in-aid to the states, to encourage forest fire fighting on private land. Presumably, there is a sufficient public service in this to justify the expenditure of public money. However, the cost of fire fighting on federal land is borne entirely out of annual appropriations, and thus its full cost appears as an expenditure against these lands. If the same subsidy or grant-in-aid were available to federal land as is available to private land, the cost chargeable against the federal land would be lower on this account.

A similar situation exists with respect to soil conservation and range improvement practices of various kinds. The federal government makes technical aid available free to farmers through the Soil Conservation Service, and it extends direct financial aid to farmers to carry but soil conservation and improvement practices through the Agricultural Conservation Program. In contrast, similar activities on federal land must be paid entirely from appropriations, except as the private users of these lands make voluntary contributions to their improvement. Ranchers can obtain payments covering up to roughly half the costs of range reseeding, range land contouring, stock pond building, and various other practices on their own lands.

Another type of indirect subsidy arises out of the fact that the federal government pays the full cost of building roads on some types of federal lands, notably national parks. Those who use these roads buy gasoline and pay state taxes on it. The states concerned gain the full value of the tax for the gasoline used on these roads and bear no share of the roads' original cost or of their upkeep. It is true that the federal government makes grants to states to build other roads and that the state benefits from the value of the gas tax to the extent the roads are used; but in such cases the state usually bears part of the road's construction cost and all of its maintenance cost.

Later in this chapter an attempt will be made to estimate the rough magnitude of these items. Rough as they necessarily are, these estimates may serve to give some idea of the extent to which the federal land is discriminated against through federal subsidies to private land.

A second level of indirect benefit from federal lands is the contribution the lands make to the local or regional economy. This is true for much lumbering and ranching, for instance; and for recreation, too, where national parks and forests attract people to a locality. The productivity of the federal land is translated into private income and private profit, and through the taxation of private property, into taxes for the support of local government. The costs of the federal lands to the communities in which they are located must be balanced against such benefits, the extent of which has yet to be measured.

A third level of indirect benefits is the contribution of the federal lands to the national economy. This is, in general, far less than the sum of the indirect contribution to the various local and regional economies. To some extent the use and productivity of federal lands in one locality merely substitutes for the use and productivity of other lands in other ownerships in other localities. If no grazing were allowed on any federal lands, the livestock of the country would find feed somewhere else—perhaps fewer livestock, and perhaps at higher cost. Measurement is impractical. But to the extent that there are no alternatives for federal lands—as might well be argued for some of the more outstanding national parks—or to the extent that the alternatives are poorer in quality or lower in productivity, the federal lands may be said to make a direct contribution to the national welfare.

Revenues from and Expenditures on National Forests [2]

The pattern of analysis used here for the national forests will be followed subsequently, insofar as data and nature of programs permit, for each of the four major types of federal land administered by the four major land managing agencies—Bureau of Land Management, Fish and Wildlife Service, Forest Service, and National Park Service.

REVENUES FROM NATIONAL FORESTS

Rapidly increasing revenues (shown in figure 14 and in appendix table 5) [3] reflect the increased use made of national forest resources in recent years. Receipts alone, however, do not tell the whole story of use, for they exclude such major uses of these lands as recreation and watersheds.

---

[2] The charts showing revenues, expenditures, and related financial items for the national forests and other types of federal land management units discussed in this chapter have been drawn to two different scales. An effort has been made to use, wherever possible, the same horizontal and vertical scales for comparable charts. The two vertical scales, designated A and B, are so drawn that scale B is one tenth as large as scale A. Readers are warned to observe the scales carefully before making comparisons between charts. In each case comparisons between total revenues and total expenditures are on the basis of the B scale to permit comparisons between types of land and also, in figures 27 and 28, a summation of all federal lands.

It should be noted that all revenue projections assume normal or trend-line conditions in 1960 and 1980; actual revenues might be unusually high or unusually low in a particular year.

[3] In addition to the revenues, shown in appendix table 5, there were revenues from the formerly controverted O & C lands, which are shown in appendix table 13. These have been included in figure 14.

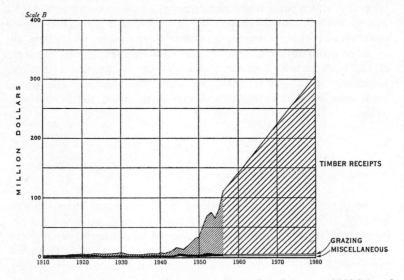

FIGURE 14. *Sources of receipts from the national forests, 1910-56 and projections for 1960 and 1980.*

In recent years cash revenues from national forests have been dominated by the sale of timber. Up to about 1920 cash revenues from grazing fees and timber sales were roughly equal; through the 1920's timber sale receipts were generally higher, sometimes twice as high as grazing fees; and they were roughly equal again in the early 1930's, when timber sales were greatly reduced. After that, timber sale cash receipts increased tremendously until in 1956 they were roughly thirty-five times as large as grazing receipts. Approximately half of the fifteen-fold increase in total revenues from 1942 to 1956 is due to a rise in the general price level; the rest largely reflects increased output. Throughout the whole period there have been minor cash receipts from miscellaneous sources, including some from the land utilization areas transferred to the Forest Service from the Soil Conservation Service in 1953.

Projections of future revenues from the national forests depend almost entirely upon estimates of timber sales since these are now so nearly the total of all revenues. These, presented in chapter two (figure 8), envisage a sale of 9 billion board feet of timber in 1960 and 15 billion feet in 1980. Stumpage prices have averaged about $15.00 per thousand board feet in recent years and will probably continue to rise even given a stable general price level.[4] No attempt to make a careful statistical analysis of the probable extent of this price rise is involved here, but on a purely judgment basis, an average price of $15.00 and $20.00 per thousand board feet is assumed for 1960 and 1980 respectively. This would yield $135 million in 1960 and $300 million in 1980 from timber sales. Adding to this the revenues from the formerly controverted O & C lands and miscellaneous receipts, including grazing fees, total cash revenues may be estimated at $148.8 million and $318 million respectively.[5]

It should be emphasized that these are *cash* revenues only; in addition, there are certain revenues that can best be described as "in kind," the nature and amount of which will be described later. There are also major products from the national forests of great economic importance which do not produce cash revenues. The Forest Service in 1949 estimated that for 1948 the value of water, recreation, and other miscellaneous services provided free amounted to $337 million.[6] While its estimate may have been high, there is little doubt that the values are large and probably exceed by a wide margin the cash revenues. These cash revenue data also omit increases in inventory value of the growing timber and of the land itself. In the same study, the Forest Service estimates that for 1948 this amounted to $65 million.

DISTRIBUTION OF CASH REVENUES

With few exceptions, 25 per cent of the cash receipts from the national forests is distributed to the counties within which the national forests lie, 10 per cent is returned to the Forest Service for expenditure on roads and trails, and the remaining 65 per cent is deposited in the Treasury's general fund. (The pertinent data are in appendix tables 7 and 52.) Receipts from that part of the national forests which was formerly controverted O & C land are distributed accord-

[4] U. S. Department of Agriculture, Forest Service, *Timber Resource Review* (preliminary review draft subject to revision), September, 1955 see chapter I, Summary, and chapter VI, Future Domestic Requirements for Timber. Also *America's Demand for Wood, 1929-1975*, Stanford Research Institute to Weyerhauser Timber Company, 1954.

[5] After the above analysis was completed, the President's budget for fiscal 1958 was presented to the Congress. It includes estimates of sale of 8.75 billion board feet of timber for $148,750,000 from national forests (including formerly controverted O & C lands) and $156,400,000 total cash revenues in fiscal 1958.

[6] U. S. Department of Agriculture, *National Forest Protection and Management*, "P & M" Budget Study [processed], July, 1949.

ing to the formula prescribed for the O & C lands. These revenues have been small compared with other national forest receipts.

Since the distribution has been on the same percentage basis throughout, the trends in the various items are the same as the trend in total cash receipts. The amounts paid to the counties did not exceed $2 million annually until 1943; from 1951 to 1955 they exceeded $15 million annually, and in 1956 exceeded $28 million. If the projections of cash revenues are realized, and if present laws as to revenue distribution are unchanged, the counties will be getting $35 million by 1960 and $77 million by 1980.

The significant consideration is the interpretation put upon these amounts distributed out of revenues. The 10 per cent road and trail fund is, in practice, merely a part of the total appropriation for national forests and is supplemented by other appropriations for roads and trails. While its amount may be more predictable than that of other appropriations, and while it may be more secure, these are not basic differences.

The 25 per cent fund paid to the counties and other payments out of receipts can be considered as payments in lieu of taxes. Their legislative history shows rather clearly that this was their purpose. The fact that they are calculated as a share of revenues lends further weight to this interpretation. On the other hand, expenditures made by the Forest Service on national forest lands include amounts for roads, fire control, and other purposes, which the counties would be required to make if the federal government did not. The Forest Service has estimated that these are greater than taxes. To this extent, taxes are included in expenditure data.[7]

EXPENDITURES ON NATIONAL FORESTS

Funds expended to manage, conserve, and improve the resources on national forests come from several sources. First, there are the

[7] The authors are aware that some students of this matter consider such payments simply a subsidy to counties granted by the federal government and not comparable to taxes on private land. We believe this is an erroneous interpretation. Payment of a share of gross cash revenues to the counties is, in our view, the political equivalent of the legal necessity of a private owner paying a share of his income to government at different levels in the form of various taxes. If this interpretation is correct, then gross cash receipts are comparable to receipts from private property or business before taxes; and net cash receipts, after payments to counties, are comparable to those same receipts after taxes but before deducting the costs of managing the property or the costs of business. The propriety of this type of payment is an entirely different matter. The topic is discussed at much greater length on pp. 235-37.

various direct appropriations for protection and management, fire fighting, roads and trails, etc. A second source of funds is the 10 per cent of receipts available for roads and trails, previously mentioned, which is appropriated annually. A third type of funds are those which arise out of timber sales. Among these are the previously described K-V funds which are retained from the sale of timber and used by the Forest Service to restore the logged site to a productive condition. The Forest Service may require timber purchasers to deposit funds to pay for the disposal of slash and brush or it may require the purchaser to do this himself. Timber purchasers have the option of entering into co-operative agreements with the Forest Service, wherein the purchaser pays for the cost of certain erosion control measures or road maintenance and the Forest Service does the work. Fourth, when it is necessary to build access roads to take out the timber they have bought, timber purchasers may build and pay for the roads themselves but the improvements become the property of the United States when the timber sale is completed. Fifth, local governments voluntarily make expenditures on national forest lands—more commonly for recreational purposes—which will benefit their citizens. Sometimes private citizens or groups make similar expenditures but usually they turn the funds over to the Forest Service to pay for the work. Total expenditures on national forests, falling under the first three of the sources listed above, are shown in appendix tables 9 and 10 [8]; funds that come from private sources are shown in appendix table 6. The value of the roads built under the fourth source of funds is shown as a footnote to appendix table 8. Expenditures for other purposes made from such funds are not shown in any of the appendix tables. The amount of funds in the fifth class, for 1950 and 1954, is shown in appendix table 11.

Expenditures for all operating purposes have risen considerably in recent years, as may be seen from figure 15 and appendix table 9. These operating expenditures were roughly $25 million during the early war years and rose to about $65 million in 1956. Since a rough doubling of all prices occurred during this period, the real increase has been modest—far less than the increase in use of the forests. A real increase in expenditures has occurred for timber use, fire control (including presuppression and suppression together), and also for the control of insects, rodents, and disease. But even these real increases are probably less than proportional to the increase in use of

---

[8] Expenditures include those on the formerly controverted O & C lands.

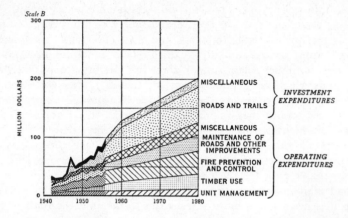

FIGURE 15. *Expenditures on the national forests, 1942-56 and projections for 1960 and 1980.*

the forests. This is clearly true for timber use, for which there is a quantitative measure. While somewhat larger in monetary terms, other items of expenditure show a decrease in real terms, while the uses of the forests have risen. This is especially serious for recreation, wildlife management, and some other aspects of national forest management. Direct operating expenditures for recreation in 1953-55 averaged about $750,000 annually or about 2 cents per recreation visit. A drop in effective funds accompanying a rise in workload has created serious problems for national forest administration.

Expenditures for investment purposes have risen sharply in recent years. They were very low during the war and rose erratically immediately afterward. Since 1950 there has been a steady rise in investment expenditures. A predominant share of these expenditures has been for roads and trails (see appendix table 10). From an annual level of about $5 million in 1950, sums for these items have risen to nearly $22 million. In addition, substantial sums of private money have been used for roads and trails, as can be seen from the footnote to appendix table 8. In the six years from fiscal 1951 to 1956, inclusive, over $120 million was spent in this way, exceeding the expenditures of appropriated funds for this purpose.

Apart from expenditures for roads and trails, there has been no increase in the level of real investment on the national forests in recent years, in spite of increased use of the forests. Investment for recreational purposes has lagged particularly.[9]

The amount of private funds spent by the Forest Service for improvement and protection of national forests is shown in appendix table 6. These funds have risen from about $1 million annually during the war to $10 million annually in 1956. They are a form of receipt "in kind." That is, a timber purchaser is required to pay certain sums in cash for the timber he buys and also to agree to carry out certain improvement activities on the land. The sale might have been handled in such a way that he paid the entire sum in cash in the form of a higher price for the product, and direct appropriations would be used to pay the cost of the necessary improvement on the land. It seems logical to expect that the cash price he actually paid took account of the cost of the improvements he was required to make, and that if he had not been required to make them the cash price he was willing to bid would have been higher. However, if he had paid a higher cash price, a share of this would have been paid to the counties. The use of these funds is one way of escaping the ill effects of revenue sharing, as far as the optimum level of investment in the land is concerned. In the discussion of the balance between revenues and expenditures, which follows later, it is necessary to add these "in kind" receipts to cash revenues in order to get a fair balance.

If the national forests are to be used in the future as our projections would indicate, it is clear that more funds for their management and improvement will be needed. The projected figures shown in appendix tables 9 and 10, and in figure 15 are more or less arbitrary; nevertheless, they are based on carefully analyzed trends. A modest increase in unit management, less than proportional to the expected increases in total national forest use, has been projected for 1960 and 1980. Timber use expenditures fully proportionate to the anticipated increases in volume of timber sold are projected, with a modest allowance for a higher cost per unit of sale. There is some evidence of a trend in this direction. Higher real wages and shorter working weeks

[9] Included in the budget request for fiscal 1958 is an item of $11.5 million, of which $6.6 million is for capital investment, for recreational purposes. This is part of a five-year program, "Operation Outdoors," developed by the Forest Service and calling for investments totaling $54.4 million and operation and maintenance costs of $30.6 million over the period, or an average of $17 million per year. $424,000 was obligated for investments in fiscal 1956 and the total present investment is less than $30 million. See U. S. Forest Service, *Operation Outdoors,* Part I, January, 1957.

in the future are likely to mean higher costs per unit. Expenditures for insect, disease, and rodent control should increase, both because of the greater intensity of forest management contemplated for the future, and because with timber more valuable, greater expenditures to protect it will be wise. Fire control costs are expected to rise also because more people using the forests will create a greater fire hazard, and because larger timber sales will mean more slash. The maintenance of roads and trails will increase as more roads are built; therefore expenditure has been projected in proportion to the projected increase in road mileage. The investment in roads is projected at a much higher level than in the past. An average of $50 million per year might well be spent for roads but it is assumed that expenditures could not rise to this level by 1960. A lower expenditure than projected could be made if a large proportion of the roads were built with timber sales; but the large size of individual timber sales necessary to get the roads built has the undesirable result of reducing the competition for the timber, with the result that the price is lower than it would otherwise have been. It has been assumed that the necessary funds for all major and for many secondary timber access roads would be available from appropriations.

The total projected expenditures for national forests, including funds provided by timber purchasers, are about $130 million in 1960 and about $200 million in 1980, compared with slightly less than $100 million in 1956.[10] Projections of this sort obviously have a large margin of possible error; this is particularly true of the individual items. The total expenditure projection may be more accurate than the individual items that compose it.

SUBSIDIES AVAILABLE IF NATIONAL FORESTS
WERE PRIVATELY OWNED

Certain items of cost are higher on federal land than on private land because the private land is eligible for federal subsidies. If the federal grants-in-aid to states for fire control on private land were applicable to federal land, this would amount to about $3.2 million annually at present levels of fire control and expenditure on national forests. However, it is doubtful if the states and private owners would

[10] The President's budget requests for fiscal 1958 contemplate a total expenditure of approximately $135 million for the same purposes.

attempt to provide as high a degree of fire control on the lands now in national forests if they were privately owned. Williams [11] has estimated that they would spend about 70 per cent as much as now. On this basis, assuming the same relative sharing of costs, the lands now in national forests would receive a federal subsidy, through grants-in-aid to states, of about $2.2 million.

If the national forest lands were in private ownership and thus were eligible for agricultural conservation payments, they would receive an estimated $1.9 million for forest land improvement and up to $0.7 million for range improvement, if private landowners carried out these practices at present levels. To the extent that this level would not be attained—a probable event—the subsidy would be less.

The states and counties receive some revenue from the gas tax resulting from travel over forest roads and trails built by the Forest Service. The amount of this gas tax may be as much as $0.5 million annually.

These various items amount to more than $6 million at current levels of national forest management expenditures. This is to be compared with total expenditures of nearly $100 million. Thus, the receipts or subsidies which would accrue to national forest lands if they were in private ownership is something like 6 per cent of present management expenditures on these lands. The amount is not large, but it is not unimportant. Presumably it was smaller in the past and will be larger in the future as the level of national forest management expenditures rises.

BALANCE OF REVENUES AND EXPENDITURES

Striking a balance between revenues and expenditures is not simple because there are items on each side of the equation which can be looked at in different ways.

For some years the Forest Service has prepared a condensed statement of receipts and expenditures. This type of summary statement is valuable because it separates expenditures into operating and investment items, and shows revenues. It also shows an estimated depreciation of real estate improvements which in 1956 was only slightly more than half of total new investments. This permits a calculation

---

[11] Williams, Ellis T., "National Forest Contributions to Local Governments," *Land Economics*, Vol. XXXI, No. 3, August, 1955.

Condensed Statement Receipts and Expenditures, National Forest Programs, Fiscal Year 1956

	Receipts	Expenditures	
		Operating	Investments
National forest protection and management & land utilization projects		$34,172,615	$ 3,593,372
Fighting forest fires		12,417,974	
Blister rust control		1,668,475	13,179
Forest pest control		3,130,391	7,635
Co-operative range improvements		388,945	296,878
Smokejumper facilities			2,722
Road & trail system—construction & maintenance		9,185,353	22,090,928
Acquisition of land		6,889	402,316
Flood prevention & watershed protection		422,929	450,460
Co-operative deposits (including timber deposits for stand improvement)			
Operating .... $ 711,460			
Investment 7,207,620	$ 7,919,080	700,551	5,454,625
National forest & land utilization area receipts			
Forest Reserve Fund	111,739,132		
Oregon & California lands (national forests)	2,485,782		
Tongass National Forest, Alaska (escrow account)	568,184		
Land utilization areas (Title III Farm Tenant Act)	2,204,059		
Other miscellaneous receipts	808,704		
Total	$125,724,941*	$62,094,122 (1)	$32,312,115
Less co-operative deposits investment receipts	7,207,620		
Total operating receipts & expenditures	$118,517,321	$94,406,237	
(1) a. Operating expenditures $62,094,122			
b. Estimated annual depreciation on roads, trails and other improvements in place on June 30, 1955 17,192,000			
Total	$ 79,286,122		
Amount by which receipts exceed operating expenditures plus estimated depreciation	$ 39,231,199		

* This does not include amounts collected by Federal Power Commission for power licenses and by Department of Interior for mineral leases on national forest lands.

of the balance of cash inflow and cash outflow as well as something
approaching a net balance figure in the private business sense of
the term. This figure is incomplete, however, since it does not include
inventory changes.

The summary balance statement is deficient in ignoring the payments to states and counties out of receipts. This is done apparently
on the theory that these are a general federal subsidy to local
government rather than in-lieu-of-tax payments. On the basis of
this statement, the national forests in 1956 had a cash inflow of
$24 million more than their cash outflow, and the amount by which
receipts exceeded operating expenditures plus estimated depreciation
was $39 million. But if the $30.7 million paid to counties out of
receipts in that year is deducted, these amounts become a minus $6.7
million and a plus $8.3 million, respectively. The favorable showing
of the national forests is possible only by ignoring their taxes—something which private landowners find impossible to do.

A summary of the revenue and expenditure situation and a balance
between them is shown in figure 16 and table 7. The gross revenues
shown are cash revenues only. To these should be added revenues
"in kind" to get a full picture of monetary returns, and the value of

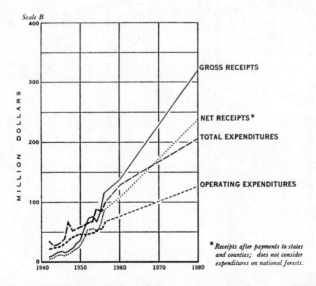

FIGURE 16. *National forest receipts and expenditures, 1942-56 and
projections for 1960 and 1980.*

TABLE 7. *Net Balance of Receipts and Expenditures on National Forest Land 1942-56 and Projections for 1960 and 1980*
(in millions of dollars)

Fiscal year	Cash receipts			Expenditures [1]			Net balance [2]			
	Gross receipts [3]	Payments to states and counties [4]	Net receipts [5]	Total	Operating	Investment	Gross receipts minus		Net receipts minus	
							All expenditures	Operating expenditures	All expenditures	Operating expenditures
1942	7.2	1.7	5.5	33.8	22.9	11.0	− 25.3	− 14.4	− 27.0	− 16.1
43	10.1	2.5	7.6	27.5	24.5	3.0	− 16.5	− 13.5	− 19.0	− 16.0
44	15.9	4.4	11.5	29.6	26.9	2.7	− 12.6	− 9.9	− 17.0	− 14.3
1945	16.3	4.2	12.1	30.4	28.6	1.8	− 12.8	− 11.0	− 17.0	− 15.2
46	14.2	3.7	10.5	37.5	32.7	4.8	− 21.8	− 17.0	− 25.5	− 20.7
47	18.7	4.8	13.9	65.6	40.0	25.6	− 44.7	− 19.2	− 49.5	− 24.0
48	25.0	6.6	18.4	51.5	40.4	11.1	− 23.3	− 12.2	− 29.9	− 18.8
49	32.1	8.5	23.6	54.1	44.5	9.6	− 17.9	− 8.3	− 26.4	− 16.8
1950	34.6	9.1	25.5	58.5	48.7	9.8	− 19.7	− 9.9	− 28.8	− 19.0
51	57.6	15.1	42.5	62.1	47.0	15.1	− 0.7	+ 14.4	− 17.8	0.7
52	71.5	18.7	52.8	68.7	49.2	19.5	+ 8.4	+ 27.9	− 10.3	+ 9.2
53	76.0	19.4	56.6	67.6	49.2	18.5	+ 14.9	+ 33.3	− 4.5	+ 13.9
54	69.0	18.0	51.0	85.6	54.0	31.6	− 8.4	+ 23.2	− 26.4	+ 5.2
1955	81.1	21.0	60.1	82.8	53.3	29.5	+ 8.3	+ 37.7	− 12.7	+ 16.7
56	117.0	30.7	86.3	97.6	65.5	32.2	+ 29.4	+ 61.5	− 1.3	+ 30.8
1960 [6]	148.8	40.2	108.6	129.9	76.9	53.0	+ 32.4	+ 85.4	− 7.8	+ 45.2
1980 [6]	318.0	84.0	234.0	202.5	126.5	76.0	+ 133.5	+ 209.5	+ 49.5	+ 125.5

[1] Expenditures from 10 per cent of receipts road fund and from direct appropriations; includes expenditures out of private funds. Is equal to expenditures shown in appendix tables 9 and 10.

[2] In calculating the net balance, the expenditures from private sources as shown in appendix table 6 have been added to both gross and net receipts since they represent a noncash receipt. Estimate for expenditures from private sources: $13.5 million for 1960 and $18.0 million for 1980.

[3] Taken from appendix tables 5 and 7 and revenues from formerly controverted O & C lands as shown in appendix table 13.

[4] Taken from appendix table 7. Includes estimated payments out of receipts from formerly controverted O & C lands as shown in footnote 1, appendix table 7.

[5] Includes 10 per cent roads and trails funds and land acquisition funds as well as those deposited in general fund, U.S. Treasury. Is difference between gross receipts and payments to states and counties.

[6] Projections of authors.

services furnished free to get full production from the forests.[12] The net revenues are the gross revenues minus the direct cash payments to counties and states. The operating and investment expenditures are those previously discussed. The net balance includes the value of revenues in kind since these same items are included on the expenditure side, but it does not include inventory changes or value of free services. Four kinds of net balance have been computed as follows:

(1) gross receipts minus all expenditures,
(2) gross receipts minus operating expenditures only,
(3) net receipts minus all expenditures, and
(4) net receipts minus operating expenditures only.

The history of net balances shows three distinct periods: (1) For all years of record (and almost surely for all earlier years for which detailed data were not assembled) up through fiscal 1950, both the total and operating expenditures exceeded both gross and net revenues. The amount by which expenditures exceeded revenues depends upon the measures of each, and varied from year to year. (2) From 1951 through 1955, inclusive, gross revenues and total expenditures on the national forests played tag with one another—sometimes one was ahead, sometimes the other. Gross revenues exceeded operating expenditures in all years in this period, net revenues equalled or exceeded operating expenditures in all years (except for a tiny deficit in 1951), and net revenues failed by varying amounts to equal all expenditures in all years of this period. (3) Beginning in 1956 and extending well into the future, as far as we can see, gross revenues will exceed total expenditures on the national forests by a large margin, and net revenues will exceed operating expenditures by a roughly equal margin. However, at present and for roughly ten years into the future, net receipts will not meet total expenditures, although thereafter they will do so by a rather large and increasing margin. This simply means that the scale of investment we have projected cannot be borne out of projected net receipts, although there will be substantial sums available from net receipts for investment. If this scale of investments is to be made, appropriations varying from very small up to as high as $10 million per year must be used to supplement net cash revenues. If investment is limited to

---

[12] If an accrual type of accounting system is used, the change in values represented by net changes in inventory should also be included here.

that possible out of net cash revenues, plus the expected investment of private funds, total investment would run from $30 million to $40 million annually from 1956 to 1965; while this is smaller than we have projected as desirable, it is larger than in any year through 1955.

Revenues from and Expenditures on Grazing Districts,
Other Public Domain, O & C Lands, Acquired Lands,
and Submerged Areas of Outer Continental Shelf [13]

The situation with respect to these various areas is much more complex than for the national forests. A large body of diverse legislation is applicable to them, each of which has its own specific provisions as to revenue and its uses. Again as compared with the national forests, revenue is obtained from more sources and in different proportions; it is also shared differently.

REVENUES FROM THESE AREAS

The history of revenues from the public domain reaches back to the very beginning of our nation (figure 17 and table 8). Variations in revenue from sale of public domain present an interesting picture of boom and depression. Until 1900 nearly all of the revenue was from the sale of the public lands. This revenue was not income in any meaningful economic sense of that term, but was the turning into cash of capital assets. By 1909 over $350 million had been received from the sale of public lands. By that time various miscellaneous sources of revenue began to come into the picture—fees and commissions charged for various applications for public land, trespass charges of various kinds, some revenue from Indian lands sold, and minor amounts from leases and permits of various kinds. By 1913 the sales of public land had fallen off greatly and were actually exceeded by these miscellaneous sources of revenue, which had increased.

Then the Mineral Leasing Act was passed in 1920, and from that date through fiscal 1954 the revenue under it dominated the entire revenue picture from these lands. This revenue is in one sense a

[13] Detailed data for this section are found in appendix tables 13 to 35 inclusive. See footnote 2, p. 259, for details necessary to the reading of charts appearing in this section.

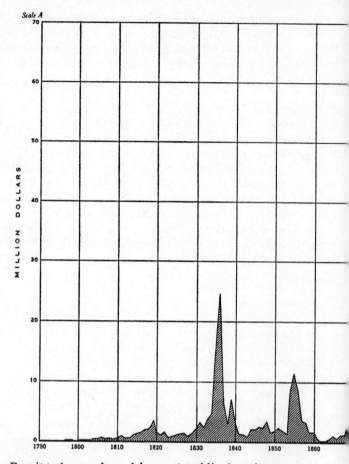

FIGURE 17. *Receipts from sale and lease of public domain, revested and acquired lands and their products, 1796-1952. This figure does not account for all receipts prior to 1881, notably fees, commissions, and the sale of Indian lands—items which make up the miscellaneous*

selling of capital assets, since it is derived from a nonrenewable resource. The latest and most dramatic addition to revenues from the areas considered in this section is the $142 million received as bonuses, rentals, and royalties on leases for submerged land areas, in fiscal 1955,

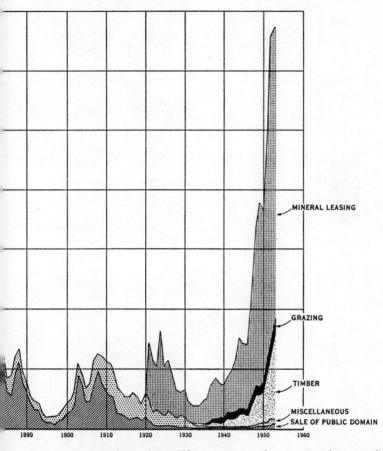

category from 1881 to date. These same receipts for recent years, beginning with 1930 and drawn to scale B, are shown in figure 18. Projections for 1960 and 1980 are also shown there.

and the $111 million received from the same source in fiscal 1956.[14] Including these amounts, nearly $870 million has been received from mineral leasing; excluding them, over $600 million.

[14] These amounts exclude revenues from Section 6 leases, placed in escrow. See footnote 3, appendix table 21.

TABLE 8.   *Revenues from Public Domain, Revested, and Acquired Land, and Submerged Areas of Outer Continental Shelf, by Periods, 1785-1956, and Projections for 1960 and 1980*

(in millions of dollars)

Period	Total	Sales of public domain	Grazing fees and rentals [1]	Timber sales (O & C, and public domain) [1]	Mineral Leasing Act receipts— public domain and acquired land [1]	Mineral leasing, submerged areas of outer continental shelf	Miscellaneous [2]
1785-1880	208.1	204.0	…	…	…	…	4.1
1881-1890	99.3	76.9	…	…	…	…	22.4
1891-1900	33.5	21.3	…	…	…	…	12.2
1901-1910	94.1	64.8	…	…	…	…	29.3
1911-1920	67.0	27.9	…	…	…	…	39.1
1921-1930	104.5	6.7	…	…	76.4	…	21.4
1931-1940	58.0	1.4	3.2	3.7	46.0	…	3.7
1941-1950	199.4	2.4	11.5	24.9	158.0	…	2.6
1951-1956	709.2	8.8	12.5	94.4	335.0	253.6	4.9
Total	1,573.1	414.2	27.2	123.0	615.4	253.6	139.7
1960 [3]	251.0	[4]	3.0	41.1	107.0	95.0	[4]
1980 [3]	551.0	[4]	7.6	63.2	265.5	210.0	[4]

[1] Revenues for earlier years included under "Miscellaneous."

[2] Includes fees and commissions, sales of Indian lands, various rentals and permits, and a varied assortment of minor items. For the period roughly 1910-20 it contains relatively minor amounts from mineral leases of various kinds. For the period roughly 1910-45 it contains minor amounts from sale of dead, down, or damaged timber, including trespass damages for timber cutting; and for the period roughly 1910-34 it includes minor amounts for grazing, including grazing trespass damages. From 1916 through 1932 it also includes receipts from sale of O & C timber.

[3] Projections of authors, at annual rate.

[4] Not estimated separately; assumed to total $5 million annually.

Although some revenue had been received from the sale of dead, down, or damaged timber in earlier years, the lack of any law for the sale of live timber from public domain kept timber sales to a minimum until the passage of a temporary act in 1944 and permanent legislation in 1947. Authority to sell O & C timber had existed since 1916, but a lack of markets had hampered sales. Although receipts from timber sales from all types of land discussed in this section were less than $1 million in 1937, they increased very rapidly to $25 million in 1956. Since these lands are managed on a sustained yield forestry basis, this money is clearly income in the economic sense of the word.

Grazing began to contribute revenue after the passage of the Taylor Grazing Act in 1934, but in total has been responsible for only about $27 million of cash revenues, and thus is decidely minor in the whole revenue picture. It is true that grazing fees have been low, but had they been four times as high revenues from them still would not have equalled timber sale receipts. The area used for grazing is large, but production per acre is small.

The magnitude of the increase in receipts from these areas in recent years is amazing. The revenues collected in the six years beginning with fiscal 1951 have been nearly as large as the total revenues for the preceding 165 years. This is specific statistical evidence of the beginning of the era of intensive federal land management, which was discussed in chapter one. A substantial part of this increase has come from the offshore areas, but mineral leasing receipts from onshore areas in these same six years were considerably more than revenues from land sales in the first 115 years. The great increase in oil and gas leasing since the war, the increased number and acreage of producing leases, and a steady but rapid rise in the output of oil and gas have been the factors behind this great increase in revenues. The rapid increase in revenues in recent years and the dominance of oil and gas is shown in figure 18.

In addition to the cash revenues from the lands dealt with in this section, there have been some revenues "in kind" (appendix tables 33 and 34), most of which have been for grazing land and have consisted of range improvements of various kinds. As in the case of the national forests, the revenues in kind are exactly matched by the expenditures of private parties and local government on these lands.

The data projected for 1960 and 1980 on acreages in leases, oil and gas production, timber cut, and the like, presented in chapter two, are here translated into revenue projections. In making these estimates a stable price level at approximately the present level is assumed; no

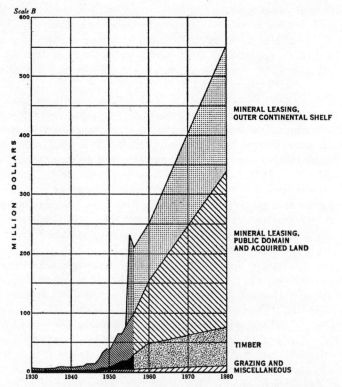

FIGURE 18. *Sources of receipts on grazing districts, other public domain, O & C lands, acquired lands, and submerged areas of outer continental shelf, 1930-56 and projections for 1960 and 1980.*

formal analysis of prices has been undertaken. Royalty rates and oil prices are taken to be about as they were in 1955 and 1956. For reasons discussed in the last section, some increase in timber prices is anticipated.

Estimates of future revenue from mineral leasing of lands and submerged areas are as follows:

	1955	1956	1960	1980
1. Oil and gas leasing on the public domain:				
total area under lease (mil. acres)	73	73	90	150
rentals and bonuses on nonproducing areas (mil. $) ..	20	20	30	50
royalties from producing leases (mil. $)	40	43	68	202
2. Revenue from other mineral leasing on public domain				
(mil. $)	5	4	5	7
3. Revenues from acquired lands (mil. $)	2	2	4	6

4. Submerged areas:

total area under lease (mil. acres)	1.6	2.3	5	8
area in producing leases (mil. acres)	.3	.6	3	5
rentals (mil. $)	3.8	4.8	5	7
royalties (mil. $)	3.4	6.5	75	188
bonuses (mil. $)	140	109	15	15
Total revenue from mineral leasing (mil. $)	214	189	202	475

In addition there may be substantial revenues, not here allowed for, from leasing of submerged areas for minerals other than oil and gas. These amounted to over $1 million in 1955.

The outlook for revenues from timber sale is also sharply upward.

	1960	1980
1. O & C lands:[1]		
volume of timber sold (mil. bd. ft.)	700	950
price per 1,000 bd. ft. ($)	40	45
total revenue (mil. $)	28	42.7
2. Public domain in the states:		
volume of timber sold (mil. bd. ft.)	275	300
price per 1,000 bd. ft. ($)	26	35
total revenue (mil. $)	7.1	10.5
3. Alaska:		
volume of timber sold (mil. bd. ft.)	75	1,200
price per 1,000 bd. ft. ($)	1.8	5
total revenue (mil. $)	.1	6
Total timber revenue (mil. $)	35	59

[1] Excluding the formerly controverted lands, which are included in national forest receipts.

Revenue from grazing will increase moderately; only moderate increases are expected in volume of grazing, although some increases in fees and rentals also are likely. An estimate is 15 million AUM at 20 cents for $3 million revenue in 1960, and 19 million AUM at 40 cents for $7.6 million revenue in 1980. To these must be added revenues from miscellaneous sources, such as sale of land, fees and charges of various kinds, and other minor items, which might total $5 million in 1960 and in 1980.

All these estimates of revenues from the various land uses total $245 million for 1960 and $548 million for 1980.[15][16] These may seem to be very large revenues, but a few comparisons may be helpful. If one goes back to 1954, before the submerged lands yielded any revenue,

[15] These figures are slightly higher than the projections shown in appendix table 51, because they include some revenue from mineral leasing on acquired lands which also is included under the revenues from other types of land.

[16] The President's budget request for fiscal 1958 includes an estimate of $237 million from these sources.

total revenues were over $78 million. By 1980, roughly twenty-five years, this would increase about seven times, including revenue from the submerged lands. If this seems extreme it should be noted that the increase from 1933 to 1954, twenty-one years, was fifteen times. Even though prices rose considerably in this latter period, whereas for the 1960 and 1980 estimates no change from present prices has been assumed, the real increase from 1933 to 1954 was great. Moreover, for the future there is the new factor of the submerged lands from which a substantial revenue is certain by 1980. There seems little doubt that total revenues from the whole group of areas dealt with here will rise tremendously in the next twenty-five years.

DISTRIBUTION OF RECEIPTS FROM AREAS CONSIDERED IN THIS SECTION

Distribution of receipts from the areas we are considering here is much more complex than it is for the national forests. With minor exceptions, national forest revenues are distributed according to a single formula. But for the public domain, O & C, and submerged areas, several different formulae are followed.[17] Using the figures shown in table 9, it can be seen that for the whole period 1785-1956, 53 per cent of the receipts have gone into the general fund, 26 per cent to the Reclamation Fund, 20 per cent to the states and counties, and 1 per cent to miscellaneous places. These figures are considerably influenced by the very large revenues from the submerged lands in 1955 and 1956, all of which went into the general fund. If these are omitted, then total receipts are 16 per cent less; in these circumstances the general fund would have received 46 per cent, the Reclamation Fund 30 per cent, and the states and counties 23 per cent, with 1 per cent going to miscellaneous places.

The distribution of receipts has varied greatly at different periods, depending largely upon the source of the revenues. In the earliest periods, when the receipts were nearly all from the sale of public land, the states received 5 per cent and the other 95 per cent went into the general fund. More than half of all receipts into the general fund accrued before 1933—78 per cent if the large revenues from the submerged areas in 1955 and 1956 are excluded. With the passage of the Reclamation Act in 1902, 95 per cent of the receipts from public land in the "reclamation" states went into the Reclamation Fund; after the passage of the Mineral Leasing Act of 1920, 52.5 per cent of

[17] See chapter four, pp. 233-41, for detailed discussion.

TABLE 9. *Distribution of Receipts Collected by Bureau of Land Management and Predecessor Agencies, from Sale and Use of Various Public Lands, Including Submerged Areas, 1785-1956, and Estimated Annual Figures for 1960 and 1980*

(in millions of dollars)

Period	Total receipts	Reclama-tion Fund	States and counties	Miscel-laneous	General Fund, U.S. Treasury
1785-1932	615.5	125.1	56.0	[1]	434.4
1933-1940	49.0	21.9	19.0	1.1	7.0
1941-1950	199.4	84.2	73.7	4.4	37.1
1951-1956	709.2	174.4	167.1	14.8	353.3
Total	1,573.1	405.6	315.8	20.3	831.8
1960 [2]	251.0	62.0	60.0	4.0	125.0
1980 [2]	551.0	147.0	130.0	7.0	268.0

[1] Minor items may have fallen in this category; if so, they are in the general fund amount.

[2] Estimates by authors at an annual rate based on projected revenues and present laws as to disposition of receipts.

the mineral receipts went there also, with the appropriate states receiving 37.5 per cent of the receipts. In recent years prior to 1955, revenues have been distributed roughly as follows: 40 per cent to the Reclamation Fund, 37 per cent to the states and counties, and 20 per cent to the general fund, with 3 per cent going to miscellaneous places (figure 19). About 40 per cent of the money paid into the Reclamation Fund from various sources has come from the public lands. Power sales from the dams and other installations, repayments of construction costs of the irrigation projects, and other revenues to the reclamation program have contributed the other 60 per cent.

Using the projected revenues and the present legal basis for the distribution of the receipts, the following is the probable distribution for 1960 and 1980. The Reclamation Fund, which has averaged about $30 million annually since 1951, would receive $62 million in 1960 and $147 million in 1980. States and counties would receive $60 million in 1960 and $130 million in 1980. The largest relative increases would be to the general fund of the Treasury, and would be due to the large increases in revenues from the submerged areas, none of which is as yet earmarked for any special purpose. Approximately $125 million would be deposited to the general fund in 1960 and $268 million in 1980.

Of the $316 million paid to states and O & C counties during the entire period 1785-1956, about $242 million have gone directly to the

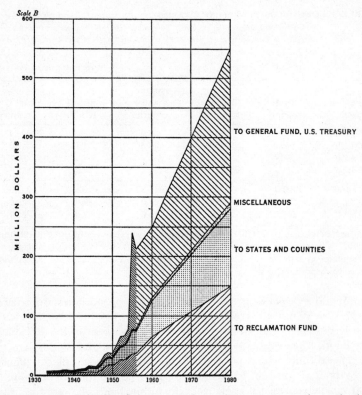

Scale B

MILLION DOLLARS

TO GENERAL FUND, U.S. TREASURY

MISCELLANEOUS

TO STATES AND COUNTIES

TO RECLAMATION FUND

FIGURE 19. *Distribution of total receipts from grazing districts, other public domain, O & C lands, acquired lands, and submerged areas of the outer continental shelf, 1933-56 and projections for 1960 and 1980. Projections are based on previous projections of total revenue and on present laws relating to revenue sharing.*

states and $74 million directly to counties. Although all of the public land states have received some revenue, the distribution among states is highly variable (table 10). Of the total, 36 per cent has gone to Wyoming, 21 per cent to California, 14 per cent to New Mexico, and 10 per cent to Colorado, or a total of 81 per cent to these four states. Their large share reflects primarily the distribution of receipts under the Mineral Leasing Act and the occurrence of oil discoveries on the public lands up to now. It should be recognized that the smaller sums accruing to the middle western and southern states were all

TABLE 10. *Total Payments to States from Receipts from Public Domain, up through 1956*

(in thousands of dollars)

Region and state	Total	Sale of public lands 1803-1956	Taylor Grazing Act 1934-1956	Mineral Leasing Act 1920-1956
		Paid to state from		
East North Central				
Ohio	999	999	...	...
Indiana	1,040	1,040	...	...
Illinois	1,188	1,188	...	*
Michigan	616	593	...	23
Wisconsin	592	591	...	1
Subtotal	4,435	4,411	...	24
West North Central				
Minnesota	597	597	*	...
Iowa	634	634	...	...
Missouri	1,061	1,061	...	...
North Dakota	1,175	542	12	621
South Dakota	901	355	62	484
Nebraska	632	580	4	48
Kansas	1,448	1,129	*	319
Subtotal	6,448	4,898	78	1,472
South				
Florida	210	198	...	12
Alabama	1,186	1,097	...	89
Mississippi	1,091	1,078	*	13
Arkansas	396	362	*	34
Louisiana	1,042	473	*	569
Oklahoma	247	68	2	177
Subtotal	4,172	3,276	2	894
Mountain				
Montana	9,758	627	620	8,511
Idaho	1,559	361	646	552
Wyoming	87,960	346	1,662	85,952
Colorado	24,456	563	478	23,415
New Mexico	34,670	170	923	33,577
Arizona	916	69	559	288
Utah	10,329	206	1,025	9,098
Nevada	3,358	80	933	2,345
Subtotal	173,006	2,422	6,846	163,738
Pacific				
Washington	607	500	56	51
Oregon	1,620	925	504	191
California	51,265	1,298	473	49,494
Subtotal	53,492	2,723	1,033	49,736
Total	241,553	17,730	7,959	215,864

* Less than $500.

received in much earlier times, when money had a higher purchasing power, and when such sums were more important to the finances of local government than they would be now.

Payments are made directly to the eighteen counties of western Oregon in which the O & C lands lie. Since the passage of the O & C Act of 1937 they have received 50 per cent of the revenues from these lands—an average, over the forty-one years since title to the lands reverted to the United States, of about $1.8 million annually (see table on page 325). Averages in this case however, are highly misleading. Payments in recent years have been as follows:

1956	$12.0 million	1953	$6.5 million
1955	14.2 million	1952	6.1 million
1954	6.6 million	1951	3.2 million

These total to $48.6 million in the last six years—65 per cent of the forty-one-year total, and an average of $8.1 million annually over the six years. The payment was unusually large in 1955 when the accumulated funds from the "controverted" lands, which had been held in escrow, were distributed to the counties according to the O & C formula, following court and Congressional action. However, the relatively large payment to the counties in 1956, which was made entirely out of revenues received that year, is noteworthy. A later section of this chapter will deal in more detail with these payments to O & C counties (see pages 324-29).

If the $74 million paid to O & C counties is added to the $242 million paid to the states, then the shares of individual states are different from those found previously when the shares were of revenues paid only to the states. Wyoming still leads, with 28 per cent; but Oregon is now second, with 24 per cent of the total, followed by California with 16 per cent, New Mexico with 11 per cent and Colorado with 8 per cent—a total of 87 per cent for these five states.

EXPENDITURES ON GRAZING DISTRICTS, O & C LANDS,
AND OTHER AREAS CONSIDERED IN THIS SECTION[18]

Although both area and the revenues of the public domain and revested lands are roughly equal to those of the national forests,

---

[18] The expenditure data in appendix tables 30 to 35 inclusive and in this section do not include expenditures by the Forest Service in the administration of the formerly controverted O & C lands.

expenditures on these lands have been much lower (figure 20). Expenditures were roughly $5 million annually through World War II, and have now risen to nearly $20 million, but both levels of expenditure are less than a quarter of those made on the national forests in corresponding periods.

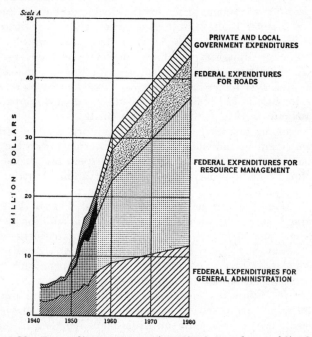

FIGURE 20. *Expenditures on grazing districts, other public domain, O & C lands, acquired lands, and submerged areas of the outer continental shelf, 1942-56 and projections for 1960 and 1980. For a comparison with cash receipts, see figure 21. Expenditures are shown there on scale B.*

The differences in expenditures reflect, of course, the differences in physical characteristics, but even more, the differences in intensity of management applied to the two types of land. The lower expenditures on the public domain do not necessarily imply greater efficiency of management or a more desirable public policy. On the contrary, the lands have not been intensively administered and many students of land management would argue that through lack of funds they have been insufficiently managed. The doubling of expenditures from 1942 to 1951 is believed to have kept pace with rising costs of administration due to higher prices. Beginning in 1951 or 1952, however, the rise in expenditures has been greater than the rise in prices. In the earlier period federal expenditures were divided somewhat equally between (1) general administration, including mineral leasing activities, supervision of mineral leases (by the Geological Survey), cadastral surveys, and general administrative activities; and (2) resource management, including range management, forestry, fire control, and the like, and some capital expenditures for these purposes, excluding roads. In the latter period, expenditures for resource management activities increased somewhat relative to those for the more administrative functions. Expenditures for roads began in a comparatively major way only in 1952, but are still fairly small.

In view of the low level of federal expenditure, the comparatively large sums spent by individuals and local governments on the public lands may have significance. Most has been spent on grazing lands, chiefly for range improvements, soil conservation activities, weed control, and the like. Expenditures for these purposes represent a receipt "in kind," as they do on national forests. That is, the users of the grazing land, chiefly within grazing districts, in addition to paying grazing fees have spent cash or labor in the improvement of these ranges. It may be assumed that they have gained at least as much as they have spent or they would not have made the expenditures.

It is difficult to estimate the amount of expenditures that will be needed in the future if the estimated revenue is to be obtained and if the lands and resources are to be managed at a reasonable level. The present level of management, while far better than in the past, is still not intensive. Demands of nearly all kinds upon these and other federal lands will increase. Merely to achieve the higher revenues previously estimated would require considerable additional expenditure. A rough estimate suggests that federal expenditures should rise from the $20 million in 1956 to perhaps $28 million in 1960 and $44 million in 1980.[19] These estimates assume a more intensive management of the forests and grazing lands in the future than has been the case in the past, involving a larger annual investment on timber access road construction, reforestation, grass reseeding, soil erosion control, and weed control measures.

[19] The President's budget for fiscal 1958 contains a request for $30 million for these same items.

SUBSIDIES AVAILABLE IF LANDS WERE PRIVATELY OWNED

As with the national forest, these lands would be eligible for certain subsidies if they were in private ownership. Based on current levels of fire protection, federal grants-in-aid for fire control today would be about $315,000. For range reseeding, erosion control, and reforestation work now being undertaken, federal subsidies would be about $1.53 million, supposing no limit were set to the amount one landowner could receive. Similarly, if adequate appropriations were now available for a full-scale program, federal subsidies would be about $2.86 million. On the basis of the program assumed for the future, all these subsidies would increase. Gas tax monies collected by the states on roads built by federal funds amount to too little to warrant estimating.

BALANCE OF RECEIPTS AND EXPENDITURES

Much the same limitations apply here, in the matter of balancing receipts against expenditures, as apply to national forests. The balance between cash receipts and expenditures again in no sense measures income, annual operating costs, or profits from these areas. Some receipts and some expenditures are in kind. In addition, some of the expenditures are for capital improvements, not for annual operating costs. If these limitations are kept in mind, the net balance comparisons have some value.

With comparatively large gross receipts and comparatively small expenditures, the grazing districts, O & C lands, and other areas considered in this section might be expected to show substantial net balances in the federal Treasury of cash revenue over cash outlay. However, this is not the case because such a large proportion of the gross revenues is used for payments to the states and counties and to the Reclamation Fund. If a comparison is made between gross revenues and expenditures, a comparatively large net balance has existed since 1930. This can be seen from figure 21. The net balance existing in earlier years is not shown. (See also appendix tables 54 and 55.) The projection of probable gross receipts from all areas and probable expenditures into the future show still larger net balances, approximating $215 million in 1960 and $500 million in 1980.

However, as pointed out for the national forests, the payments out of receipts to states and counties are politically the equivalent of taxes

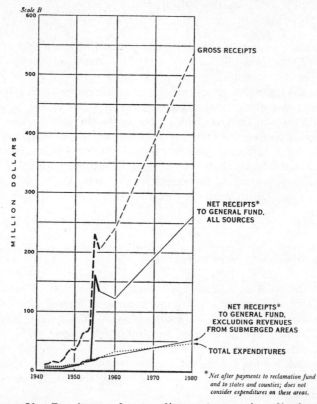

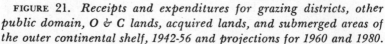

FIGURE 21. *Receipts and expenditures for grazing districts, other public domain, O & C lands, acquired lands, and submerged areas of the outer continental shelf, 1942-56 and projections for 1960 and 1980.*

—they are part of the political price of federal land administration, just as income taxes are part of the legal price of private business. Accordingly, any realistic calculation of net balance must exclude them, at least in principle, although there may be argument about the reasonableness of a particular system of calculating such payments. Payments into the Reclamation Fund are in a different category. They have always been primarily for the benefit of the reclamation program rather than a condition imposed upon federal land management.

For the period 1942 through 1947 expenditures were roughly double the net revenues. For the period 1948-51, expenditures and net revenues were roughly equal. The differences each year were less than

TABLE 11. *Net Balance of Revenues from and Expenditures on the Public Domain, 1955-56 and Projections for 1960 and 1980*

(in millions of dollars)

Revenues and expenditures	History [1]		Projections [1]	
	1955	1956	1960	1980
Gross cash revenues:				
Land areas [2]	86	96	146	326
Submerged areas	142	111	95	210
Total	228	207	241	536
Paid to:				
States and counties	33	37.	56	125
Reclamation Fund	36	37	64	149
Total	69	74	120	274
Net cash receipts to Treasury:				
Land areas only	17	22	26	52
Submerged areas	142	111	95	210
Total	159	133	121	262
Expenditures from the federal Treasury (including roads and other capital items)	17	20	28	44
Net balance of net cash revenues over cash expenditures:				
Land areas only	0	2	—2	8
Submerged areas [3]	142	111	95	210
Total	142	113	93	218

[1] See appendix tables 51, 52, 53; revenues in kind and equal expenditures by nonfederal sources, as shown in appendix tables 33 and 34, excluded.

[2] Excluding formerly controverted O & C areas.

[3] Putting all costs of administration of these areas (which are relatively small) against land areas.

$1.5 million, and in some years revenues and in others expenditures were more. Beginning with 1952, a substantial cash net balance was received each year with one minor exception. If net receipts exclude those from the submerged areas and if expenditures include those on roads, the net balance was negative by about $0.5 million in 1955 and positive by $2.5 million in 1956. If the receipts include those from submerged lands, a very large net balance existed in 1955 and 1956—especially large because there is no outside claim on this source of revenue. Nearly all the expenditure on roads has been for construction, with only a little so far for maintenance. If this clearly capital outlay is excluded (regardless of the fact that some other small outlays were also for capital items),[20] the positive net balance has been larger each year, and is growing, even if the revenue from submerged land is excluded.

Although the foregoing analysis of net balance of receipts and expenditures is as accurate as the authors can make it, it is in many ways highly misleading because of the changed composition of the Reclamation Fund. As has been pointed out in chapter four (page 241), today payments into the Reclamation Fund from public lands are practically meaningless as support for the reclamation program, but they seriously distort the picture as to the net balance of receipts and expenditures on the public land.

Considering the most disadvantageous comparison of net cash receipts and expenditures—excluding revenues from submerged areas and including an allowance for more road building and other capital improvement in the future than in the past—these public domain and related lands will barely pay their own way. If the payments into the Reclamation Fund were to be discontinued, these areas would show much larger annual net balances, even over desirable capital investment, running to over $150 million annually by 1980. Sums of this magnitude would pay a large part or all of the annual operating and investment costs on other types of federal land, such as national parks, which in themselves do not produce much revenue. If the revenues from the submerged areas are included, even retaining the Reclamation Fund payments on the present basis, still larger net balances seem likely. Considerable question might be raised as to the use of the revenues from the submerged areas for federal land management functions, yet the possibility exists. If the revenues from submerged areas are included and if the payments to the Reclamation Fund are discontinued, the net balance figure rises tremendously to over $350 million annually by 1980.

Revenues from and Expenditures on the National Park System [21]

The national parks and monuments are not primarily revenue producing in purpose. Their main product is recreation. The use of

---

[20] None of these outlays were for land acquisition.

[21] Detailed data for this section are found in appendix tables 36 to 42 inclusive. See footnote 2, p. 259, for details necessary to the reading of charts appearing in this section.

these areas has traditionally been free, or at most subject to modest entrance fees which in no sense were designed to produce the maximum revenue. The park system costs the national Treasury far more than it takes in, and for that reason the revenue and expenditure features of the lands' management are important in the financial considerations of all federal lands. The indirect benefits to the nation and to the states and localities in which the national parks are located are not touched on here. In monetary terms they are immeasurable.[22]

Virtually all the cash receipts from the national park system can be considered income. On the expenditure side, however, a considerable part of the monies spent is for capital improvements, especially roads and structures. Until the last two years expenditures for these items have been relatively low, and depreciation of roads and structures built in earlier years may easily have been greater than the cash outlay for roads and structures built each year. In any case, the data which follow are cash receipts and cash expenditures only, rather than income and annual operating costs.

REVENUES FROM NATIONAL PARK SYSTEM

Revenues from the national park system have always been relatively low (see figure 22 and appendix table 37). From an annual level of roughly $2 million in prewar years, they fell to less than $1 million during the war, and since have risen to slightly above $5 million in 1955 and 1956. Where fees are charged at all, entrance fees differ considerably between the different units of the national park system. However, if each fiscal year's receipts are divided by the number of visitors to the whole national park system in the preceding calendar year, the average receipts-per-visit figure has been remarkably steady at about 10 cents per visit. In view of the substantial rise in general price level since 1940, it is evident that the real income per visit has been roughly halved.

An estimated use of the park system in the future of 60 million visits in 1960 and 135 million visits in 1980, and an allowance of only modest increases in average receipts per visit, would produce a gross revenue of $7 million in 1960 and $20 million in 1980.[23] If fees were raised substantially, use would be cut somewhat but revenues would

[22] Indirect benefits are discussed rather fully in chapter four, pp. 257-59.
[23] The President's budget for fiscal 1958 includes an estimate of $5.5 million total receipts in 1958.

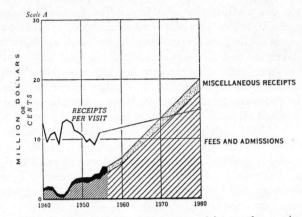

FIGURE 22. *Receipts and receipts per visit to the national park system, 1940-56 and projections for 1960 and 1980. The scale on the left should be read in cents for statistics on receipts per visit. These were determined by dividing fiscal year receipts by visitors in previous calendar year. To compare national park receipts with receipts from other lands, see figure 24 which is on the same scale as figures 16 and 21.*

almost surely increase. However, this is a matter both political and social, which goes beyond the restrictions of financial analysis.

The national park system has been the recipient of many gifts over the years. These are not revenues in any sense; they are not even revenues "in kind" comparable to those so designated from national forests, because the givers have not associated them with specific park uses. And yet in some ways they are analogous: they represent values seen in the park system for which some people voluntarily surrender cash or assets. As shown in appendix table 42, cash gifts have amounted to $7.2 million since 1920. While small in relation to total federal expenditures on the national parks, these gifts have often been crucial to the development of the park system we have today. The gifts of land, which have been major, are not shown in the appendix table.

DISTRIBUTION OF REVENUES FROM NATIONAL PARK SYSTEM

Virtually all the receipts from the national park system go into the general fund of the U. S. Treasury. There is no sharing of receipts with states and counties, except for very limited payments to the state of Wyoming for Grand Teton National Park. As can be seen in appendix table 38, small sums are used from the revenues to aid in providing educational facilities for the dependents of Park Service personnel located at Yellowstone, Crater Lake, and Mammoth Cave national parks. Small sums from the revenues of certain properties are available for use in the management and improvement of these properties; a part of the receipts from Mammoth Cave National Park is available for the purchase of privately owned properties within the boundaries of the park. With these exceptions, which in 1956 totaled only $203,000, all the revenues from the national park system go into the general fund.

EXPENDITURES ON NATIONAL PARK SYSTEM

The changes in expenditures on the national park system, shown in figure 23, give an impression of rugged peaks and deep valleys similar to those found in the most mountainous of national parks. Expenditures totaled roughly $5 million annually during the war, a substantial decline from the $15 to $20 million or higher level of the preceding years. Construction was halted, maintenance activities were reduced to a minimum, and even management expenditures were reduced. This was possible because of the great decline in park use during the war. Since then, general administrative and protection and management expenditures have risen slowly—very slowly in terms of real purchasing power, and far more slowly than the increase in park use. Maintenance expenditures have also risen, but irregularly; the really erratic increases have been for construction, primarily of roads. When put on a per-visit basis, expenditures show no real trend since the war. Annual expenditures in the early 1950's mostly averaged 60 to 80 cents per visit, as they had during the war. Prior to that, appropriations were occasionally more than $1.00 per visit. If the general rise in prices is considered, expenditures in relation to use as late as 1954 were only about half or less than half what they had been before the war when the level of services was not extravagant. Since the war facilities in the parks, including roads, have not increased adequately to care for the greatly increased numbers of visitors; many facilities have been inadequately maintained and the level of service to the visitors has fallen off. With 50 million visits annually now, there are no more facilities and no more services than when visits numbered only 20 million.

It was a consideration of this situation which led the National Park

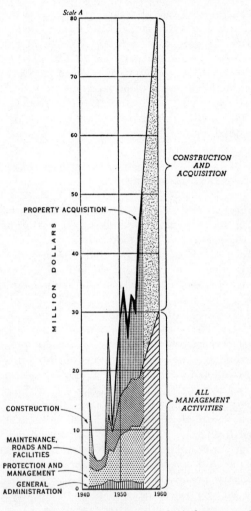

FIGURE 23. *Expenditures on the national park system, 1942-56 and projections for 1960. Projections for 1980 are shown in figure 24 but are plotted on scale B.*

Service to develop its "Mission 66"—a plan for the national park system.[24] It estimates that use of the system will reach 80 million visitors by 1966, the Service's fiftieth anniversary.[25] Plans for facilities and services to care for this number of visitors have been prepared, and estimates made of the costs of providing them. Since there is a substantial backlog of postponed construction, appropriations for construction during the next few years will have to be at a higher level than may later be necessary. The Mission has estimated a total appropriation of $83.6 million for 1966; $35.5 million of this sum would be spent on management in the broadest sense of the term, and $48.1 million on construction of various kinds. It is notable that appropriation of this order would approximately restore the $1.00-per-visit level of appropriation which prevailed before the war; however, with the present purchasing power of the dollar, the real level proposed is lower than this, even though higher than has existed since the war.

Our estimate of needed appropriations, if the relatively modest estimates of use based on the 1952-55 trend are to be realized, and if visitors are to be properly cared for, is as follows:

	1956	1960	1980
	(in millions of $)		
Total appropriations	51	80	135
For construction of all kinds and land acquisition	30	50	50
For management in the broadest sense	21	30	85

The total for 1960 is high [26] relative to other figures, because of the construction backlog already referred to. If use of the national park system increases in line with higher estimates, based on more rapid growth periods of the past, still larger appropriations will be needed.

SUBSIDIES IF NATIONAL PARKS WERE PRIVATELY OWNED

Because they are federally owned, the national parks and monuments are ineligible for certain subsidies or revenues which would accrue if they were in private ownership or if certain services were asumed by the states. A major item here is the revenue from gasoline

[24] National Park Service, *Mission 66 for the National Park System* [processed], January 1956.
[25] Our estimates of the number of visitors in 1966 allow for as many as 135 million visitors if the 1947-54 trend continues.
[26] The President's budget for fiscal 1958 includes a request for $64 million for these purposes.

taxes paid by persons driving over the park roads which are built entirely with federal funds. An estimate based on a year's car mileage in four parks is given in appendix table 39. It averages out to 33 cents per car entering the national parks—a total in 1955 of about $1.7 million for all parks. The estimate is necessarily rough, but it is likely to be of the correct magnitude. If the fire-fighting subsidy available to private lands through the Clarke-McNary funds applied to national parks, it would amount at present to about $167,000 annually. If the various land treatment subsidies were available, they would amount only to about $30,000.

BALANCE OF RECEIPTS AND EXPENDITURES

In showing that the national parks have had a deficit of cash revenues over cash expenditures, no suggestion is intended that this is undesirable—the matter of the proper level of revenues, touched upon later, will be based on other considerations. First, however, an explicit consideration of the actual history of cash revenues in relation to cash expenditures seems desirable.

For the years since 1942 cash revenues have met from one-fourth to one-third of the cash operating costs, excluding construction and land acquisition (see figure 24). But cash expenditures, even for operation, have been much too low for proper service to park visitors; hence, the present level of entrance fees will not over the long run return this large a share of cash operating costs. Receipts are an even smaller proportion of the total cash expenditures if construction and land acquisition are included—more on the order of one-sixth to

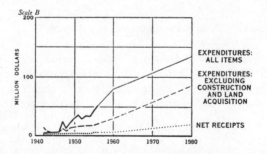

FIGURE 24. *Receipts and expenditures for the national park system, 1942-56 and projections for 1960 and 1980.*

one-tenth in recent years.[27] Since the beginning of 1950 the cash deficit has averaged over $31 million annually if all costs are included and nearly $15 million if construction and land acquisition costs are excluded. If future use develops along the lines estimated, if entrance fees increase moderately as shown in figure 22, and if sufficient appropriations are made to care properly for the visitors, cash deficits in 1960 and 1980 will be as follows:

	1956	1960	1980
	(in millions of $)		
Above all expenditures	46	73	115
Above expenditures, omitting construction and land acquisition	16	23	65

ENTRANCE FEE POLICY

Implicit in the figures cited above is the question of whether the level of entrance fees to national parks should be reconsidered. The question is complex. Certainly, any move to raise entrance fees sharply would be unpopular; so would be the Administration sponsoring it. Nevertheless, the facts should be weighed carefully. First, the United States today has a booming national economy—real incomes per capita are rising and give every prospect of continuing to do so for many years. People have money to pay for what they want to a degree never before known. Second, the use of the national park system is also booming—booming at a rate at least twice or three times that of the growth in real income. There is no need today to coax people to use the national parks. They are using them, "loving them to death," as some commentators have noted. Third, entrance fees to all national parks are low or nominal and are absent for some. It has been pointed out that for several years total receipts have averaged about 10 cents per visit for all visits to all areas, and that car entrance fees for the whole system have averaged less than $1.00 per car. Auto entrance fees for a fifteen-day period at Yellowstone are $3.00, at Yosemite they are also $3.00, and at Grand Canyon they are $1.00; for the calendar year, entrance fees are $6.00, $6.00, and $2.00, respectively. A carload of people can enjoy the resources of one of these parks for many days for less than the cost of a movie or of a single meal. Fourth, for most visitors the entrance fee is an extremely small part of the total cost of visiting most national parks. Recalling data presented earlier, the

[27] The situation varies greatly between parks; Carlsbad and Yellowstone have about met expenses whereas others have a ratio below average.

average party of visitors to Shenandoah Park spends $125 for the whole trip; for the Grand Canyon the figure is over $500. It is true that in many cases such vacation trips may include more than one national park or other major sightseeing area. Nevertheless, since the average party spends $15.00 to $30.00 per day if it stays overnight in the park, by this yardstick, too, the entrance fee is a minor expense. Entrance fees within the range of $10.00 to $20.00 per car would still be small in relation to the total cost of visiting a major national park.

Perhaps the most important consideration is the over-all use of the national parks—how widely it is distributed among the total population. Data on numbers of visits throw no light at all on this matter. What we need to know is: How many persons used the national park system in any one year, or over a period of several years? If the total number of persons is high and more or less evenly distributed over the country and among the various income classes, then low entrance fees with costs met out of general taxes may be both equitable and efficient. But use concentrated among relatively smaller groups argues for a higher entrance fee, permitting a larger share of the costs of national park administration to be borne by the actual users. More information is needed to guide sound decisions.

Revenues from and Expenditures on Federal Wildlife Management [28]

The Fish and Wildlife Service has a complex and integrated program for the protection and management of wildlife of all kinds. The management of wildlife refuge lands is only one part of this program.[29] A brief consideration of the Service's various activities is necessary in order to understand where land management, as such, fits into the larger program.

One major activity is the enforcement of certain game laws, especially as they relate to migratory waterfowl, and of certain treaties with other countries as to waterfowl. Prevention, or at least minimization, of illegal and excessive hunting is necessary if gains from the provision of better refuges and other aspects of the program are not

[28] Detailed data are found in appendix tables 43 to 50 inclusive. See footnote 2, p. 259, for details necessary to the reading of charts appearing in this section.

[29] The discussion in this section is concerned with the Fish and Wildlife Service as it was organized until July 1, 1956.

to be thrown away. Research into mammal, bird, and other wildlife problems is also a major activity which, in its narrower sense, is closely related to wildlife management. The Fish and Wildlife Service administers a system of grants to states for provision of wildlife refuges and for other purposes. The state and the federal wildlife refuges complement each other. The Service has special responsibilities in Alaska and in some of the islands off Alaska. All of these and other varied activities are closely correlated. Wildlife refuge management is an integral part of the whole, but only a part.

Several sources of revenue have been tapped and utilized directly for various parts of the whole program of wildlife management. The ingenious methods adopted are successful not only in raising substantial sums but also in imposing charges more or less in proportion to the benefits received by various groups of users. Charges of this type are usually in the public interest.

Since 1949 no receipts from the various sources have gone into the general fund of the Treasury; they are made available for the purposes authorized by law only by specific annual appropriation. This, plus the fact that some direct appropriations are made each year, gives the Congress continued control over the content and the scope of the program of the Fish and Wildlife Service. One of the strongest arguments against earmarking receipts for specific activities is that it robs Congress of its control over federal agency activities. In this case, however, Congressional control seems to have been retained, while governmental activities are largely paid for by the beneficiaries of the activities.

The management of the wildlife refuges themselves is similar to that for other types of federal land in that its primary purpose is not profit or maximum revenue. The primary purpose for these lands is to provide a suitable habitat for certain kinds of mammals and waterfowl. The comments in earlier sections of this chapter concerning the nature and limitations of the available data apply also to these lands.

SOURCES AND USES OF REVENUE FOR WILDLIFE MANAGEMENT

Because the use of the various revenues is so closely linked to their source, it is necessary to look at the source, amount, and use of each of the major revenues in turn, beginning with revenues most directly related to refuge management and proceeding to those not directly related.

1. Receipts from the refuges themselves. As can be seen from figure 25, and from appendix table 47, these have increased from about $100,000 in 1942 to $2.3 million in 1956. They have come principally from oil and gas leases in the past, but there is some doubt that oil royalties will continue equally high in the future. The receipts include small sales of timber and other minor sources of income. Twenty-five per cent of these funds is paid to the counties in which the refuges lie; in this respect the revenues are similar to those from national forests. Where they differ is in the fact that the expenses of making sales are deducted first, so that the sharing of revenues is

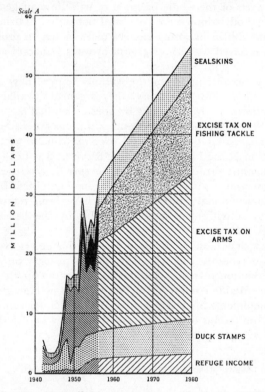

FIGURE 25. *Funds available for state and federal wildlife management programs, 1942-56 and projections for 1960 and 1980. Projections are based on present prices and taxes. To compare income from wildlife refuges only with revenues from the national forests and other federal lands, see figure 27 where all data are plotted on scale B.*

partially on a net basis. However, because the costs of various management practices are not deducted, earlier criticisms of the principle of revenue sharing apply here also. Through fiscal 1948 the rest of the receipts went into the general fund of the Treasury, but beginning in 1949 this remainder was made available for management of refuges and enforcement of migratory bird treaties. A modest increase is the most reasonable outlook for receipts from the refuges.

2. Revenue from the sale of duck stamps. Each duck hunter is required by federal law annually to purchase a duck hunting stamp, the price of which has risen in recent years from $1.00 to $2.00 a year. Since 1942 revenues from the sale of duck stamps have varied from slightly more than $1 million to as high as $5 million. All these revenues are available for wildlife refuge administration, which includes land acquisition. When the duck stamp act was passed in 1934, and when the price of the stamps was raised in 1949, it apparently was intended that most of the funds would be used to acquire and improve refuges for migratory waterfowl. In practice, however, after 15 per cent is set aside to pay for administering the act and printing the stamps, most of the remainder has gone into refuge administration and management. The outlook is for a modest increase of revenues at the present price per stamp.

3. An excise tax of 11 per cent on sporting arms and ammunition, generally known as the Pitman-Robertson funds. This tax yielded only $1 million to $2 million annually, during the war, when hunting was infrequent. More recently it has amounted to some $10 million annually, and was up to $15 million in fiscal 1956. In 1952 the Korean war led to a run on sporting arms and ammunition which brought in nearly $18 million in the form of tax receipts. A growing population and the prospects for greater leisure can mean greater revenues from this source in the future. The use of these funds is discussed below.

4. An excise tax of 10 per cent on fishing tackle. Instituted in fiscal 1952, revenues from this tax have already passed the level of $5 million annually. Some increases in the future seem reasonable. The excise taxes on both arms and ammunition and fishing tackle can be used in small amount for administrative costs by the federal agency, after which over 90 per cent of the funds are available to the states as grants for development of fishing and for wildlife management and protection, including the provision of state refuges and other areas. There is one interesting feature of these grants: if not spent or obligated within two years from the date made, the funds revert to the federal

government and are available to the Fish and Wildlife Service for land acquisition of refuges and other purposes. In practice, however, comparatively little has actually reverted for federal use.

5. Receipts from the sale of sealskins from the seals on Pribilof and adjacent islands off Alaska. This is a special activity with a dramatic history behind it—a wildlife species once faced with extinction, brought back by careful management to a level about as great as its environment will support, and maintained, with harvest of the natural increase, by the same careful management. The skins from the natural increase of animals are taken and sold, producing a revenue which has varied from about $0.5 million to nearly $5 million. Revenues from this source are available to administer the seal herd and the islands and to provide some governmental services to the inhabitants of the islands. These activities are not federal wildlife refuge management in the usual sense of the term, but they are part of the complex integrated wildlife program previously discussed. No material increase in revenue from this source seems probable.

The total of all these sources of revenue increased from about $3 million during World War II to an average of some $25 million for the past few years. If present laws and rates of tax remain in effect, increases in total revenues to perhaps $36 million in 1960 and $56 million in 1980 seem probable. If the need for additional funds to acquire, improve, and manage federal wildlife refuges becomes acute, and if direct appropriations are not forthcoming on a larger scale than in the past, it is possible that the rates of tax will be raised.

EXPENDITURES ON WILDLIFE REFUGE MANAGEMENT
AND CLOSELY RELATED ACTIVITIES

Because the wildlife management program consists of many parts, several of which receive funds from more than one source, expenditures on wildlife refuge management cannot precisely be determined without accounting procedures too detailed for the scope of this book. As an example, there are activities, such as some river basin studies or some waterfowl investigations, that could equally well be included in or excluded from wildlife refuge management (see appendix tables 49 and 50). And there are also difficulties connected with apportioning overhead expenditures between wildlife refuge management and other functions. Accordingly, the estimates of expenditures used in figure 26 are only approximate. They are shown in total in appendix table 53, the footnotes to which give the detailed origin of amounts.

The funds in figure 26 show a rise from less than $3 million annually during the early war years to over $7 million in 1955 and slightly less in 1956. Since wages and other costs roughly doubled during this period, the increase in actual purchasing power was relatively small. Sums have been used in all years for land acquisition, and larger sums have been used to complete the development of lands acquired during the 1930's. Each of the three sources of funds has shown a general

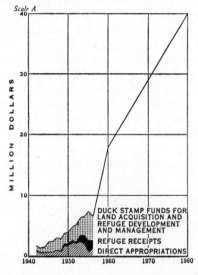

FIGURE 26. *Funds available for federal wildlife refuges only, 1942-56 and projections for 1960 and 1980. See text for an explanation of some of the items shown here and for the basis of projections. For comparison with expenditures on national parks and on grazing districts and other public domain, see figures 23 and 20, which also use scale A.*

increase, although direct appropriations have declined since fiscal 1953.

The data are neither precise nor adequate enough to provide the basis for judging the adequacy of the funds available for refuge management and related activities. Had more funds been available perhaps a more intensive job could have been done. Certainly, the degree to which these activities have been able to tap sources of revenue from those who benefit from them, and to become self-supporting, does not necessarily mean that the resulting funds have been adequate to meet all the needs.

If refuge management and related activities are to preserve desirable wildlife species by providing suitable habitat and protection against indiscriminate hunting, and still satisfy future demands for hunting and fishing, substantial additional funds must be made available. It has been estimated that the federal wildlife refuges should contain 7.5 million acres, instead of the present 3.5 million acres, in order to supplement the areas owned and developed by the states. It has also been estimated that it would cost $40.00 per acre or $160 million in total to buy the necessary lands, and an additional $80 million to develop them for good wildlife management.

Figure 26 shows that total expenditures for wildlife refuges desirably should rise to $18 million in 1960 and to $40 million in 1980, of which $3 million and $10 million, respectively, would be for land acquisition and development. If the latter is actually realized, it would permit by 1980 about half of the estimated necessary expansion in refuge area. Such estimates, obviously general in nature, rest upon several assumptions, the most important of which is that such an expansion is desirable. No attempt has been made in figure 26 to indicate the source of the necessary funds.

SUBSIDIES AVAILABLE IF REFUGES WERE PRIVATELY OWNED

Wildlife refuges, like other types of federal land, are excluded from the various subsidies available to private land. If the fire-fighting (Clarke-McNary) subsidy were available, it would amount at present to about $50,000 a year. If the various land treatment subsidies were available, they might amount yearly to $150,000.

BALANCE OF REVENUES AND EXPENDITURES

As with other federal lands discussed in this chapter, the balance between cash receipts and cash expenditures does not show net profit, nor is it an evaluation of the soundness of the management program. The net balance between cash receipts to the general fund and direct appropriations from the same fund has been negative in all years. From 1942 through 1948 net receipts tended to reduce the direct appropriations slightly; since 1949 all direct appropriations have been a net adverse balance because there have been no net receipts. The negative balance has varied from $1.5 million to $5.5 million each year, and since 1949 has exceeded $3.5 million each year. Including expenditures made out of receipts from the sale of duck stamps, the negative net balance of refuges is increased by from nearly $1 million to nearly $5 million. If the foregoing estimates of future revenues and future expenditures are realized, the negative net balance will be about $16 million in 1960 and about $40 million in 1980. It may be argued that a direct appropriation of the latter size will never come about. The duck stamp tax was adopted, and accepted by the public, on the grounds that the revenues from it were to be used to improve wildlife conditions. There has been considerable objection to the use of these funds for management instead of for land acquisition. If larger appropriations were made, there might be public acceptance of higher duck stamp fees.

Revenues from and Expenditures on All Federal Lands [30]

Looked at as a whole, the data we have been examining on revenues and expenditures for all four types of federal land lead to conclusions that underline the importance of these lands in the nation's economy.

1. There has been a tremendous upswing in receipts from federal land. How great an upswing can be seen in figure 27, table 12, and, in greater detail, appendix table 51. The rate of growth of revenues from national forests and public domain has been almost equal if one excludes the submerged areas, and these two dominate the whole revenue situation. The rate of growth of each and of the total has been as much as between 17 and 19 per cent annually for the past fifteen years. Even if half this growth rate has been due to higher prices for the products sold, this still leaves a substantial rate of growth derived from the sale and harvest of more products. The increase in volume of timber cut and in volume of oil produced (as well as in numbers of recreational visits, which produce little revenue) was about 10 per cent annually. Total revenues in 1954 were about eight times—or, in real price terms, probably four times—what they were in 1942. In 1955 and 1956, when substantial revenues

[30] Detailed data for this section are found in appendix tables 51 to 55. See footnote 2, p. 259, for details necessary to the reading of charts appearing in this section.

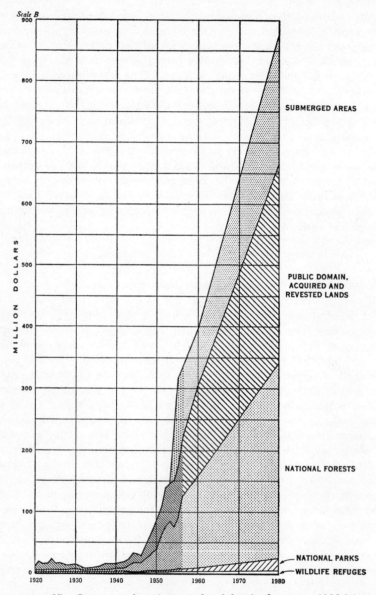

FIGURE 27. *Gross receipts from federal lands, by type, 1920-56 and projections for 1960 and 1980.*

were obtained from the submerged areas, the increase was much greater.

2. There is a strong probability of major increases in revenue in the future. If revenues from the submerged lands are included, the prospect for 1980 is for nearly $900 million cash revenue; if these revenues are omitted, the total cash revenue may still exceed $650 million. In view of the fact that total cash revenues were less than $100 million only five or six years ago, these forecasts may perhaps seem extreme. But these projections have been built up from a consideration of each major land use on each major type of federal land, and its revenue prospects. Moreover, they contemplate a much lower *rate* of increase in the future than in the past. A proportionate extension of the past rate, omitting the revenue from the submerged lands, would lead to a higher revenue in 1980 than is estimated here, even when the latter are included. These revenue projections assume a generally stable price level and are based on present pricing arrangements for the uses and products of federal land. If maximum revenues were the objective, and higher prices were charged with this in mind, considerably more revenue could be obtained.

3. Expenditures from all sources on these lands have also risen (see table 12 and appendix table 53). Total expenditures from all sources have risen roughly three times from the war years to 1955, and somewhat further in 1956. If the rough doubling in prices and costs during this period is taken into account, management has less than doubled on these lands, in spite of the greatly increased demand for the land and its products. The funds presently available for management of all types of federal land are inadequate in relation to the magnitude of the present management job. The major part of the funds available in the past has come from direct appropriations, and a small part has come from receipts and from private or local government sources. Roughly one-fourth of total expenditures in 1942-56 were used for capital outlays such as road and other construction and for land acquisition, and about three-fourths for annual operating purposes. It is obvious that expenditures must rise in the future, because increasing demands for the land and its products, if met, will require more management, and because greater expenditures will be needed if the increased revenues estimated are actually to be achieved. An increase of about 50 per cent from 1956 to 1960 is considered necessary, and another increase of about 65 per cent above the 1960 level will be needed by 1980.

4. The greatest rise of all has been in the payments to states.

TABLE 12.   *Summary of Revenues and Expenditures for all Federal Lands 1942-56 and Projections for 1960 and 1980* [1]

(in millions of dollars)

Fiscal year	Gross cash revenues from all federal land [2]	Payments out of revenues to [3]		Net cash revenues [2,4]	Contributions from private sources [5]	Expenditures on land [6]		Net cash balance to Treasury			
								Above gross revenues [7]		Above net revenues [8]	
		Reclamation Fund	States and counties			Total	Excluding major investment items	All expenditures	Expenditures other than major investment	All expenditures	Expenditures other than major investment
1942	19.2	4.0	5.5	9.7	1.7	55.6	35.9	— 34.7	— 15.0	— 44.2	— 24.5
43	21.7	4.2	6.5	11.0	1.2	39.6	36.2	— 16.7	— 13.3	— 27.4	— 24.0
44	31.8	6.2	10.1	15.5	1.4	41.2	38.2	— 8.0	— 5.0	— 24.3	— 21.3
1945	31.4	5.9	9.7	15.8	1.7	43.2	40.4	— 10.1	— 7.3	— 25.7	— 22.9
46	29.9	5.9	9.0	15.0	1.9	51.5	46.0	— 19.7	— 14.2	— 34.6	— 29.1
47	42.8	8.6	12.9	21.3	2.8	101.6	61.6	— 56.0	— 16.0	— 77.5	— 37.5
48	60.8	13.8	18.7	28.3	3.6	72.0	58.9	— 7.6	+ 5.5	— 40.1	— 27.0
49	72.6	16.5	21.9	34.2	4.5	86.0	68.1	— 8.8	+ 9.1	— 47.3	— 29.4
1950	74.3	15.8	21.9	36.6	5.7	99.5	76.9	— 19.5	+ 3.1	— 57.2	— 34.6
51	109.9	20.8	32.7	56.4	5.1	111.3	78.2	+ 3.7	+ 36.8	— 49.8	— 16.7
52	139.3	24.5	41.9	72.8	7.1	115.8	84.0	+ 30.6	+ 62.4	— 35.9	— 4.1
53	146.8	25.5	44.0	77.3	8.8	123.2	88.1	+ 32.4	+ 67.5	— 37.1	— 2.0
54	150.3	30.9	46.2	73.2	10.5	141.2	93.6	+ 19.6	+ 67.2	— 57.5	— 9.9
1955 [9]	317.0	35.9	54.7	226.3	12.0	152.8	95.1	+ 176.1	+ 233.8	— 85.5	+ 143.2
1955 [9]	*174.6*	*35.9*	*54.7*	*84.0*	*12.0*	*152.8*	*95.1*	*+ 33.8*	*+ 91.5*	*— 56.8*	*+ .9*
1956 [9]	331.3	36.9	67.9	226.5	11.7	176.5	110.4	+ 166.5	+ 232.6	— 61.7	+ 127.8
1956 [9]	*220.1*	*36.9*	*67.9*	*115.3*	*11.7*	*176.5*	*110.4*	*+ 55.3*	*+ 121.4*	*— 49.5*	*+ 16.6*
1960 [10]	399.3	64.0	96.8	238.5	16.5	258.9	147.9	+ 156.9	+ 267.9	— 3.9	+ 107.1
1960 [9,10]	*304.3*	*64.0*	*96.8*	*143.5*	*16.5*	*258.9*	*147.9*	*+ 61.9*	*+ 172.9*	*— 98.9*	*+ 12.1*
1980 [10]	877.0	149.0	209.8	518.2	22.0	425.5	282.5	+ 473.5	+ 616.5	— 114.7	+ 257.7
1980 [9,10]	*667.0*	*149.0*	*209.8*	*308.2*	*22.0*	*425.5*	*282.5*	*+ 263.5*	*+ 406.5*	*— 95.3*	*+ 47.7*

[1] Includes national forests, national parks, wildlife refuges, public domain, acquired and revested land, and submerged areas only; omits other types of federally owned or federally controlled land.

[2] See appendix table 51.

[3] See appendix table 52.

[4] Net cash revenues are gross cash receipts less payments to Reclamation Fund and to states and counties.

[5] See appendix tables 6 and 33. On national forests includes K-V funds and voluntary contributions by timber operators, livestockmen, and local associations, if for the benefit of national forest lands and if spent by the Forest Service. On grazing districts, includes primarily funds contributed by livestockmen and spent by the Bureau of Land Management. Does not include expenditures for timber access roads made under timber purchase contracts. While these sums were expended on federal land, they are also and equally in the nature of receipts "in kind."

[6] See appendix table 53. Includes national forest 10 per cent road fund, range improvement fee in grazing districts, and other miscellaneous items available for expenditures from receipts, as well as expenditures from direct appropriations and from contributed funds. Excludes forest highways but includes other roads and trails built by the federal agencies.

[7] See appendix table 54.

[8] See appendix table 55.

[9] Italicized figures show revenues and expenditures if the submerged areas of the outer continental shelf are excluded.

[10] Projections of authors.

counties, and the Reclamation Fund (see appendix table 52). From under $10 million in 1942, they have risen to over $100 million by 1956, ten times in fifteen years. This great increase is largely due to increasing revenues from the leasing of oil and gas; 90 per cent of these revenues are given to either the Reclamation Fund or the states. It also reflects the increase in revenues from timber sales; 25 per cent of these from national forests and 50 per cent or more from O & C lands are paid to counties. Unless the present law is changed, the amounts going to these purposes will rise 53 per cent from 1956 to 1960, and more than double again by 1980. The rationale of continued major financial aid from federal lands to the reclamation program has been challenged frequently throughout this book.

5. Four measures of the balance between revenues and expenditures are possible. Two apply to revenue—gross revenues before any payments to states, counties, and the Reclamation Fund have been deducted, and net revenues, after deduction of these payments. And two apply to expenditure—total of all items including investment, and operating expenses as far as the major investment items can be eliminated. Each of the two measures of revenue can be compared with each of the two measures of expense, thus providing four measures of net balance (see table 12, figure 28, and appendix tables 54 and 55).

If gross revenues are compared with all expenditures, negative balances are evident through fiscal 1950. Thereafter there is a positive balance. This shift from a negative to a positive balance in 1950 is one indication of the transition then taking place from custodial to intensive management. The size of the positive balance increases almost every year, even with the revenues from the submerged lands excluded. When these are included the balance in 1955 and 1956 becomes very large.

When gross revenues are compared with operating expenses only, a negative balance appears through fiscal 1947, and thereafter a positive balance exists. The size of the negative balances is smaller, and that of the positive balances larger, than in the former comparison, by the amount of the gross investment each year. A substantial net balance shows up each recent year until the addition of revenues from the submerged areas in 1955 leads to a very large positive balance.

In our judgment, these two comparisons are somewhat misleading because they do not take account of the payments to states and counties, and the Reclamation Fund. As we have pointed out previously, for the federal agencies at least the first of these are the political equivalents of taxes paid by private business.

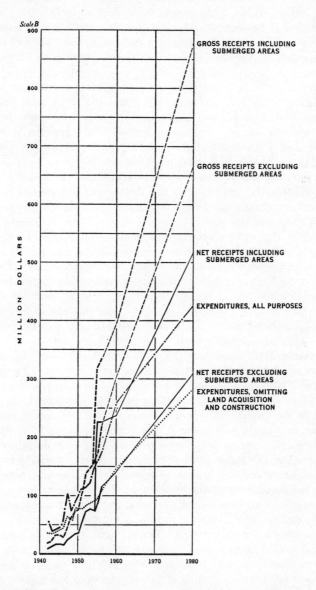

FIGURE 28. *Gross receipts, net receipts, and expenditures for all federal lands, 1942-56 and projections for 1960 and 1980.*

When net revenues are compared with total expenditures, a substantial minus shows up each year until 1955 and 1956, but in those years also the balance would have been negative without the submerged area revenues. The negative balance has averaged about $50 million annually for several years if the submerged area receipts are excluded.

If net revenues are compared with operating expenditures only, there is still a negative balance each year until fiscal 1955, although the trend is downward and the amount in some years small. In 1955, even excluding the submerged areas, there was a very small positive balance which increased slightly in 1956. Thus, without the submerged areas the federal lands in total are now just able to carry their operating costs with little or nothing for investment, while making substantial payments to the Reclamation Fund and to states and counties. If the submerged lands are included, the positive balance becomes substantial.

6. When the future balance between revenues and expenditures is considered, several alternatives are possible. These depend largely on whether revenues from the submerged areas are included or excluded, and on whether present arrangements for payments into the Reclamation Fund remain unchanged. Pricing methods for the sale of products and uses are also a factor. Starting with the least favorable financial situation and progressing to others more favorable, four distinct possibilities appear.

If revenues from the submerged areas are excluded and if payments to states, counties, and the Reclamation Fund remain as at present, the federal lands in total can meet all operating costs and leave from $12 million to $50 million available annually for investment. This should be compared with the $110 million to $140 million annually we have estimated as desirable if the federal lands are to make their maximum contribution to the total national income and welfare. The revenues from the lands alone simply cannot make a major financial contribution to the reclamation program and at the same time make substantial investment on the land itself.

If revenues from the submerged areas are excluded and payments into the Reclamation Fund are abolished, a substantial sum for investment on the land would remain after deducting operating costs. For 1955 and 1956, and until after 1960, this sum would be less than actual investment has been during the past few years and less than projected investment for future years, by sums ranging from $13 million to $35 million annually. By 1980, however, a surplus in excess of $50 million annually would appear. For the whole period ahead to 1980, deficits below the projected investment in the early years roughly would be offset by surpluses above it in the later years. Thus, freed of the Reclamation Fund the federal lands could cover reasonably adequate investment in addition to operating costs.

If the revenues from the submerged areas are included and payments to the Reclamation Fund are left on the present basis, a substantial surplus appears in 1955 and 1956. But in 1960 there would be a small deficit not only because of the relatively high level of investment projected, but also because revenue from the submerged areas, now largely from bonuses in the sale of leases, is expected to fall off until the areas come fully into production. This is unlikely before 1960. By 1980 a surplus of over $100 million annually appears. Use of revenues from the submerged areas for the federal lands would thus make possible the land's continued substantial subsidy to the Reclamation Fund; in effect, the result would be much as if the revenues from the submerged areas were themselves used to subsidize the reclamation program.

If revenues from the submerged areas are included and payments into the Reclamation Fund are discontinued, quite sizable surpluses would result—in 1955 and 1956, $100 million or over in each year; in 1960, about $60 million; and in 1980, about $250 million.

It should be recalled that the foregoing analysis of projected balance of revenues and expenditures is based on current pricing practices as to the products and uses of federal land, and on current methods of making payments to states and counties. No attempt has been made to compare balances between gross revenues and measures of expenditure in the way that we have applied these measures to net revenues, because we consider comparisons based on gross revenues to be misleading. However, comparisons of this kind can be made using the data shown in table 12.

At various points in this chapter we have mentioned the subsidies which landowners could receive if the lands which at present are federal were in private ownership. In total, these would amount to about $10 million annually.

Payments to States and Counties

The states and particularly the various units of local government, such as counties and school districts, raise a substantial part of their revenues by means of a general property tax. The federal government has much property in some states and counties. Why should it escape taxation? This is a natural question, especially to a local official harassed with inadequate revenues. The situation is aggravated in those cases where the federal property brings to a locality more people who require more local governmental services. If, under these circumstances, the federal property does not contribute to the cost of local government, the local unit of government feels it has been twice imposed upon—once by loss of normal revenue, once by imposition of extra costs.

The problem has application far wider than to the federal lands dealt with in this book. It may be found in especially aggravated form, for instance, in small towns where there is urban federal property, or in areas where there are federally financed water developments. The whole matter has been of some concern at various levels of government.[31]

Any suggestion that federal lands or other property be taxed as though privately owned runs into both legal and administrative or operational objections.

On the legal side, local governments are not permitted to impose taxes or financial burdens upon the federal government without its consent. On several occasions, however, the federal government has consented to local governments levying taxes, or charges closely similar to taxes, upon its property. The legal objection can, therefore, be met if the federal government so chooses.

The administrative or operational objection concerns the methods of applying taxes on federal land. How can its value for tax purposes be established? Much land is in federal ownership precisely because it has uses and values other than the usual commercial ones. How could the land in a national park be valued, for instance? Should values be established on the basis of the land's suitability for grazing, forestry, and other commercial uses, or on the basis of the area's value for scenic and other qualities which were decisive in its estab-

---

[31] Legislative Reference Service, Library of Congress, *Federal Land Ownership and the Public Land Laws,* report on taxes and other in-lieu payments on federal property, prepared for use of the Committee on Interior and Insular Affairs, House of Representatives, Committee Print No. 23, 83rd Congress, 1954; Council of State Governments, *Federal-State Relations,* Report to Commission on Organization of the Executive Branch of the Government, Senate Document No. 81, 81st Congress, 1st Session, 1949; The Commission on Intergovernmental Relations, *Report,* June 1955; *Payments in Lieu of Taxes and Shared Returns,* Study Committee Report submitted to Commission on Intergovernmental Relations, June 1955. This last report contains a good bibliography, a history of this general matter, and rather detailed discussion of revenue sharing for federal lands.

lishment as a park? If the latter, how are these noncommercial values to be established?

Even if it is possible to agree upon a formula for valuing federal lands for local taxation purposes—and the problem should not be considered insoluble in spite of the difficulties—the federal government probably could not safely allow local assessors unlimited authority to assess federal lands for local taxation. The temptation to kill the goose that laid the golden eggs might prove too strong.

FEDERAL-LOCAL GOVERNMENT RELATIONSHIPS

The federal government is in an unusual role as a landowner, partly because of its unique legal status, and partly because of its very size as a landowner. The federal government provides on its lands many of the services, such as roads and fire protection, that other landowners expect and receive from local government. If the federal government were to pay taxes or tax equivalents on its land, some adjustment would certainly have to be made for the cost of these services.

Recognizing the reasonable basis for their claims the federal government has made various arrangements to meet the need of local governments for revenues from federal land. It allows taxes to be levied, or at least payments directly in lieu of taxes to be paid. It shares revenues in ways discussed in some detail in chapter four. In making certain grants to states, it bases the size of grant partly on the amount of federal land in the state.

This last arrangement may be illustrated by grants-in-aid under the federal highway program. Under the formula which applied from 1921 through 1951, the federal government's share of the cost of federal-aid highways was 50 per cent "plus a percentage of such estimated cost equal to one-half of the percentage which the area of the unappropriated public lands in such state bears to the total area of such state." Nontaxable Indian lands were added to unappropriated public domain by later amendment. Under the 1952 Federal Highway Act, the largest of four separate funds established by the act continued to be distributed according to this formula. Applied to Nevada, this has resulted in 83.68 per cent of the cost of federal-aid highway construction being borne by the federal government, and it has been estimated that over a two-year period Nevada received $4,605,156 in federal aid through this formula, which it would not have received if the public domain and Indian lands were privately owned and taxed.[32] This sum is to be compared with $746,000 paid to Nevada by the Forest Service and Bureau of Land Management in 1955, and with the figure—which may be too high—given later in this subsection, of $2,515,000 full tax equivalent of these lands in 1955. This provision of assistance on federal-aid highways has been of very great value to the state itself for the grant has gone to it, whereas if the lands were privately owned, the taxes would have gone primarily to the counties. For other western states, where the percentage of public domain is less than in Nevada, the amounts paid would probably be less important but still significant.

DISADVANTAGES OF REVENUE SHARING

Sharing the receipts from federal lands may have some advantages over taxes as a means of compensating states and counties, but it also has major disadvantages. Revenue sharing is appropriation sharing. Even though increased appropriations for road building or more intensive resource management will yield revenues larger than the appropriations, the states and counties receive a share of the gross revenues which may return less to the Treasury than that which was spent. It is as though a part of the appropriation were given direct to the state or county. How this has inhibited appropriations for and investments in the federal lands and how it can operate to the disadvantage even of local government, has been pointed out in chapter four (pages 242-44).

A share of revenues may be far more, or far less, than taxes would be; but the distribution of revenues in time and space is not necessarily the same, or as equitable, as the distribution of taxes.

NATIONAL EDUCATION ASSOCIATION STUDY
FOR ELEVEN WESTERN STATES

A few years ago the National Education Association attempted a study of this problem, using data for 1948.[33] In each of the eleven

---

[32] Statement by William Brussard, Reno (Nevada) Chamber of Commerce, *Proceedings of the Western Chambers' Conference on Federal Lands*, Natural Resources Department, Chamber of Commerce of the United States, 1953, p. 85.

[33] Committee on Tax Education and School Finance, *Status and Fiscal Significance of Federal Lands in the Eleven Western States*, Washington, D. C.: National Education Association of the United States, 1950.

TABLE 13. *Estimated Taxes on Federal Land in Eleven Western States, 1948* [1]

State	Area of federal land [2] (1,000 acres)			Assessed value of federal real estate (million dollars)			Estimated taxes on federal real estate ($1,000)		
	Total	Under five federal agencies [3]	Other	Total	Land under five federal agencies [3]	Other	Total	Land under five federal agencies [3]	Other
Arizona	50,274	25,845	24,429	131.1	67.2	63.9	2,464	1,262	1,202
California	45,679	41,317	4,362	901.0	686.0	215.0	34,979	26,629	8,350
Colorado	25,018	23,375	1,643	78.8	73.7	5.1	2,609	2,440	169
Idaho	35,807	33,357	2,450	113.1	105.4	7.7	3,387	2,983	404
Montana	34,251	26,776	7,475	48.3	29.4	18.9	4,173	2,543	1,630
Nevada	59,410	53,530	5,880	95.7	86.2	9.5	2,838	2,557	281
New Mexico	35,308	25,422	9,886	64.5	43.9	20.6	1,578	1,074	504
Oregon	32,935	30,886	2,049	346.0	321.5	24.5	15,963	14,833	1,130
Utah	37,718	32,475	5,243	88.0	75.6	12.4	3,358	2,885	473
Washington	15,038	11,359	3,679	471.3	311.8	159.5	18,768	12,433	6,335
Wyoming	32,597	29,100	3,497	86.4	77.7	8.7	2,649	2,206	443
Total reported	404,036	333,443	70,594	2,424.2	1,878.4	545.8	92,766	71,845	20,921

[1] Estimates based on 1950 study by National Education Association of the United States, *Status and Fiscal Significance of Federal Lands in the Eleven Western States*. Data on areas, on total assessed values, and on total estimated taxes taken directly from report. Also data on taxes for land under five agencies for Idaho and Wyoming taken directly from report. For other states, assessed value estimated for "other" lands on basis of (1) average assessed value per acre of all land for land under Bureau of Reclamation, Bureau of Indian Affairs, and National Military Establishment (except civil lands), plus (2) 10 times (in California 100 times and in Nevada one time) average value of all land, for land under Veterans Administration, Public Buildings Administration, Public Housing Administration, Bonneville Power Administration, and miscellaneous; assessed value of land under five agencies is total assessed value minus assessed value of "other" lands; estimated taxes divided proportionately to assessed values.

[2] As reported by this study; for slightly different figures, see appendix table 1.

[3] Bureau of Land Management, Fish and Wildlife Service, Forest Service, National Park Service, and Soil Conservation Service.

western states local assessors and other tax officials were asked to estimate the taxes on all federal property in their state. The results of this study almost certainly are biased upward, for three reasons: (1) No restraints other than their own general honesty and competence were placed on the estimators; yet it would be natural to expect both local assessors and local school people to be anxious to show how large the taxes from the federal property might be. (2) Apparently no account was taken of the value of services provided by the federal agencies on the lands they administered, similar to those services that local governments would normally provide to privately owned land. (3) No account was taken of the fact that a larger total assessed property base in a county or other unit of local government would produce a lower rate per $100 of assessed value, if the level of government services remained the same.

For each of the western states, the NEA report gave estimates of the area in each type of federal land holding, including Indian reservations and urban property, and for each state it gave a total assessed

TABLE 14. *Estimated Values and Taxes for Federal Land in Eleven Western States, 1948*

State	All federal land in state			Land under five agencies [1]
	Value per acre	Tax per acre	Tax per $100 value	Tax per acre
	$	¢	$	¢
Arizona	2.61	4.9	1.88	4.8
California	19.72	76.6	3.88	64.5
Colorado	3.15	10.4	3.31	10.4
Idaho	3.16	9.5	2.99	8.9
Montana	1.41	12.2	8.64	9.5
Nevada	1.61	4.8	2.97	4.8
New Mexico	1.83	4.5	2.45	4.2
Oregon	10.51	48.5	4.61	48.0
Utah	2.33	8.9	3.82	8.9
Washington	31.34	124.5	3.98	109.5
Wyoming	2.65	8.1	3.07	7.6
Average	6.00	23.0	3.83	21.5

[1] Bureau of Land Management, Fish and Wildlife Service, Forest Service, National Park Service, and Soil Conservation Service. The latter is included because these lands have since been transferred to other agencies, particularly to the Forest Service.

value and a total estimated tax for all federal property. For Idaho and Wyoming, the report also gave the assessed value and the estimated tax by types of federal land. In table 13, we have estimated the assessed value and the tax for all types of federal land with which we are here concerned. It is probable that in the process of separating out Indian reservations and urban land, our estimates for federal rural lands are too high, even accepting the accuracy of the report in general. Some basis for judging the soundness of these NEA estimates can be found in the figures shown in table 14, calculated from the report. On the whole, while values and taxes may be estimated too high, these data do not seem unreasonable.

The NEA report estimates taxes for all federal property in the West in 1948 at about $93 million. Against this, payments of over $29 million, or 31.4 per cent of the estimated taxes, were made by the federal government. It estimates further that the taxes on federal land were 8.95 per cent of total property taxes in the eleven western states. On the basis of our estimates, taxes on the federal lands we are considering in this book would be nearly $72 million if the general estimates of the NEA report are accepted.

The data in the NEA study relate to 1948. In general, taxes on privately owned land have gone up since that year. An index of taxes paid on farm property, by states and by years, calculated by the U. S. Department of Agriculture, is given in appendix table 56. The estimates of taxes for federal land by years and by states, given in the same table, are calculated from this same index. It should not be overlooked, however, that these latter calculations have their origin in the NEA study and suffer from any deficiencies it may have. On the basis of these data and estimates, taxes on the federal land have gone up from about $38 million in 1938 to slightly over $100 million in 1955—a rise of slightly more than two and a half times. The rise was not regular from year to year—in fact, there were slight decreases until 1943 and no major rise until 1945. After the war all real estate taxes rose rapidly and the process has apparently not yet run its course, since 1955 was about 10 per cent above 1954 and that in turn was above 1953. The rise in taxes during those years was part of the general rise in nearly all prices in the same period.

Payments out of receipts from the lands administered by the Forest Service and Bureau of Land Management have increased from well under $10 million annually during the war to about $60 million in 1956 (see appendix table 57). On the basis of these figures, 1944 payments out of receipts were 19.5 per cent of estimated taxes; by

1956 they were nearly 60 per cent of estimated taxes. The amount of the payment per state varies greatly among the states, as does the trend in payments per state. Payments in 1956 were eight times those in 1944 for the eleven western states as a whole, but this increase ranges from Oregon (nearly seventeen times) to Montana (about four times). The changes in payments reflect income changes from the federal land in the different states, particularly the production of oil and gas and the sales of timber.

If the trends from 1944 to 1956 are extended, payments by 1963 will equal taxes with each at a level of about $240 million annually. However, it is doubtful that these trends will continue without change, since a substantial part of each was due to the upward movement of the general price level, which gives signs of being more stable in the future. If the general price level stabilizes at about the present level, estimated taxes can be expected shortly to level off not far above the 1955 figure.

The NEA study reveals great discrepancy between estimated taxes and payments out of income or otherwise from the federal agencies when the comparison is made on a state by state basis. Some of this discrepancy may be due to the methods used in the study. It does seem probable, however, that payments out of income are not closely proportional to estimated taxes. One of the major disadvantages of the revenue-sharing arrangements is that sale and harvest of resources from the federal lands is often irregularly distributed geographically and in time.

Despite their limitations, the estimates in appendix tables 56 and 57 provide the basis for comparison between states. Estimated taxes and payments by states for 1955 are shown in figure 29. At the top of the list is New Mexico, where payments are nearly four times estimated taxes; next is Wyoming, where payments nearly triple taxes; in Colorado they are almost exactly equal, and in Oregon not greatly different.[34] In all the other states payments are less than taxes, ranging down to California where they are only 17 per cent of estimated taxes.

The NEA estimates may be seriously in error in failing to allow for the value of the federal services that the states and counties would otherwise have to provide. In some cases such contributions amount to more than estimated taxes, and for many types and tracts of federal land they are substantial in relation to possible taxes. Neither,

[34] A different conclusion for Oregon is presented on pp. 324-29.

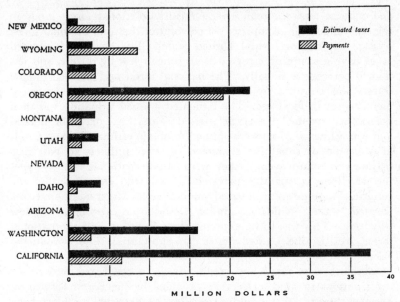

FIGURE 29. *Payments made by the Bureau of Land Management and the Forest Service in lieu of taxes to the eleven western states or their counties in 1955, compared with an estimate of taxes on the federal lands within each state. Probably this estimate is too high. The states are arranged in descending order of the ratio of payments to estimated taxes.*

as far as the authors know, have these states officially accepted the NEA estimates. While we consider the estimates to be too high, some of the states might contend they are too low. Certainly, the foregoing analysis should be regarded as suggestive rather than definitive in treatment.

ESTIMATED TAXES ON NATIONAL FORESTS

A study of estimated taxes on national forests for 1952 has been made by the Forest Service,[35] based on a sample of 135 out of the 652 counties that contain national forest land; the counties were chosen at random within some thirty-four strata based on location

[35] Williams, Ellis T., *op. cit.*

and natural and economic characteristics. National forest lands in the sample counties comprised 40 per cent of the total national forest acreage in the continental United States. The data for estimated taxes have a sampling error of 8 per cent or less by regions and less than 6 per cent nationally. The national forest area of each sample county was classified by local Forest Service officials into the assessment classes in local use. The estimated assessed valuation was then determined by use of average assessed values for each class of land and prevailing tax rates were applied to obtain estimated taxes. Lands of a barren or subalpine character, or types unlikely to pass into private ownership even if they were not in national forests—types for which no comparable privately owned land existed within the counties—were given an assessed value of zero. Much additional area merited "waste," "wild," or similar classifications carrying a very low valuation. This was to be expected since less than half the national forest area in the United States has substantial timber-producing value.

Estimates were made and credit was given the Forest Service for contributions in kind, or services provided by the Forest Service on national forests "that could reasonably be expected to have been made by state, county, or other local governments in the absence of national forest expenditures." Expenditures were not included merely because they were useful, but because, in their absence, local government could and would have spent funds to continue the same services. Nearly half of the contributions in kind were for the construction and maintenance of forest highways, about 30 per cent were for fire control, and about 20 per cent for roads and trails.

In addition to estimated taxes and contributions in kind, consideration was given to the revenue-sharing payments—the 25 per cent of gross receipts from each national forest paid to the states in which national forest lands are located and spent for the benefit of county schools and county roads.

The general results of this study were summarized as follows:

	Million dollars	Cents per acre
Estimated taxes, calendar year 1952	29.7	19
25 per cent fund payments, fiscal year 1952	17.4	11
Contributions in kind, fiscal years 1950-52, average annual	38.8	24

It is thus evident that direct cash payments to these counties in this year were nearly 60 per cent of the estimated taxes. The study points out that payments under the 25 per cent fund have risen from less than 1 cent per acre for the entire national forest system before the war, to over 10 cents per acre in 1952. On the basis of data presented in appendix table 52, the figure in 1955 was over 12 cents per acre, and in 1956 about 17 cents. The striking thing, however, is the value of the services rendered by the Forest Service on the national forests—a value greater than the total estimated taxes.

If these figures are correct, state and local governments are actually better off with these lands in federal ownership and management, even if they received no revenues at all, than to have them on the tax roll and be forced to pay for the necessary services. Some may doubt if the Forest Service was realistic in applying its criteria, i.e., that the cost of such services was included only if the local governments would have been both willing and able to pay for the cost of the services involved. But even if its estimate is heavily discounted, the total of payments made and services rendered is greater than estimates of taxes. The importance of the value of the services rendered on these lands underlines the importance of their omission from the NEA study previously discussed.

	United States	Northern	Southern	Rocky Mountain	Pacific Coast
		(cents per acre)			
Estimated tax per acre.........	18.6	14.1	13.5	6.8	47.5
25% fund payments per acre....	10.9	6.0	27.8	3.2	25.8
Contributions in kind per acre..	24.3	22.5	23.1	15.9	43.7

The situation differed in different parts of the country: In the South, the 25 per cent fund payments were roughly twice as much as estimated taxes; elsewhere they were roughly half as much. In every region except the Pacific Coast the contributions in kind were greater than the estimated taxes per acre, and even on the Pacific Coast they were nearly as great. In every region the total of the 25 per cent fund payments and contributions in kind was materially more than estimated taxes.

On the basis of this Forest Service study, it is apparent that *in total* local government is not losing because the national forest lands are not on the tax rolls. Individually, however, some counties may receive relatively little revenue or contributions in kind, compared with estimated taxes on the same land; other counties may receive appreciably more than the estimated taxes.

Particular interest attaches to the payments out of federal land revenue to the eighteen counties of western Oregon in which the O & C lands lie. In recent years Oregon has received considerably more payments out of federal land revenues than has any other western state—in some years, more than the two next largest states combined (appendix table 57). Nearly all of the payments to Oregon have gone to these eighteen counties. The rate of increase in payments to Oregon has been especially rapid—about a tenfold increase in eight years.

Payments to these eighteen O & C counties come in large amounts from O & C lands and from national forest lands. While no comprehensive study of the probable taxes on these federal lands has ever been made, some significant data do exist. It will be recalled that the O & C counties receive more than 50 per cent of the receipts from O & C lands, and would get 75 per cent if the cost of roads were not deducted from their share; and that they receive 25 per cent of national forest receipts.

The distribution of the O & C payments follows the formula established in the 1937 act based on the relative assessed value of the O & C lands in 1915 when they were last upon the tax rolls as private property. Each county receives a percentage of total receipts which is the same each year, irrespective of the origin of the receipts, but the shares are not equal.

As will be seen from the figures below, well over half of the total goes to three counties: Douglas county, with about 25 per cent; Jackson county, with about 17 per cent; and Lane county, with nearly 16 per cent. Since the relative importance of O & C lands differs greatly between counties, this formula may distribute the revenue more or less proportionately. Certainly it is an advantage that the counties can depend on receiving the same sum every year. Totalled together, O & C payments and national forest payments to these eighteen counties have risen from $1.3 million in 1945 to over $18 million in 1955 (appendix table 58). A strong upward trend in payments from the federal agencies is evident.

Total county taxes from private lands in these same counties increased over these same years, as has been generally true throughout the nation. A fourfold increase from $23 million in 1945 to $91 million in 1955 contrasts with the fourteenfold increase in payments from federal agencies. In 1945 payments from the federal agencies

County	Total payments received 1916-56 [1] ($1,000)
Benton	2,450
Clackamas	4,148
Columbia	1,306
Coos	5,367
Curry	1,180
Douglas	18,982
Jackson	12,431
Josephine	7,040
Klamath	1,522
Lane	11,486
Lincoln	331
Linn	2,254
Marion	1,216
Multnomah	914
Polk	1,899
Tillamook	499
Washington	540
Yamhill	609
Clark (Washington)	4
Total	74,175

[1] Including payments on Coos Bay Wagon Road Grant lands.

were less than 6 per cent of taxes on private property; by 1955 they were 20 per cent. The tax figure is heavily dominated by Multnomah county in which Portland lies. If this county is omitted, payments from the federal agencies in 1945 and 1955 are 10 per cent and 31 per cent of taxes on private land.

The counties differ greatly in the share of their revenues from the federal land. At one extreme is Josephine county, which in 1955 received 143 per cent from the federal agencies as from the taxes it raised on all private property. Other counties receiving comparatively large payments are Douglas, with 89 per cent as much from this source as from taxes in 1955, and Jackson with 63 per cent as much. Even Lane county received 34 per cent as much from federal lands as from taxes on private land.

Another approach to this problem is possible. Since 1946 county assessors in Oregon have been required by law to report the value of all tax-exempt property, including federal property. Their estimates of the value of *all* tax-exempt federal property are shown in appendix table 59. Since these estimates include all federal property, they are too high when applied to O & C, national forest, and public

domain lands alone; the extent by which they are too high varies
from county to county, being greatest in largely urban counties and
least in counties with smaller urban centers. These estimates of
assessed value exhibit some erratic variations from year to year—
for instance, in Clackamas and Douglas counties in 1950, Multnomah
county in 1948, and Marion county in 1952. But perhaps they give
a rough idea of the value of the tax-exempt federal property in the
group of counties, if not in each. The totals rose from $247 million
in 1946 to $306 million in 1954 if Multnomah county is included,
and from $169 million to $245 million if it is excluded. These rises
are at least roughly in line with the increases in taxes on privately
owned land, the upward trend of which was largely due to higher
assessed values.

These assessed values become more meaningful when related to
the foregoing data on payments from O & C, national forest, and
public domain lands. The assessed values are inflated for this purpose by the inclusion of Multnomah county, which is largely urban
in character. The payments figures are too low because they do not
include payments from other types of land or federal property. Accordingly, total payments to the eighteen O & C counties have been
related to the assessed values of all federal property in these counties,
omitting Multnomah. The resulting payments per $100 of assessed
valuation are as follows:

1946	$0.65
1948	2.30
1950	1.45
1952	4.04
1954	3.62
1955 (est.)	7.25
1956 (est.)	7.13

The results of this comparison are slightly erratic, rising in some
years and falling in others. But a strong upward trend is evident.
The 1955 figure shows a sharp rise over the preceding year because
of the payment of the impounded funds from the previously controverted lands in that year; part of this unusually large sum is
properly creditable to earlier years. But the total payment in 1956
was still larger, although the payment per $100 of assessed value was
slightly less. On the basis of these data it would appear that, beginning with 1952, the counties were getting in cash the full tax
equivalent or more from these lands; tax rates on private property

as high as $5.00 per $100 assessed value are considered nearly confiscatory, and rates above $3.00 are considered high. These cash payments make no allowance for the value of services provided by the federal agencies, that the counties otherwise would be required to furnish.

In the county comparisons which follow the 1955 and 1956 payments have been divided by the 1954 estimated assessed value, to obtain the following payments per $100 of assessed value:

	1955	1956
Benton	$ 14.65	$ 13.26
Clackamas	5.00	5.52
Columbia	1,014.28	890.48
Coos	8.78	7.87
Curry	10.68	11.98
Douglas	18.40	18.39
Jackson	17.64	15.47
Josephine	65.96	54.61
Klamath	8.42	8.73
Lane	2.98	3.53
Lincoln	11.58	16.73
Linn	4.76	6.54
Marion	1.28	1.62
Multnomah	0.58	0.47
Polk	274.31	240.37
Tillamook	7.83	9.72
Washington	96.77	82.80
Yamhill	66.85	66.85
Average payments per $100 of total assessed value in eighteen counties	5.91	6.05
Average payments per $100 of total assessed value excluding Multnomah	7.25	7.45

These results are clearly erratic for some counties. Although, for reasons explained previously, the 1955 payment was large, all counties were affected about equally by this fact, since the same percentage distribution of O & C funds between counties existed in all years. The variations between counties were due to other factors. Payment per $100 of assessed value was almost equally high in 1956. At one extreme is Columbia county, where the payment was more than ten times the reported assessed value, and Polk county where it was nearly three times; at the other extreme is Marion county with a payment little more than $1.00 per $100 assessed value, and Lane

county with less than $3.00. It would appear that some of the as-
sessed values, if not all of them, may have been carelessly arrived at.
On their face, however, they show that in 1955 and 1956 these counties were getting substantially more than tax equivalent from the
lands.

The Coos Bay Wagon Road Grant lands can shed further light
on the matter of tax-equivalent payments from federally owned forested lands in western Oregon. In physical characteristics these lands
are similar to the forested O & C and national forest lands; they are
intermingled with them, or closely adjacent. However, since their
reconveyance to the United States in 1919 the Coos Bay lands have
paid a tax-equivalent payment to the counties—a payment based, as
nearly as could be estimated by county and federal officials, on what
these lands would have paid if in private ownership. The lands lie
chiefly in Coos county and to a lesser extent in Douglas county; fiscal
conditions in these counties are possibly not identical with those
in other western Oregon counties.

For fiscal years 1940-55 inclusive, payments in lieu of taxes have
been slightly less than 10 per cent of gross receipts from the Coos
Bay lands. Beginning with fiscal 1950, when sales of timber increased
substantially over previous lower levels, payments in lieu of tax
through fiscal 1955 averaged about 7 per cent of gross receipts. In
estimating tax-equivalent payments, no account was taken of services
provided by the federal government on these lands, which were small.
To the extent the situation on these lands is typical of all federally
owned forested lands in western Oregon, it appears that the 50 per
cent of gross receipts for O & C lands and the 25 per cent for national
forests is excessive.

These data in themselves are not proof that payments from the
federal land are too high in these counties, but they are highly suggestive. A definitive finding would have to be based on careful and
consistent appraisal of land in these federal ownerships and in private
ownership, and of the extent of the governmental services provided
by the federal agencies.

The data do show that the relationship between payments from
federal land and taxes on private land has changed materially in
the past few years; that, in fact, federal lands have become a major
source of revenue to these counties—an almost dominant source for
a few of them. Not many years ago these same counties received
relatively little from the large areas of federal land lying in their
midst. Local newspapers have reported that in some southwestern

Oregon counties taxes on privately owned forest land have been sharply reduced. In some of these counties new courthouses and other major structures have been built in recent years. One county is reported to have about $1 million invested in other securities, on which it earns interest. All of these items are suggestive that the counties have prospered greatly from their share of federal land revenues.

POSSIBILITY OF DIRECT IN-LIEU TAX PAYMENTS
FROM FEDERAL LAND

The general situation we have outlined with respect to payments from federal lands to states and counties leads to speculation about the possibility of making direct tax-equivalent payments on the federal land. To accomplish this a procedure somewhat along the following lines might be set up: (1) local units of government would be encouraged to make tax assessments and tax-equivalent calculations for the federal land within their boundaries on the basis of assessments applicable to the most nearly comparable types of privately owned land; (2) from the taxes so estimated the local officials would deduct their estimated cost of services provided by the federal agencies for agreed-upon types of services ordinarily performed by local government for privately owned land; (3) the federal agencies would be empowered to pay the tax-equivalent bill so rendered if in their judgment they considered it reasonable; and (4) in the event of dispute, the issue could be decided by some method of arbitration. Some mechanism, possibly an interagency committee, would be required to insure reasonable consistency on the part of the federal agencies. A flexible procedure of this kind could be adapted to the revenue needs in each unit of local government and to the amount contributed by the federal agencies to the cost of local governmental services. Local initiative would be encouraged, but the federal government would be protected against unreasonable assessments.[36]

If something like the foregoing were to be done, any enabling legislation would have to define most carefully the terms and procedures, especially as to the kinds and intensities of services rendered by the

---

[36] A proposal to create a federal review board, to serve essentially the same purpose, is made in a Study Committee Report, *Payments in Lieu of Taxes and Shared Revenues,* submitted to the Commission on Intergovernmental Relations, June 1955.

federal agencies. What would be the probable consequences? First, it is not possible to say with certainty, on the basis of evidence in hand, whether the payments in lieu of taxes would be as large as, or larger than, the present payments out of revenues. There is a good probability that they would not be larger than at present, and a virtual certainty that tax equivalents would be less than the present share of receipts in the near future, as revenues from the federal lands increase. Second, it is certain that distribution of tax-equivalent payments to states and counties would be different—in some cases materially different—from the payments now made out of revenues; some states and counties would gain, others would lose. Third, payments of fixed sums by the federal agencies would remove the appropriation-sharing objection to revenue sharing. Payment would no longer depend upon the intensity with which a federal agency managed its land. Fourth, payments equal to taxes, minus expenses that local government itself estimates it would otherwise have to undertake, would remove much of the cause for complaint by states and counties as to the nontax-paying status of the federal lands in their midst. Fifth, this arrangement would permit flexibility in raising revenues to meet local needs more than would any fixed formula basis.

It is recognized that many factors, including those of administrative feasibility and general acceptance, will govern any change from the present basis of revenue sharing with states and counties. Nevertheless, a re-examination of the whole system at this time would seem to be desirable.

Need for Better Data and Better Analysis

The experience of assembling revenue and expenditure data on the federal land provides the basis for some suggestions for the future. A great need exists for better data on the revenues from and expenditures on federal lands of all types, and for better analysis of the data that exist or that could be readily developed in the future.

Existing data on revenues and expenditures are badly scattered. The most readily available sources of information are the annual budget submissions and annual reports of the various agencies. But by no means all the data needed are to be found in these two places. There is little historical background against which to judge the significance of such data as are given in any single source; and these are not always comparable from year to year and rarely from agency to agency. Even for students of the management of the federal lands, data on revenues and expenditures have been nearly nonexistent in readily available, consistent, sensible form. The authors spent the equivalent of nine man-months assembling, analyzing, and revising the data given in the appendix tables. The time spent would have been longer had it not been for the familiarity brought to the subject matter and for the helpful co-operation of the various agencies.

Nonetheless, there are serious gaps in the available data. Some of them are evident in the appendix tables; some are concealed by the form of the tables which was determined in large part by the availability of data.

One serious deficiency in data concerns the operations of the Mineral Leasing Act. The records are kept partly in the Bureau of Land Management, partly in the Geological Survey; for the convenience of the oil industry many records of the latter are on a calendar-year rather than a fiscal-year basis. The data that are tabulated are not made available through consistent and detailed public releases. Data by fiscal years on numbers of leases, acreages of leases, and on royalty, bonus, and rental income separately, each for producing and for nonproducing leases, have generally not been publicly available in the past. The Geological Survey has provided some of these data for this book; they are given in appendix tables 15 to 22.

As with the data, so with analysis: the various agencies make only a limited analysis of the revenue and expenditure situation for the lands under their jurisdiction. Some analysis is to be found in annual reports and budget submissions, but often it is incomplete, rarely has it real historical perspective, often it is not comparable for the same agency from year to year—virtually never from agency to agency. On the whole, the Forest Service has a better record in this regard than have the other federal land managing agencies. It may well be that some agencies, in their concern for broad resource management policies, prefer to limit the emphasis given to fiscal aspects of their operations, believing that a contrary course would react adversely on their budget requests. The form of most agency records has been influenced more by operational problems than by needs for economic analysis.

Reports and data are especially deficient in analyzing the relation between additional outlays and additional revenues, what the economist would call the marginal-revenue–marginal-cost relationship.

If an additional $1,000 is spent on a particular type of land, for specified purposes, will the additional revenue be more or less than the additional expenditure? It is generally accepted among economists, accountants, and businessmen that additional expenditures should be made as long as additional revenues are greater than the expenditures; it can readily be shown that at this point net revenues (or profits) are the greatest. It is often true that the relation between marginal expenditure and marginal revenue is far different from the relation between average expenditure and average revenue; that is, an activity may be returning a handsome margin of revenue over expenditures, but additional expenditure would return insufficient additional revenue to cover the cost. Another activity might be returning less revenue than present expenditure, but additional sums spent would be far more than returned.

Examination of the data presented in this chapter, personal knowledge of the authors, and statements of agency administrators all give reason for supposing that the level of expenditures on the federal lands is far below the maximum revenue-minus-expenditure point; and even farther below a point where nonrevenue-producing activities would be adequately provided for. Apparently no competent analysis of this matter exists in published form, if it exists at all, which seems doubtful. The usual form of budget request seeks to demonstrate that the amount requested is needed or is reasonable. Work load statistics, job performance standards, manpower and material requirements, and various other management devices are used, especially in the better managed agencies. These devices are valuable, but they are generally not directed toward the marginal net revenue problem; they are used to support requests for funds to perform an intensity of management which is judged desirable on other grounds. A careful and adequate analysis of the financial results of applying different levels of expenditure to the federal lands has yet to be made. Responsibility for deficiency must be shared at several levels of government. Funds necessary to employ personnel to collect the needed data and to make the desired analyses have generally not been provided. Full analyses have not been required of the responsible federal agencies by the Bureau of the Budget or by the Congress, and such analyses as have been made have often had rather superficial consideration. It is doubtful if in the past even the best of analyses would have materially influenced the budget considerations. But the seriousness of the deficiency will be more marked as the intensity of use of the federal lands increases and as both expenditures and revenues rise. If the deficiency is to be made good, effort and time at several levels of government will be necessary.

In the management of the federal lands the type of balance-sheet analysis and analysis of future profit prospects which characterizes the management of well-run private companies is generally lacking. The nearest approach are the annual reports of the Forest Service; but it is doubtful if well-managed private business concerns would consider them adequate. Money is spent and money is collected, sometimes with a favorable balance, sometimes with an adverse one. Capital accounts are mostly lacking or incomplete. There is little or no analysis of the relation between marginal costs at present and those in the recent past; above all, there is almost no consideration of the future. It is understandable that federal agencies may hesitate to volunteer forecasts of future revenues. The appropriations process may tie their hands: Will appropriations be cut if future revenues exceed their forecasts? Will they be penalized if revenues fall short of forecasts? However unwise, bureaucratic caution may dominate the interests of broad public resource management.

When one considers federal land in total, the scarcity of data and analysis is aggravated by a total lack of co-ordination between agencies. No consolidated balance sheet of revenues and expenditures is now prepared, nor, so far as is known, has one been attempted. As a matter of fact given the present structure of government, it would be difficult to find a place in government where a consolidated summary could be prepared. No single land administering agency could do it, and there is no force encouraging the agencies to do so co-operatively. The Bureau of the Budget or a Congressional committee might prepare a summary, but it is unlikely that either is equipped with the staff necessary for such an undertaking. As far as revenues and expenditures are concerned, the over-all view of federal land management is totally missing.

CHAPTER SIX

What of the Future?

THE FOREGOING CHAPTERS HAVE PRESENTED A great deal of information about the federal lands today, and their history. This book has not been history for history's sake, but was written because we assume that the lessons of the past have relevance for the future. Using such wisdom and knowledge as the lessons of the past have taught with respect to the federal lands, what can we foresee for their future?

Before beginning a more detailed consideration of possible future developments, we wish to stress again our basic assumption set forth in the Introduction: there will be no major change in the net acreage of land in federal ownership, as we have used the term. The reasons for this assumption and its meaning were outlined in the Introduction. As a consequence, we have ruled out consideration of transfer of substantial parts of the federal land to nonfederal ownership, or major increases in federal landownership or land management activities. One theoretical solution to some of the problems of federal land management would be to turn over all or large parts of these lands to other ownership. We believe this is not a practical solution. In the discussion of future federal land management problems which follows, as well as in specific statistics of future situations, this assumption is basic.

A New Era in Federal Land History

Federal lands have entered into a new era in their history—that of intensive management. The major characteristics of this new era are greatly increased intensity of use, much greater revenues than in the past, and the need for larger investments and expenditures for current management. These changes are so large in degree as to mean a change in kind; the management of federal lands in the future will be significantly different from their management in the past. Although eras do not begin and end precisely in a single year, in fiscal 1951, for the first time in modern federal land history, gross revenues from all federal lands equalled total expenditures on them; hence 1950 may serve as well as any year to mark the beginning of the new major era.

SUMMARY OF PAST AS BASIS FOR FORECASTING THE FUTURE

The major impression emerging from a study of federal land management is growth—growth in use, growth in revenues.

A number of the measures of use of federal lands show strong growth trends. The volume of timber cut, the quantity of oil and gas produced, and the numbers of recreation visits, each show growth trends roughly approximating 10 per cent per year. In each case the growth is a logarithmic or percentage one; the more the lands are used, the faster is the growth in their use in absolute terms. While there have been minor deviations, the uniformity in the rates of growth of these major factors for the whole period is striking. There is no clear evidence of their slowing down. While it would be impossible to continue a 10 per cent annual growth rate for long, growth in these major forms of federal land use has been at this rapid rate from as early as 1905 in some cases, and as late as 1924 in others, until the present.

In this picture of growth in use of federal lands only grazing shows a major decline; mining of metals has probably not increased and perhaps has decreased considerably, but no reliable quantitative figures exist to measure changes in this use.

While water and its conservation have become increasingly more important, data on watershed use are lacking. The stream flow and water use data available do not differentiate between flows that would have existed without special watershed management and those which are in some degree attributable to such management. Such information as does exist, however, shows that the value of water from the federal lands has increased greatly over recent years. Some estimates of the value of the water rising from federal lands suggest a total value of water as great as the value of all the products sold from these lands. While these estimates have not been subjected to the scrutiny of critics and hence are not as yet fully accepted, it does seem probable that one of the most valuable products of federal land is water.

The increase in revenues from the federal lands has been even more startling than the increase in their use. Revenues have increased from a $20 million to $30 million annual range during the war to a $300 million to $350 million level at present—a more than tenfold rise in ten years. Almost overnight, in the historical sense, federal lands have become big business in the American sense of the term; in 1955 revenues from all federal lands were large enough to have put them within the hundred largest industrial corporations of the nation, if the lands had been privately owned in one combined enterprise.[1] The general price level roughly doubled in these years, and thus the rise in real revenues was half as large—but still a growth of five times in ten years is hardly slow. With the great increase in physical output from the federal lands, it could not have been otherwise. Then too, some prices rose more than the rise of the general price level. This was especially true of lumber and stumpage prices, which advanced at least seven times in monetary terms and three to five times in real terms in these years.

The dramatic new development in the federal "land" field is the submerged areas of the outer continental shelf. Considered both valueless and inaccessible only a few years ago, and then retarded in development by legal and political struggles over their ownership, they are now clearly federal (although some dispute still continues as to some part of them) and available for exploitation. Dramatic new technological and engineering developments now permit oil well drilling in many feet of water, thus opening these areas to practical use. Oil and gas leases sold at public sale have yielded bonuses of over $250 million to date. Although yet largely an unknown or at least an unproven factor, especially from the economic viewpoint, these areas may be a major future source of oil for the United States as well as a major future source of oil royalties to the federal government.

Increased expenditures have been necessary to achieve these greater revenues and to permit the increased uses of the federal lands. Total annual expenditures have risen from the $40 million to $50 million

[1] See p. 383 for further details.

range during the war to a level between $150 million and $170 million now. These sums also reflect the rough doubling of prices, so that the rise in expenditures in real terms has been somewhat less than twice. A fivefold increase of real revenues while real expenditures were doubling in ten years would be a financial feat of no mean proportions, if that were all the story. In fact, expenditures have lagged seriously, especially for some functions, and services to the public have been correspondingly impaired. In view of the experience of the past few years, it would appear that a somewhat larger volume of business on the federal lands could be handled without a proportionate rise in expenditures; this may especially be so for timber sale, oil leasing, and other functions involving revenue. But the funds available for recreation have been seriously deficient—a deficiency from which the Park Service seems about to escape, and possibly the Forest Service as well.

This serious lag in expenditures grows out of the equally great lag in appropriations, and this in turn largely grows out of the built-in lags in the appropriation process. Appropriations have been rising, in dollar terms; the loss of much of the apparent rise to higher prices and costs, and the need for much greater rises in real terms, have been less apparent. The lag in appropriations has been particularly serious for investment funds; in the past four or five years substantially more money has been appropriated, at least for timber access roads, but the amounts available for this function are still too small in relation to need and there has been no major increase for other functions until the last year or two.

With revenues rising at a rate much faster than expenditures, it was inevitable that the situation in which revenues were substantially below expenditures which prevailed during the war should give way to one at present where gross revenues (even excluding the submerged areas) exceed total expenditures. Up through 1947, both gross revenues and revenues net after payments to states, counties, and the Reclamation Fund were less than either total expenditures or operating expenditures. From 1951 through 1955, the situation as to revenues and expenditures was somewhat confused. Beginning in 1951, gross revenues (even excluding submerged areas) exceeded total expenditures, but net revenues (after payments to states, counties, and the Reclamation Fund) did not exceed operating expenditures until 1955, and then only by a very small amount. At no time through 1956 did net revenues (excluding submerged areas) exceed *all* expenditures, that is, operating expenses plus investment. This comparatively poor showing of net revenues is due, in no small part, to the large disbursements made to states and counties and even more to the large diversion of land revenues to the Reclamation Fund.

Beginning with 1955 the situation changed greatly, if the submerged areas are included. Now, both gross and net revenues far exceed all expenditures, and obviously exceed operating expenditures even further. This vastly more favorable financial picture is due not only to the large revenues secured from the submerged areas, but also to the fact that, thus far at least, neither states nor counties nor Reclamation Fund has managed to get a cut out of them.[2]

The interest or pressure groups most concerned about federal lands fall into four occupational groups: those interested in forestry and timber harvest; those concerned with grazing; the mineral development groups; and a group best characterized as recreation-conservation-general resources. Each such group is further divided according to whether its primary orientation is that of the professional society, that of the semi-professional – general-public group, or is industry oriented, or is a nonprofit research foundation. Still other groups normally take little interest in federal land management, but can sometimes be rallied to a position or a course of action because of the actions of some of the directly interested groups. The industry groups are often in a better position to give continued attention to matters concerning them, but less able to rally large-scale popular support, than are the organizations interested in recreation and conservation of resources in general. The mass of the general public is uninformed and normally uninterested in federal land management. Each interest group tries to influence action at the legislative and administrative level in directions favorable to it.

The two major governmental processes by which the will of the public, or at least the interested portions of it, is translated into action are the budget-appropriation-allocation and legislative processes. Each involves both the Executive and Legislative branches of government. The most serious shortcoming of the appropriation process is that it tends to reflect past conditions too much, and to adapt too slowly to new situations. For resource management it has another basic deficiency: appropriations for this purpose are considered in nearly the same light as are appropriations for general governmental functions, and do not sufficiently consider the revenue-

[2] The situation differs considerably for the different types of federal land; the reader is referred to chapter five for information on each type.

producing aspects of resources and the economic tests inherent in revenue production. There are other serious difficulties, particularly as to timing, inflexibility, and various hampering restrictions. These disadvantages are especially serious for investment appropriations, because the ill effects of inadequate investments are less immediately felt; hence the need for appropriations for this purpose are even more underestimated. The level of investment greatly affects the kind of management that is possible; many desirable management practices require investment. The fullest future economic use of the federal lands will require substantially greater investments than have been made in the past.

The federal lands suffer in the legislative process from the necessity of obtaining essentially unanimous agreement, or of generating sufficient interest to permit effective competition for the time and attention of the Congress in the resolution of issues on which complete agreement is not possible. Federal land law is in general a tangle. Many laws are highly detailed, others have great breadth and generality, and the total is encumbered with parts more or less obsolete and yet not decently buried. Each of the four major industry or occupational groups seems sufficiently strong to block proposals of any other group to which it feels really strongly opposed, and no group seems to have sufficient strength to push legislation to enactment over the determined opposition of another group.

The many demands for the federal land and its products, and the diverse physical and economic conditions on and around them, complicate the decision-making process. To best satisfy the demands and to protect the public interest in the lands, the philosophy of multiple-use management has evolved for most of the federal lands. Its essence is the simultaneous use of the same or of closely intermingled areas for two or more purposes, on a carefully planned and co-ordinated basis. Forestry, grazing, recreation, watershed management, and many other types of federal land use, and varying forms of use within these major types, are each considered and as far as possible provided for.

The decision-making process is further complicated because in many instances the federal land manager must substitute his decision for that of the market place. In no instance is the decision between major uses of federal land or between the relative emphasis upon different major uses made in the market place, and only for most timber sales and a few mineral lease sales is the choice between individual applicants based upon the competitive bidding of the various applicants. In all other cases the administrators, through applicable regulations, on the basis of various factual analyses, and by the exercise of personal judgment, decide upon the major kinds of land use, or the degree of one use compared with others, and upon the individual or individuals who shall use the federal lands.

This method of allocating the uses of federal lands and their products has been a rather conscious one. In spite of criticisms of it by those not fully satisfied with its results, there would be major opposition to a wholesale use of the competitive bid. Nevertheless, this system makes for a more complicated, red-tape encumbered, and slower administration than would otherwise probably be necessary. Competitive bidding does not eliminate all decision making, however, for the terms of sale are often as important as the monetary price, and these can be modified or manipulated to ends other than maximum revenue.

While the whole process of federal land management, and especially of investment on these lands, has not been guided primarily by economic considerations and economic analysis, especially in the budget-appropriation-allocation process, yet one must admit that there is one major obstacle to the application of economic considerations to the level of appropriations for management, and especially for investment on these lands. This is the present arrangement for sharing of gross revenues with states and counties, and even more with the diversion of revenues to the Reclamation Fund. Private businesses are subject to real estate taxes and taxes based upon net incomes, and these are sometimes denounced for their adverse effects on economic activity. But the federal lands pay what amounts to a gross income tax, ranging from 25 per cent to 75 per cent in most cases. An expenditure for more intensive management or for investment will return to the federal Treasury its direct cash cost only if the gross return is from 1.33 to 4.0 times the outlay. This is a standard often impossible to meet, even for activities which private business finds highly profitable.

The revenue-sharing provisions of federal land law will be a major handicap to the investment of additional funds on these lands. One solution would be to put the federal lands, in effect, upon the local tax roll. The total cost to the federal government would probably be no more than at present, the local units of government would be dealt with more equitably, and the inhibiting effect of revenue sharing on appropriations would be removed. Another remedial action would be to abolish the transfer of funds from federal lands receipts to the Reclamation Fund.

PROJECTIONS FOR THE FUTURE SUMMARIZED

Projections of future use and revenue grow naturally out of past experience on federal lands.[2] Projections for the future are at best subject to a considerable margin of error, but they do make explicit what seems implicit in past trends. Underlying our projections have been assumptions of a rising population, rising real income per capita, more leisure for the average person, absence of devastating war, and continued technological advance but nothing so radical as to make less valuable most of the conventional natural resources. For the economic projections, a reasonably stable general price level has been assumed. The level of use and productivity of the federal lands will depend in considerable measure upon the availability of funds for their management, especially funds for investment; the projected expenditures are the minimum that will produce the projected revenues, and provide for the projected uses of the land, and maintain or increase the productivity of the resources.

The projections are summarized in table 15. In general, the federal lands will produce a larger share of the total national supply in the future than in the past. An approximate doubling of timber sales by 1980 is projected and is within the sustained yield concept. Although it would require more intensive forestry than at present, it would still be considerably short of the biological potential of these lands. From about 15 per cent of the national timber harvest at present, the share from the federal lands would rise to about 30 per cent by 1980. This projected rate of increase in timber sales for the future would be much below the rate for the past.

A much greater increase in recreational use of federal lands seems probable. The extent of the increase is difficult to predict. Two projections have been made for the national park system: a high level based upon the 1947-54 trend, and a lower one based on the 1952-55 trend. Possibly past trends will slacken in the future, although there is little solid evidence of it now. Since comprehensive recreation statistics are not available, it is impossible to estimate the relative share of federal lands in the whole recreation picture. It seems reasonable to expect, however, that use of these recreational resources will rise faster than the use of most other recreational resources.

---

[2] For details of these projections by types of federal land, the reader is referred to chapters two and five.

TABLE 15. *Summary of Projections for 1960 and 1980, all Federal Lands* [1]

Item	Unit	History		Projections	
		1955	1956	1960	1980
Timber sales:					
national forests	billion bd. ft.	6.6	7.0	9.0	15.0
O & C	billion bd. ft.	.7	.7	.7	1.0
Recreation:					
national forests	million visits	46	53	65	360
national parks system	million visits	50	55	80[2] / 60[3]	440[2] / 135[2]
Oil and gas production:					
federal lands	million barrels	160	168	275	800
submerged areas	million barrels	13	23	300	750
Gross cash revenues:					
excluding submerged areas	million dollars	175	220	304	667
including submerged areas	million dollars	317	331	399	877
Net cash revenues: [4]					
excluding submerged areas	million dollars	84	115	144	308
including submerged areas	million dollars	226	226	238	518
Contributions from private sources [5]	million dollars	11	12	16	22
Expenditures:					
all purposes	million dollars	153	176	259	426
operations only	million dollars	95	110	148	282

[1] Includes national forests, national parks, wildlife refuges, public domain, acquired and revested land, and submerged areas only; omits other types of federally owned or federally controlled land.

[2] High projections.

[3] Low projections.

[4] Net after payments to states, counties, and Reclamation Fund, but expenditures are not deducted.

[5] These are an additional revenue, "in kind" rather than in cash; must be added to cash revenues for comparisons with expenditures. Latter include expenditures of contributed funds.

Oil and gas production will probably rise rapidly both from the land areas and from the submerged areas. If these projections are realized, oil production in 1980 from the land would be five times what it was in 1955. On the submerged areas present production is so low that the percentage rise is very great indeed, but by 1980 the actual volume would be nearly that projected for the land. In total, these two types of federal property would be producing about 1.5 billion barrels of oil, or its equivalent in gas, annually by 1980. This might represent roughly 15 per cent of total petroleum production by that date.

Accompanying these very great projected increases in uses, major increases in revenue are anticipated. Gross revenue, excluding the submerged areas, is projected to rise nearly 50 per cent above the 1956 level by 1960, and to more than double in the following twenty years. Gross revenue including the submerged areas will rise relatively more slowly, because the large bonuses received in fiscal 1955 and 1956 are not likely to be repeated, at least not on that scale; but by 1980 the submerged areas are projected to produce more than $200 million annually. Federal land and submerged areas would be nearly a billion dollar business by 1980, according to these projections.

Net revenues are also projected to rise considerably. The rise from the lands only would be smaller in dollar terms than for gross revenues because under existing law such a large share of these revenues are paid to states, counties, or the Reclamation Fund. A change in any of these revenue-sharing arrangements might affect this picture greatly. Net revenues, when the submerged areas are included, rise by the amount of the increase in gross revenues from these areas. Even with the substantial deductions from gross revenues, net revenues by 1980 would be a very tidy sum.

Expenditures on the federal lands are projected to rise materially from the present level. Operating expenses would increase more than two and a half times from 1956 to 1980, going from $110 million to $282 million then. An approximately equal relative rise in investment expenditures from $66 million in 1956 to $144 million in 1980 would also be necessary.

On the basis of these projections, certain broad conclusions as to the net financial balance of the federal lands can be drawn: [4]

1. If present revenue-sharing arrangements continue, the lands alone, excluding the submerged areas, cannot pay operating expenses and at the same time support the projected level of investment. They can meet operating expenditures with only a few million dollars to spare each year for investment.

2. If the large-scale financial support from the federal lands to the reclamation program were discontinued, the situation would change greatly. The deficiency of revenue for all early years would be greatly reduced, making possible a substantial rate of investment, but below the projected level, out of net revenues as they would then be defined. In the later years a surplus would develop.

3. If the submerged areas are included with the land areas, net

[4] See table 12, p. 308, for more detailed data by types of land areas.

revenues in the early years will about meet all expenditures, including the level of investments projected, and in the later years a substantial surplus will develop.

4. Gross revenues, excluding the submerged areas, provide an even larger margin over total expenditures than did net revenues including the submerged areas. However, for reasons set forth previously, we believe it illogical to make comparisons based on gross revenues.

These comparisons are based upon present pricing methods of the various products sold and, except as explicitly noted with respect to the Reclamation Fund, upon present distribution of revenues to states, counties, and the Reclamation Fund. We have pointed out in chapter four that it would be possible, if it were desired to do so, to charge higher grazing fees, to obtain somewhat higher prices for timber sold, to secure substantial additional sums through higher rentals for nonproducing oil and gas leases, and to obtain somewhat more revenue from higher charges for recreation. In total, these various measures might yield as much as 30 per cent more revenue from the same resources; there are important policy considerations in higher charges, and there may be sound reasons for not obtaining the maximum revenue.

The use of the revenues could be changed also, if that were desired. Payments into the Reclamation Fund could be discontinued. for reasons previously set forth. The present revenue-sharing arrangements with states and counties are estimated to yield them now as much revenue as they could secure from taxes if the land were privately owned, when allowance is made for the value of the services performed by the federal agencies for the benefit of the local governments. On the basis of projected revenues, payments to states and counties will increase nearly 50 per cent by 1960, and nearly treble by 1980, over 1956 levels. While some increase in equivalent taxes is probable, it seems highly doubtful if increases of this magnitude will occur. The level of payments to states and counties under present laws will surely rise well above that of equivalent taxes. Is it equitable that it should?

Considering these various factors, we conclude that the federal lands *could* be made to earn enough cash to pay not only their operating but also their investment costs, after a fair tax equivalent. If all feasible steps to bring about a balance of revenues and expenditures on the federal lands were taken, it appears that the revenues from the submerged areas would not be needed, even to finance investment on the land. However, this tentative conclusion may well prove wrong in practice, because there inevitably is a large margin of error in any estimates of future revenue and expenditure. Revenues from the submerged areas would surely provide a large margin of safety for such errors of estimate, and would be needed if not all the steps suggested were taken. On the other hand, if these steps were taken the revenues, including those from the submerged areas, would be sufficient to finance some additional activities, such as federal grants-in-aid to states and other local government for recreation development. Recreation on lands under the control of such units of local government is closely related to recreation on the federal lands; and as our population becomes more mobile, good-quality parks tend to be used increasingly by people not resident in the taxing area which established the park. There is some rationality to the use of income from the sale of nonrenewable resources, for investment in resources which will serve permanently large sectors of the entire population.

There is another aspect to the continuation of federal land income payments into the Reclamation Fund. We have pointed out that the original reason for this arrangement is gone, and that today payments from land into this fund have no measurable effect upon the reclamation program. In the last year or two, substantial investments in the national park system have begun, and still larger ones are contemplated for the future. These investments may well be of the same rough magnitude as the payments from federal lands into the Reclamation Fund. If the latter payments are continued, direct appropriations out of the general revenues of the United States must be made to the national park system; if these payments were discontinued, a long step would be taken toward having all federal lands stand on their own financial feet. In effect, the direct appropriations for improvement of the national parks would merely replace the transfer of revenue from federal lands to the Reclamation Fund. One argument in favor of use of land income for the Reclamation Fund has been that the western states, where most of this income arises, get it spent back within their borders to their benefit, but this would be largely true also for investments in the national park system. It may also be argued that it is immaterial where taxes and other funds are raised, and where money for management and improvement of lands comes from—that it is all one big federal purse, and that there neither is nor should be a connection between revenues from a source and expenditures on it. Realistically, however, the Congress will almost surely appropriate more money for a function if the income from that function is equally large and is rather directly related to the expenditures, than if the money must come from general funds.

Since the federal lands are so largely located in the West, these revenue and use projections, and the chances of realizing them, are of particular significance to the West. If the full timber or oil harvest projected is not realized, the nation suffers to some extent because of a restricted supply of these raw materials, but the West suffers a more direct and relatively larger income loss. The West is particularly interested that the necessary appropriations be made; but if they are made, this region will produce from the federal lands a net balance of revenue for the federal Treasury.

The prospects for revenue may change from those on which these projections are based; and the need for expenditures, and hence the balance between the two, may likewise change. It will be possible, however, to make new estimates of probable revenues and expenditures at yearly or perhaps longer intervals. If there should be a move to tie expenditures and revenues more closely together, as is suggested in one alternative later in this chapter, there will be ample opportunity to re-examine revenue and expenditure prospects at intervals, and to make new financial plans based on the latest outlook.

CHARACTERISTICS OF THE NEW ERA

These projected major increases in the uses of federal lands and in the revenues from them are the basis for the characterization of the period from 1950 onward as a new major era in federal land history—the era of intensive management. The intensity of federal land use in the past few years has so much exceeded that of a few years ago, and promises to be so much greater in the future, as to constitute a different management problem. The same basic concern for conservation of the resources and for making them available widely to all people will continue in the future, as in the past. But the scale of activities will be several times as great as at even the end of the era of custodial management.

In this new era of intensive management substantially more capital must be invested in the federal lands, and substantially more money must be expended on their management each year. This will be necessary if the demands on their use are to be met, and if they are to make their maximum contribution to the national income and welfare. At the same time, these investments and expenditures promise to pay off well from a purely financial viewpoint as well as from a broader one.

If the new era develops even approximately as we have projected it, it will also intensify existing problems. Management problems and problems of appropriation and of use of revenues will become more difficult as the intensity of use rises. More groups will be seeking increased uses which will be incompatible with all that other groups seek. The range and complexity of policy and management decisions will increase. At the same time, the public support for a continuation of federal landownership may well rise above the present level, which we have judged to be great enough to prevent any move for major disposal of federal lands. While the lumberman might prefer private ownership of forested lands now federally owned, he would prefer federal ownership of these lands to their ownership by recreation groups; and vice versa. While each of the interest groups would perhaps like to see greater attention given to its use of federal lands, each may be forced to accept more compromise with the demands of others, and all may prefer that the federal agencies serve as the balance wheel.

If these projected uses of the federal lands are to be realized, what does this mean in terms of an administrative organization, at all levels of the federal government? How can the more difficult management problems be met? What are the alternatives? The rest of this chapter is concerned with these matters. Several alternatives are presented; perhaps other major alternatives will occur to others, and certainly there are many variations of each major alternative.

Federal Land Corporation

From an economic viewpoint, the basic need for federal land management in the future is for a more careful appraisal of expenditures and revenues; for larger appropriations, especially for investment, in order to make the lands more fully productive; and for generally less restrictive methods of resource management. At the same time that these basic needs are met, the methods of land administration must preserve the nonmonetary values of the federal lands, and must also be compatible with the American system of government. The administration of these lands must be not only responsible but also responsive to the wishes of the public.

The government corporation is a form of operation adopted for many essentially business operations undertaken by government. It has been used by states and municipalities as well as the federal government. Its advantages over the traditional bureau lie in its greater freedom and flexibility of operation. One of its greatest advantages lies in its flexibility with regard to expenditures—authority to expend revenues, to establish systems of accounts adapted to its needs, to make budgets of a general program nature rather than of great detail, and to have made audits comparable to those of business enterprises. As a legal entity, it has special powers not available to regular government agencies. The make-up of its governing body may also permit representation of divergent or varying interests.

Since the strong points of the government corporation largely match the shortcomings of federal land management by the existing bureaus, the possibility of establishing a federal land management corporation merits consideration.[5] For the coming period of intensive management during which revenues are expected to increase rapidly and the federal lands to emerge as truly big business, it makes sense to examine rather carefully that kind of government organization, namely the federal corporation, which would seem to offer maximum opportunity for dealing successfully with these economic, business-type problems. Here in this section we seek to do this in sufficient detail that the major characteristics of the corporation will be clear, while at the same time leaving many details of a possible corporation open for later consideration.

The criteria which a government corporation should normally meet are:

1. Its program is predominantly of a business nature.
2. Its activities are revenue-producing and potentially self-sustaining.
3. Its work involves a large number of business-type transactions with the public.
4. It requires greater flexibility than the customary type of appropriation budget ordinarily permits.[6]

The facts presented in this book show that federal land manage-

[5] A recent proposal for a federal forest land corporation is made in *The Forest Products Industry of Oregon*, Part 2, a report of the Business Executives' Research Committee sponsored by Lewis and Clark College and Reed College, Portland, Oregon, September, 1956.

[6] These criteria originally appeared in President Truman's Budget message for 1948.

ment meets these criteria at least in large measure. It should be noted that the criteria do not include the objective of maximizing net revenues, and in fact this is not the objective of most government corporations. If these criteria are the chief basis upon which decisions as to establishment of a federal land corporation are made, the federal lands would seem to meet them. However, other considerations may well be dominant.

The corporate form of organization has been used by the United States government for more than fifty years. Several of a temporary nature were created during World War I. The next big expansion occurred during the severe depression of the early 1930's. At that time, many corporations were created by government agencies without specific Congressional approval, which led to much severe criticism in Congress and elsewhere. As a result, the Government Corporation Control Act was passed in 1945. It established uniform rules for such corporations and required specific Congressional approval for the establishment of new ones. A major feature of that act was the provision for a business-type budget and commercial audit. With the passage of this act, the government corporation may be considered to have come of age.[7]

The government corporation has been used extensively for agricultural credit for many years, and is worth looking at briefly at this point. The federal land bank system began in 1916, the intermediate credit bank system was begun in 1923, and the production credit and co-operative credit system in 1933. Each of these involved corporations. The general principle has been initial government aid, by means of interest-free capital and technical supervision, and gradual transfer of control to the borrowers as they gain financial equity and experience. The various parts are under the supervision of a Farm Credit Administration, which was a separate agency from its creation in 1933 until 1939, when it became a bureau of the Department of Agriculture, and which again became a separate agency in 1953. It is now a government corporation, with special powers and privileges, and a unique method of selecting its management board. This is a complex and intricate system, composed of different units for different types of credit and in different areas, but the whole makes a well-

---

[7] Two recent references relating directly to the federal government corporation are: Sidney D. Goldberg and Harold Seidman, *The Government Corporation: Elements of a Model Charter*, Chicago: Public Administration Service, 1953; *Controlling Government Corporations*, New York: The Tax Foundation, Inc., August, 1955.

integrated setup. At the bottom are borrower associations of different types, which elect directors of the twelve District Boards for each type of lending institution, and also nominate men from whom the President selects directors of the national organization. One man from each of the twelve districts is appointed to the National Board, and in addition the Secretary of Agriculture names one director. The Board of Directors selects a Governor, subject to the approval of the President, and all direction of the agency is in his hands, subject to general policy review by the Board. He also appoints two directors to each District Board of Directors, but when the government capital has been repaid will appoint only one. The system as a whole has now become largely borrower-owned, and it is expected that in a few years it will be wholly so owned. The various banks and associations use their own funds as a basis for loans, and also borrow in the general credit markets of the nation. Their borrowings are not guaranteed by the federal government. The whole system pays its own expenses (except for interest on the government capital remaining, some free office space, and government contributions to employee retirement), and obtains no direct appropriations from the Treasury.

This is a major example of successful operation of the government corporation idea, and a recent instance of a move from regular bureau to government corporation.

ELEMENTS OF A CHARTER FOR A FEDERAL LAND CORPORATION [8]

Before considering the problems and policy issues involved in establishment of a federal land corporation, it seems necessary to consider the elements of such a corporation as briefly as is consistent with a reasonably clear picture of the advantages and difficulties. Corporations can take many forms and have widely varying powers. The merits or the weaknesses of a particular corporation will depend in no small measure upon the various details of its charter.

The main elements of a charter for a federal land corporation would include the following:

1. *Formal parts.* This would include the introductory paragraph creating the corporation; later paragraphs specifying the length of life for the corporation, which for federal lands presumably would be perpetual, since their administration is not a temporary matter;

---

[8] This discussion follows very closely after Goldberg and Seidman, *op. cit.*

provisions as to the location of offices, residence, and venue of the corporation, particularly in anticipation of possible later legal actions. These parts of the charter could be comparatively brief, but are highly important for any government corporation.

2. *General powers.* These are the matters which are more or less common to all government corporations, although their precise form may vary considerably from one corporation to another. This would include such general matters as the power of the corporation to acquire and dispose of property. This is most important to the federal land corporation, because its basic purpose is management of real property. Any act establishing a federal land corporation should spell out very carefully which lands were transferred to the corporation; if the definition were the same as used in this book, these would include the national forests, the grazing districts, other public domain, revested and reconveyed lands, submerged areas of the outer continental shelf, the entire national park system, wildlife refuges, and perhaps other miscellaneous areas. Since there are many types of areas, especially areas under one form of withdrawal or another, this specification of lands would have to be drawn with the greatest care.

Among the general powers might be included authority to borrow funds from the private money market and from the Treasury. A federal land corporation would require an initial working capital, which might well be provided by appropriations. In addition, it would need substantial sums for investment, especially in roads. It might be highly desirable that the corporation could borrow for this latter purpose, its borrowings to be repaid out of future increased receipts.

Another general power would include all phases of contracts, for all authorized functions of the corporation. The charter would also specify the particular authority of the corporation to employ various kinds of personnel, including attorneys and agents. Presumably the federal land corporation would take over the present personnel of the federal land managing agencies, so that these people could retain their status, their civil service rights, their pension rights, and other privileges. Recruitment for the future should also include these same features. Provision might be made for a very few employees without regard for civil service and other restrictions, for the major policy positions.

A basic general power relates to expenditures. The typical government corporation exercises wide latitude in this connection—this is in fact one of the basic reasons for incorporation. But the precise powers of the federal land corporation should be spelled out carefully. Perhaps particular attention should be given to limitation of the corporation's authority to buy land. Some additions to federal land holdings may be highly desirable, even though relatively small in area and even though fully or more than offset by disposals of land.

Another general power of a government corporation is to sue and be sued in its own name. There are many ramifications to this power, but it would be particularly significant with respect to forest access roads. The land management corporation should have the power of eminent domain to condemn rights of way for roads, or even existing roads, if necessary for harvest of the federal timber. At the same time, the corporate structure would enable private timber operators to sue the federal government over road and right-of-way matters in ways that are not now possible.

3. *Specific powers.* In contrast to the foregoing powers which apply more or less equally to any corporation, the powers for a particular government corporation would have to be set forth in detail and with care. For new government corporations this is often the most difficult and controversial part of the charter. For the federal land corporation, however, this would be relatively easy. Federal land management is a going activity, with many years of successful experience behind it; the charter for the corporation would largely incorporate the best of current law and practice, some merely by reference to the appropriate land laws. The corporation's responsibilities would include protection of the federal lands from loss by fire, trespass, disease, insects, erosion, and other forces which would impair the value of the resources if not checked. It surely would also be authorized and directed to make the products and uses of the federal lands widely available, under terms to be set forth in the charter or taken over from existing law. This would require the setting of prices, where this is not done by competitive sale, and the collection of money due the corporation. Surveys or studies for the best management of the resources would be necessary; and the corporation would require authority to enter into co-operative agreements with other units of government, federal, state, and local, and even with private groups, for these purposes.

The corporation probably should also be given at least as many rule-making powers for federal lands as the Secretaries of the respective departments now have, and possibly somewhat additional powers. In any case, its charter should specify the way in which rules or regulations will be formulated, including such matters as public hearings, publication in the Federal Register, and the like. The corporation might also be given the authority to develop, announce, and enforce land use plans for federal lands, such as reservations for recreational use, and the like. Particular guidance to the corporation on land disposal matters should be given in its charter. Ideally, the welter of old land disposal laws would be clarified and simplified, but this might be a large task. Where existing law permits administrative discretion as to disposal, some general policy guides to the corporation would be helpful and wise.

4. *Management.* The method by which the management of a government corporation is chosen is equally critical with its powers. Various forms of top management are open to the government corporation. The two most common are administrators appointed by the President or by a department Secretary, and boards of directors chosen in different ways. For reasons discussed later, a policy-making board of directors seems preferable for a federal land corporation. We believe that the board should be made up of part-time members who have other major occupations, and that it should be moderately large but not excessive in numbers—something in the range of ten to twenty directors. If this were done, the enabling legislation should clearly specify that the board would serve as a policy-making and general directing board, not as a governing one, and specify that day-to-day management be carried out through a manager appointed by, and responsible to, the board.

The President must have appointment and removal power over a majority of the board. However, the act might provide some guides as to membership on the board; for instance, it might specify that as far as possible consideration be given to a balanced regional representation on the board, and that the various user groups concerned with the federal lands be represented to a degree. The President might appoint some members of the board, perhaps federal officials, to serve at his pleasure; others, especially from the general public, might be appointed for definite and overlapping terms, during which these members would not be removable, so that there would always be some continuity to the board. The President would normally name the chairman of the board, and its vice chairman.

Such a corporation in any event would have to develop a working relationship with the Congress. This suggests the possibility that each House might be permitted to name a few directors, as long as the number so named was clearly in the minority on the board. The possibility that even members of the Congress might be named as directors of the corporation need not be ruled out. An objection can be made to this suggestion, on the ground that it diffuses the responsibility for the conduct of the affairs of the corporation, and that the President cannot be held responsible unless he can control the entire membership of the board of directors. But this objection overlooks the fact that in any federal program there is always a sharing of responsibility between the Executive and the Legislative branches. No federal program can long function without the support of some influential members of the Congress. The corporation would need to have a working partnership with its dominant interest group in the Congress. Split authority over land management functions or death of the corporation may be the realistic alternatives. If actual participation on the board of directors by members of the Congress or their representatives is not desired, then some other form of close liaison between the corporation and the Congress will be necessary. Possibly a joint House-Senate committee could be established, after the pattern of the Joint Atomic Energy Committee.

A government corporation with land management responsibilities scattered over the entire nation would encounter some problems of local relationships, and would require some local flexibility. A continuation of the presently dominant decentralized operations of the federal land managing agencies would help solve this problem. It might also be possible to establish regional advisory groups with diverse membership, to provide the corporation with localized advice and counsel.

5. *Financing.* One of the major differences between a government corporation and a regular agency is in the method of financing. At the extreme, the corporation may have occasional appropriations of fairly large sums, available for use until expended, and may have use of its receipts. Even such broad authority is limited by an annual budget program, but this may be in rather general terms and may be approved in its entirety, rather than in detail. From this relatively broad grant of authority, actually adhered to in practice, the powers and the practice with respect to a particular corporation might be modified and reduced until there was little more flexibility than in the operations of a regular federal agency. Thus, the precise terms of the charter of a federal land management corporation would be extremely important. If the federal land corporation were permitted to use its prospective large revenues it would have a large measure

of freedom from annual appropriations. In practice, the corporation's operations would depend in very large measure on the degree of confidence that the Congress had in its management. The ability to spend available funds to meet resource management problems, and to operate through the busy summer season without a hitch because a fiscal year ended in the middle of it, would be great advantages to the corporation. If at the same time there were sufficient funds for investment on an economically rational scale, the situation of the corporation would be immeasurably better than that of the present agencies.

As a practical matter, the necessary local political and popular support for higher charges for use of federal land and its products would probably be forthcoming only if there was reasonable assurance that the added revenue would be spent back on these lands. The possibility of making the land (excluding submerged areas) fully self-supporting, both as to operating expenditures and as to investment, thus may be linked with the establishment of a corporation or with provision of approximately equal powers to regular bureaus.

6. *Miscellaneous provisions.* These would include the right of Congress to amend the charter of the corporation, provision that services of other government agencies could be used upon repayment, and other matters. The major item under this general heading relates to taxes. While important for all government corporations, it is especially so for the land corporation because of its large real estate holdings. There would be substantial advantages from a business viewpoint in paying tax equivalents directly, with some allowance for the value of the services provided by the corporation to local government. This would greatly facilitate more intensive resource management on the federal lands. On the other hand, the present revenue-sharing arrangements could be continued, although it is to be hoped that some of the more glaring inequities could be corrected. Possibly revenue sharing could continue as an interim measure for a limited number of years, pending the working out of procedures for direct tax payments.

POLICY ISSUES WITH RESPECT TO CORPORATION CHARTER

Policy issues may arise with respect to any of the foregoing elements of a corporation charter, because the details of a corporation's powers and structure largely determine its capacity to carry out its broad goals. But three policy issues seem major; two of them apply to all government corporations and one is peculiar to land management: breadth of powers, form of management and control, and relations to agency activities other than land management.

The first policy issue is that of broad versus restricted powers, especially with respect to use of revenues and other financial matters, and in promulgation of regulations. Innumerable details would arise if a corporation were to be seriously debated, but their full exploration would require too much space here. Yet the combined effect of these details might be critical. The authors would consider the full powers conferrable under the Government Corporation Control Act to be relatively wide for a land corporation; they might be much restricted from this. If the corporation's powers were severely restricted, question might well be raised as to the wisdom of establishing a corporation. The extent of the powers which the Congress would grant, and perhaps should grant, to the corporation is related to the next major issue, that of form of management and control.

The management and control of the corporation might be in a government agency, with a single administrator for the affairs of the corporation. This may make for prompt, clear-cut, and decisive action; it may also centralize power too much, subject it to too few controls, and lead to behind-the-scenes power struggles. A board of directors presents an opportunity for breadth of interest, for representation of political and other minority interests without strangling paralysis, and for policy formation separate from but related to administration. The Congress and the public could perhaps safely entrust more power to a corporation with a broadly based membership than would be wise or politically feasible to a corporation with a single administrator. The all-important matter of relationships between the Congress and the corporation might be resolved more easily with a board. Another device might be to permit certain steps of the corporation to become effective only after a specified interval after announcement of its intentions, during which the Congress could reverse the proposal if it chose; this would be analogous to the arrangement whereby the President may make administrative reorganizations provided the Congress does not reverse his decisions. In seeking breadth of interest among its directors, the corporation would have to avoid cumbersome and inefficient management; this is the reason why part-time rather than full-time directors were proposed earlier, and why the corporation should actually function through a single manager.

We have purposely refrained from suggesting the origin of the federal employees named to the board, or the location of the corporation within the federal structure. A natural suggestion would be that the latter be in either the Department of the Interior or in the Department of Agriculture, and that the federal members of the board be drawn from that department. But this would immediately initiate a power struggle between the departments. If the authority to appoint directors rested with the President, he could select directors where he chose, perhaps some from one department, some from the other, and some elsewhere, as from the Bureau of the Budget or from his own staff. The corporation might thus be given a chance to function without initially deciding the thorny issue of administrative reorganization which, as is shown later, has wrecked previous reorganization proposals.

A major policy issue of a different kind relates to those functions and activities of the present federal land managing agencies that are not concerned with land management. As we pointed out early in this book, each of the federal land management agencies has such responsibilities. In the case of the Bureau of Land Management and the National Park Service, they are relatively small—maintenance of basic land records and cadastral survey, and general recreational planning, respectively. If a federal land corporation were set up, these activities could be transferred to it, along with the rest of the respective bureaus, with no major problems. For the Forest Service and the Fish and Wildlife Service—even as the latter is evolving in fiscal 1957—the situation is different. The Forest Service has three major functions: management of the national forests, research, and co-operative relations with the states, especially on fire control. The Fish and Wildlife Service has research functions, enforcement of certain game laws and treaties, and also co-operative relations with the states.

One solution would be to transfer all functions to the new corporation; but this would considerably widen its powers, would include some functions of the types not normally included in government corporations, and would require substantial annual appropriations for these activities. A different solution would be to split the Forest Service and Fish and Wildlife Service, transferring to the corporation only those parts relating to land management and leaving the rest as bureaus in their respective departments. To some of the loyal supporters of each, this suggestion is rank heresy; they feel that the effectiveness of the agency and its programs requires no modification of the present organization. However, all forestry in the federal government is no longer in the Forest Service, nor is even all forestry of the Department of Agriculture in that agency. A good argument can be made that the research work of the Forest Service would be more effective and more generally accepted by the private forest industry if it were not tied to the land managing function of that agency.

Relationships between federal agencies and states exist in many fields where there is little or no operating function in the federal agency concerned. Whatever might be the decision on this issue, some objection and some objectors would surely be found, and there might be as much turmoil stirred up over it as over major administrative reorganization. The mineral lease supervisory function of the Geological Survey also presents a problem; possibly this function could be detached from that agency and transferred to the corporation. A complication is that the same unit performs similar activities on Indian lands and also other limited functions, but perhaps these could be transferred to the corporation also. This problem of other activities within the federal land managing agencies is not basically different, whether the proposal is to establish a single federal land management corporation or by administrative reorganization to bring all of this function into one department.

POSSIBLE DIFFICULTIES WITH THE CORPORATION

The foregoing discussion has been largely on the basis that a federal land corporation, if established, would have all the best features of government corporations and that in practice it would work well. Realistically, we must expect that ideal conditions will not always prevail. What are the most likely dangers that a corporation would face?

The corporation might be severely restricted by the Congress, so that in practice it would not have the freedom to act that the corporate form is designed to provide. This restriction might take place in the enabling legislation which sets up the corporation, or it might occur later. A common experience of government corporations has been some later loss of freedom to act. The Congress is understandably jealous of its rights and powers, and often takes action to prevent the assumption of those powers by parts of the Executive Branch. If the Congress, or influential members of it, became suspicious that the corporation was managing the federal lands in ways not contemplated by the enabling legislation, numerous means to restrict the activity of the corporation could be found. Most would probably center on the appropriations and use of funds; restrictions could easily be placed which would largely nullify the apparent advantages of the corporation. We have pointed out earlier that the corporation, no less than a regular agency, must develop friendly working relations, based on trust and confidence, with the Congressional committees and members with whom it works. This is essential, and some price might have to be paid for it; an effort to operate without regard for the interests and concerns of the Congress is short-sighted, and in the end is likely to mean less rather than more freedom.

A government corporation is likely to experience some restricting efforts by some of the regular departments and bureaus, including the Bureau of the Budget. The corporation might exercise more power than the regular federal agency; jealousy might be a factor, but honest concern that this greater power is not abused would be the chief basis for agency efforts to enforce conformity upon the corporation. In numerous small ways which could total to serious proportions the powers of the corporation might be restricted and confined.

The corporation itself might go astray. Perhaps the greatest danger is that it would become too commercial in its viewpoint. We have argued that greater attention should be given to the financial side of federal land management, and more concern directed to the revenue-expenditure relationships. But we have suggested this always within the framework of sound resource management for many purposes, including those which produce no revenue as well as those which do. It has been our conviction that more attention to economic problems and management with more concern for the business aspects of federal land management would actually strengthen the other aspects of such management—would yield funds to develop recreational resources, for instance. Yet it must be recognized that a danger exists that the corporation management would become excessively commercial in its approach. If our suggestions about personnel were followed, it seems fairly clear that there would be no serious danger from this source as long as the present individuals and ideals remain dominant. There would be less incentive to achieve the last possible penny of profit, if the funds actually obtained were adequate to permit the type of administration that the officers of the corporation thought necessary. In this case, the situation would be not unlike that of the present agencies. Greater incentive would exist if the receipts were inadequate to carry out needed management and improvement; then there would be much incentive to squeeze out the greatest possible profit. The importance of sound financial analysis of the prospects for revenue and of the need for expenditure, and of flexible financial arrangements, is evident. While the authors feel that the risk of commercialism is not serious, it must be admitted that such risk does exist. It is considered further in the following section.

Alternatives to a Federal Land Corporation

There are various ways whereby the federal lands may be managed in the future, other than by a federal land corporation; and a consideration of the characteristics, advantages, and disadvantages of some of the principal ones is necessary. The chief alternatives which we will examine are a minimum of change from the present, a basic reorganization of the land agencies, and a federal land review board. The weaknesses or objections to a federal land corporation perhaps provide a beginning point for review of other alternatives.

The federal land corporation would involve a substantial change from present methods of managing federal lands. While the corporation is an accepted governmental device, the idea of combining all federal lands into a single organization with the wide authority typical of government corporations would appear undesirable to many.

There are two main objections to a federal land corporation: (1) the noneconomic ends of federal land management and related activities are too important and too likely to be mishandled in a corporation; and (2) while the corporation is desirable, it is practically unattainable.[9]

The noneconomic ends of federal land management and related activities fall into two broad classes. There are on one hand the recreation, watershed management, game and other wildlife, and perhaps other aspects of federal land management which produce little or no revenue. The danger exists that such ends would be neglected or inadequately provided for under a corporation which operated out of the revenues it was able to obtain from the land. It may be

[9] The authors will concede that some may oppose a corporation because they think it would not accomplish as much as we have outlined as possible under the corporate form.

argued that in the search for revenues the corporation would become excessively commercial in its approach, to the neglect of these non-revenue functions. On the other hand, there are the agency functions other than land management. These include research in the Forest Service and Fish and Wildlife Service, co-operative work with the states on fire control in the Forest Service, co-operative work on game and other wildlife refuges in the Fish and Wildlife Service, enforcement of game laws and treaties in the latter, and perhaps other activities. Each of these is important. To some, there would appear a danger that these activities would suffer if transferred to the corporation, or if split off and carried on under a separate agency.

To these rather specific fears about the operations of a federal land management corporation must be added general fears of any new method or approach in government. Some will fear that something undesirable will arise from a corporation, without being able to name specifically the undesirable results feared. Others will fear that existing balances of political strength and interest group power will be disturbed by the creation of the corporation.

For all of these, and perhaps for other reasons, the idea of a corporation may be rejected.

Others will argue that although corporations may be desirable they are practically unattainable. A realistic estimate of probable attitudes toward a corporation suggests that it may encounter more opposition than support. The federal land managing bureaus are more likely to oppose than support it, for they will fear loss of agency or personal power and independence; the departments in which the bureaus lie are likely to resist it for much the same reason. The Bureau of the Budget is likely to prefer the present arrangements as giving it more control over federal activities and funds. Congressional committees are likely to be wary of the proposal as threatening some of their prerogatives and powers. The various interest groups are more likely to see possible loss of advantage to them than general gain. There may well be substantial support for a corporation in each of these groups, but the preponderance of strength is likely to be against it. If a federal land corporation is ever to be set up, it may well be only under strong Presidential leadership, such as Theodore Roosevelt gave to the national forests and Franklin Roosevelt gave to several conservation programs. Clearly, if the federal land corporation is ever to come into being an active minority must sell the idea to the passive majority, as has been the case in every previous major step in federal land history.

If it is argued that people do not want a land corporation, or want it but cannot get it, then what are the future alternatives for coping with the increased managerial problems which the increased use of the federal lands seems sure to bring?

One alternative for the future is to change the management of federal lands to the minimum extent made necessary by changing times and circumstances. Since there is always opposition to change, and inertia to be overcome, minimum change may be the most probable alternative. Some change is virtually certain, since all government organizations respond to some degree over a period of time to new needs and situations. Substantial changes in land management have occurred in the past fifty, or twenty-five, or ten years, and further changes in like periods in the future are certain. The impetus for change comes partly from the course of events in the nation's economy and society, and partly from the initiative of the persons in government at all levels.

Since evolution to some degree is almost inevitable, it is a little difficult to describe what natural evolution may be. Perhaps it is easier to say what natural evolution is not: it excludes a federal land corporation; it excludes any other major effort to change the basic structure and methods of functioning of the federal land management agencies; it excludes major administrative reorganization; and it excludes sharply different financial bases for federal land management, including different methods of revenue sharing.

On the positive side, natural evolution of governmental procedures and methods for federal land management includes a continuation of the present federal land managing agencies, each with approximately its present range of functions and areas of land. It also includes the present methods of budgeting and appropriation, subject to perhaps limited modification and improvement over the years. Included also are the present lags in the appropriation process, between need and availability of funds, or at least something roughly like the present. There might well be some new legislation affecting the federal lands, but no repeal of any present major land law or enactment of any major new one. The agencies might in time begin to obtain better economic data from their own records or elsewhere, and subject them to more and better economic analysis, and to improve their financial planning as a result. In all of these, and in other ways, natural evolution will bring some changes in federal land management; but the emphasis will be upon gradualism and the avoidance of major change.

Increased use of the federal lands will create greater public awareness of the problems and the potentialities of federal land management. Vastly more people than now will enjoy the recreational resources of the federal land, federal land will provide more builders a major part of their lumber supply, and oil from federal properties will be a greater part of the total supply—to mention some of the major ways in which greater use of the federal lands will touch larger numbers of the total population. A greater general public awareness, and the attendant greater activities of the various special interest groups, will bring the federal lands more directly and more frequently to the attention of the Congress, the President, the Secretaries of departments, and others than is now the case. This in itself will constitute some pressure for gradual evolution of federal land management.

As we define natural evolution of federal land management, after twenty years or so it would be still recognizable to anyone familiar with its present operations. While some changes would be clearly evident to any Rip Van Winkle of federal land management who might come back in 1980 from twenty years' sleep, any former official would have no great difficulty in quickly adjusting himself to the new regulations, procedures, and methods.

In thus describing the natural evolution of federal land management for the next two decades or so as the most likely in the absence of a major effort to change it, it should be recognized that this is, on the whole, not a bad alternative. As federal activities and agencies go, federal land management and its agencies have been good, sometimes even distinguished. In many ways federal land management compares favorably with the best that is done on private land. The agencies are staffed with competent professional personnel, who are idealistically motivated toward their jobs; they are public spirited to a high degree, and their morale is good. There is every reason to believe that these people, and new ones that will be recruited, will strive to improve federal land management.

If change in federal land management is suggested, a case cannot be made to rest upon the severe shortcomings or dismal failure of the present setup; it must rest rather upon the fact that better possibilities exist. It is always hard to argue for something better than what is now reasonably good, and this is the major reason why natural evolution of present federal land managing agencies is the most likely alternative. If there were major public dissatisfaction with federal land management today, there would be a stronger push to change it.

If there is a desire to modify federal land management in order to meet the needs of the future more efficiently, but within the broad framework of the present governmental structure, one possibility is an administrative reorganization of the existing agencies. When several federal agencies are performing what appear to be similar functions, a natural suggestion is their administrative reorganization and combination. It is easy to argue that simplification and economy can be achieved in this way, and that duplication and overlapping can be avoided.

A federal land corporation such as outlined earlier in this chapter would include a reorganization of present land agencies; however, the basic purpose of the corporation is not a different form of organization, but significantly different powers and methods of management and policy formation. It would be possible to establish corporations for some if not all of the various types of federal land now administered by separate bureaus, although we think this would not be a constructive move and hence do not explore it in detail. Administrative reorganization as such does not involve significantly different powers and authorities to the agencies, but merely reassigns responsibilities or regroups operating units.

Nearly every commission or committee that has studied the organization of the federal government, and many individuals, have advanced proposals for reorganization of various parts of the federal establishment, including the land managing agencies. Reorganization proposals have had wide publicity, and there has been much support in some quarters for them. Accordingly, it seems necessary to examine the possibilities of administrative reorganization in some detail, even though in practice the difficulties of administrative reorganization are greater, and the possible advantages less, than often appear to the outsider, and there is usually more opposition to change than one would expect.

Evolution of departments of the Interior and of Agriculture. Recent or prospective proposals for administrative reorganization must be reviewed in the light of past changes and proposals. Few recent proposals have been completely new, and it is hard to imagine that many future proposals will be; it may be instructive to inquire why similar proposals in the past have or have not worked or been tried.

The federal departments and bureaus have evolved over the decades, usually not in a simple and direct manner to their present form, but often slowly and haltingly, with a long interval between the initial suggestion for a change and its final consummation. A full history of reorganization proposals which resulted in change would be far too long for this book, but some of the major parts of the history of the departments of Agriculture and the Interior may be helpful as a background for considering possible future changes. In an earlier day, when the scope of federal activities was much more restricted, functions or bureaus were often assigned to departments for the simple reason that there was no more logical place to put them.

This is illustrated by the evolution of the Department of the Interior. Created in 1849, it was briefly known also as the Home Department, and its function was largely the administration of various domestic programs not clearly belonging in other departments then existing. The Office of Indian Affairs and the General Land Office were in it from the beginning, and continuously (though now under different names) to the present; but it originally included the Pension Office, the Census Office, and the Patent Office, the latter of which was not transferred to the Department of Commerce until 1925. Over the years, the Geological Survey was added, in 1879; the Reclamation Service in 1902, renamed Bureau of Reclamation in 1907; the Bureau of Mines was created in 1910, transferred to the Department of Commerce in 1925, and back to Interior in 1934; the National Park Service was created in 1916, and major additional functions transferred to it in 1933; the Grazing Service (first as the Grazing Division) was established in 1934, and consolidated with the General Land Office to form the Bureau of Land Management in 1946; the Bureau of Biological Survey was transferred to it from the Department of Agriculture in 1939, and the Bureau of Fisheries from the Department of Commerce at the same time, to form the Fish and Wildlife Service the following year; [10] Bonneville Power Administration was added in 1937, and the Southwest Power Administration in 1943. Consideration of these changes shows that the Department was gradually working toward a function of natural resource research and administration. But there were other changes, not so clearly in this direction at first. The Office

---

[10] In the discussion in this section, the Fish and Wildlife Service is considered as it was prior to July 1, 1956.

of Education was added in 1869; Howard University in 1891; Columbia Institution for the Deaf, St. Elizabeth's Hospital, and Freedmen's Hospital in later decades—and all of these remained in the Department until 1939 or 1940. A Soil Erosion Service to combat erosion on farm lands was created in Interior in the early 1930's, and transferred to the Department of Agriculture in 1935; but this activity on certain public lands was transferred back again in 1940. The only major change involving the Department of the Interior which was not in the direction of resource management was the transfer of the Forest Reserves from it to the Department of Agriculture in 1905.

The Department of Agriculture has had an evolution too. The Weather Bureau was added to it in 1891 by transfer from the War Department, and remained there until its transfer to the Department of Commerce in 1940; the Bureau of Public Roads was created in the Department in 1918, out of units which had been in the Department since 1893, because in those days federal roads were largely rural roads, and it stayed there until its transfer to the Federal Works Agency in 1939; the Food and Drug Administration was set up in the Department in the 1920's out of the Bureau of Chemistry, because in the earlier periods most federal chemists were in Agriculture, and it was transferred out only in 1940 to the new Federal Security Agency. The establishment of the Forest Service in 1905 to administer the newly transferred Forest Reserves, and the transfer of the Bureau of Biological Survey out of the Department in 1939, have already been mentioned. The Forest Service had antecedent organizations going back to 1881 in the Department. While these changes were taking place, the Department was greatly extending its research, educational, and direct action programs affecting farming—price reporting for agriculture is in the Department of Agriculture, not in the Department of Commerce; regulation of agricultural processors and marketers is in Agriculture, not in the Federal Trade Commission; and agriculture has its specialized credit agencies. The Department of Agriculture today contains nearly all of the federal programs directly affecting agriculture and farmers.

Reorganization proposals made, but not adopted. In addition to these major changes, many other proposals that directly affect federal lands have been made but not adopted. It would be an impossible task to trace all of these, or to trace proposals which later resulted in the actions listed above. There follow some of the major proposals made over the past fifty years, which have not been translated into action.

In 1905 Gifford Pinchot tried to get at least some of the remaining public domain reserved for grazing purposes, and to have its administration put in the Department of Agriculture.[11] In 1920 a voluntary private organization, known as the National Budget Committee of New York, presented a comprehensive plan for reorganization of the federal government, which attracted considerable attention at the time. Its plan proposed to abolish the Department of the Interior and to establish instead a department of public works; into this would have been put the resource-administering functions of Interior, plus the Forest Service and Bureau of Public Roads, as well as certain water development functions from the War Department.[12] In 1923 the Brookings Institution published a comprehensive plan for reorganization of the federal government; it would have created a new department of public works and public domain, which would also have included the Forest Service and Bureau of Public Roads. In December, 1932, President Hoover submitted comprehensive reorganization proposals to the Congress, but all were rejected by it. His plan would have established a division of land utilization within the Department of Agriculture, to which would have been assigned the Forest Service, General Land Office, Bureau of Biological Survey, Bureau of Chemistry and Soils, and other miscellaneous units.

In 1936 a Senate committee, popularly known as the Byrd Committee, after its chairman, presented a reorganization plan. It recommended that the General Land Office and the Geological Survey be in the same department, that grazing on public lands and in national forests be brought under common direction; that there be closer co-ordination in the development of recreational facilities in national parks and national forests; that the O & C lands and national monuments within national forests be transferred to the Forest Service; and made other miscellaneous recommendations affecting federal land. In the same year the Forest Service prepared a document known as *The Western Range*,[13] in which it advanced strongly the argument that the public domain grazing areas should be transferred to its jurisdiction. In 1937 the President's Committee on Administrative Man-

---

[11] Peffer, E. Louise, *The Closing of the Public Domain,* Stanford: Stanford University Press, 1951, p. 86.

[12] Except as specifically otherwise noted, this discussion is based upon W. Brooke Graves, *Basic Information on the Reorganization of the Executive Branch 1912-1948,* Legislative Reference Service, Library of Congress, Public Affairs Bulletin No. 66, February, 1949.

[13] *The Western Range,* Senate Document No. 199, 74th Congress, 2nd Session, 1936.

agement recommended the creation of a department of conservation, which would "administer the public lands, parks, territories, and reservations" and presumably but not specifically include the Forest Service.

In a reorganization plan which was adopted in 1939, President Roosevelt said that he was considering the problem of certain public lands insofar as they presented overlapping jurisdiction between the departments of the Interior and Agriculture. This was a time when Secretary of the Interior Ickes was making an insistent effort to obtain the Forest Service, and when the latter was resisting equally insistently. It is generally accepted that the President seriously considered this transfer but was dissuaded because it was believed that the plan would be defeated in the Congress.

In 1949 the First Hoover Commission made recommendations on this matter.[14] Its Task Force on Natural Resources had recommended a department of natural resources, into which would be put the Forest Service; its Task Force on Agriculture had recommended an agricultural resources conservation administration in the Department of Agriculture, into which would be put the Fish and Wildlife Service as well as the administration of the forested and grazing lands of the public domain and O & C areas. The Commission itself split, with eight members favoring the recommendation of its Agriculture Task Force and four members favoring its Task Force on Natural Resources. The Second Hoover Commission limited itself to a recommendation that the President appoint a committee from federal and state governments, and from various interest groups concerned with the federal lands, to make a study of them and the laws affecting them, and to make recommendations for their improved management.[15] It also recommended a uniform policy for all agencies involved in control of federal rural lands.

This brief review of past reorganization proposals for the federal government shows that there have been many proposals affecting federal lands which have not been adopted. The most common proposals have dealt with the Forest Service or with the functions now in the Bureau of Land Management, or both; the idea of getting all these functions in one department is an attractive one, but there has never been full agreement on which department it should be. Bureaucratic

---

[14] Commission on Organization of the Executive Branch of the Government, *Department of the Interior,* a report to the Congress, March, 1949.

[15] Commission on Organization of the Executive Branch of the Government, *Real Property Management,* a report to the Congress, June, 1955.

and interest group opposition to any administrative reorganization has been sufficiently strong in the past to prevent any action. As one contemplates this history, one cannot be hopeful (or fearful, depending on one's viewpoint) that administrative reorganization will actually occur. It has been proposed too many times, and failed of achievement each time, for one to have confident expectations that it will occur.

General outline of possible reorganizations. Suggestions for reorganization of federal land management fall into two broad categories or combinations of ideas: those involving shifts or changes between departments, and those involving shifts or changes between bureaus or agencies. The first category includes shifting the Forest Service from the Department of Agriculture to the Department of the Interior, or shifting all or part of the Bureau of Land Management to the Department of Agriculture. Most recent suggestions for interdepartmental shifts have not included the National Park Service or the Fish and Wildlife Service since the latter was placed in Interior. Another major type of reorganization involving changes in departments is to combine both Agriculture and Interior into a new "super" department, roughly analogous to the combination of Army, Navy, and Air Force into a Department of Defense. In such a super department there would be subdepartments, of which lands or resources might be one.

Regardless of departmental reorganization, some shifts of functions or activities might be made between bureaus. For instance, all federally owned land of commercial forest type might be shifted to the Forest Service; this would include the O & C lands, some tracts of commercial forest within grazing districts or other public domain, and the forested lands of interior Alaska. At the same time, or irrespective of the foregoing, all lands primarily usable for grazing might be shifted to the Bureau of Land Management. Such shifts could not completely eliminate forestry problems from the grazing agency, nor grazing problems from the forestry agency; some land is more or less equally usable for forestry and grazing, and some land primarily useful for one or the other has some values for the minor use. But it would be possible to greatly reduce the amount of secondary or minor use, through a reorganization of lands according to primary usefulness.

If some lands were to be shifted from the jurisdiction of their present bureaus to that of another, a classification of the land to determine its physical suitability would be a desirable first step.

All of the recent suggestions for administrative reorganization are, with one exception, speculative. That is, someone argues that a new organization would be more efficient than the present one. In such arguments much is often made of the inefficiencies or shortcomings of the present organization, and of how the new organization will cure such inefficiencies or shortcomings.

But this is only a judgment or opinion, which may or may not work out in practice; and rarely does the suggester face the possibility that his ideas would bring into existence wholly new problems, perhaps more serious ones.

The one exception to the foregoing is the suggestion that has been made in several quarters, including the majority of the First Hoover Commission, that the mineral leasing, land title, land disposal, and cadastral survey work of the Bureau of Land Management be split off from the administration of forest and grazing resources, and each put in a different organization. This reorganization would restore essentially what existed from 1934 to 1946, when the General Land Office and the Grazing Service operated in essentially this way. The proven difficulties of having two agencies administer the same tracts of land, one for the surface resources and the other for the mineral resources and title activities, led to the creation of the Bureau of Land Management in 1946. Much is often made of the "duplication" of having two federal agencies administer adjacent or closely located land, sometimes of different physical type, such as the Bureau of Land Management administering grazing districts and the Forest Service administering adjoining national forests; but the inefficiencies and difficulties that arise in this case are only a small fraction of those which arise when two agencies carry out different, but interrelated, functions on the same tract of land. No informed observer would today argue that the Bureau of Land Management is less efficient than the General Land Office and the Grazing Service; rather, there is much evidence that the reverse is true. Management of federal land must be management of all its resources, the different functions being closely interrelated and necessarily co-ordinated if a good job is to be done. Any reorganization proposal that involves the grazing districts and other public domain should keep this basic fact and experience in mind; and this might well affect proposals for reorganization at a departmental level, for inclusion of the mineral activities would lead the Department of Agriculture afield from its present core of interest.

Limited Role of Administrative Reorganization. Administrative reorganization is limited to reassignments of functions and activities and of administrative units; it does not affect basic legislative authority for functions, is unlikely easily to affect administrative policy built on such legislative authority, does not affect use of revenues and methods of appropriation and expenditure, and is unlikely to change materially public pressures for and against maximum revenues from the federal lands. If changes in these matters are desired, more drastic action than administrative reorganization alone is required.

Administrative reorganization does not change the laws under which the lands are administered and the agencies operate, nor does it directly change the popular support which led to those laws. Some writers on this matter have cited the different laws and regulations affecting grazing use of national forests and of grazing districts, as reason for administrative reorganization of the agencies responsible for this work. If either the Forest Service or the Bureau of Land Management were solely responsible for the administration of grazing on national forests and grazing districts both, either agency would find it necessary to observe the laws relating to the two types of land and, until they could be changed, the regulations applicable to each. Moreover, it is certain that there would be major opposition to change in either laws or regulations, although there might well be support for change of either; after all, both laws and regulations were worked out over a considerable period of time, were subject to much debate and to suggestions from numerous people, and have been modified over the years as the needs seemed to indicate. This is not to say that either is perfect or unchangeable, but it does say that administrative reorganization is neither the only nor the major factor involved.

Some of the writing on this matter has been very naive. The Agricultural Task Force for the First Hoover Commission, for instance, cited the discrepancy in the distribution of receipts to counties, as between the national forests and O & C lands, as argument why the administration of the O & C lands should be shifted to the Forest Service. If such reorganization were made, that agency would be forced to carry out existing law concerning the receipts from O & C lands; moreover, it would find it most difficult to get the law changed. As a matter of fact, the Forest Service, in order to get settled the issue over the formerly "controverted" O & C lands and in order to obtain continued administration of these lands, accepted a continuation of the previous arrangements with respect to distribution of O & C receipts. Many other examples could be cited, to the effect that administrative reorganization changes neither law nor the popular support which led to present law. One Secretary is reported once to have described a reorganization he had made of his department as essentially a shifting of furniture within a home—"and, after all, they are the same old bureaus."

Administrative reorganization alone does not change the amount of appropriations for federal land administration, nor does it remove some of the problems of the appropriation process discussed above. Administrative reorganization alone does not change the essential lack of economic analysis at all levels in the administration of federal lands, nor does it affect the fact that investments on such land are now largely regarded as though they were annual outlays, without adequate regard for their long-term effect. A large portion of the shortcomings in the administration of federal lands may be traced to these difficulties.

Administrative reorganization alone is unlikely to result in significantly more local support for increased grazing fees, maximum stumpage prices, higher rentals on oil and gas leases, and other parts of a program of larger financial returns from the federal land. Such support might be forthcoming to either corporation or agency that could assure expenditure of the increased revenue to build up productivity in the federal lands locally, or to make investments that would open them for easier local use. While the corporation might be able to give such assurance, the reorganized bureaus could not without further grants of authority.

To those who fear or oppose the idea of a corporation, these limitations on administrative reorganization are not disadvantages. We have argued that the basic economic problem in federal land management is lack of adequate funds for investment and management, and existence of hampering restrictions in the usual governmental process; if this view is accepted, the limited role of administrative reorganization is a serious argument against putting much faith in its efficacy. But to those who prefer limitations on the operations of federal land management agencies, rather than broader powers with the risks that these entail, the limited role of administrative reorganization is an advantage.

Problems created by reorganization. Administrative reorganization of federal land managing agencies may create new problems as well as fail to solve old ones. Two new problems come particularly to mind.

First, any consolidation of federal land managing agencies is a step in the direction of monopoly. The disadvantages of two or more land managing agencies with similar responsibilities but differing laws or procedures or policies have often been mentioned; but this pattern does at least provide something of a standard or guide to judge each by the other. For instance, a recent Congressional committee report analyzes differences in timber sale practices among federal agencies.[16] If all such activity were in one agency, with only one method of operation, one might suspect that some other management practices would be better, but direct evidence would be lacking. Moreover, in some parts of the western United States, if all federal lands were in one agency that agency would have great economic power, in a local sense. These disadvantages of administrative reorganization may be less than the advantages, but at least they should be considered.

The federal land corporation would suffer from this same disadvantage, perhaps to an even greater degree. Its authority to operate out of revenues, if it had such authority, would make it less immediately dependent upon the will of the Congress and the people. The greater power of the corporation would have to be matched by better mechanisms for control over its policies, to insure that the public benefit was uppermost in its considerations. This is another reason why the make-up and operations of the board of directors are extremely important. While greater economic power, possibly tending toward undesired monopolistic practices, would be a serious facet of the corporation, that same increased authority might enable it to do a better job of resource management.

Second, administrative reorganization of federal land managing functions would create difficult problems for the other functions now carried on by these agencies. As we have seen, each federal land managing agency has other functions, although their relative extent varies considerably among the agencies. If the National Park Service were to be transferred from Interior to another department, presumably its functions other than land management could also be transferred without much trouble. The Bureau of Land Management could be transferred intact without great difficulty, but this would bring a new set of functions to the Department of Agriculture, if it were taken there. Unless the Conservation Division of the Geological Survey were transferred to the same department as the Bureau of Land Management, closely related functions would be split. The greatest difficulties arise with the Forest Service and the Fish and Wildlife Service, however. The Forest Service has the threefold functions of research, land

---

[16] *Federal Timber Sales Policies,* Thirty-first Intermediate Report of the Committee on Government Operations, House Report No. 2960, 84th Congress, 2nd Session.

management, and co-operative relations with states, including fire control. The Fish and Wildlife Service has functions of game law and treaty enforcement, research, and co-operative relations with states, as well as land management. In each case, the necessary adjustments could be made, whether the present agency were kept intact or whether the land management function only were transferred elsewhere; but each would involve some problems not apparent when one considers only the land management function. This problem of administrative reorganization is akin to, but possibly less serious than, the same problem if a corporation were established.

Potentialities of reorganization. In spite of its limited role, administrative reorganization of federal land management would have some favorable effect which, especially over a period of years, might be considerable. First of all, it would reduce, but not eliminate, purely bureaucratic obstacles to change of laws, regulations, and procedures. Such things as varying bases of payments to counties, or different laws and regulations for granting of grazing privileges, or different procedures for sale of timber from federal land, might be brought into more consistent arrangements as a result of administrative reorganization. The "might" is stressed, because it is by no means certain that these things would happen. If administrative reorganization brought single functions within single agencies, or brought various agencies under single departmental direction, some of the bureaucratic obstacles to change would be reduced and improvements might be possible. But it would often take Congressional approval to effect needed changes.

Co-operation between agencies on all land management matters might be better after reorganization than now; however, it should be emphasized that at present, co-operation on matters of mutual interest among the federal land managing agencies is good, although this has not always been true in the past and may not always be true in the future. Development of recreation programs on all federal lands would probably be greatly facilitated if all such lands were in one agency or in one department, for instance. While not negligible, such benefits would almost surely be less than the proponents of reorganization usually assume.

One of the benefits often alleged for administrative reorganization is that it will produce substantial economies in administration. For the most part, this is an illusion. The cost of administering federal land is largely determined by the area and location of the land, by the amount and kind of use, and by the intensity of management, at least as long as administration is as efficient as it is at present; these factors are not related to the kind of administrative organization. If the national forests and grazing districts, which are intermingled in many western states, were under single administration, some economies could be achieved by using personnel, equipment, and other factors to better advantage than when there are two administrative organizations. Slight savings at national and regional headquarters would be possible. But the total economies that might be achieved would be small relative to the total cost of administration.

This section on administrative reorganization might be summarized by saying that a really well-conceived administrative reorganization of federal land management, if it could be achieved without crippling controversy, would produce some benefits, but that it would not greatly affect many of the major land management problems, nor would it produce major economies. The precise nature of the reorganization is perhaps less important than the spirit in which it is done and the earnestness with which further improvements are sought by the new organization. Administrative reorganization would perhaps do more to set the stage for more basic changes in federal land management than it would to bring about changes itself.

It has been difficult to arouse much popular support for any single plan of federal land reorganization because it has appeared to so many people what it is in part—a power struggle among departments and bureaus and pressure groups over who does what. The authors would suggest to those interested in land agency reorganization that they consider additional steps that would strengthen the land management function, and that they combine these with reorganization. A broader appeal can perhaps be built upon a broader approach. Some specific suggestions are included in the two sections which follow.

PERMANENT FEDERAL LAND REVIEW BOARD

Thus far we have considered three rather distinctly different and mutually exclusive alternatives for future federal land management— a government corporation, minimum change from the present arrangements, and administrative reorganization. We come now to two additional possibilities which do not so logically fall into this classification, for they are not mutually exclusive with all of the foregoing. These two are (1) the establishment of a permanent federal land review board, and (2) a deliberate and rather basic attempt to obtain the advantages of a corporation within the framework of regular bureaus. If a corporation were set up, neither of these would be needed; if either were adopted, it would to some extent modify the minimum change proposal; but either could be adopted with or without administrative reorganization. Moreover, these two are not in themselves mutually exclusive; either or both could be adopted. At the expense of logical nicety, these suggestions of practical measures should be considered.

A useful device in federal land management might be a permanent federal land review board to which would be attached a federal land fund. The function of the board would be to gather facts about federal land management, analyze them in significant ways, and make reports and otherwise publicize its findings. It would have no direct administrative powers.

As this suggestion is visualized, the board would gather facts about federal land management from the federal land agencies directly, but also from other federal and state sources, and in some instances perhaps even from members of the general public itself. It would try to persuade the various agencies to keep their records and tabulate their data in ways that would be most revealing for economic analysis. The co-operation of the Bureau of the Budget and of the Congressional committees would be needed in this endeavor. Great emphasis would be placed on uniform methods between agencies so as to permit consolidated statements for all federal lands. The board might seek to analyze the data about federal lands much as we have done in this book; but, at least after a few years, the analysis should be more accurate, better directed toward significant issues, and more authoritative than it has been possible for us to make it. It would probably also be desirable to think in terms of comparable analyses for each state, or at least for the states with relatively large areas of federal land. The authors hazard the guess that the board would find it more difficult to make this type of analysis for any state than for the nation as a whole—the differences in agency records would become more bothersome at the local level. But the western states, with half or more of their area in federal ownership, have a direct and legitimate interest in a summary of federal land management for their area. The board might also undertake the study of various special problems, on its own initiative, or they might be referred to it by the agencies themselves, by the President or one of his staff agencies, by the Congress through one of its committees, or even by an interest group or the general public. Almost any type of land management problem might be studied, as long as emphasis was upon ascertaining relevant facts. But one major focus of the various studies would be the economic one, with particular emphasis upon the economic margin— what would be the effect upon revenues and costs of any particular program, method, or procedure? The board would need a substantial degree of freedom to decide for itself what studies to undertake, how to carry them out, and what presentation of the results to make.

A useful device of the board would be the federal land fund. This would be a mere accounting fund, not an operating one. It would include on the one side all the revenues collected by the federal land managing agencies, including those we have characterized as "in kind," and on the other side it would list all the expenditures out of revenues, including payments to states, counties, and the Reclamation Fund, and also all expenditures on the federal lands, from whatever source. If the agencies could provide it with adequate data, the board might well include in the fund an allowance for changes in the value of federal land, including timber and minerals. Consideration should also be given to the amount of investment in federal lands, and to the interest charges on such investment. The fund would thus in time become a financial balance sheet for the federal lands, in total and for each type, in the sense that the best private business firms prepare financial balance sheets. An analysis of changes in revenues and expenditures, and of the factors underlying the changes, would be a most useful tool for the board to employ in studying and dramatizing the land management problems. The board would surely wish on occcasion to make projections or forecasts of future revenue, under most probable conditions or on the basis of other specified assumptions.

Since the board would have no direct administrative powers, its influence would depend very largely upon the competence and relevance of its analyses. It could not command, but it might lead. It would give wide circulation to its findings in most cases, although on occasion it might direct its reports only to one or more of the agencies concerned. The board would be authorized to recommend on such matters as appropriate level of budgets, appropriate level of fees and charges, and the like; but the major emphasis would be upon letting the facts speak for themselves. The fund would probably become the central core of its analysis, even though it was a purely bookkeeping device. Every major administrative or legislative policy would have its effect upon the fund, and analysis of this effect would be a useful means of emphasizing the importance of the various programs and policies.

If a permanent federal land review board were established, how should it be organized and to what part of the federal governmental structure should it be attached? Why should it be a board, rather than a regular division or branch of an established agency? To these and other questions, various alternative answers are possible. If it were part of the Executive Branch, it rather clearly could not be part of a federal land managing bureau, or even of one of the two major federal departments with land management functions. Since these are the major objects to be studied by the board, objective study from a new viewpoint would then be unobtainable, in addition to which the present division of activities between several bureaus and two departments would create impossible difficulties if one were given power to study and report on the others. The board might be attached to the Bureau of the Budget, but, after all, Budget's actions in the land management field should also be subjected to objective scrutiny.

It is possible that the board might be attached to the Congress. Some might even argue that its functions could be taken over by a regular committee and its staff. However, a Congressional committee is not a study group in the sense that this board is expected to be. Moreover, the board should be in a position to criticize Congressional action and to propose changes. There is no obvious place where such a board might be attached to the Congress.

A third major alternative would be to make the board largely independent, with members from various sources—some named by the President, perhaps including some from the Executive Branch but at least some from the public, and perhaps some named by the Congress. There might even be provision for direct nomination of members by some of the major interest groups. The precise make-up of the board might not be too significant, as long as its freedom to ascertain and publicize facts was not impaired. A board of diverse interests might have many advantages.

In any case, a board would function through its full-time staff, and the competence and creativeness of that staff would largely determine the results and public acceptance of the board. It would not be necessary to have a large staff. The board's independence, and hence possibly its effectiveness, would perhaps be enhanced if it received its funds in some automatic fashion—possibly one-tenth of one per cent of gross revenues from federal land, or in some other more or less automatic fashion. In this way, the board would have assured funds and a chance to see what it could do; it could always be abolished by new legislation, and should be if its work did not seem to advance knowledge and understanding of federal land management.[17]

What disadvantages would attach to the federal land review board and what dangers might there be in its creation? In the absence of experience, it is necessary to speculate on this question. Two opposite tendencies may be noted. First, in spite of a lack of direct administrative power, it might become such an effective instrument of analysis and publicity that it would acquire great power to influence legislative, appropriation, and administrative action. Thus it might become to some extent a spokesman for the region of the country in which most of the federal land lies. If it did acquire such power, it would seriously interfere with the operations of the management agencies and of the Congress. Second, the opposite fate might befall it—lacking administrative powers, it might be ignored and become futile. Advisory or study units of government have often found themselves relatively impotent. The authors feel that the second danger is more real than the first, although each is a possibility. The quality of the leadership and staff of the board, if one were established, would be highly important in influencing its role.

ACHIEVING ECONOMIC ADVANTAGES OF A CORPORATION
UNDER BUREAUS AND DEPARTMENTS

The second possibility that does not fit into the mutually exclusive categories of corporation, minimum change, and administrative reorganization, is to devise methods of attaining some of the advantages of the corporation while retaining the regular bureau form of organization. The suggestions which follow could be adopted with or without administrative reorganization; they would possibly give administrative reorganization that strength which it seems to have lacked thus far.

Some students of government argue that it is possible to achieve the probably realizable advantages of a government corporation, and perhaps even all of the hoped-for advantages, under the regular bureau and department structure of government. There is unquestionably considerable flexibility under the latter—the relative success of the

[17] A proposal to establish a permanent federal lands commission is advanced in a study Committee Report, *Natural Resources and Conservation,* submitted to the Commission on Intergovernmental Relations, June, 1955. That proposal was directed mainly to the studying of federal landownership and administration, and to recommending legislation or other action as it deemed desirable. Its primary function would not be economic analysis as we have outlined it. Other somewhat similar proposals have been made elsewhere.

federal land management agencies in the past is additional proof on this point. A comparison of theoretical advantages is one thing, a comparison of the probable advantages another. Some who argue that federal bureaus and departments can do anything that government corporations can do will admit that in practice they are unlikely to be able to do so.

The following list includes the steps that would be necessary if the regular bureaus were to accomplish all that a well-functioning corporation is capable of; achievement of any part of this list would help the agencies, and might accomplish as much as a poorly or moderately effective corporation:

.1. A more detailed and relevant annual economic and financial analysis of the federal land management function than has been available in the past would be necessary. It should consider future financial prospects as realistically as possible, and should face explicitly the effect of different management and pricing policies upon future finances. The corporation, if it were to operate largely or wholly from its revenues, would be forced to make such analyses. The bureaus and departments have not done so to date, at least not upon the scale and intensity required, and such analyses as they have made have not been widely distributed to the public. It should be pointed out again that they have been neither required nor encouraged to do so by the Bureau of the Budget and the Congressional committees. Such economic and financial studies take manpower and cost money, although they should not be costly compared with the potential revenues involved. If the federal land review board and federal land fund, previously described, were set up, these might provide the basis for such an analysis. In their absence, no single agency could provide the combined analysis of all federal lands that would be necessary, unless all of the federal land managing agencies were united through an administrative reorganization.

2. The budget procedure would have to be changed considerably if the bureaus and departments were to achieve what the government corporation is theoretically capable of doing. The device of budget ceilings in specific monetary terms would have to be abolished for land managing agencies. In their place, the general principle would be established that appropriations should be at the point where maximum net revenue could be obtained from the revenue-producing activities, and at alternative levels for the other activities. If appropriations are really at the maximum net revenue point, there can be no excuse for a lower appropriation, regardless of how "tight" the federal budget may be—in fact, the tighter it is, the more essential

that no revenue-producing activity be slighted. The Bureau of the Budget would have to establish tests and procedures to insure that this objective was in fact reached. For the nonrevenue activities, the agencies could perhaps present alternative budgets, in general terms, with corresponding degrees of performance and with their recommendations as to the optimum level of intensity of activity. The Bureau of the Budget would thus have a better basis for decision as to appropriations for such activities; and the agencies might be permitted to introduce as evidence their requests for levels of intensity other than the one chosen by the Bureau of the Budget, when the appropriation hearings were held before the Congressional committees. Much less irrelevant detail should be included in all budget requests.

3. Appropriations actually conforming to these principles would be needed. This would require acceptance of these ideas by the Bureau of the Budget and by the Congress; it would also require much greater boldness in appropriations, especially for roads and other construction items, than has prevailed in the past.

4. Much greater flexibility in use of appropriated funds than is now possible would be needed if the bureaus were to achieve what the government corporation ideally might do. For instance, the agencies might be given general authority to shift a small percentage, say 10 per cent, of their appropriations from any function to any other function, and in addition to add as much as 10 per cent to the total expenditure, above specific appropriation. Such authority could be limited to those activities for which needs on a significant scale could not always be foreseen at the time the budget requests were made up. This would in large part overcome the inflexibility caused by the long time-lag between budget preparation and fund expenditure. It would be effective only if the level of appropriations was adequate. Perhaps other and more effective devices to serve this general purpose could be devised.

5. The appropriation-expenditure procedures would have to be changed to permit the carry-over from one fiscal year into the next of sums up to perhaps 15 per cent of the appropriation. This would introduce an additional degree of flexibility into operations, and would overcome much of the inefficiency due to the delays in making annual appropriations and to the fact that the fiscal year begins in the middle of the major field season. At the same time, the fact that the carry-over was limited in amount and to a single fiscal year after the year to which the appropriation initially applied would keep control over agency activities in the Bureau of the Budget and the

Congress. The effectiveness of this device would also depend largely upon the adequacy of the level of appropriations—there is not much gain from spreading poverty.

6. The bureaus would be authorized to make more longer-term commitments than has been possible in the past. This would be especially the case for roads, reforestation, range reseeding, insect control, and other activities which require expenditures many months or even years in advance of actual application on the ground and which must be continued over long periods of time in order to be fully effective. A greater use of contract authorization than has been made in the past, plus the previously suggested changes, would go far toward meeting this need.

7. If the land management programs are to be on a more rational economic basis, it is essential that the present gross-revenue sharing be replaced by a direct in-lieu-of-taxes system of payments, along the lines we have previously suggested. This would remove the substantial barriers to more intensive resource management that now exist, if management is on the basis of economic calculations.

8. In the whole structure there would be need for greater pressures for maximum reasonable revenues from the revenue-producing aspects of federal land management. The corporation, with its more or less directly linked expenditures and revenues, would have substantial local support for raising grazing fees, lease rentals on nonproducing oil and gas leases, and the like. The agencies now lack but need this type of support. Gentle and continued insistence from the Congress and the Bureau of the Budget would be helpful, but local support is also needed. It could perhaps be developed, if the Congress, the Bureau of the Budget, and the agencies continually pressed home to local advocates for expenditures that revenues should be at the maximum reasonable level from the revenue-producing activities. A major requirement of the development of such local support would be increased appropriations for various land management activities when additional revenues were raised; preaching for more revenues is not as effective as rewarding them.

Federal Lands in Retrospect and in Prospect

Federal land management has become big business—not giant business, but big business. Considered as a business activity, the management of all federal land runs well behind the largest American private business operations, and behind such giants of federal government business as the Post Office Department, the Atomic Energy Commission, and the Commodity Credit Corporation. But an activity with a gross revenue in 1955 and in 1956 of roughly $350 million if the revenues from submerged areas are included, or of roughly $200 million if they are excluded, and a gross expenditure of the latter general magnitude, can lay claim to being moderately big business even on the American scene.[18] The size of the federal land management job is obscured in part because the job is divided among four major agencies.

Federal lands are managed for purposes other than maximization of revenues and profits; but the revenue-expenditure aspects of federal land management are important. The magnitude of revenues and expenditures sharpens the situation today. Before the war annual gross revenues were roughly $20 million or less, and total expenditures not more than roughly double this amount. Now, if the submerged areas are included, revenues are over $330 million and total expenditures are up to about $175 million. The prospect for 1980 is for total revenues of nearly $900 million. These are important figures, even in the magnitudes of federal government in the second half of the twentieth century.

The big business aspect of federal land management has slipped upon most of us, unawares. Many persons familiar with federal land have known that the uses of these lands and their revenues have been increasing, especially since the war. But few have realized how rapid

---

[18] In July, 1956, *Fortune* released its second annual compilation of the largest industrial corporations in the United States. Companies were ranked according to net sales (or gross operating revenues). A listing of these companies to which the federal agencies are comparable dramatizes the big business aspect of federal land management. All federal lands, including submerged areas, had gross income of $339.8 million in fiscal 1955. If in a single private corporation, this revenue would have earned them 98th place among industrial corporations. They would have been neighbors to such industrial giants as Singer Manufacturing, Phelps Dodge, United Merchants and Manufacturers, Pillsbury Mills, Standard Oil (Ohio), American Radiator and Standard Sanitary, Deere, and Hormel. If the submerged areas are excluded, the $198.7 million gross revenue would have put them in 182nd place, near Anheuser-Busch, National Distillers Products, Time Inc., Timken Roller Bearing, Mack Trucks, and Cannon Mills. The Bureau of Land Management, with its gross revenues of $98.4 million excluding submerged areas, would have been in 310th place (even without the submerged areas), among Interchemical, Interstate Bakeries, Interlake Iron, Plymouth Oil, Allied Mills, and Kendall Co. The Forest Service, with gross revenues of $79.5 million, would have been in 375th place, near Midland Steel Products, Harbison-Walker Refractories, Hazel-Atlas Glass, Island Creek Coal, Lukens Steel, Superior Oil, and Square D.

the increases have been, how much they have been shared by all types of land and all agencies, and how large they have been in total. The absence of considered forecasts for the future has left most of us ill-prepared for the size of the increases that seem altogether probable. Unless the experiences of the past have no meaning for the future, the federal lands will continue to become bigger business.

Some parts of the management of the federal lands have scarcely kept pace with the growth of use and revenues. The technical, public service, and resource management aspects of federal land management have always been of a high standard. The agencies are now struggling to care for the flood of people that enter the federal lands and the mounting demands for the lands' products. By and large, they have done a wonderful job. Their personnel have high professional competence and high standards of public service; in general, morale is high. But the business aspects of management of the federal lands have lagged. To a degree, all agencies are aware of the revenue and expenditure situation, but the problems it involves become vastly different as the scale of expenditure and revenue grows. Some of the tools of analysis used by well-run private businesses have not been applied to federal land management.

One of the great needs of the future in federal land management is to marry the best features of enlightened private business managment with sound, tested features of public resource management as these have evolved over the years. The latter must be extended to meet the new demands imposed by the immensely greater uses of the federal lands. The former are necessary in any conscious and explicit consideration of the financial aspects of federal land management today.

In the opinion of the authors, the demands and the possibilities of the new era point to the urgent need for a fresh re-examination of the whole system of federal land management. In some respects, the situation today is not unlike that of fifty to seventy-five years ago. Then, a substantial dissatisfaction with the policy of unrestricted disposal of the public domain led to new policies and new social instruments—a policy of reservation of certain lands for continued public ownership, then a policy of their use under careful management, and the creation of the new federal agencies, and their staffing with professionally trained and publicly dedicated people, to effectuate these new policies. In retrospect, these policies and new administrative devices seem so eminently sound that now we may wonder why they were once considered so novel, and why they were so strongly opposed in some quarters. But it is at least questionable if the devices and procedures largely established roughly fifty years ago are the best than can be devised today to meet tomorrow's problems—possibly those responsible for creation of the present arrangements would themselves propose something different today, if they contemplated tomorrow's needs.

The present report has sought to bring together accurate and full information on the management and use of the federal lands, and to present some suggestions of the problems and opportunities of the future. It has not sought to advocate a program, but to provide the basis for discussion and consideration by the many groups interested in and concerned over federal land management. We suggest that it is time to take a careful, critical, but imaginative look at the idea of a federal land corporation, at administrative reorganization, and at the other ideas outlined in this chapter—and at any others that may be suggested. No individual or group has the full answer to all the future problems of federal land management, but enlightened discussion may lead to a consensus more constructive than any individual approach.

APPENDICES

Laws and Regulations

THE PURPOSE OF THIS APPENDIX IS TO PRESENT A general idea of the main laws affecting federal land management, and to give information on where the laws and the regulations may be found for the benefit of those who would like to acquire more specific information about particular laws and regulations.

Federal laws relating to disposal of land usually have specified in detail the size and price of the tracts to be sold, even when the law was of general application. In addition, however, a comparatively large number of private-land laws relate to specified tracts of land and have provided the means whereby specified individuals or groups could secure this land. These private-land laws are not discussed here.

There has been a notable tendency to legislate for specific situations rather than to amend previous general law and make it more broadly applicable. A dozen or more laws, for instance, provide for the acquisition of rights of way across federal land. Specific legislation of this kind has not in all cases repealed the earlier legislation which it replaced, thus sometimes leading to further confusion.

Basis of Federal Land Law

"The Congress shall have Power to dispose of and make all needful Rules and Regulations respecting the Territory or other Property belonging to the United States." This single reference in the Constitution to the Public lands has been interpreted by the Supreme Court as giving the Congress complete control over the public domain.[1] Statutes, court decisions, executive orders of the President, and agency regulations have spelled out the public policies in detail, beginning with the Continental Congress and, in particular, its Ordinance of 1785. The bulk of the laws and regulations now applicable have been codified in two reference sources: statute law, reorganization plans, and certain Executive Orders in the *United States Code;* other Executive Branch rules and regulations in the *Code of Federal Regulations.*

Laws now in effect pertaining to the national forests, national parks, wildlife refuges, and the protection of wildlife are grouped in the *United States Code* under Title 16, Conservation. Title 30, Mineral Lands and Mining, contains the laws relevant to that subject while the laws relating to grazing, homesteading, sale of isolated tracts, the management of the Oregon and California Revested Lands, and other matters pertaining to the public domain within the continental United States are compiled under Title 43, Public Lands.

Laws having special application to public land in Alaska are under Title 48, Territories and Insular Possessions. Title 25, Indians, contains those laws relating to ceded Indian lands, and Title 18, Crimes and Criminal Procedure, details the punitive measures for those violating the regulations for use of wildlife refuges, trespassing on public lands by cutting timber, mining coal, grazing and other unauthorized activities, or engaging in other unlawful activities with reference to public lands. Title 33, dealing with Navigation and Navigable Waters, contains statutes relating to flood control in chapter 15.

The applicable titles in the *Code of Federal Regulations* are: Title 25, Indians; Title 30, Mineral Resources; Title 36, Parks, Forests, Memorials; Title 43, Public Lands; and Title 50, Wildlife.

Compilations of laws in handbook form also exist, some of relatively recent issue and others which require considerable revision to bring them up to date.[2] For a detailed discussion of forest and range policy development as well as a chronology of laws, Executive Branch activities and other significant landmarks in the history of federal landownership, Dana's *Forest and Range Policy* is excellent.[3]

---

[1] Article IV, Sec. 3, second paragraph.

[2] Greene, Daniel M. (comp.), *Public Land Statutes of the United States,* Washington, D. C.: U. S. Government Printing Office, 1931.

Irion, Harry (comp.), *The Principal Laws Relating to the Establishment and Administration of the National Forests and to other Forest Service Activities.* U. S. Department of Agriculture Handbook No. 20, 1951.

Lewis, Elmer, A. (comp.), *Oil Land Leasing Act of 1920 with Amendments and other Laws Relating to Minerals Lands.* Washington, D. C.: U. S. Government Printing Office, 1952.

Tolson, Hillory O. (comp.), *Laws Relating to the National Park Service.* Washington, D. C.: U. S. Government Printing Office, 1933. Supplements 1944, 1949, 1950.

[3] Dana, Samuel T., *Forest and Range Policy—Its Development in the United States,* New York: McGraw-Hill Book Co., 1956.

Methods of Land Disposal

Public lands are not offered for public sale, except for small tracts, isolated and disconnected fractional tracts, and certain other lands for which there has been express authorization for sale by the Congress (43 USC 671).[4] Land patents may be granted, when suitable land is available, under the provisions of several different laws. Homestead entries, in which title to the land passes to the applicant upon his paying a filing fee and satisfying the requirements of settlement, residence, and cultivation, may be made under provisions of the Homestead Act (43 USC 161-301). However, the land must be classified as suitable for the particular type of homestead before entries will be permitted.[5] Various types of homesteading are permitted: the 160-acre homestead; the enlarged homestead of 320 acres; and the reclamation homestead on reclamation project land. Forest homesteads are permitted on national forest lands that the Secretary of Agriculture determines to be suitable for agriculture (16 USC 506-12), and on Oregon and California Railroad and Coos Bay Wagon Road revested lands when classified for such purpose by the Secretary of the Interior (43 USC 1181 c).

Desert land entries may be made on 320-acre tracts or less and a patent granted if the required expenditures for irrigation facilities are made and at least an eighth of the land is irrigated and cultivated and a sum of $1.25 an acre is paid (43 USC 321-39). Permits are authorized, in Nevada only, to explore for underground water with the subsequent right to patent no more than 640 acres of the land upon development of a water supply adequate to produce crops profitably on a minimum tract of 20 acres. The fee is one cent per acre on the tract to be explored with no more than 2,560 acres to be included in the tract (43 USC 351-60). Grants of desert land to the states for purposes of irrigation are made under the Carey Act (43 USC 641). Other grants to states for public purposes are covered in chapter 20 of Title 43 of the code. The laws relating to the grants of land made for railroads and wagon roads are found in chapter 21 of Title 43.

Small tracts of any vacant unreserved public land, 5 acres or less, primarily valuable for home, business, recreation or health sites, may be leased or sold (43 USC 682a). and the sale of lots in town sites reserved from the public lands is also authorized (43 USC 712). Isolated tracts of land, not exceeding 1,520 acres, may be sold at not less than appraised value (43 USC 1171), and tracts of land too rough for cultivation, up to 760 acres, may also be sold even though the tract is not isolated. Only an adjoining owner may apply for the sale of such land but anyone may then bid on it, or the federal government may exercise the initiative and offer such a tract for sale. Timber lands and stone lands not previously reserved were also available for purchase

---

[4] The citations used here are to the 1952 edition of the *United States Code* and Supplements.

[5] Classification of the land is not required prior to homesteading on lands in Alaska.

in 160-acre tracts at a price no lower than $2.50 per acre, until the act was repealed on August 1, 1955.

Mineral rights in known mineral lands are available for sale only in those instances where the mining laws apply and claims can be patented (30 USC 22-48, 612). The surface rights of land that has been classified as mineral land containing oil, gas, coal, phosphate, potash, nitrate, oil shale, and asphaltic minerals may be disposed of through homesteading or sale, but the mineral rights are reserved to the federal government (30 USC 81, 83, 85, 86, 90, 121-24). If other minerals are involved, gold for instance, the surface rights may not be homesteaded or sold. Inasmuch as the mining laws refer only to the public domain, they have for the most part been interpreted as not applying to the acquired lands.

In general, when a mining claim is patented it conveys title not only to the minerals but to the surface as well. This has been a source of trouble where the surface resources, such as timber, may be more valuable than the mineral deposits and would not otherwise be available except through the sale of the surface resources themselves at a price reflecting their true value. To remove the incentive for using mining claims to obtain timber, mining claims *located* after July 23, 1955 are not to be used prior to patenting for purposes other than prospecting, mining, and processing operations, and other reasonably related uses. Before patenting, the United States reserves the right to manage and dispose of the surface resources other than the mineral being mined (30 USC 612).

On lands within certain watersheds and on lands where the protection of scenic values has been an objective, all mining patents issued on claims established since the date of the respective acts convey title to the mineral deposits within the claim, together with the right to use as much mature timber as is required for their mining operations, provided it is cut according to national forest rules and regulations. But each patent reserves to the United States all title in or to the surface of the claim and the surface resources (16 USC 482, a, f, h, p).

Reservation of Public Land

The disposal of federal land is further limited by other reservations in the public interest. Both the Congress and the President exercise the power to reserve or withdraw public land. The President may withdraw or reserve land for water power sites, for irrigation projects, to classify the land, and for other public purposes (43 USC 141). These powers in turn are delegated to the Secretary of the Interior by Executive Order 10355, issued in 1952. Reservations of the public domain remain in force until revoked by the Secretary of the Interior or by act of Congress.

Prior to 1907 the President could create national forests, and until 1910 he could enlarge an existing forest on public lands in any state or territory. From time to time since then, these powers have been restricted. Now, an Act of Congress is required before this can be done in the states of California, Oregon, Washington, Idaho, Colorado, Wyoming, New Mexico, and Arizona (16 USC 471, 471a, 471b).

Some of the national parks and monuments, military parks, and the related areas administered by the National Park Service have been created by the reservation of public land for this use. Others have been redesignated as parks or monuments after having first been part of a larger national forest reserve. National monuments may be established on federally owned lands anywhere other than Wyoming at the discretion of the President (16 USC 431). Congress also establishes national monuments and has the sole authority to establish national parks and other areas. A considerable body of law has been written in establishing these areas, much of it for specific parks and monuments (16 USC 21-460).

By special acts, the Congress has established or permitted the President to establish reservations for the protection of wildlife on vacant public land as well as upon lands previously reserved for national forests (16 USC 671, 673-75, 680, 682, 684, 688, 689, 692, 693). But the Congress has specified that "it is not intended that the lands so designated shall cease to be parts of the national forest within which they are located, and the establishment of such game sanctuaries or refuges shall not prevent the Secretary of Agriculture from permitting other uses of land under and in conformity with the laws and regulations applicable thereto so far as such uses may be consistent with the purposes for which such game sanctuaries or refuges are established" (16 USC 692). A similar provision was written into the general authority given the President to establish such areas in any of the national forests (16 USC 694). This multi-use authorization is also found in the law directing any federal agency which is impounding or diverting water to make "adequate provision consistent with the primary purposes" of the development "for the conservation, maintenance, and management of wildlife" (16 USC 663, 665 a).

The most recent large-scale withdrawal of public lands was that accomplished by the Taylor Grazing Act in creating grazing districts on the "vacant, unappropriated and unreserved lands of the public domain" (43 USC 315). While homesteading is not precluded on these lands, no entries are allowed until the land has been classified and is opened to entry. They are then restricted to 320 acres, in effect repealing the stock-raising homestead act although the law remains on the books (43 USC 291-97). The lands remain available, however, for entry under the mining laws.

Acquisition of Privately Owned Land

When in the public interest it is desirable that lands not presently in federal ownership be available for use or management for forest, park, grazing, or wildlife refuge purposes, or to permit the consolidation of scattered land holdings, provisions have been made for the purchase, lease, or exchange of land, and the acceptance from donors of gifts of money and land. Land purchases are authorized for the establishment of national forests by the Secretary of Agriculture when approved by the National Forest Reservation Commission and consented to by the state legislature concerned (16 USC 513-17, 521). The Congress also permits the exchange of national forest land or timber for privately owned land within the exterior boundaries of a national forest, if both tracts are within the same state and if the value of the land conveyed does not exceed the value of the land received (16 USC 485-86, 516). Reservation by either party of the mineral rights on the lands exchanged is permitted. The Secretary of Agriculture, acting for the federal government, may accept donations of land, subject to the reservation by the donor of the present stand of merchantable timber or of mineral or other rights for a period not exceeding twenty years. The rights retained or reserved by the donor are subject to the tax laws of the state in which the lands are located (16 USC 569).

Similarly, the Secretary of the Interior has authority to accept gifts of privately owned grazing land and to exchange land with private individuals or with states (43 USC 315g).

The laws relating to the national parks provide for the general acceptance of donated lands and money (16 USC 6, 6a), but authority to purchase property for park purposes or to make land exchanges, when granted, has been for specific parks. Similarly, the authority to purchase land or to accept donation of it for wildlife refuges is to be found in legislation for specific acquisitions. General authority has also been granted the Secretary of the Interior to acquire leaseholds or to purchase or exchange land in order to provide refuges for wildlife (16 USC 695, 715d). Leaseholds on grazing lands in private or state ownership may be acquired and integrated with public land in a grazing district to permit the intermingled lands to be managed as a unit (43 USC 315 m-1).

Management and Protection

Limited free use of coal, timber, grazing, stone, gravel, etc., is permitted under several laws to bona fide settlers, prospectors, miners, and residents, for domestic use or mining operations (16 USC 45c, 477, 604, 607-613). To use these resources in violation of the regulations governing their free use subjects the user to the penalties of the criminal code (18 USC 1851-1857, 1863). These provisions apply to all public lands of the United States and include restraints against such acts as unlawfully removing coal and timber; destroying or injuring trees; wilfully and without authority setting fire to timber, underbrush or grass, or leaving a fire unattended, or permitting it to spread beyond control; destroying fences, etc.; and illegally entering and grazing, and trespassing on national forest lands. Timber cut in trespass may be seized (16 USC 602) and the equipment and weapons used to kill or capture birds or animals in national parks may be seized and are forfeited to the United States (16 USC 65). Wildlife in refuges is protected (18 USC 41, 16 USC 689b, 690d, 690e, 694, 694a, 694b), and employees of the Interior Department and the Forest Service have the power to arrest, without warrant, those violating the laws and regulations in their presence (16 USC 559).

The Secretary of Agriculture has the authority to protect the national forests from fire and depredation and to make the necessary rules and regulations and to enforce them (16 USC 471, 551). The Secretary of the Interior has the authority to make and publish and enforce rules and regulations for the use and management of the parks, monuments, and reservations under the jurisdiction of the National Park Service (16 USC 3), and similar powers to protect, administer, regulate, and improve the public land in grazing districts (16 USC 315a). He is also authorized to protect the timber on all public land under his jurisdiction from fire, disease, and insects (16 USC 594).

The Forest Pest Control Act (16 USC 594-1–594-5) established the policy of protecting all forest land, whether private or public, from forest insects and diseases. Similarly, to protect the livestock industry it is the policy of the Congress to appropriate funds for eradication of the poisonous range weed *Halogeton glomeratus* on all lands irrespective of ownership (7 USC 1652).

The administrators of the public lands are allowed, and to some extent required, to permit certain limited uses of the lands for a nominal fee or none at all. The free use of coal, timber, stone, and other materials, when in accordance with the established rules and regulations, has already been mentioned.

On the lands under the National Park Service jurisdiction the Secretary of the Interior is permitted to cut and sell or dispose of timber where necessary to control attacks of insects or diseases or to protect natural or historic objects or conserve the scenery. He may grant concessions to permit the accommodation of visitors. He may grant grazing privileges when such use is not detrimental to the primary purpose of the tract (16 USC 3). In the management of wildlife refuges similar uses are permitted. No power development within the parks or monuments is permitted without Congressional authority, however (16 USC 797).

On the other lands of the public domain under his jurisdiction and on the O & C revested lands, the Secretary of the Interior has similar authority. Sand, stone, gravel, yucca, cactus, timber or other forest products, and other materials of like nature may be removed from unreserved public lands subject to the regulations of the Secretary (43 USC 1185, 1186). He may lease tracts for airport use (49 USC 211-14), and to state and local governments for recreational purposes (43 USC 869). He may lease O & C lands for grazing purposes (43 USC 1181d). He may permit rights of way across the public lands for various purposes and under various conditions (chapter 22, Title 43 and 16 USC 5).

The Secretary of Agriculture may, with respect to national forest lands, sell without advertisement small quantities of timber, cordwood and other forest products when the value does not exceed $2,000, and timber for domestic use of farmers and settlers at actual cost (16 USC 476, 489). He may permit leasing, for not more than thirty years, tracts of 5 acres or less within the forests for summer homes and stores, and tracts of 80 acres or less for hotels and resorts and such facilities for industrial or commercial purposes related to or consistent with other uses on the forests. States or local governments and other public or nonprofit agencies may use and occupy tracts of 80 acres or less for the same period of time (16 USC 497 as amended June 28, 1956, 70 Stat. 708).

Resource Use

Protecting the timber, grass, mineral, wildlife, recreational, and esthetic values of the public lands is important only in relation to the ultimate availability of these resources for the purpose of satisfying human needs. The statutes already mentioned which allow limited free use and small sales are not sufficient for the fullest use of these resources. However, more extensive use is permitted.

The sale of standing timber from the national forests, the Oregon and California and Coos Bay lands, and the public domain is authorized by section 476, Title 16 and sections 1181 and 1185, Title 43 of the U.S. Code. Prior to the passage of these acts, sales were generally limited to dead and down timber. Both the Secretary of Agriculture and the Secretary of the Interior are authorized to set up co-operative sustained-yield units with owners of private timber, treating the combined federal and private holdings as a single unit and prescribing the rate and method of cutting timber. The private timber owner who enters into a co-operative sustained-yield agreement may be given the privilege of buying federal stumpage without competitive bidding at not less than appraised value (16 USC 583-583i). The sustained-yield limit on the annual cut of timber on the Oregon and California and Coos Bay lands is written into the law in section 1181 of Title 43 as well as the permission granted to the Secretary of the Interior to establish sustained-yield forest units. Upon the sale of any federally-owned timber, the needs of the state or territory have priority in the marketing of the timber (16 USC 616).

Although grazing permits have been issued since 1900, grazing on national forest lands was not specifically mentioned in any law until 1950. Permits were issued under the general authority of the Secretary of Agriculture to regulate the use and occupancy of the forests. They are now issued under the Granger-Thye Act of 1950 which also provides legal status for the grazing advisory boards and specifically authorizes the issuance of permits for periods of not more than ten years (16 USC 580).[6] Most special-use permits are still issued under the more general authority given the Secretary of Agriculture to regulate the use and occupancy of the national forests (16 USC 551).

Grazing on the unreserved public domain, unregulated and free until the passage of the Taylor Grazing Act, is governed by the provisions of that act (43 USC 315-315r), and the regulations of the Secretary of the Interior published in Title 43 of the Code of Federal Regulations. There are important differences, both in the fees charged and the regulations in effect, between grazing lands managed by the Forest Service and those managed by the Bureau of Land Management.

In those states and for those minerals not subject to the mining laws, mineral rights owned by the federal government and the mineral deposits on the public domain are developed under permits and leases (30 USC 181-94, 201-9, 211-14, 223-29, 241, 251, 261-63, 271-76, 281-86 and 48 USC 432-52). The act does not apply to national parks, monuments, etc. Mineral deposits on other lands acquired by the United States, in particular the lands purchased for national forests, may be leased (30 USC 351-59). The submerged lands of the outer continental shelf are dealt with in separate legislation which also provides for the development of their mineral resources under a leasing arrangement (43 USC 1334-43).

The mineral leasing law does not apply to national parks (30 USC 181) and, with only a few exceptions, mining, under the mining laws, is limited to those claims which were in existence before the park or monument was created.

Resource Development

The recognition that the continued use of certain resources would not be possible without definite investments for their development has led to policy declarations by Congress and legislation to permit and encourage such investment. For the range lands, both in national forests and on the unreserved public domain, provision has been made for setting aside a portion of the grazing receipts to be used for range improvement (16 USC 580h and 43 USC 315b, 315i).

Measures to prevent soil erosion, including engineering operations, methods of cultivation, and the growing of vegetation, may be undertaken on any federally owned or controlled lands (16 USC 590b), and the funds appropriated for this purpose may be used for revegetation, watering facilities, fencing, and other projects.

The Congress has declared its policy with respect to a continuing invest-

[6] The difficulties of regulating grazing and the tests of its constitutionality are related by Dana, *op. cit.,* pp. 115-16 and 144-47.

ment in national forest lands by authorizing specific appropriations for reforestation and revegetation (16 USC 581j, 581k). This step followed an earlier act which authorized the establishment of forest tree nurseries and permitted the Secretary of Agriculture to require any purchaser of national forest timber to deposit funds in addition to payment for the timber, these funds to be used to replant or treat the cutover area to improve the future stand of timber (16 USC 576-576b). A similar act permits the Secretary to require a deposit of funds by timber purchasers to be used to cover the cost of disposing of brush and debris resulting from their cutting operations (16 USC 490).

Appropriations for the construction and maintenance of forest roads and trails on national forest lands are available from two sources: 10 per cent of the receipts from the national forests (16 USC 501); and funds available from the Federal Highway Act as amended (23 USC 23). Funds are authorized for the construction and maintenance of forest access roads on the Oregon and California revested lands on the basis of the authority of the Secretary of the Interior to sell the timber and protect it as well as the specific authority of the appropriation acts. Roads, trails, and parkway construction and maintenance in relation to the national park system are specifically authorized in several acts (16 USC 8-8d, 403h-11, 460). Approach roads outside of park and monument boundaries are included in this authorization.

Development and maintenance of refuges for migratory waterfowl also are specifically provided for (16 USC 718, 718i).

Disposition of Receipts [7]

No single act governs the disposition of receipts from the various public lands, and often within one agency several nearly physically identical tracts of land will be administered under as many different laws, each prescribing a different formula for the use of receipts.

The disposition of nearly all receipts from national forest lands is governed by sections 500 and 501 of Title 16 of the U.S. Code which specify a 25 per cent distribution to the state within which the revenue was earned and a 10 per cent distribution to the Forest Service to be used for forest roads and trails. The remainder of the receipts goes to the general fund of the Treasury. Receipts from a portion of the Superior National Forest are handled in a slightly different fashion (16 USC 577g), while receipts from the lands within national forest boundaries that at one time were a part of the land grant to the Oregon and California Railroad are handled in the same fashion as those O & C and Coos Bay lands administered by the Bureau of Land Management (43 USC 1181d, 1181f-1181i). The revenues from mineral leases and royalties

[7] See chapters four and five.

are not regarded as receipts from national forests unless the forest was created by purchasing the land rather than reserving it while a part of the public domain (30 USC 355).

Revenues under the Mineral Leasing Act on lands other than those acquired and the naval petroleum reserves (34 USC 524) are divided between the states, the Reclamation Fund, and the general fund of the Treasury (30 USC 191, 285). Revenues from the mineral leases on the outer continental shelf are not shared but deposited in their entirety to the general fund of the Treasury (43 USC 1337g).

Two different methods are used in sharing grazing receipts with the states, depending upon whether the land is within a grazing district or is under lease outside a district (43 USC 315i). Grazing revenues from the O & C lands and Alaskan lands are handled in yet different ways (43 USC 1181f, 48 USC 471).

Receipts from sales of timber, sand, gravel, and other materials from the public domain and of public domain land are shared with the states to the extent of 5 per cent (31 USC 711). In the reclamation states, the remaining 95 per cent of receipts from sales is deposited to the credit of the Reclamation Fund (43 USC 391). In the remaining states this portion of the receipts is deposited in the general fund of the Treasury.

Receipts from the national parks are primarily deposited to the general fund of the Treasury (16 USC 54, 452) with certain exceptions, the major ones being payments for educational expenses in Yellowstone and payments in lieu of taxes in Grand Teton National Park (16 USC 40a, 406d-3).

Revenues from lands administered by the Fish and Wildlife Service are shared with the states in which they are earned, the states receiving a 25 per cent share after the cost of sales has been deducted (16 USC 715s). The remaining 75 per cent of the receipts is used for development and maintenance of refuges and sanctuaries as well as for enforcement of the laws protecting wildlife.[8] Receipts from sale of the migratory waterfowl hunting stamp are administered by the Fish and Wildlife Service (16 USC 718d) and are available for enforcement purposes and land acquisition for refuges (16 USC 718, 718i). Funds from federal taxes on firearms and on sport fishing equipment which are granted to the state for projects to restore fish and wildlife, if not spent, are available to the Fish and Wildlife Service (16 USC 669b, 777b).

[8] Prior to fiscal year 1951, these receipts were deposited to the general fund of the Treasury. The General Appropriation Act, 1951, September 6, 1950, contained the authorization for the Fish and Wildlife Service to use these funds in that and in future fiscal years.

Statistical Appendix

Code of symbols:

　　... none
　　– not available or beyond the scope of the study
　　* less than half of the unit indicated

Statistics have been included in another column if column has been shown blank.

Because of rounding, details in both text tables and appendix tables may not add to totals.

Operating costs shown in these tables are the funds obligated for expenditure by the agencies concerned rather than the actual expenditures. Actual expenditures can be expected to be slightly less than the obligations, but since obligated funds are available for expenditure for two years comparable figures on an expenditure basis for the most recent years are not available.

APPENDIX TABLE 1. *Rural Land in Federal Ownership by State and by Administering Agency 1950*

(all areas in thousand acres)

Region and state[3]	Total land area	In federal ownership		Dept. of the Interior[1]						Dept. of Agriculture[1]			Dept. of Defense	Other
		Area	% of total	Bur. of Land Management	Nat'l. Park Service	Fish and Wildlife Service	Bur. of Indian Affairs	Bur. of Reclamation	Sub-total[1]	Forest Service	Soil Conservation Service[2]	Sub-total[1]		
United States[3]	1,903,786	455,625	23.93	179,093	13,956	4,129	57,280	9,928	264,379	160,582	7,415	167,998	21,458	1,791
New England	40,422	1,128	2.79		28	34			62	968	4	971	87	8
Maine	19,866	134	.68		28	22			51	63	4	67	13	3
New Hampshire	5,771	683	11.84			*			*	670		670	13	*
Vermont	5,938	226	3.81			2			2	210		210	14	1
Massachusetts	5,035	52	1.03			10			10	2		2	38	2
Rhode Island	677	19	2.79			*			*	11		11	8	1
Connecticut	3,135	14	.44			*			*	12		12	1	1
Middle Atlantic	64,327	1,084	1.61		6	65	87		159	520	22	543	289	43
New York	30,684	354	1.15		2	53	86		141	15	17	33	155	25
New Jersey	4,814	96	1.99		1	12			13				79	4
Pennsylvania	28,829	584	2.03		3	*	1		4	505	5	511	55	14
East North Central	156,715	6,086	3.88	22	134	310	480		946	4,468	7	4,476	613	51
Ohio	26,240	251	.96		*	*			*	134	*	135	106	11
Indiana	23,171	341	1.47							125		125	209	7
Illinois	35,798	450	1.26			51			51	220		220	159	21
Michigan	36,494	2,801	7.68	16	134	94	27		270	2,473	7	2,481	42	8
Wisconsin	35,011	2,242	6.40	6		165	453		624	1,516		1,516	97	5

APPENDIX TABLE 1—continued

Region and state	Total land area	In federal ownership		Dept. of the Interior[1]						Dept. of Agriculture[1]			Dept. of Defense	Other
		Area	% of total	Bur. of Land Management	Nat'l Park Service	Fish and Wildlife Service	Bur. of Indian Affairs	Bur. of Reclamation	Subtotal[1]	Forest Service	Soil Conservation Service[2]	Subtotal[1]		
West North Central	326,812	17,969	5.50	543	221	645	7,851	71	9,333	5,331	2,227	7,556	1,001	79
Minnesota	51,206	3,829	7.48	93	*	205	863	...	1,161	2,658	...	2,658	3	7
Iowa	35,869	107	.30	...	1	22	5	...	28	5	2	7	71	1
Missouri	44,305	1,646	3.72	1	*	40	...	...	41	1,346	14	1,359	213	33
North Dakota	44,836	2,681	5.98	98	59	189	1,094	11	1,451	1	1,085	1,085	145	*
South Dakota	44,983	8,644	17.65	319	159	50	5,779	30	6,337	1,115	886	2,001	296	11
Nebraska	49,064	740	1.51	29	2	139	74	19	264	206	137	343	111	22
Kansas	52,549	322	.61	3	...	*	36	11	51	...	103	103	163	5
South Atlantic	171,507	10,830	6.32	24	928	892	136		1,980	5,889	549	6,439	2,209	202
Delaware	1,266	40	3.17	...	...	14	...	...	14	...	5	5	21	*
Maryland	6,324	216	3.42	...	16	14	...	...	30	43	2	45	127	14
Virginia	25,532	2,074	8.12	...	250	13	...	...	263	1,482	...	1,482	321	8
West Virginia	15,411	947	6.15	...	*	*	...	...	*	911	8	919	26	2
North Carolina	31,422	1,931	6.15	...	253	134	56	...	442	1,134	14	1,148	258	83
South Carolina	19,395	952	4.91	...	4	126	...	...	130	585	56	641	128	53
Georgia	37,429	1,841	4.92	...	16	371	...	...	387	660	162	822	623	9
Florida	34,728	2,829	8.15	24	389	220	80	...	714	1,074	302	1,377	705	33
East South Central	115,192	4,783	4.15	45	304	117	15	...	482	2,785	123	2,907	878	516
Kentucky	25,513	989	3.88	...	51	65	...	...	115	469	15	484	364	26
Tennessee	26,750	1,347	5.04	...	240	11	...	...	251	649	1	650	127	319
Alabama	32,690	966	2.95	27	1	...	*	...	28	621	11	632	180	126
Mississippi	30,939	1,480	4.00	18										

West South Central	403,...	10,007	3.33	136	1	122				259	2,352	86	2,438	328	24
Arkansas	33,712	3,049	9.05		1	*	*	...			560	31	591	233	9
Louisiana	28,904	1,064	3.68	7	*	224			231	560	31	591	233	9
Oklahoma	44,180	3,769	8.53	26	1	79	2,852	13	2,970	178	101	278	484	37
Texas	168,648	2,723	1.61	...	692	75	4	5	776	658	131	789	1,012	146
Mountain	548,669	309,036	56.32	145,844	6,129	1,037	40,640	6,909	200,558	92,560	3,994	96,554	11,539	385
Montana	93,362	34,307	36.75	6,783	1,141	489	6,502	240	15,155	16,531	1,953	18,484	593	75
Idaho	52,972	34,444	65.02	11,350	79	11	865	779	13,084	20,282	126	20,408	916	37
Wyoming	62,404	32,723	52.44	17,586	2,309	70	2,081	1,022	23,068	8,566	584	9,150	501	4
Colorado	66,510	25,094	37.73	8,410	518	1	731	737	10,397	13,706	626	14,332	241	125
New Mexico	77,767	34,793	44.74	15,702	235	187	7,328	212	23,614	9,066	664	9,730	1,340	107
Arizona	72,688	50,749	69.82	13,958	1,445	*	19,457	2,188	37,048	11,486	2	11,488	2,205	8
Utah	52,701	37,919	71.95	24,477	286	74	2,534	456	27,827	7,870	39	7,909	2,175	8
Nevada	70,265	59,008	83.98	47,578	116	255	1,142	1,275	50,366	5,053	...	5,053	3,568	21
Pacific	204,698	94,145	45.99	32,448	5,503	527	5,214	2,929	46,623	44,315	139	44,455	2,784	284
Washington	42,743	15,381	35.98	493	1,133	86	2,798	776	5,287	9,680	...	9,680	175	239
Oregon	61,642	32,772	53.16	15,065	161	417	1,733	344	17,720	14,779	112	14,891	147	13
California	100,314	45,993	45.85	16,890	4,209	24	683	1,809	23,616	19,856	27	19,883	2,461	33

Note. In some instances the data in the above table do not conform precisely with the records of some of the federal agencies. The Fish and Wildlife Service, in particular, has raised this point. Such discrepancies may be due to differences in definition or to changes occurring since the source data were assembled. Data on federal landownership are notoriously difficult to obtain on an accurate, comparable, inclusive, and nondouble-counting basis. This is largely because, until recently, no single inventory or other record of all federal land holdings existed. Moreover, since some tracts of lands are under the jurisdiction of two or more agencies for different purposes, and since some lands are withdrawn for special uses or purposes, a compilation of federal land may or may not include them, depending on definitions used. Recently, however, the General Services Administration conducted two inventories of federal real property (see table 2, p. 39. The GSA will continue to do this annually and in time its reports will provide up-to-date information on holdings by the various agencies. Meantime, Circular No. 909 represents a painstaking attempt to gather the data on a comparable basis; the data is used here as a very close approximation of the correct situation.

[1] Of enumerated agencies; additional small areas under other agencies included in "Other."

[2] Most of this land has been transferred to the Forest Service since 1950.

[3] Total includes 7,550 acres not allocated as to state; also included in "Other."

Source: R. D. Davidson, *Federal and State Rural Lands, 1950,* U.S. Department of Agriculture, BAE Circular No. 909; and *Statistical Abstract of the United States, 1955.* For precise definition of areas included, see appendix table 17, Circular No. 909.

APPENDIX TABLE 2. National Forest Lands: *Grazing Receipts, Grazing Fees,*
and Paid-Permit Grazing, 1905-56

(receipts in thousands of dollars;
numbers and animal-unit months in thousands;
fees in cents per AUM)

Year[1]	Receipts into Treasury	Use of range by domestic livestock and game					Grazing fee	
		Cattle, horses, & swine	Sheep & goats	AUM for all animals[2]	AUM for domestic livestock	AUM for game animals[3]	Cattle	Sheep
1905	–	692	1,710	–	–	–	–	–
06	513	1,015	5,762	–	–	–	–	–
07	857	1,200	6,657	–	–	–	–	–
08	947	1,382	7,087	13,952	13,952	–	–	–
09	1,023	1,586	7,820	–	–	–	–	–
1910	970	1,498	7,649	–	–	–	–	–
11	928	1,448	7,449	–	–	–	–	–
12	961	1,503	7,552	–	–	–	–	–
13	999	1,557	7,868	15,612	15,612	–	–	–
14	1,002	1,620	7,619	–	–	–	–	–
1915	1,130	1,727	7,284	–	–	–	–	–
16	1,210	1,861	7,886	–	–	–	–	–
17	1,550	2,054	7,636	–	–	–	–	–
18	1,726	2,243	8,512	20,365	20,365	–	–	–
19	2,609	2,234	7,996	–	–	–	–	–
1920	2,486	2,121	7,325	–	–	–	–	–
		[4]96	[4]557	–	–	–	–	–
21	2,132	2,080	6,980	–	–	–	–	–
22	1,316	1,987	6,892	–	–	–	–	–
23	2,341	1,864	6,712	18,349	17,179	1,170	–	–
24	1,916	1,753	6,597	–	–	–	–	–
1925	1,725	1,621	6,432	–	–	–	–	–
26	1,422	1,559	6,503	–	–	–	–	–
27	1,531	1,486	6,704	–	–	–	–	–
28	1,714	1,415	6,784	14,262	12,672	1,590	–	–
29	1,740	1,399	6,964	–	–	–	–	–

APPENDIX TABLE 2—continued

Year [1]	Receipts into Treasury	Use of range by domestic livestock and game					Grazing fee	
		Cattle, horses, & swine	Sheep & goats	AUM for all animals [2]	AUM for domestic livestock	AUM for game animals [3]	Cattle	Sheep
1930	1,943	1,358	6,714	–	–	–	–	–
31	1,961	1,376	6,608	–	–	–	–	–
32	830	1,397	6,321	–	–	–	–	–
33	1,498	1,399	6,162	15,173	12,943	2,230	9.05	2.05
34	1,359	1,419	6,161	–	–	–	7.51	2.39
1935	1,151	1,345	5,691	–	–	–	8.04	2.71
36	1,442	1,311	5,645	–	–	–	13.05	3.36
37	1,580	1,284	5,485	–	–	–	12.55	3.66
38	1,696	1,250	5,307	13,912	11,062	2,850	14.98	4.24
39	1,574	1,209	5,132	–	–	–	13.4	3.3
1940	1,463	1,177	4,949	–	–	–	14.89	3.68
41	1,429	1,176	4,787	–	–	–	15.97	3.85
42	1,595	1,191	4,758	–	–	–	18.90	4.6
43	1,973	1,212	4,539	13,252	9,842	3,410	23.0	5.5
44	2,459	1,225	4,280	–	–	–	26.0	6.25
1945	2,159	1,206	3,889	12,756	9,136	3,620	24.8	6.03
46	2,060	1,203	3,713	–	–	–	27.0	6.25
47	2,294	1,247	3,403	11,889	8,149	3,740	31.0	7.5
48	2,898	1,226	3,322	–	–	–	40.0	10.0
49	3,276	1,126	3,092	11,615	7,645	3,970	49.0	11.0
1950	3,385	1,092	3,006	–	–	–	42.0	10.75
51	4,166	1,088	3,013	11,768	7,338	4,430	51.0	12.25
52	5,023	1,096	3,000	11,762	7,332	4,430	64.0	15.25
53	4,416	1,108	2,964	12,126	7,376	4,750	54.0	11.75
54	3,107	1,008	2,910	12,285	7,285	5,000	35.0	9.00
1955	2,954	1,106	2,822	12,452	7,232	5,220	37.0	9.00
56	2,906	1,095	2,730	–	7,126	–	35.0	8.75

[1] Fiscal years throughout, except for use of range by domestic livestock and game which, since 1921, has been reported on a calendar year basis.

[2] Estimates prior to the first use of animal-unit months in 1926.

[3] Big game population estimates not available prior to 1921.

[4] Last 6 months of the calendar year.

Source: Compiled from U.S. Forest Service data.

APPENDIX TABLE 3.   National Forest Lands: *Timber Receipts, Volume and Value of Timber Cut by Class of Sale, 1905–56 and Projections for 1960 and 1980*

(volume in millions of board feet; receipts and value in thousands of dollars)

Year [1]	Timber receipts [2]	Total		All timber cut								
				Commercial sales		Cost sales [4]		Land exchanges		Forest products [5]	Free use	
		Volume	Value [3]	Volume	Value	Volume	Value	Volume	Value	Value	Volume	Value
1905	73	68	86	68	86							
06	237	139	203	139	203							
07	654	195	338	195	338							
08	811	525	964	393	794						132	170
09	702	458	847	353	678						105	169
1910	1,011	484	1,082	379	906						105	176
11	952	498	1,040	375	843						123	197
12	1,028	555	1,139	432	943						123	196
13	1,271	617	1,267	495	1,074	1	1				121	192
14	1,311	747	1,454	617	1,264	10	7				120	183
1915	1,183	689	1,386	547	1,165	19	14				123	207
16	1,422	714	1,439	575	1,240	20	14				119	185
17	1,640	850	1,683	716	1,518	21	15				113	150
18	1,630	827	1,655	709	1,511	21	16				97	128
19	1,535	796	1,635	686	1,500	19	14			8	91	113
1920	2,045	893	1,887	783	1,748	22	16			10	88	113
21	1,770	981	2,081	776	1,878	25	18			8	180	177
22	1,813	812	1,859	702	1,736	21	16			8	89	99
23	2,722	1,092	2,680	975	2,553	20	18			11	97	98
24	3,036	1,233	3,203	1,128	3,080	16	15			14	89	94
1925	2,940	1,100	2,895	1,005	2,793	17	15			5	78	82
26	3,367	1,281	3,477	1,177	3,356	16	14			10	88	97
27	3,253	1,442	3,944	1,146	3,293	15	14	199	540	6	82	91
28	3,325	1,354	3,610	1,151	3,194	17	15	104	299	12	82	90
29	4,109	1,583	4,456	1,335	3,876	17	15	144	437	30	87	98
1930	4,390	1,769	4,930	1,470	4,324	18	17	165	449	23	116	117
31	2,608	1,390	3,527	1,080	2,871	18	17	174	460	17	168	162
32	1,049	882	1,767	526	1,309	19	17	67	193	21	270	227
33	783	740	1,333	522	823	18	15	84	239	19	266	237

Year												
36	2,203	1,314	2,892	795	2,100	20	19	206	471	30	293	272
37	2,924	1,608	3,505	1,078	2,723	19	17	193	449	39	318	277
38	2,518	1,589	3,539	1,055	2,644	20	18	213	546	52	301	279
39	2,857	1,558	3,687	999	2,668	18	17	273	690	52	268	260
1940	3,943	2,066	5,168	1,347	3,803	24	21	369	982	58	326	304
41	4,737	2,352	6,084	1,530	4,509	22	20	515	1,233	62	285	260
42	5,094	2,424	6,429	1,540	4,505	20	18	645	1,586	79	219	241
43	7,610	2,529	8,907	1,848	6,819	17	16	495	1,837	60	169	175
44	12,623	3,514	14,517	2,821	12,399	19	17	493	1,739	149	181	213
1945	11,587	3,299	13,291	2,712	11,663	20	19	413	1,334	104	154	171
46	10,554	2,868	11,811	2,470	10,494			260	997	150	138	170
47	15,421	3,962	16,780	3,472	14,955			363	1,445	183	128	197
48	20,487	3,875	21,389	3,451	19,842			307	1,212	145	116	189
49	26,927	3,854	29,163	3,380	26,928			360	1,821	224	114	190
1950	29,379	3,623	31,140	3,195	29,084			307	1,630	211	121	215
51	51,099	4,794	48,227	4,422	46,533			266	1,284	178	106	232
52	63,723	4,516	59,759	4,232	58,275			186	1,066	193	98	225
53	69,252	5,261	71,039	4,982	69,727			179	889	226	101	196
54	61,289	5,474	65,887	5,180	64,149			185	1,259	255	109	224
1955	73,187	6,434	71,231	6,225	70,105			103	656	266	106	204
56	107,070	7,020	97,839	6,813	96,565			94	775		104	...
1960 [6]	135,000			9,000	135,000							
1980 [6]	300,000			15,000	300,000							

[1] Fiscal year throughout, except for free use where fiscal year is used for data, 1905 to 1920 and 1933 to 1956. Calendar year data, 1922 to 1932. Figures for 1921 are for 18-month period, July 1, 1920 to Dec. 31, 1921. Figures for *both* 1932 (calendar year) and 1933 (fiscal year) include data for 6-month period, July 1 to Dec. 1, 1932.

[2] Receipts covered into Treasury are credited to the year deposited rather than the year earned. Receipts from the Tongass National Forest are excluded here but are shown in appendix table 5. Receipts from formerly controverted O & C lands not included here, but timber cut and receipts from these lands are shown on appendix table 13.

[3] This value does not correspond to the value of receipts shown in the first column because it contains the value of stumpage exchanged for land and the value of timber taken under free-use permits, neither of which values are treated as receipts.

[4] Cost sales included with commercial sales from 1946 through 1956.   [6] Projections of authors.

[5] Includes materials not measurable in board feet.

Source: Compiled from U.S. Forest Service data.

APPENDIX TABLE 4.   National Forest Lands: *Recreational Use, 1924-56 and projections for 1960 and 1980*

(all figures in thousands)

Year[1]	Total use of recreational resources		Visits to areas improved by public funds	Visits to all other areas[2]	Big game killed by hunters	
	Man days	Visits			Deer	Other
1924	–	4,660	3,460	1,200	–	–
1925	–	5,623	4,217	1,406	–	–
26	–	6,044	4,460	1,584	–	–
27	–	6,136	4,469	1,667	–	–
28	–	6,550	4,783	1,767	–	–
29	–	7,132	4,959	2,173	–	–
1930	–	6,911	5,253	1,658	–	–
31	–	8,074	5,959	2,115	–	–
32	–	7,896	6,227	1,669	–	–
33	–	8,166	6,576	1,590	–	–
34	–	8,581	6,953	1,628	–	–
1935	–	9,719	7,722	1,996	–	–
36	–	10,781	8,233	2,548	–	–
37	–	11,831	8,810	3,021	–	–
38	–	14,496	10,810	3,686	–	–
39	–	14,332	11,466	2,866	–	–
1940	–	16,163	13,062	3,101	190	26
41	–	18,005	10,688	7,317	198	38
42	–	10,407	6,066	4,341	193	35
43	–	6,274	3,412	2,862	158	27
44	–	7,152	3,585	3,567	181	32
1945	–	10,074	5,072	5,002	222	43
46	–	18,241	8,763	9,478	233	42
47	–	21,331	10,506	10,825	238	41
48	–	24,011	12,391	11,620	270	48
49	37,538	26,080	13,277	12,803	302	51
1950	38,932	27,368	13,061	14,307	305	53
51	43,789	29,950	14,857	15,093	354	62
52	45,861	33,007	15,929	17,078	363	45
53	48,750	35,403	17,199	18,204	400	52
54	54,847	40,304	19,747	20,557	426	53
1955	62,103	45,713	22,317	23,396	488	63
56	69,714	52,556	25,053	27,503	–	–
1960[3]		65,000				
1980[3]		360,000				

[1] All years are calendar years except 1933-38, which are on a fiscal year basis.
[2] Unimproved public areas, e.g., wilderness areas, and a few public areas improved by nonfederal means. Does not include persons who drove over highways through forest lands but made no other use of the areas.
[3] Projections of authors; for basis, see text, pp. 71-74.

Source: Compiled from U.S. Forest Service data.

APPENDIX TABLE 5. National Forest Lands: *Summary of Receipts from All Sources on National Forests and Land Utilization Areas, 1905-56 and Projections for 1960 and 1980*

(in thousands of dollars)

Fiscal year	Receipts from all lands	National Forest Lands [1]					Land utilization areas [4]
		Total receipts	Timber receipts	Grazing receipts	Miscellaneous use receipts [2]	All receipts Tongass National Forest [3]	
1905	73	73	73	...	...	...	...
06	758	758	237	513	7	...	...
07	1,530	1,530	654	857	19	...	...
08	1,788	1,788	811	947	30	...	...
09	1,766	1,766	702	1,023	42	...	...
1910	2,041	2,041	1,011	970	60	...	...
11	1,969	1,969	952	928	89	...	...
12	2,109	2,109	1,028	961	120	...	...
13	2,392	2,392	1,271	999	122	...	...
14	2,438	2,438	1,311	1,002	124	...	...
1915	2,481	2,481	1,183	1,130	168	...	...
16	2,824	2,824	1,422	1,210	192	...	...
17	3,457	3,457	1,640	1,550	267	...	...
18	3,575	3,575	1,630	1,726	219	...	...
19	4,358	4,358	1,535	2,609	214	...	...
1920	4,793	4,793	2,045	2,486	263	...	...
21	4,152	4,152	1,770	2,132	250	...	...
22	3,422	3,422	1,813	1,316	292	...	...
23	5,336	5,336	2,722	2,341	272	...	...
24	5,252	5,252	3,036	1,916	300	...	...
1925	5,000	5,000	2,940	1,725	334	...	...
26	5,156	5,156	3,367	1,422	367	...	...
27	5,167	5,167	3,253	1,531	382	...	...
28	5,442	5,442	3,325	1,714	403	...	...
29	6,300	6,300	4,109	1,740	451	...	...
1930	6,752	6,752	4,390	1,943	419	...	...
31	4,993	4,993	2,608	1,961	425	...	...
32	2,294	2,294	1,049	830	415	...	...
33	2,626	2,626	783	1,498	345	...	...
34	3,315	3,315	1,522	1,359	434	...	...
1935	3,289	3,289	1,729	1,151	408	...	...
36	4,063	4,063	2.203	1,441	418	...	...

APPENDIX TABLE 5—continued

Fiscal year	Receipts from all lands	National Forest Lands [1]				All receipts Tongass National Forest [3]	Land utilization areas [4]
		Total receipts	Timber receipts	Grazing receipts	Miscellaneous use receipts [2]		
37	4,936	4,936	2,924	1,580	431	...	...
38	4,671	4,671	2,518	1,696	457	...	...
39	4,908	4,903	2,857	1,574	472	...	5
1940	5,863	5,859	3,943	1,463	453	...	3
41	6,638	6,630	4,737	1,429	464	...	8
42	7,171	7,165	5,094	1,595	475	...	7
43	10,071	10,056	7,610	1,973	473	...	15
44	15,629	15,617	12,623	2,459	535	...	13
1945	16,076	16,048	11,587	2,159	2,302	...	28
46	13,920	13,875	10,554	2,060	1,261	...	45
47	18,397	18,372	15,421	2,294	658	...	24
48	24,388	24,374	20,487	2,898	858	131	14
49	31,320	31,208	26,927	3,276	873	132	111
1950	33,738	33,672	29,379	3,385	830	77	66
51	56,355	56,293	51,099	4,166	883	146	62
52	70,003	69,955	63,723	5,023	975	235	49
53	75,613	74,939	69,252	4,416	1,064	207	673
54	67,787	66,014	61,289	3,107	1,311	307	1,773
1955	79,868	78,250	73,187	2,953	1,524	585	1,618
56	114,511	112,307	107,070	2,906	1,763	568	2,204
1960 [5]	142,800	140,500	135,000	2,500	2,000	1,000	2,300
1980 [5]	309,000	306,500	300,000	2,000	2,500	2,000	2,500

[1] Excludes receipts from the controverted Oregon and California lands which appear with other Oregon and California receipts in appendix table 13.

[2] Largely special permits and receipts from mineral leases on acquired lands collected by the Bureau of Land Management. See appendix table 29.

[3] These receipts are deposited to a separate account which until July 24, 1956 could only be used to settle Indian claims but now may be used in part for roads and trails and for payments to the Territory of Alaska. Tongass Timber Act, August 8, 1947, 61 Stat. 92, and Public Law 758, 84th Congress, July 24, 1956.

[4] Lands purchased under Title III, Farm Tenant Act, for retirement of submarginal land. Includes only those areas administered by the Forest Service in the years shown. The area under Forest Service supervision was enlarged by transfer of such lands to it from the Soil Conservation Service in 1953.

[5] Projections of authors.

Source: U.S. Forest Service.

APPENDIX TABLE 6.   National Forest Lands: *Distribution of Expenditures of Funds Available from Nontax Sources, 1940-56 and Projections for 1960 and 1980* [1]

(in thousands of dollars)

Fiscal year	Total expenditures	Construction and maintenance			Sale area betterment	Brush disposal
		Total	Road maintenance	Other improvements		
1940	500	302	–	–	36	162
41	675	375	–	–	43	257
42	1,266	866	–	–	96	304
43	931	590	–	–	58	283
44	1,127	540	–	–	64	523
1945	1,345	592	–	–	91	662
46	1,478	642	–	–	145	691
47	2,194	811	–	–	371	1,012
48	3,203	1,056	–	–	948	1,199
49	4,060	1,409	–	–	1,423	1,228
1950	4,162	1,274	245	1,029	1,613	1,275
51	3,819	916	498	418	1,863	1,040
52	5,586	953	616	337	2,970	1,663
53	6,477	845	502	343	3,322	2,310
54	8,171	1,130	769	361	4,377	2,664
1955	8,946	1,026	678	348	5,100	2,820
56	9,954	1,178	828	350	5,455	3,321
1960 [2]	13,500					
1980 [2]	18,000					

[1] Financed from deposits required of timber purchasers or improvements made by timber purchasers. These expenditures are included in appendix tables 9 and 10.
[2] Projections of authors.

Source: Compiled from U.S. Forest Service data.

APPENDIX TABLE 7. National Forest Lands: Distribution of Receipts, 1905-56 and Projections for 1960 and 1980

(in thousands of dollars)

Fiscal year	Total receipts	Payments to states, territories and counties [1]					Allotments to Forest Service			General Fund, U.S. Treasury			
		From Forest Reserve Fund receipts			From Tongass National Forest [3]	From Land Utilization area receipts [4]	Total	For roads and trails	For land acquisition [5]	Total	Forest Reserve receipts	Tongass receipts [6]	L.U. areas
		Total payments	25 per cent fund [2]	Arizona & New Mexico school fund									
1905-09	5,915	1,117	1,117	...	...	...	...	...	...	4,798	4,798	...	...
1910	2,041	511	510	1	...	...	...	...	...	1,530	1,530	...	...
11	1,969	515	485	30	...	...	...	...	...	1,454	1,454	...	...
12	2,109	554	518	36	...	...	207	207	...	1,348	1,348	...	...
13	2,392	633	587	46	...	...	235	235	...	1,524	1,524	...	...
14	2,438	640	599	41	...	...	240	240	...	1,558	1,558	...	...
1915	2,481	649	611	38	...	...	244	244	...	1,588	1,588	...	...
16	2,824	737	696	41	...	...	278	278	...	1,809	1,809	...	...
17	3,457	911	849	62	...	...	340	340	...	2,206	2,206	...	...
18	3,575	946	876	70	...	...	351	351	...	2,278	2,278	...	...
19	4,358	1,149	1,070	79	...	...	428	428	...	2,781	2,781	...	...
1920	4,793	1,253	1,180	73	...	...	472	472	...	3,068	3,068	...	...
21	4,152	1,083	1,023	60	...	...	409	409	...	2,660	2,660	...	...
22	3,422	882	846	36	...	...	339	339	...	2,201	2,201	...	...
23	5,336	1,371	1,321	50	...	...	529	529	...	3,436	3,436	...	...
24	5,252	1,347	1,302	45	...	...	521	521	...	3,384	3,384	...	...
1925	5,000	1,271	1,243	28	...	...	497	497	...	3,232	3,232	...	...
26	5,156	1,299	1,286	14	...	...	514	514	...	3,343	3,343	...	...
27	5,167	1,311	1,285	26	...	...	514	514	...	3,342	3,342	...	...
28	5,442	1,387	1,351	36	...	...	541	541	...	3,514	3,514	...	...
29	6,300	1,606	1,565	41	...	...	626	626	...	4,068	4,068	...	...
1930	6,752	1,719	1,678	41	...	...	671	671	...	4,362	4,362	...	...
31	4,993	1,272	1,241	31	...	...	496	496	...	3,225	3,225	...	...
32	2,294	589	568	21	...	...	227	227	...	1,478	1,478	...	...
33	2,626	679	651	28	...	...	260	260	...	1,687	1,687	...	...

Year											
36	4,065	1,028	970	32	...	461	378	65	2,574	2,574	...	...
37	4,936	1,243	1,215	28	...	545	486	59	3,148	3,148	...	...
38	4,671	1,167	1,136	31	...	526	454	72	2,978	2,978	...	...
39	4,908	1,217	1,192	24	1	587	477	110	3,100	3,104	...	4
1940	5,863	1,457	1,433	23	1	678	573	105	3,726	3,728	...	2
41	6,638	1,558	1,533	23	2	1,088	613	475	3,986	3,992	...	6
42	7,171	1,695	1,670	23	2	1,130	668	462	4,341	4,346	...	5
43	10,071	2,507	2,476	27	4	1,117	990	127	6,436	6,447	...	11
44	15,629	4,180	4,139	38	3	679	1,655	—976	10,760	10,770	...	10
1945	16,076	4,046	4,003	36	7	1,601	1,601	138	10,408	10,429	...	21
46	13,920	3,474	3,424	39	11	1,508	1,508	137	8,904	8,938	...	34
47	18,397	4,602	4,547	49	6	1,956	1,879	138	11,821	11,839	98	18
48	24,388	6,106	6,012	57	4	2,543	2,405	1	15,631	15,739	98	10
49	31,320	7,919	7,797	61	28	3,102	3,101	...	20,299	20,117	99	83
1950	33,738	8,515	8,407	72	17	3,404	3,346	58	21,712	21,819	58	49
51	56,355	14,178	14,019	107	15	5,729	5,590	139	36,293	36,448	109	46
52	70,003	17,607	17,404	132	12	7,085	6,945	140	45,098	45,311	176	37
53	75,613	17,085	18,742	123	168	7,290	7,480	—190	48,578	49,238	155	505
54	67,787	17,063	16,440	103	443	6,569	6,559	10	42,595	44,155	230	1,330
1955	79,868	20,124	19,459	114	405	7,650	7,766	—116	50,442	52,094	439	1,213
56	114,511	28,761	27,939	129	551	11,169	11,159	10	72,502	74,581	426	1,653
1960 ⁷	142,800	35,700				14,280			92,800	92,800		
1980 ⁷	309,000	77,250				30,900			200,850	200,850		

¹ Does not include payments to counties from receipts of the sales from the formerly controverted O & C lands. An estimate of what these payments would have been if paid (prior to 1955) in the year in which receipts were collected follows:

Thousands of dollars

1942 4	1945 169	1948 469	1951 950	1954 904
1943 18	1946 186	1949 621	1952 1,086	1955 945
1944 188	1947 245	1950 610	1953 322	1956 1,864

² Includes payments to three Minnesota counties based upon the assessed valuation of wilderness area of the Superior National Forest.

³ Payments to Alaska not authorized until 1956, at which time payments out of prior year receipts were authorized. Here they are shown as if they were paid during the year they were received.

⁴ Payments are estimated on the basis of 25 per cent of receipts of the current fiscal year rather than the legal formula of 25 per cent of receipts of the preceding calendar year.

⁵ Negative entries indicate that funds previously withheld for acquisition of land have been distributed in payments to states, territories, and counties, for roads and trails, and to the U.S. Treasury.

⁶ Not paid into the general fund but held in a special escrow account.

⁷ Projections of authors; based on present law and projected revenues.

Source: U.S. Forest Service.

APPENDIX TABLE 8. National Forest Lands: *Total Reported Investments by Type of Investment, End of Fiscal Year, 1941-56* [1]

(in millions of dollars)

Fiscal year	Total	Tree planting	Timber stand improvement [2]	Range [3]	Acquisition of land	Buildings [4]	Telephone and radio	Fire control improvements	Recreation use improvements	Roads and trails [5]	Equipment	Other
					Reported investment at end of fiscal year							
1941	444.4	19.5		13.1	85.7	30.8	13.7	10.2	25.9	207.0	27.6	10.9
42	454.9	20.7		13.7	87.4	32.1	14.1	10.3	27.5	210.6	27.8	10.7
43	451.4	20.8		13.9	88.3	32.2	14.0	10.4	27.5	212.4	21.5	10.4
44	451.3	20.2		14.3	88.5	32.0	13.9	10.4	27.2	213.4	21.6	9.8
1945	450.5	20.3		14.5	88.5	32.1	13.9	10.4	27.2	214.1	20.5	9.0
46	454.3	20.7		14.8	88.5	32.3	13.8	10.4	27.4	216.5	21.5	8.4
47	466.9	21.4		15.5	90.2	32.4	13.7	10.4	27.6	223.4	24.0	8.3
48	473.5	22.6		16.2	91.4	32.8	13.4	10.2	27.6	225.1	26.4	7.8
49	488.0	23.9		17.4	92.0	33.3	13.0	10.1	27.5	234.0	28.6	8.2
1950	495.5	25.0		18.7	92.8	33.7	12.8	10.2	27.6	236.5	29.7	8.5
51	522.9	26.2	1.5	19.5	93.2	34.1	12.4	10.2	28.6	255.8	31.1	10.1
52	541.6	27.3	3.7	20.4	93.7	34.5	12.9	10.0	28.7	270.3	31.0	9.2
53	589.0	28.5	5.9	21.6	93.7	35.2	14.2	9.9	28.5	307.5	30.5	13.4
54	658.5	29.9	9.0	22.7	93.8	35.7	13.7	9.6	28.4	363.2	33.4	19.0
1955	700.0	31.2	12.7	23.1	93.6	36.8	13.1	9.6	28.3	404.9	33.8	12.8
56	750.3	32.8	16.5	24.0	93.8	37.5	12.4	8.1	28.7	446.3	35.5	14.4

[1] Includes land utilization project areas which were minor in area until fiscal 1953. Includes also formerly controverted O & C lands.

[2] Activity treated as an operating expenditure rather than an investment prior to 1951.

[3] Includes revegetation from 1946 to date together with other range improvement activities.

[4] Includes dwellings and related improvements, warehouses, offices, shops, etc.

[5] Value of Tongass National Forest Highway, for which $7,000,000 was appropriated over the 2-year period 1951-52, has not been included. Includes value of roads built annually as part of timber sales as follows: 1951—$13,835,000; 1952—$6,554,000; 1953—$25,937,000; 1954—$37,894,000; 1955—$16,296,000; 1956—$20,889,000. Excludes general use forest highways which are part of the regular federal highway system.

Source: Compiled from U.S. Forest Service data.

APPENDIX TABLE 9. National Forest Lands: *Operating Expenditures, 1942-56 and Projections for 1960 and 1980* [1]

(in thousands of dollars)

Fiscal year	Total expenditures for national forest administration [2]	Subtotal	Operating expenditures							
			Unit management	Timber use	Insect, disease, and rodent control	Fire prevention and pre-suppression	Fire suppression	Maintenance of improvements	Maintenance of roads and trails	Miscellaneous
1942	33,848	22,878	4,453	1,794	855	4,598	1,541	1,219	2,815	5,604
43	27,509	24,466	5,206	2,076	976	6,829	1,448	1,230	3,790	2,912
44	29,572	26,881	6,041	2,173	1,016	6,849	1,336	1,431	4,991	3,045
1945	30,351	28,592	6,200	2,781	1,362	6,794	1,842	1,505	4,941	3,168
46	37,492	32,697	6,291	2,871	1,466	7,215	3,540	1,706	6,002	3,606
47	65,618	39,992	7,000	3,825	2,887	8,012	3,310	2,922	7,649	4,386
48	51,485	40,385	6,829	4,390	2,743	8,401	4,541	2,816	6,727	3,987
49	54,067	44,451	7,244	5,170	2,533	9,351	2,677	3,208	9,692	4,575
1950	58,480	48,693	7,386	5,477	3,495	9,491	6,579	3,196	9,545	3,523
51	62,068	46,952	7,354	4,531	4,891	9,127	5,888	2,973	8,730	3,458
52	68,734	49,195	7,776	5,429	3,418	9,782	7,994	3,009	8,739	3,050
53	67,639	49,176	7,975	7,289	3,734	10,155	4,692	3,492	8,657	3,184
54	85,608	53,982	7,916	8,109	3,189	9,906	9,285	3,444	8,285	3,849
1955	82,750	53,251	8,013	8,906	5,502	10,295	4,877	3,356	8,034	4,269
56	97,621	65,452	8,675	10,932	4,293	12,634	10,686	4,085	9,121	5,027
1960 [3]	129,900	76,900	9,500	14,900	7,000	25,000		4,500	10,000	6,000
1980 [3]	202,500	126,500	12,000	27,000	12,000	40,000		5,500	20,000	10,000

[1] Includes land utilization project lands which were minor in area until fiscal 1953. Includes expenditures out of 10 per cent of receipts for roads and trails, contributions made by timber users and others when funds benefit national forest lands (see appendix table 6), and regular appropriations. Includes expenditures on the formerly controverted O & C lands.

[2] Includes total investment expenditures shown in appendix table 10.

[3] Projections of authors; assuming average fire years.

Source: Compiled from U.S. Forest Service data.

APPENDIX TABLE 10. National Forest Lands: Investment Expenditures, 1942-56 and Projections for 1960 and 1980 [1]

(in thousands of dollars)

Fiscal year	Total	Tree planting	Timber stand improvement [2]	Range revegetation	Buildings [3]	Recreational use improvements	Range use improvements	Roads, trails, and bridges [4]	Miscellaneous [5]
				Investment expenditures					
1942	10,971	2,642			858	751	418	3,075	3,227
43	3,043	83			124	30	219	1,972	615
44	2,691	52			87	12	283	1,931	326
1945	1,758	55			96	4	305	952	345
46	4,795	262			97	22	339	3,750	326
47	25,626	639			282	127	685	20,695	3,199
48	11,100	1,097		548	314	66	277	7,285	1,513
49	9,616	1,138		775	584	111	466	5,083	1,458
1950	9,787	1,031	1,654	712	504	130	602	5,447	1,362
51	15,116	1,108	2,141	687	600	65	280	9,715	1,007
52	19,539	1,367	2,372	689	405	132	273	13,589	943
53	18,463	1,235	3,181	665	743	56	378	11,456	1,555
54	31,626	1,308		583	559	150	335	23,732	1,777
1955	29,499	1,522	3,794	506	753	144	174	21,219	1,388
56	32,169	1,708	3,998	726	1,051	424	336	21,934	1,992
1960 [6]	53,000							40,000	
1980 [6]	76,000							60,000	

receipts for roads and trails, contributions made by timber users and others when funds benefit national forest lands (see appendix table 6), and regular appropriations. Includes expenditures on formerly controverted O & C lands.

² Included as an operating expense under timber use prior to 1951.

³ Includes dwellings as well as warehouses and similar structures.

⁴ Includes appropriations of $2,000,000 and $10,900,000 for access roads from National Housing Agency in 1946 and 1947, and $3,500,000 each year for the Tongass Forest Highway in Alaska in 1951 and 1952. Not included are general use forest highways, part of the regular federal highway system within national forest boundaries. A total of $163,037,000 was appropriated for these purposes for fiscal years 1942 through 1955.

⁵ Includes large expenditures for acquisition of lands for two years: 1942—$1,581,000; 1947—$2,124,000.

⁶ Projections of authors.

Source: Compiled from U.S. Forest Service data.

APPENDIX TABLE 11. National Forest Lands: *Value of Services or Contributions by Local Governments for Maintenance and Improvement of Recreational Facilities for Two Recent Years*

(in thousands of dollars)

Fiscal year	Total	Clean-up	Maintenance	General supervision of areas	Construction of improvements	Road construction	Snow clearance	Purchase of land	Other
1950	976	55	110	58	241	205	157	112	38
1954	1,240	142	227	125	271	177	207	55	36

Source: Hearings, U.S. Congress, House Appropriations Subcommittee on Department of the Interior and Related Agencies, 84th Congress, 1st Session, 1955, p. 692.

APPENDIX TABLE 12. Public Domain Lands: *Grazing Receipts, Use of Range, and Level of Fees, 1935-56*[1]

Fiscal year	Total receipts	Receipts covered into U.S. Treasury (1,000 dollars)			Amount of grazing in districts[2] (1,000 AUM)[3]			Monthly grazing and range improvement fees in district (cents per head)		
		Grazing districts	Pierce Act	Land outside districts	Cattle and horses	Sheep and goats	Total	Cattle	Sheep and goats	
1935	1	1	...	...			6,507	5	1.0
36	48	48	...	...			11,106	5	1.0
37	488	415	...	73			14,383	5	1.0
38	850	800	...	49			13,376	5	1.0
39	1,038	886	...	152			13,789	5	1.0
1940	747	595	...	152			13,832	5	1.0
41	1,113	922	...	191			15,369	5	1.0
42	1,095	900	...	195			15,271	5	1.0
43	979	785	...	194			15,061	5	1.0
44	1,015	813	...	202			15,745	5	1.0
1945	996	765	...	231			15,572	5	1.0
46	964	736	...	228			15,254	5	1.0
47	1,046	819	6	221	9,195	5,798	14,993	8	1.6
48	1,415	1,165	6	244	9,078	5,648	14,726	8	1.6
49	1,239	1,060	6	173	9,117	5,405	14,522	8	1.6
1950	1,534	1,146	5	383	9,205	5,256	14,461	8	1.6
51	1,694	1,382	6	306	9,211	5,120	14,331	12	2.4
52	1,985	1,658	5	322	10,157	5,246	15,403	12	2.4
53	2,095	1,764	3	328	10,483	5,297	15,780	12	2.4
54	2,039	1,678	2	359	10,371	5,315	15,686	12	2.4
1955	2,219	1,879	1	339	10,186	5,181	15,367	[4]15	[4]3.0
56	2,386	2,050	1	335	10,223	5,078	15,301	15	3.0

[1] Excludes grazing on reclamation land, land utilization projects where not part of a grazing district, O & C lands, and Alaskan grazing, but includes lands rented and sublet under the Pierce Act (43 USC 315m). See appendix table 27 for all receipts from grazing.

[2] Includes free use, crossing, and trailing permits in addition to regular paid use.

[3] One animal-unit month represents the forage required to maintain 5 sheep or goats or 1 horse or cow for a month.

[4] Effective January 1955.

Source: Compiled from reports of the former Grazing Service and General Land Office and of the Bureau of Land Management.

APPENDIX TABLE 13. Oregon and California and Coos Bay Revested Lands: *Cash Receipts from All Sources and Volume and Value of Timber Cut and Sold, 1916-56 and Projections for 1960 and 1980*

(in thousands of dollars and millions of board feet)

Fiscal year	Receipts covered into U.S. Treasury[1]			Volume and value of resources sold or leased on noncontroverted lands by the Bureau of Land Management					Timber cut on controverted lands under sales by Forest Service		Total cut on all lands under the administration of the Bureau of Land Management and the Forest Service	
	Total all sources	By Bureau of Land Management from noncontroverted lands	By Forest Service from controverted lands[2]	Timber sold[3] Volume	Timber sold Value	Timber cut[4] Volume	Timber cut Value	Sale & lease of other resources[5]	Volume	Value	Volume	Value
1916-1935	-	-	…	2,809	6,623	-	-	-	…	…	-	-
36	318	318	…	188	306	-	-	16	…	…	-	-
37	785	785	…	431	743	-	-	55	…	…	-	-
38	615	615	…	294	569	-	-	27	…	…	-	-
39	421	421	…	345	662	-	-	12	…	…	-	-
1940	850	850	…	595	1,196	-	-	8	…	…	-	-
41	1,158	1,158	…	494	1,106	-	-	3	…	…	-	-
42	1,174	1,168	6	486	1,364	456	-	3	-	-	456	-
43	1,541	1,517	24	394	1,498	415	1,221	6	-	-	415	1,221
44	2,045	1,795	250	368	1,274	414	1,329	8	26	-	440	-
1945	1,990	1,764	226	435	1,837	433	1,470	10	46	-	476	-
46	1,689	1,441	248	345	1,501	336	1,262	12	42	111	378	1,373
47	3,363	3,039	324	449	3,085	469	2,197	21	54	338	523	2,535
48	5,292	4,667	625	400	4,176	596	3,647	14	76	287	672	3,934
49	4,417	3,588	829	264	2,919	414	3,992	16	40	410	454	4,402
1950	4,818	4,005	813	395	4,810	308	3,055	18	112	1,234	420	4,289
51	7,984	6,717	1,267	416	9,002	435	5,683	17	76	1,059	511	6,742
52	9,889	8,440	1,449	419	10,503	363	8,001	19	62	1,156	425	9,157

APPENDIX TABLE 13—continued

Fiscal year	Receipts covered into U.S. Treasury[1]			Volume and value of resources sold or leased on noncontroverted lands by the Bureau of Land Management					Timber cut on controverted lands under sales by Forest Service		Total cut on all lands under the administration of the Bureau of Land Management and the Forest Service	
	Total all sources	By Bureau of Land Management from noncontroverted lands	By Forest Service from controverted lands[2]	Timber sold[3]		Timber cut[4]		Sale & lease of other resources[5]				
				Volume	Value	Volume	Value		Volume	Value	Volume	Value
53	13,420	12,991	429	552	12,579	494	11,301	25	75	1,312	569	12,613
54	13,521	12,315	1,206	615	11,519	493	10,549	23	61	852	554	11,401
1955	15,608	14,337	1,271	645	18,337	665	14,730	20	90	1,540	755	16,270
56	23,088	20,602	2,486	665	25,024	612	18,251	18	108	2,346	720	20,597
1960[6]	34,000	28,000	6,000	700	28,000				150	6,000	850	34,000
1980[6]	52,700	43,700	9,000	950	43,700				200	9,000	1,150	52,700

[1] Receipts are credited to the year in which they were deposited in the Treasury rather than for the year in which they were earned. While primarily from the sale of timber, they also include receipts from the sale or lease of other resources.

[2] The administration of these lands was the subject of controversy between the Forest Service and the Bureau of Land Management. A solution was arrived at when the 83d Congress declared the lands "to be revested Oregon and California railroad grant lands; and said lands shall continue to be administered as national-forest lands . . . subject to all laws, rules, and regulations applicable to the national forests." Public Law 426, June 24, 1954, 43 USC 1181g. The receipts had accumulated in a suspense fund until passage of the act in 1954.

[3] Timber sales are reported for the year in which the sale was made although actual cutting may not be completed within the same year. Small sales of forest products and timber cut in trespass are not included.

[4] Includes small sales and timber cut in trespass but does not include timber cut under free-use permits.

[5] Includes receipts from grazing, miscellaneous leases of land, and the sale of land and materials.

[6] Projections of authors.

Source: Compiled from the Reports of the Director of the Bureau of Land Management, Statistical Appendices; and U.S. Forest Service data.

APPENDIX TABLE 14.   Public Domain Lands: *Cash Receipts from Sale of Timber and Other Materials, and Quantity and Value of Timber Sold, 1946-56 and Projections for 1960 and 1980*[1]

(All values and receipts in thousands of dollars and all quantities in millions of board feet)

Fiscal year	Cash receipts covered into U.S. Treasury	Timber sales			Miscellaneous receipts [2]
		Number	Volume	Value	
1946	6	139	22	47	...
47	6	200	52	78	...
48	50	204	32	166	...
49	332	265	61	585	12
1950	365	493	51	396	23
51	1,061	631	84	1,348	6
52	1,124	647	94	1,183	45
53	831	808	91	1,100	69
54	1,115	814	77	1,055	87
1955	1,654	843	110	1,489	108
56	1,843	882	223	2,331	79
1960 [3]	7,100		275	7,100	
1980 [3]	10,500		300	10,500	

[1] Sales of timber outside of Alaska were limited to the sale of dead and down trees until World War II, and receipts until 1949 were shown as part of the receipts from the sale of public land. This explains the large difference between sales and cash receipts in this table prior to 1949 where the cash receipts are largely those of sales made in Alaska.

[2] Sale of soil, sand, gravel, and similar materials.

[3] Projections of authors.

Source: Reports of the Director of the Bureau of Land Management, Statistical Appendices.

APPENDIX TABLE 15. Public Domain Lands: Oil and Gas Leasing Receipts, Number and Acreage of Leases and Volume of Production, 1921-56 and Projections for 1960 and 1980[1]

Fiscal year	Receipts covered into U.S. Treasury (1,000 dollars)			Leases in effect June 30 (1,000)			Acreage under lease June 30 (1,000)			Volume of output			
	Total	Estimated rentals & bonuses[2]	Royalties	Total	Producing	Nonproducing	Total	Producing	Nonproducing	Petroleum (million barrels)	Natural gas (billion cu. ft.)	Natural gasoline & butane (million gallons)	Total crude oil equivalent[3] (million barrels)
1920-30	–	–	59,400	–	–	–	–	–	–	260	198	390	302.3
1931-40	–	–	43,700	–	–	–	–	–	–	328	698	759	462.4
1941	5,280	419	4,861	5.3	0.7	4.6	5,482	256	5,226	43	82	52	57.9
42	6,345	662	5,683	4.3	0.7	3.6	3,292	264	3,028	45	88	71	61.4
43	6,615	549	6,066	4.5	0.8	3.7	2,810	225	2,585	50	87	90	66.6
44	10,298	3,373	6,925	5.3	0.9	4.4	3,106	249	2,857	54	80	78	69.2
1945	9,366	1,980	7,386	7.0	1.2	5.8	4,586	367	4,219	56	96	250	78.0
46	9,323	1,040	8,283	8.8	1.5	7.3	6,034	483	5,551	60	96	121	78.9
47	14,509	2,185	12,324	12.5	1.8	10.7	8,071	646	7,425	64	98	126	83.3
48	24,067	2,891	21,176	13.4	1.9	11.5	10,703	857	9,846	74	124	152	98.3
49	28,444	4,926	23,518	21.3	1.9	19.4	19,012	875	18,137	76	124	158	100.5
1950	26,682	4,257	22,425	28.9	2.0	26.9	23,554	893	22,661	76	126	145	100.5
51	34,343	7,940	26,403	42.5	2.2	40.3	32,889	1,060	31,829	82	123	141	105.9
52	46,750	19,204	27,546	63.2	2.4	60.8	48,554	1,227	47,327	92	152	179	121.6
53	43,766	12,810	30,956	78.8	2.8	76.0	59,928	1,631	58,297	94	173	184	127.2
54	53,596	15,457	38,139	87.7	3.0	84.7	66,025	2,062	63,963	105	223	197	146.9
1955	59,955	19,622	40,333	96.4	3.3	93.1	73,287	2,043	71,244	111	261	211	159.5
56	62,782	20,282	42,500[4]	100.4	3.6	96.8	73,097	2,171	70,926	118	272	203	168.3
1960[5]	98,000	30,000	68,000				90,000	2,880					272.0
1980[5]	252,500	50,000	202,500				150,000	6,000					810.0

[1] Excludes military and naval reserves and the outer continental shelf submerged lands.

[2] Estimated by deducting reported royalties from total receipts.

[3] Includes gasoline and butane on an equal basis with petroleum (42 gallons per barrel), and 6000 cubic feet of natural gas equal to one barrel of petroleum.

[4] Estimated on the basis of the relation of 1955 royalties to production in terms of total crude oil equivalent.

[5] Projections of authors; see discussion in text, pp. 99-101, for basis.

Source: Compiled from Reports of the Director of the Bureau of Land Management, Statistical Appendices; and reports and records of Geological Survey.

APPENDIX TABLE 16. Public Domain Lands: *Oil and Gas Well Activity,*
1941-55 and Projections for 1960 and 1980 [1]

		Wells as of December 31			
Year [2]	Total	Active producer, oil and gas	Shut in producing oil and gas	Drilling, active & suspended	Abandoned
1941	9,657	4,258	929	277	4,193
42	10,058	4,521	923	255	4,359
43	10,852	4,824	914	279	4,836
44	11,355	5,084	983	260	5,028
1945	12,036	5,407	1,134	231	5,264
46	12,381	5,772	1,047	252	5,310
47	13,118	6,099	1,121	312	5,586
48	14,160	6,866	1,068	309	5,917
49	14,650	6,924	980	550	6,196
1950	15,629	7,743	1,070	304	6,512
51	16,970	8,294	1,186	431	7,059
52	18,193	8,964	952	558	7,719
53	19,550	10,045	935	471	8,099
54	21,404	11,027	1,126	442	8,809
1955	23,020	11,740	1,389	512	9,379
1960 [3]		20,160			
1980 [3]		60,000			

[1] Includes activity on the outer continental shelf from 1954 to date.

[2] Calendar year.

[3] Projections of authors; for basis, see discussion in text, pp. 105-6.

Source: Compiled from Geological Survey data.

APPENDIX TABLE 17. Public Domain Lands: Relationship of Producing Oil and Gas Leases to All Such Leases and to Volume of Output, 1941-56 and Projections for 1960 and 1980 [1]

Fiscal year	Percentage of all leases producing	Percentage of all leased acreage producing	Acres per lease		Output of crude oil equivalent [2] (barrels)		Active wells		Production per active well (1,000 barrels)
			All leases	Producing leases	Per producing lease	Per producing acre	Per producing lease	Per 1,000 acres of producing leases	
1941	14	4.7	1031	351	79,000	226	5.8	16.6	13.6
42	17	8.0	761	358	83,000	232	6.1	17.2	13.6
43	17	8.0	628	296	88,000	296	6.3	21.5	13.8
44	17	8.0	584	275	76,000	278	5.6	20.5	13.6
1945	17	8.0	654	307	65,000	213	4.5	14.7	14.4
46	17	8.0	690	325	53,000	164	3.9	12.0	13.7
47	14	8.0	645	365	47,000	129	3.4	9.4	13.7
48	14	8.0	793	453	52,000	115	3.6	8.0	14.3
49	9	4.6	893	454	52,000	115	3.6	7.9	14.5
1950	7	3.8	815	453	51,000	113	3.9	8.7	13.0
51	5	3.2	773	487	49,000	100	3.8	7.8	12.8
52	4	2.5	769	514	51,000	99	3.7	7.3	13.5
53	4	2.7	760	573	45,000	82	3.5	6.2	12.6
54	3	3.1	753	683	49,000	71	3.6	5.3	13.4
1955	3	2.8	761	614	48,000	78	3.5	5.7	13.8
56	4	3.0	727	601	46,000	77			
1960 [3]		3.2						7.0	13.5
1980 [3]		4.0						10.0	13.5

[1] Calculated from original unrounded data, rather than from data in appendix tables 15 and 16.
[2] Calculated by dividing production during year by number and acreage of producing leases at end of year.
[3] Projections of authors; see discussion in text, pp. 99-101, for basis.

APPENDIX TABLE 18. Public Domain Lands: *Receipts and Production from Miscellaneous Minerals, 1943-56 and Projections for 1960 and 1980*

(in thousands of dollars and thousands of short tons)

Fiscal year	Total rents and royalties	Coal		Sodium salts		Potassium salts		Phosphate rock		Other minerals
		Rents and royalties	Production	Rents and royalties	Production	Rents and royalties	Production	Rents and royalties	Production	Rents and royalties
1943	1,175	–	7,000	–	134	–	3,000	–	107	...
44	1,494	846	9,061	1	158	637	3,493	8	44	...
1945	1,653	905	10,117	1	244	734	3,776	13	81	1
46	1,796	930	9,282	1	276	846	3,920	16	101	3
47	1,756	828	8,661	1	373	910	4,122	19	124	1
48	2,042	850	7,978	2	464	1,163	4,594	26	150	...
49	2,082	806	8,025	1	542	1,245	4,950	31	268	*
1950	2,052	787	7,072	1	457	1,202	4,598	61	275	1
51	3,323	1,122	8,946	4	663	2,122	5,394	71	69	3
52	2,913	992	8,106	10	613	1,797	5,402	110	257	4
53	3,537	929	7,017	13	613	2,459	7,857	183	509	4
54	3,850	1,007	7,185	26	663	2,613	7,481	201	545	3
1955	4,529	894	5,589	476	742	2,967	7,876	189	570	3
56	4,330	785	5,703	122	856	3,081	9,416	338	1,070	4
1960 [1]	5,000									
1980 [1]	7,000									

[1] Projections of authors.

Source: Compiled from Geological Survey data.

APPENDIX TABLE 19. Acquired Lands: Oil and Gas Leasing Receipts, Number and Acreage of Leases, and Volume of Production, 1947-56 and Projections for 1960 and 1980

Fiscal year	Receipts covered into U.S. Treasury (1,000 dollars)			Leases in effect June 30		Volume of output		
	Total	Rentals and bonuses[1]	Royalties[1]	Number (1,000)	Area (1,000 acres)	Petroleum (million bbl.)	Natural gas (billion cu. ft.)	Gasoline and butane (million gal.)
1947	–	–	–	0.2	233	–	–	–
48	368	183	185	0.2	218	0.7	0.4	2.0
49	395	205	190	0.4	456	0.7	0.3	2.1
1950	354	54	300	0.5	549	0.8	0.2	1.6
51	711	11	700	0.6	628	1.7	0.5	1.1
52	1,348	121	1,227	1.2	1,116	3.3	4.7	0.8
53	1,816	401	1,415	2.0	1,881	4.2	3.4	4.1
54	2,297	299	1,998	2.9	2,759	4.1	3.3	0.1
1955	2,172	904	1,268	3.2	3,008	2.9	7.4	0.1
56	2,611	611	2,000	4.2	3,853	6.5	13.5	0.2
1960[2]	4,000							
1980[2]	6,000							

[1] Estimated.
[2] Projections of authors.

Source: Compiled from Geological Survey data.

APPENDIX TABLE 20. Acquired Lands: *Miscellaneous Mineral Production and Receipts from Rents and Royalties, 1948-56* [1]

(all receipts in thousands of dollars and all production in thousands of short tons)

Fiscal year	Rents and royalties	Production									
		Coal	Sand & gravel	Quartzite	Feldspar	Fluorspar	Phosphate rock	Asbestos	Bentonite clay	Manganese	Rock and stone
1948	63	29	...	109	*	22	...	*	...	...	*
49	38	8	...	132	*	17	...	*	...	...	*
1950	28	67	5	79	1	9	...	...	...	...	*
51	77	73	6	131	2	11	*	...	14	...	1
52	55	62	33	136	7	11	4	*	...	...	1
53	57	9	25	105	...	10	3	1	*	*	1
54	118	86	8	132	16	16	5	*	1	5	1
1955	134	92	98	56	21	10	4	1	1	7	*
56	167	25	*	147	31	13	4	*	18	3	10

[1] Small quantities of zinc and mica also produced in different years.

Source: Compiled from Geological Survey data.

APPENDIX TABLE 21.   Outer Continental Shelf Lands: *Oil and Gas Leasing Receipts, Number and Acreage of Leases, and Volume of Production, 1954-56 and Projections for 1960 and 1980*

Item	Unit	Historical record, fiscal year			Projections [1]	
		1954 [2][3]	1955 [3]	1956 [3]	1960	1980
Cash receipts covered into U.S. Treasury:						
Royalties	$1,000	2,148	3,353	6,468	75,000	188,000
Rentals	1,000	2,823	3,784	4,759	5,000	7,000
Bonuses	1,000	...	139,736	108,529	15,000	15,000
Total	1,000	4,971	146,873	119,756	95,000	210,000
Leases in effect June 30:						
Section 6 ("state") leases						
Producing	number	−	79	130		
Nonproducing	number	−	299	237		
Total	number	401	378	367		
Section 8 ("federal") leases						
Producing	number	...	...	8		
Nonproducing	number	...	109	222		
Total	number	...	109	230		
All leases						
Producing	number	−	79	138		
Nonproducing	number	−	408	459		
Total	number	401	487	597		
Acreage under lease June 30:						
Section 6 ("state") leases						
Producing	1,000 acres	−	312	523		
Nonproducing	1,000 acres	−	785	927		
Total	1,000 acres	−	1,097	1,450		
Section 8 ("federal") leases						
Producing	1,000 acres	...	...	36		
Nonproducing	1,000 acres	...	462	829		
Total	1,000 acres	...	462	865		
All leases						
Producing	1,000 acres	−	312	559	3,000	5,000
Nonproducing	1,000 acres	−	1,247	1,756	2,000	3,000
Total	1,000 acres	−	1,559	2,315	5,000	8,000
Volume of output:						
Petroleum	million bbl.	2.5	3.5	7.9		
Natural gas	billion cu. ft.	50.8	58.3	88.4		
Gasoline and butane ..	million gal.	...	...	...		
Total petroleum equivalent [4]	million bbl.	11.0	13.2	22.6	300	750

[1] Projections of authors.

[2] Act (43 U.S.C. 1334) became effective August 7, 1953.

[3] Receipts as shown here include sums received on Section 6 leases; title to these lands has been claimed by Louisiana and Texas, and is the subject of suit. Receipts from these leases have been placed in escrow. They amount to $4,971,000 in fiscal 1954, $4,469,000 in fiscal 1955, and $8,532,000 in fiscal 1956. Appendix tables 27, 28, 29, 51, 54, and 55 exclude these receipts in escrow.

[4] See footnote 3, appendix table 15.

Source: Compiled from Geological Survey data.

APPENDIX TABLE 22. Outer Continental Shelf Lands: *Receipts from Sulfur Lease Royalties and Rentals, 1954-56*

(in thousands of dollars)

Fiscal year	Total	Royalty	Rental	Bonus
1954	...	...	...	...
1955	1,283	...	50	1,233
1956	50	...	50	...

Source: Compiled from Geological Survey data.

APPENDIX TABLE 23. Public Domain Lands: *Area of Land on which Original and Final Entries Were Made, 1908-56*

(in thousands of acres)

Fiscal year	Original entries [1]	Final entry [1]
1908	19,090	–
09	19,893	–
1910	26,391	–
11	19,211	–
12	14,575	–
13	15,867	–
14	16,523	–
1915	16,861	–
16	18,708	–
17	16,202	–
18	10,147	–
19	11,871	–
1920	16,437	9,778
21	15,632	8,772
22	10,367	8,074
23	6,415	6,201
24	4,564	5,229
1925	3,641	4,489
26	3,243	3,962
27	3,595	3,011
28	3,726	2,168
29	4,613	2,030
1930	5,435	1,577
31	5,219	1,537
32	4,552	1,333
33	3,118	980
34	3,585	1,225

APPENDIX TABLE 23—continued

Fiscal year	Original entries [1]	Final entry [1]
1935	1,759	1,772
36	426	1,938
37	125	2,026
38	131	1,478
39	302	1,198
1940	54	756
41	76	491
42	135	252
43	63	168
44	91	85
1945	40	60
46	27	62
47	76	53
48	117	57
49	134	117
1950	142	149
51	121	199
52	113	165
53	310	176
54	306	239
1955	251	250
56	151	267

[1] These are not total disposals of all federal land, but include only those types, such as homestead and desert land entries, where the applicant must carry out certain settlement, irrigation, or other improvement in order to get title to land. Prior to 1934 they are nearly the total of disposals; for more recent years, see appendix table 24.

Source: Compiled from the Reports of the Director of the Bureau of Land Management, Statistical Appendix.

APPENDIX TABLE 24. Public Domain Lands: *Disposal and Land Exchange Activities, 1941-56*

Item	Unit	1941	1942	1943	1944	1945	1946	1947	1948	1949	1950	1951	1952	1953	1954	1955	1956
Original entries allowed:[1]																	
Homestead	Number	425	285	213	158	185	144	475	689	684	571	415	460	483	474	482	455
Desert land	Number	17	18	11	30	13	4	26	56	78	146	224	165	256	731	486	315
Other	Number	180	272	167	208	76	74	102	111	122	93	60	110	188	162	85	106
Total	Number	622	575	391	396	274	222	603	856	884	810	699	735	927	1,367	1,053	876
Final entries approved:[1][2]																	
Homestead	Number	1,473	821	499	318	249	254	243	168	335	418	660	357	353	370	340	330
Desert land	Number	49	52	39	22	22	10	24	14	25	60	75	47	76	84	100	148
Public auction	Number	256	233	256	135	149	104	75	162	338	514	773	637	578	854	911	839
Mineral	Number	147	107	93	87	87	59	57	81	87	89	113	114	176	118	43	50
Small tract	Number	282	172	489	330	239	278	258	212	404	349	460	1,026	1,472	2,199	4,172	4,827
Other	Number	—	—	—	—	—	—	—	—	—	—	—	—	—	—	16	258
Total	Number	2,207	1,385	1,376	892	746	705	657	637	1,189	1,430	2,081	2,181	2,655	3,625	5,582	6,452
Area of final entries approved:[1]																	
Homestead	1000A.	437	203	114	54	37	34	30	21	42	49	71	42	44	46	39	43
Desert land	1000A.	7	7	5	3	2	1	3	2	3	10	11	7	13	11	16	26
Public auction	1000A.	30	21	22	11	11	10	8	15	36	62	101	88	77	121	155	154
Mineral	1000A.	11	11	8	8	8	8	5	14	31	23	13	22	35	42	13	13
Small tract	1000A.	6	10	19	9	2	9	7	5	5	5	3	6	7	19	26	18
Other	1000A.	—	—	—	—	—	—	—	—	—	—	—	—	—	—	1	35
Total	1000A.	491	252	168	85	60	62	53	57	117	149	199	165	176	239	250	289
Number of exchanges:[3]																	
National forest[4][5]	Number	140	146	126	109	65	75	74	61	20	32	35	42	42	23	37	28
Other	Number	23	198	150	66	76	49	106	150	143	211	158	81	126	149	112	149
Total	Number	163	344	276	175	141	124	180	211	163	243	193	123	168	172	149	177
Area received in exchange:[3]																	
National forest[4]	1000A.	210	485	224	362	197	110	405	288	157	172	152	82	40	46	117	54
Other	1000A.	34	196	266	147	56	55	176	188	320	272	115	169	208	192	91	147
Total	1000A.	244	681	490	509	253	165	581	476	477	444	267	251	248	238	208	201
Area patented in exchange:[3]																	
National forest[4]	1000A.	12	11	24	23	11	26	166	33	9	12	41	55	14	7	217	46
Other	1000A.	21	530	208	154	52	54	158	157	244	242	111	159	140	177	63	151
Total	1000A.	33	541	232	177	63	80	324	190	253	254	152	214	154	184	280	197
Right-of-way cases closed	Number	488	—	336	—	—	—	—	—	—	1,202	1,380	1,020	1,503	1,540	1,953	1,635

[1] Includes disposals on both public lands and ceded Indian lands.

[2] Entries approved data are comparable with entries allowed data only for homesteads and desert land entries; for public auction, mineral, and miscellaneous items included in "Other," there is no original entry corresponding to the final entry.

[3] Excludes Indian reservation exchanges, but includes O & C exchanges.

[4] National forest exchanges include both land-for-land and land-for-timber exchanges on forests created from public domain lands. Exchanges involving acquired lands are not included.

[5] From 1949 through 1956 the number of exchanges does not include the number of land-for-timber exchanges.

Source: Compiled from Reports of the Director of the Bureau of Land Management, Statistical Appendices.

APPENDIX TABLE 25.   Public Domain Lands: *Receipts from the Sale of Land, 1789-1932*

(in thousands of dollars)

Fiscal year	Receipts	Fiscal year	Receipts	Fiscal year	Receipts	Fiscal year	Receipts
Total all years: 402,081							
1789-95	0	1830	2,329	1865	997	1900	2,900
96	5	1831	3,211	1866	665	1901	2,967
97	84	1832	2,623	1867	1,164	1902	4,139
98	12	1833	3,968	1868	1,349	1903	8,960
99	0	1834	4,858	1869	4,020	1904	7,446
1800	*	1835	14,758	1870	3,350	1905	4,850
01	168	1836	24,877	1871	2,389	1906	4,885
02	189	1837	6,776	1872	2,576	1907	7,728
03	166	1838	3,082	1873	2,882	1908	9,761
04	488	1839	7,076	1874	1,852	1909	7,698
1805	540	1840	3,293	1875	1,414	1910	6,342
06	765	1841	1,366	1876	1,129	1911	5,784
07	466	1842	1,336	1877	976	1912	5,438
08	648	1843 [1]	898	1878	1,080	1913	2,747
09	442	1844	2,060	1879	925	1914	2,594
1810	697	1845	2,077	1880	1,017	1915	2,166
11	1,040	1846	2,694	1881	3,535	1916	1,770
12	710	1847	2,498	1882	6,629	1917	1,936
13	836	1848	3,329	1883	9,657	1918	2,051
14	1,136	1849	1,689	1884	10,305	1919	1,465
1815	1,288	1850	1,860	1885	6,224	1920	1,991
16	1,718	1851	2,352	1886	5,758	1921	1,546
17	1,991	1852	2,043	1887	9,246	1922	907
18	2,067	1853	1,667	1888	11,203	1923	646
19	3,274	1854	8,471	1889	8,018	1924	551
1820	1,636	1855	11,479	1890	6,349	1925	638
21	1,213	1856	8,918	1891	4,160	1926	734
22	1,804	1857	3,829	1892	3,322	1927	612
23	917	1858	3,514	1893	3,193	1928	390
24	984	1859	1,757	1894	1,653	1929	312
1825	1,216	1860	1,779	1895	1,116	1930	398
26	1,394	1861	871	1896	1,054	1931	271
27	1,496	1862	152	1897	918	1932	167
28	1,018	1863	168	1898	1,291		
29	1,517	1864	588	1899	1,704		

[1] From 1789 to 1842, the fiscal year ended December 31. Hence with the change in the fiscal year system only the months of January through June were included in fiscal year 1843.

Source: Compiled from Public Affairs Bulletin No. 76, *Natural Resources Activity of the Federal Government,* by J. R. Mahoney, Library of Congress, 1950, for the period 1789-1881; and the Reports of the Director of the Bureau of Land Management, Statistical Appendices, for the period 1881-1932.

APPENDIX TABLE 26. Public Domain Lands: *Receipts from the Sale of Land and Miscellaneous Receipts Related to the Sale and Rental of Public Lands, 1933-56*

(in thousands of dollars)

Fiscal year	Total receipts from rentals, sales of land, & related items	Sales of public lands [1]	Sales of Indian lands	Rentals [2] and permits	Fees and commissions	Other [3]
1933	436	117	26	15	255	23
34	438	108	29	18	260	23
1935	418	105	72	19	198	24
36	361	93	99	17	137	15
37	330	88	45	16	121	20
38	268	113	31	21	82	21
39	402	251	21	18	92	20
1940	272	132	28	24	66	22
41	332	200	29	29	53	21
42	259	150	6	37	44	22
43	257	139	5	35	49	29
44	266	127	7	49	50	33
1945	364	202	5	45	78	34
46	308	132	8	49	78	41
47	353	153	5	70	71	54
48	577	260	8	119	151	39
49	1,029	556	3	161	255	54
1950	1,155	462	2	281	398	12
51	1,156	539	9	217	374	17
52	1,904	845	2	200	828	29
53	1,657	1,048	2	130	439	38
54	2,149	1,279	2	236	593	39
1955	3,167	1,951	1	439	735	41
56	3,598	2,290	4	445	843	16

[1] Includes receipts from sales of town lots and reclamation lands. Includes small sales of timber for salvage until 1946. For timber receipts since then see appendix table 14.

[2] Includes rental of power sites, right-of-way payments, grazing on reclamation land, and lands in Alaska, as well as leases for all uses of public land except grazing on lands administered under the Taylor Grazing Act and the exploitation of timber and minerals.

[3] Primarily fines and penalties and the sale of government property.

Source: Compiled from the Reports of the Director of the Bureau of Land Management, Statistical Appendices.

APPENDIX TABLE 27. Public Domain, Acquired and Revested Lands: *Summary of Cash Receipts by Source, 1785-1956 and Projections for 1960 and 1980*

(in thousands of dollars)

Fiscal year	Total receipts (all sources)	Sale of land, fees, & commissions[1]	Miscellaneous permits, leases, fines, etc.	O & C and Coos Bay lands[2]	Timber on public domain	Grazing[3]	Mineral production, rents, & royalties			Other[6]
							Public domain lands[4]	Acquired lands[5]	Submerged lands	
May 20, 1785 to June 30, 1880..	208,060					...	...	...	...	...
1881-1890	99,269	99,129		...		...	...	...	...	140
1891-1900	33,493	33,203		...		...	...	...	...	290
1901-1910	94,095	91,708		...		...	–	...	...	[7] 2,387
1911-1920	67,023	63,106		...		...	–	...	...	[7] 3,917
1921	14,508	4,165					9,726			617
22	11,785	2,578					8,799			407
23	10,700	1,947					7,580			1,173
24	16,373	1,595					13,632			1,146
1925	10,766	1,539					8,279			948
26	11,414	1,974					8,385			1,055
27	9,202	1,728					6,670			804
28	6,710	1,209					4,677			824
29	6,194	1,202					3,885			1,107
1930	6,801	1,123					4,739			939
31	4,836	882					3,532			422
32	4,129	568					3,237			324
33	3,859	398	39	115			3,307			...
34	4,035	397	41	274		1	3,322			...
1935	4,800	375	43	348		2	4,032			...
36	5,195	329	32	318		49	4,468			...
37	7,400	254	36	785		530	5,795			...
38	8,447	226	42	615		866	6,699			...

Year								
41	8,052	282	30	1,158		1,114	6,052		
42	9,921	200	59	1,174		1,095	7,393		
43	[8]10,568	193	64	1,541		980	7,790		
44	15,118	184	82	2,045		1,016	11,791		
1945	14,371	285	80	1,990		997	11,019		
46	14,087	218	90	1,689	•6	965	11,119		
47	[5]21,100	229	124	3,363	6	1,111	16,267		
48	33,913	419	158	5,292	50	1,454	26,109	431	
49	37,984	814	215	4,417	332	1,246	30,526	434	
1950	36,991	862	279	4,818	365	1,551	28,734	382	
51	50,348	921	221	7,984	1,061	1,708	37,666	787	
52	65,967	1,675	214	9,889	1,124	1,999	49,663	1,403	
53	67,274	1,489	240	13,420	831	2,112	47,303	1,874	[10] 5
54	78,693	1,874	258	13,521	1,115	2,057	57,446	2,416	[10] 6
1955	231,852	2,687	460	15,608	1,654	2,240	64,484	2,306	142,405
56	212,004	3,137	451	23,008	1,843	2,440	67,112	2,778	111,224
1960 [11]	251,000			34,000	7,100	3,000	103,000	4,000	95,000 [10] 8
1980 [11]	551,000			52,700	10,500	7,600	259,500	6,000	210,000 [10] 11

[1] Includes sale of public domain lands, reclamation lands, Indian lands, and fees and commissions. See appendix tables 25 and 26.

[2] Includes receipts from controverted lands as well as the noncontroverted lands. The accumulated receipts from the former were kept in a suspense account and were not distributed until fiscal year 1955. O & C receipts included in "Other" until 1933. See appendix table 13.

[3] Includes in addition to Taylor Act grazing, grazing in Alaska, on reclamation land, and land utilization projects.

[4] Includes only the receipts from leases under the Mineral Leasing Act of 1920 up through 1932. Receipts from mineral leasing under other acts included in "Other" category until 1933.

[5] Since these receipts are ultimately transferred to the agencies administering the land, primarily Forest Service and Fish and Wildlife Service, to avoid double counting they should not be included as a receipt here in compiling a grand total of receipts from all lands. See appendix tables 19 and 20.

[6] Includes receipts from O & C and Coos Bay lands from 1916 to 1933, miscellaneous mineral leasing acts, special-use permits of land, and other sources.

[7] Includes reclamation water right charges.

[8] Excludes surplus property sale revenues.

[9] Receipts included in total receipts from the sales of land prior to 1946.

[10] Nonoperating revenues including such items as refunds and damages collected and unclaimed money. Excludes $132,000 accumulated in unsettled accounts over a 20-year period which were closed in 1956.

[11] Projections of authors; include $5 million each year from miscellaneous sources, including sale of land.

Source: Compiled from the Reports of the Director of the Bureau of Land Management, Statistical Appendices.

APPENDIX TABLE 28. Public Domain, Mineral-Producing Acquired Lands, Revested Lands, and Ceded Indian Lands: Disposition of Receipts by Source of Receipt from Sale and Use of Resources, 1943-56

(in thousands of dollars)

Fiscal year and recipient of receipts	Total	Source of receipts							
		Mineral leases and permits	O & C and Coos Bay timber sales and land use	Land and timber sales [1]	Fees and commissions [1]	Grazing fees and leases	Sale or lease of ceded Indian lands	Miscellaneous leases and permits	Other
1943:									
Reclamation fund	4,160	4,037	…	91	32	…	…	…	…
States and counties	4,043	2,853	698	2	…	490	…	…	…
Range improvement	244	…	…	…	…	244	…	…	…
Indian trust funds	9	4	…	…	…	…	5	…	…
General fund	2,087	896	819	46	17	246	…	34	29
Total	10,543	7,790	1,517	139	49	980	5	34	29
1944:									
Reclamation fund	6,200	6,089	…	97	14	…	…	…	…
States and counties	5,715	4,310	896	1	…	508	…	…	…
Range improvement	254	…	…	…	…	254	…	…	…
Indian trust funds	13	6	…	…	…	…	7	…	…
General fund	2,686	1,386	899	29	36	254	…	49	33
Total	14,868	11,791	1,795	127	50	1,016	7	49	33
1945:									
Reclamation fund	5,871	5,691	…	127	53	…	…	…	…
States and counties	5,374	3,999	871	6	…	498	…	…	…
Range improvement	249	…	…	…	…	249	…	…	…
Indian trust funds	11	6	…	…	…	…	5	…	…
General fund	2,639	1,323	893	69	25	250	…	45	34
Total	14,144	11,019	1,764	202	78	997	5	45	34
1946:									
Reclamation fund	5,900	5,737	…	93	68	…	…	2	…
States and counties	5,206	4,046	676	4	…	480	…	…	…
Range improvement	241	…	…	…	…	241	…	…	…
Indian trust funds	15	5	…	…	…	2	8	…	…
General fund	2,477	1,331	765	41	10	242	…	47	41

1947:									
Reclamation fund	8,618	8,451		93	68	5		1	
States and counties	7,968	5,984	1,461	5		518			
Transfer of funds[2]	59					59			
Range improvement	259					259	5		
Indian trust funds	17	6				6			
General fund	3,855	1,826	1,578	61	3	264		69	54
Total	20,776	16,267	3,039	159	71	1,111	5	70	54
1948:									
Reclamation fund	13,798	13,434		213	145	2		4	
States and counties	12,031	9,539	2,230	10		252			
Transfer of funds[2]	467	431				36			
Range improvement	350					350	8		39
Indian trust funds	18	6			6	4		113	
General fund	6,622	3,130	2,437	87		810			
Total	33,286	26,540	4,667	310	151	1,454	8	117	39
1949:									
Reclamation fund	16,519	15,864		491	157	4		3	
States and counties	13,317	11,330	1,783	19		185		5	
Transfer of funds[2]	441	434				2			
Range improvement	305					305	3		54
Indian trust funds	11	6			98	2		148	
General fund	6,556	3,326	1,805	378		747			
Total	37,149	30,960	3,588	888	255	1,245	3	156	54
1950:									
Reclamation fund	15,766	14,790		785	180	11			
States and counties	12,746	10,569	1,837	42		298		24	
Transfer of funds[2]	419	382				13			
Range improvement	377					377	2		12
Indian trust funds	13	7			218	4			
General fund	6,855	3,368	2,168			848		243	
Total	36,176	29,116	4,005	827	398	1,551	2	267	12
1951:									
Reclamation fund	20,828	19,463		1,356		9			
States and counties	17,460	13,909	3,202	60		289			
Transfer of funds[2]	789	787				1		1	
Range improvement	356					356	9		17
Indian trust funds	27	14				4			
General fund	9,621	4,280	3,515	183	374	1,049		203	
Total	49,081	38,453	6,717	1,599	374	1,708	9	204	17

APPENDIX TABLE 28—continued

Fiscal year and recipient of receipts	Total	Mineral leases and permits	O & C and Coos Bay timber sales and land use	Land and timber sales [1]	Fees and commissions [1]	Grazing fees and leases	Sale or lease of ceded Indian lands	Miscellaneous leases and permits	Other
1952:									
Reclamation fund	24,468	22,933		1,523		12			
States and counties	22,875	16,392	6,082	69		332			
Transfer of funds [2]	1,396	1,396							
Range improvement	361					361			
Indian trust funds	30	24				4	2		
General fund	15,388	10,321	2,358	377	828	1,290		184	29
Total	64,518	51,066	8,440	1,969	828	1,999	2	184	29
1953:									
Reclamation fund	25,476	23,985		1,478		9		4	
States and counties	24,116	17,256	6,447	67		346			
Transfer of funds [2]	1,875	1,874						1	
Range improvement	375					375			
Indian trust funds	24	17				5	2		
General fund	14,974	6,045	6,544	334	439	1,377		197	38
Total	66,840	49,177	12,991	1,879	439	2,112	2	202	38
1954:									
Reclamation fund	30,888	28,871		2,003		14			
States and counties	27,733	20,676	6,620	86		351			
Transfer of funds [2]	2,417	2,416						1	
Range improvement	388					388			
Indian trust funds	87	81				4	2		
General fund	15,968	7,818	5,695	305	593	1,300		218	39
Total	77,481	59,862	12,315	2,394	593	2,057	2	219	39
1955:									
Reclamation fund	35,854	32,933		2,906		15			
States and counties	38,310	23,605	[3] 14,223	134		348			
Transfer of funds [2]	2,308	2,306				1		1	
Range improvement	526					526			
Indian trust funds	212	207				4	1		
General fund	162,330	150,144	[3] 9,081	565	735	1,346		418	41

Reclamation fund	36,852	33,709	...	3,132	...	11	...	...
States and counties	36,579	24,256	[6] 11,974	159	...	190	...	...
Transfer of funds [2]	2,803	2,778	...	...	...	23	...	2
Range improvement	619	...	...	...	...	619	...	...
Indian trust funds	187	183	...	...	...	...	4	...
General fund	134,964	120,189	11,034	842	843	1,597	...	449
Total	212,004 [4]	181,113	23,008	4,133	843	2,440	4	451

[1] The total payment to the Reclamation Fund from the receipts of sales of public land and timber and fees and commissions is known, but prior to 1951 the amount paid from each source is only an estimate.

[2] Funds collected on acquired lands by the Bureau of Land Management and transferred to the agency holding the land.

[3] Includes that portion of receipts due the O & C counties which were collected on the controverted lands by the Forest Service and held in a Treasury suspense account for the fiscal years from 1941 until actual disbursement in 1955. Previous tables show these funds credited to the fiscal year in which they were deposited in the Treasury.

[4] Includes receipts from submerged areas.

[5] Before final settlement of all accounts.

[6] Includes a share of receipts from formerly controverted O & C lands.

Source: Compiled from the Reports of the Director of the Bureau of Land Management, Statistical Appendices.

APPENDIX TABLE 29. Public Domain and Revested Lands: *Summary of Disposition of Receipts from the Sale and Use of Resources, 1933-56 and Estimates for 1960 and 1980* [1]

(in thousands of dollars)

Fiscal year	Total receipts [2]	Reclamation Fund	States and counties [3]	Transfers to other agencies [4]	Range Improvement Fund [5]	Indian Trust Funds	General Fund
1933	3,859	1,987	1,333	…	…	40	499
34	4,035	2,034	1,486	…	…	49	466
1935	4,800	2,320	1,813	…	…	89	578
36	5,195	2,532	1,958	…	12	112	581
37	7,400	2,950	2,926	…	110	58	1,356
38	8,447	3,626	3,599	…	216	68	938
39	7,748	3,416	3,000	…	244	42	1,046
1940	7,520	3,052	2,848	…	71	37	1,512
41	8,655	3,333	3,502	…	278	35	1,507
42	9,914	4,018	3,792	…	274	11	1,819
43	10,543	4,160	4,043	…	244	9	2,087
44	[6] 14,868	6,200	5,715	…	254	13	2,686
1945	14,144	5,871	5,374	…	249	11	2,639
46	13,839	5,900	5,206	…	241	15	2,477
47	[6] 20,776	8,618	7,968	59	259	17	3,855
48	33,286	13,798	12,031	467	350	18	6,622
49	37,149	16,519	13,317	441	305	11	6,556
1950	36,176	15,766	12,746	419	377	13	6,855
51	49,081	20,828	17,460	789	356	27	9,621
52	64,518	24,468	22,875	1,396	361	30	15,388
53	[7] 66,840	25,476	24,116	1,875	375	24	14,974
54	[7] 77,481	30,888	27,733	2,417	388	87	15,968
1955	[7] 239,540	35,854	38,310	2,308	526	212	162,330
56	212,004	36,852	36,579	2,803	619	187	134,964
1960 [8]	251,000	64,000	60,000				
1980 [8]	551,000	149,000	132,000				

[1] From 1943 to 1956, inclusive, these data are the summaries shown in appendix table 28. Includes receipts from mineral leasing on acquired lands, receipts from ceded Indian lands, and receipts from submerged areas.
[2] This total does not check with the total in appendix table 27. In appendix tables 28 and 29 the receipts from formerly controverted O & C lands for the years 1942-54 are shown entirely in 1955 when they were released from escrow account, whereas in table 27 they were shown as if paid in the years the receipts were earned.
[3] Payments in lieu of taxes from receipts on all but acquired lands.
[4] Mineral receipts from acquired lands and certain right-of-way and grazing-fee collections. Disposition of these receipts determined by law within the agency administering the land. [5] Available for range improvement if appropriated. [7] Excludes nonoperating revenues.
[6] Excludes receipts from large sales of surplus real estate. [7] Excludes nonoperating revenues.
[8] Estimates based on earlier projections of revenue and on present law regarding distribution of receipts.

APPENDIX TABLE 30. Public Domain and Revested Lands: Cost to the Federal Government of Fire Protection and Suppression, 1942-56

(in thousands of dollars)

Fiscal year	Grand total	Grazing districts			Alaska			Other public domain			
		Total	Fire fighting	Fire presuppression	Total	Fire fighting	Fire presuppression	Total	Forest Service funds[1]	Contracts and special funds	O & C and Coos Bay contracts
1942	303	75	25	50	42	15	27	105	105	...	[2]81
43	682	244	138	106	168	[2]140	28	154	125	[2]29	[2]116
44	639	244	97	147	141	[2]109	32	131	125	[2]6	[2]123
1945	689	213	74	139	162	[2]128	34	199	160	[2]39	[2]115
46	635	205	70	135	138	...	138	198	...	198	94
47	652	180	105	75	164	...	164	195	...	195	113
48	597	180	130	50	71	...	71	183	...	183	163
49	676	179	90	89	142	1	141	183	...	183	172
1950	1,018	443	355	88	149	6	143	178	...	178	248
51	1,078	340	250	90	264	69	195	226	...	226	248
52	1,300	287	187	100	430	219	211	350	...	350	233
53	1,397	249	139	110	444	236	208	411	...	411	293
54	1,549	254	128	126	518	287	231	418	...	418	359
1955	1,766	404	278	126	482	240	242	445	...	445	435
56	1,667	366	215	151	411	153	258	457	...	457	433

[1] Work done by the U.S. Forest Service with funds appropriated directly to that agency.
[2] Includes special defense appropriation transferred from the Office of the Secretary of the Interior.

Source: Compiled from Bureau of Land Management data and annual Budgets of the United States.

APPENDIX TABLE 31. Public Domain and Revested Lands: Cost to the Federal Government
of Certain Activities Related to the Administration and Use of
Forest and Range Resources, 1942-56 and Projections for 1960 and 1980 [1]

(in thousands of dollars)

Fiscal year	Total cost	Range management	Range improvement	White pine blister rust control[2]	Soil & moisture conservation	Weed control	Fire[3]	Timber management	Forest development	Road building	Road maintenance	Other building	Other maintenance
1942	2,242	616	235	30	937	...	303	121	...	...	...	...	...
43	2,553	740	109	39	617	...	682	366	...	...	...	...	...
44	2,483	772	114	34	640	...	639	284	...	...	...	...	...
1945	2,551	776	156	36	579	...	689	315	...	...	...	...	...
46	2,562	778	157	54	596	...	635	342	...	...	...	...	...
47	2,597	511	231	133	678	...	652	392	...	...	...	...	...
48	2,791	566	253	93	711	...	597	571	...	...	...	...	...
49	3,433	868	307	78	987	...	676	517	...	...	...	...	...
1950	3,818	897	282	72	910	...	1,018	639	22	...	...	48	...
51	4,621	995	530	60	983	...	1,078	796	60	109	...	2	...
52	7,999	1,408	569	44	1,174	1,825	1,100	893	60	924	...	...	24
53	8,660	1,440	443	44	1,436	1,312	1,397	1,412	45	1,107	...	...	22
54	9,911	1,426	380	37	1,711	1,093	1,549	1,419	50	2,224	...	...	...
1955	10,897	1,447	532	40	1,701	647	1,766	1,477	65	3,138	35	...	49
56	12,180	1,637	535	42	2,739	699	1,667	1,599	65	3,092	35	21	49
1960 [4]	19,000									5,000			
1980 [4]	32,000									7,000			

[1] Includes, prior to 1949, some obligations which were reimbursable.
[2] Transferred from U.S. Department of Agriculture. Cost of other forest pest control work is not shown since the Forest Service performs the work on public domain and O & C lands.
[3] For detail, see appendix table 30.
[4] Projections of authors.

Source: Compiled from the annual Budgets of the United States and Bureau of Land Management data.

APPENDIX TABLE 32. Public Domain and Revested Lands: *Cost to the Federal Government of General Administrative Activities, 1942-56 and Projections for 1960 and 1980* [1]

(in thousands of dollars)

Fiscal year	Total	Leasing and disposal of lands and minerals	Cadastral surveys	General administration [2]	Oil and gas lease supervision [3]
1942	2,473	968	744	453	308
43	2,324	969	560	457	338
44	2,424	965	506	452	501
1945	2,651	1,173	495	443	540
46	2,932	1,118	599	467	748
47	3,255	1,423	646	479	707
48	3,224	1,374	515	592	743
49	3,527	1,385	629	789	724
1950	3,746	1,366	728	907	745
51	4,088	1,455	774	1,020	839
52	4,417	1,593	751	1,147	926
53	5,298	1,947	1,126	1,204	1,021
54	5,029	1,933	894	1,007	1,195
1955	6,385	2,435	1,464	1,195	1,291
56	7,347	3,469	1,540	1,270	1,068
1960 [4]	9,000				
1980 [4]	12,000				

[1] Includes, prior to 1949, some obligations which were reimbursable.

[2] Adjusted to include administrative expenses formerly charged to the agency.

[3] Services of the Conservation Branch of the Geological Survey. Includes cost of supervising some military oil lands.

[4] Projections of authors.

Source: Compiled from the annual Budgets of the United States and Bureau of Land Management data.

APPENDIX TABLE 33.   Public Domain Lands: *Contributions from Nonfederal Sources Used in the Administration of Range Resources, 1942-56* [1]

(in thousands of dollars)

Fiscal year	Grand total [2]	Soil and moisture			Range improvement			Weed control		
		Total	Range users	Others [3]	Total	Range users [4]	Others [3]	Total	Range users	Others [3]
1941	594	203	168	35	391	167	224	...	...	...
42	467	164	136	28	303	234	69	...	...	...
43	290	98	81	17	192	104	88	...	...	...
44	308	98	81	17	210	109	101	...	...	...
1945	364	132	109	23	232	155	77	...	...	...
46	396	177	146	31	219	151	68	...	...	...
47	650	170	141	29	480	225	255	...	...	...
48	421	76	63	13	345	250	95	...	...	...
49	450	104	86	18	346	281	65	...	...	...
1950	1,582	191	184	7	1,391	1,322	69	...	...	...
51	1,246	201	164	37	1,045	1,022	23	...	...	...
52	1,516	207	166	41	1,308	1,257	51	...	...	...
53	2,364	291	225	66	1,897	1,850	47	176	164	12
54	2,330	356	239	117	1,820	1,745	75	153	139	14
1955	2,009	223	193	30	1,672	1,628	44	113	97	16
56	1,701	227	193	34	1,359	1,200	159	115	70	45

[1] Includes the value of contributions of labor and materials as well as cash contributions from 1950 on.

[2] Includes improvements jointly undertaken by the federal government and others as well as improvements on public land undertaken by range users alone.

[3] Primarily state or county governments but also includes others, such as railroad companies, which would receive same benefit from the work.

[4] Prior to 1947 figures do not report the contributions made on lands outside of grazing districts, and prior to 1950 they do not show the value of labor and materials contributed.

Source: Compiled from Bureau of Land Management data.

APPENDIX TABLE 34. Public Domain and Revested Lands: *Summary of Estimated Public and Private Expenditures, 1942-56 and Projections for 1960 and 1980 (Federal obligations and state and private contributions)*

(in thousands of dollars)

Fiscal year	Total	Federal government	State and local governments [1]	Private persons [2]
1942	5,182	4,715	97	370
43	5,148	4,858	105	185
44	5,215	4,907	118	190
1945	5,566	5,202	100	264
46	5,890	5,494	99	297
47	6,502	5,852	284	366
48	6,436	6,015	108	313
49	7,410	6,960	83	367
1950	9,146	7,564	76	1,506
51	9,955	8,709	60	1,186
52	13,931	12,416	92	1,423
53	16,322	13,958	125	2,239
54	17,269	14,940	206	2,123
1955	19,290	17,282	90	1,918
56	21,228	19,527	238	1,463
1960 [3]	31,000	28,000		3,000
1980 [3]	48,000	44,000		4,000

[1] Including some private contributions from nonusers of the range.

[2] Complete reports on contributions prior to 1950 are not available.

[3] Projections of authors.

Source: Compiled from annual Budgets of the United States and Bureau of Land Management data.

APPENDIX TABLE 35. Public Domain and Revested Lands: *Cost to the Federal Government of Activities on Forested Lands, 1942-56*

(in thousands of dollars)

Fiscal year	Total obligations	Forest improvement and management	Fire protection [1]	Disease and insect control [2]	Road building	Road maintenance
1942	364	121	213	30	...	...
43	843	366	438	39	...	...
44	713	284	395	34	...	...
1945	827	315	476	36	...	...
46	826	342	430	54	...	٣...
47	997	392	472	133	...	...
48	1,081	571	417	93	...	...
49	1,092	517	497	78	...	...
1950	1,286	639	575	72	...	...
51	1,725	818	738	60	109	...
52	2,734	953	813	44	924	...
53	3,756	1,457	1,148	44	1,107	...
54	5,025	1,469	1,295	37	2,224	...
1955	6,117	1,542	1,362	40	3,138	35
56	6,134	1,664	1,301	42	3,092	35

[1] Includes services performed by the U.S. Forest Service out of its own funds and contractual services by the U.S. Forest Service and state agencies. Excludes funds spent in grazing districts.

[2] Transfer of funds from the "Control of Forest Pests" appropriation.

Source: Compiled from the annual Budgets of the United States Government and Bureau of Land Management data.

APPENDIX TABLE 36. National Park System: Number of Visits, 1904-56 and Projections for 1960 and 1980 [1]

(in thousands of visits)

Year [2]	Total visits	National parks	National monuments	Historical areas Non-military	Historical areas Military	Miscellaneous District of Columbia [3]	Miscellaneous Recreational areas [4]	Parkways
1904	121	121	...	—	—	—	...	...
05	141	141	...	—	—	—	...	...
06	31	31	...	—	—	—	...	...
07	61	61	...	—	—	—	...	...
08	69	69	...	—	—	—	...	...
09	86	86	...	—	—	—	...	...
1910	199	199	...	—	—	—	...	...
11	224	224	*	—	—	—	...	...
12	229	229	*	—	—	—	...	...
13	252	252	*	—	—	—	...	...
14	240	240	*	—	—	—	...	...
1915	335	335	*	—	—	—	...	...
16	358	356	2	—	—	—	...	...
17	490	488	2	—	—	—	...	...
18	455	452	3	—	—	—	...	...
19	811	757	54	—	—	—	...	...
1920	1,059	920	139	—	—	—	...	...
21	1,172	1,007	164	—	—	—	...	...
22	1,216	1,045	172	—	—	—	...	...
23	1,494	1,281	213	—	—	—	...	...
24	1,671	1,424	247	—	—	—	...	...
1925	2,054	1,762	292	—	—	—	...	...
26	2,315	1,942	373	—	—	—	...	...
27	2,798	2,381	417	—	—	—	...	...
28	3,025	2,569	456	—	—	—	...	...
29	3,248	2,757	491	—	—	—	...	...
1930	3,247	2,775	472	—	—	—	...	...
31	3,545	3,153	392	—	—	—	...	...
32	3,755	2,949	406	400	—	—	...	...
33	3,482	2,867	523	91	—	—	...	...
34	6,337	3,517	1,386	281	1,154	—	...	...
1935	7,676	4,056	1,332	538	1,749	—	...	...
36	11,990	5,791	1,681	749	1,156	2,613	...	...
37	15,133	6,705	1,966	967	1,900	3,206	389	...
38	16,331	6,619	2,364	956	3,026	2,801	565	...
39	15,531	6,854	2,592	761	2,136	2,575	612	...

APPENDIX TABLE 36—continued

Year [2]	Total visits	National parks	National monuments	Historical areas		District of Columbia [3]	Miscellaneous	
				Non-military	Military		Recreational areas [4]	Parkways
1940	16,755	7,358	2,817	983	2,024	2,918	656	...
41	21,237	8,459	3,745	1,765	2,259	3,268	845	896
42	9,371	3,815	1,831	885	819	1,427	338	256
43	6,828	2,054	1,578	621	446	1,784	214	131
44	8,340	2,646	1,851	726	544	2,040	264	268
1945	11,714	4,538	2,512	788	865	2,041	587	383
46	21,752	8,991	3,603	2,115	1,552	3,067	1,162	1,262
47	25,534	10,674	4,027	2,501	1,757	3,317	2,012	1,247
48	29,859	11,293	4,438	2,778	1,748	3,323	4,769	1,510
49	31,736	12,968	4,923	3,170	2,025	3,582	3,646	1,422
1950	33,253	13,919	5,310	3,201	2,153	4,123	2,551	1,996
51	37,106	15,079	6,187	4,109	2,399	4,082	2,801	2,449
52	42,300	17,143	6,807	4,994	2,689	4,295	2,814	3,558
53	46,225	17,372	7,540	5,440	2,942	4,212	3,026	5,693
54	47,834	17,969	7,805	5,390	3,075	4,121	3,407	6,067
1955	50,008	18,830	7,953	5,338	3,223	4,044	3,920	6,700
56	54,923	20,055	8,769	5,738	3,505	4,299	5,119	7,438
1960 [5]	80,000	45,000						
1980 [5]	440,000	250,000						

[1] Reorganization plans placed various monuments, memorials, and other sites and areas under National Park Service supervision. For the earlier years no statistics on visits are available. Does not include visits to areas of the National Capital Park System.
[2] Statistics are for the year ending September 30 for all years prior to 1941; thereafter for the year ending December 31. Parks and sites in Alaska, Hawaii, and Puerto Rico locations are also included.
[3] Consists of the Custis-Lee Mansion as well as House Where Lincoln Died, the Lincoln Museum, Lincoln Memorial, Jefferson Memorial, and Washington Monument.
[4] First established in 1937.
[5] Projections of authors based on 1947-54 trend; see text for discussion, pp. 117-18.

Source: Compiled from National Park Service data.

APPENDIX TABLE 37. National Park System: *Receipts from the Use of Lands and Facilities, 1940-56 and Projections for 1960 and 1980*

(in thousands of dollars)

Fiscal year	Total receipts	Auto-mobile fees	Other admission or guide fees	Business concessions	Rents, permits, and licenses	Sale of government property & products	Sale of services	Miscellaneous [1]
1940	1,900	1,213	324	99	96	135	31	2
41	2,124	1,380	357	108	68	174	33	4
42	2,030	1,272	361	118	79	161	32	7
43	1,010	374	257	64	111	170	23	11
44	755	213	130	54	110	214	22	12
1945	771	216	168	63	99	188	36	1
46	1,552	599	524	118	111	149	41	10
47	2,919	1,594	781	263	107	130	38	6
48	3,297	1,820	880	307	119	130	39	2
49	3,449	1,903	920	279	112	155	39	41
1950	3,538	2,056	892	234	110	181	48	17
51	3,542	1,973	856	306	115	231	42	19
52	3,641	2,135	911	171	117	169	39	99
53	4,240	2,375	893	473	121	216	43	119
54	4,262	2,415	860	493	105	143	12	234
1955	5,286	3,052	1,039	413	119	193	5	465
56	5,267	3,663	682	380	112	206	9	215
1960 [2]	7,000							
1980 [2]	20,000							

[1] Includes fees, forfeitures, sales of surplus real property, and for the years since 1949 those park receipts which are earmarked for the special purposes shown in appendix table 38.
[2] Projections of authors.
Source: Compiled from National Park Service data.

APPENDIX TABLE 38. National Park System: *Disposition of Receipts, 1940-56*

(in thousands of dollars)

Fiscal year	Total receipts	General fund	Educational expense [1]	Payments in lieu of taxes [2]	Management of properties [3]	Purchase of properties [4]
1940	1,900	1,900	...	...	...	...
41	2,124	2,124	...	...	...	...
42	2,030	2,030	...	...	...	...
43	1,010	1,010	...	...	...	...
44	755	755	...	...	...	...
1945	771	771	...	...	...	...
46	1,552	1,552	...	...	...	...
47	2,919	2,919	...	...	...	...
48	3,297	3,297	...	...	...	...
49	3,449	3,436	13	...	...	...
1950	3,538	3,522	16	...	...	...
51	3,542	3,528	14	...	...	...
52	3,641	3,551	71	...	19	...
53	4,240	4,124	17	49	50	..
54	4,262	4,033	26	26	177	...
1955	5,286	4,909	27	26	303	21
56	5,267	5,064	24	26	145	8

[1] A portion of visitor fees collected at the respective parks is used to provide educational facilities for dependents of employees at Yellowstone, and at Crater Lake and Mammoth Cave National Parks.

[2] Park fees are used to compensate Wyoming for tax losses on Grand Teton National Park lands.

[3] Pending establishment of Independence National Historical Park at Philadelphia, Pa., some buildings are rented and cleared sites are temporarily producing revenue as parking lots. Income from these sources is available to manage and maintain rental properties and to clear sites for the park.

[4] A portion of receipts from Mammoth Cave National Park is available to buy privately owned property within park boundaries. No use of these funds has been made to date, however.

Source: Compiled from National Park Service data.

APPENDIX TABLE 39.   National Park System: *Estimated Receipts to State Governments from Taxes Paid on Gasoline Used Driving on National Park Roads* [1]

Item	Total or average— four parks	Yellow- stone	Glacier	Crater Lake	Yosemite
Number of cars (thousand) ...	988	409	200	95	284
Car miles driven (million) ...	80.7	45.8	29.6	1.3	4.0
Miles driven per car	81.7	–	–	–	–
Gasoline mileage (miles per gallon)	14	–	–	–	–
State gasoline tax (cents per gallon) [2]	5.7	–	–	–	–
Gasoline consumption (gal- lons per car)	5.8	–	–	–	–
Gasoline tax revenue per car (cents)	33	–	–	–	–

Note: Approximately 17,750,000 visitors visited the national parks by automobile in 1955 in about 5,220,000 automobiles. If for each car 33¢ in state gasoline taxes had been paid while driving in the national parks, this would have produced a tax revenue for the states of over $1,722,600.

[1] 1955 data used for Yellowstone Park and traffic counts available from recent years, adjusted by 1955 data on visitor use. Traffic counts made in co-operative travel surveys by the National Park Service, U.S. Bureau of Public Roads, and State Highway agencies.

[2] Average of 11 western states, 1955.

APPENDIX TABLE 40. National Park System: Cost to the Federal Government of Management and Protection Activities, 1942-56 [1]

(in thousands of dollars)

Fiscal year	Grand total	Direct funds					Transferred funds [2]		
		Total [3]	Management of areas	Park recreation programs	Concession management	Forestry & fire control	Total	Soil & moisture conservation	Forest disease & insect control
1942	3,477	3,342	–	–	–	–	135	55	80
43	2,962	2,821	–	–	–	–	141	35	106
44	2,486	2,352	–	–	–	–	134	34	100
1945	2,536	2,405	–	–	–	–	131	35	96
46	2,974	2,768	–	–	–	–	206	34	172
47	5,307	4,864	–	–	–	–	443	51	392
48	4,959	4,468	–	–	–	–	491	80	411
49	6,479	5,931	4,972	333	–	626	548	95	453
1950	7,785	7,095	5,812	593	–	690	690	91	599
51	8,329	7,697	6,044	839	247	567	632	95	537
52	8,679	8,132	6,470	811	258	593	547	89	458
53	9,516	8,951	6,922	1,152	269	608	565	90	475
54	9,471	8,908	6,960	788	262	898	563	76	487
1955	9,562	9,128	7,760	507	265	596	434	51	383
56	10,829	10,340	8,678	702	246	714	489	100	389

[1] The figures shown are appropriations until 1949 and actual obligations from then on. Since the appropriated funds are not necessarily all obligated and if not obligated will revert to the federal Treasury, the appropriation figures shown may be relatively larger than the obligations shown for later years.

[2] Soil and moisture funds are now appropriated directly to the National Park Service, but forest disease and insect control funds are transferred from the U.S. Forest Service.

[3] Changes in budget and accounting procedure make it difficult to present a detailed breakdown of this total for the period before 1949.

Source: Compiled from the annual Budgets of the United States and National Park Service data.

APPENDIX TABLE 41. National Park System: *Cost to the Federal Government of All Activities, 1942-56 and Projections for 1960 and 1980* [1]

(in thousands of dollars)

Fiscal year	Grand total cost	Protection & management [2]	Construction				Maintenance [3]			Property acquisition	General administrative expense
			Total	Roads & trails	Parkways	Other	Total	Roads & trails	Facilities		
1942	14,846	3,477	8,693	3,000	5,347	346	2,295	–	–	9	372
43	5,741	2,962	399	180	167	52	1,994	–	–	...	386
44	4,782	2,486	...	...	...	...	1,644	–	–	...	652
1945	4,945	2,536	...	...	...	...	1,679	–	–	...	730
46	5,740	2,974	...	...	...	...	1,804	–	–	...	962
47	26,539	5,307	13,886	2,615	9,941	1,330	5,825	–	–	25	1,496
48	11,138	4,959	1,171	735	...	436	3,465	–	–	204	1,339
49	20,739	6,479	7,619	859	5,716	1,044	5,359	2,875	2,484	152	1,130
1950	28,080	7,785	12,296	5,271	4,213	2,812	6,509	3,534	2,975	309	1,181
51	34,295	8,329	15,457	5,069	6,994	3,394	7,307	3,776	3,531	1,921	1,281
52	28,085	8,679	8,069	2,165	3,588	2,316	7,443	3,830	3,613	2,641	1,253
53	33,014	9,516	13,676	3,674	8,315	1,687	7,994	4,134	3,860	492	1,336
54	31,895	9,471	11,130	5,114	3,163	2,853	8,125	4,159	3,966	2,020	1,149
1955	43,426	9,562	22,398	9,629	9,091	3,678	8,420	4,216	4,204	2,038	1,008
56	51,103	10,829	29,032	11,971	11,040	6,021	9,051	4,275	4,776	943	1,248
1960 [4]	80,000										
1980 [4]	135,000										

[1] The figures shown are appropriations until 1949 and actual obligations from then on. Since appropriated funds are not necessarily all obligated and may revert to the federal Treasury, the appropriation figures may be relatively larger comparable to the later figures.

[2] For detail see appendix table 40.

[3] Changes in accounting and budgeting procedure make it impossible to show the same detailed breakdown of management and protection activities and maintenance activities that is shown from 1949 through 1955.

[4] Projections of authors.

Source: Compiled from the annual Budgets of the United States and National Park Service data.

APPENDIX TABLE 42.   National Park System: *Contributions Available from*
Private Sources for Acquisition of Land and Park
Development, and the Expenditure of Such Funds, 1940-56

(in thousands of dollars)

Fiscal year	Funds received [1]	Funds available for obligation	Funds obligated
1940	60	–	–
41	77	–	–
42	77	–	–
43	33	–	–
44	30	–	–
1945	...	–	–
46	22	–	–
47	2,094	–	–
48	21	–	–
49	62	–	–
1950	44	1,798	265
51	64	1,645	495
52	770	1,991	788
53	236	1,447	851
54	232	1,049	343
1955	949	952	705
56	617	875	454

[1] Funds totaling $7,242,000 have been contributed since 1920.

Source: Compiled from National Park Service data and the annual Budgets of the
United States.

APPENDIX TABLE 43.   Wildlife Refuges: *Estimated Visitor-Days
Use of Lands, 1951-56* [1]

(1,000 visitor-days)

Year	Total visitor-days use	Visitor-days use		
		Hunting	Fishing	Other use
1951	3,443	222	1,309	1,911
52	4,261	260	1,525	2,476
53	4,687	348	1,433	2,905
54	5,202	361	1,612	3,229
55	6,974	406	2,677	3,891
56	7,555	435	2,766	4,355

[1] Data unavailable prior to 1951.

Source: Compiled from U.S. Fish and Wildlife Service data.

APPENDIX TABLE 44. Wildlife Refuges: *Peak Autumn Number of Migratory Waterfowl Using Refuges, by Flyways, 1944-53* [1]

(1,000 waterfowl)

Year	Total	Mississippi flyway	Pacific flyway	Atlantic flyway	Central flyway
1944	17,374	8,057	7,107	1,117	1,093
1945	14,270	4,526	7,563	1,088	1,093
46	16,847	5,647	8,717	602	1,881
47	18,919	4,082	12,390	850	1,597
48	17,846	4,297	10,266	931	2,352
49	17,723	5,906	8,143	1,208	2,466
1950	17,433	4,733	8,857	1,248	2,595
51	19,703	5,176	11,578	1,172	1,777
52	17,683	5,736	8,709	1,044	2,194
53	22,138	6,787	10,664	1,722	2,965
54	–	–	–	–	–
1955	–	–	–	–	–

[1] These figures were gathered from 199 separate areas covering a total of 3,368,116 acres. A compilation for recent years is not available.

Source: Compiled from U.S. Fish and Wildlife Service data.

APPENDIX TABLE 45. Wildlife Refuges: Estimated Big Game Population on Refuges and Ranges and its Relationship to the Estimated Total Big Game Population in the Continental United States [1]

Year	Antelope	Bear	Bighorn sheep	Bison	Deer [2]	Elk	Moose	Peccary
1951	4,874	104	2,350	1,343	32,088	10,086	139	325
52	3,884	92	2,380	1,391	33,971	9,036	163	375
53	3,997	122	2,532	1,467	31,090	9,557	155	375
54	3,940	102	2,354	1,608	30,049	10,270	151	505
55	3,206	146	2,198	1,660	52,122	9,785	136	510
5-year average	3,980	113	2,363	1,494	35,864	9,747	149	418
Estimated total numbers in U.S. prior to 1954 hunting season	262,262	143,086	19,438	3,858	8,603,000	303,315	12,509	119,500
Percent of total game population on refuges	1.5	0.08	12.2	38.8	0.4	3.2	1.2	0.3

[1] Estimates made of peak number on the 17 areas totaling 10,802,184 acres where big game is found.
[2] Primarily white tail deer but also includes black tail deer and mule deer.

Source: Compiled from U.S. Fish and Wildlife Service data.

TABLE 46.   Wildlife Refuges: *Major Sources of Receipts from the Economic Use of Refuges and Ranges, 1949-56* [1]

(in thousands of dollars)

Calendar year	Timber sales [2]	Grazing receipts & hay	Oil and gas leases & royalties	Lease of crop land [3]	Other [4]
1949	–	–	8	–	–
1950	–	–	14	–	–
51	–	–	411	–	–
52	177	291	963	50	–
53	136	326	1,167	28	–
54	119	355	1,604	33	146
1955	320	408	1,444	23	–
56	297	418	1,349	9	–

[1] Does not account for all receipts. Records do not show receipts by source on a fiscal year basis. Data unavailable before 1949.

[2] Does not show value of timber exchanged for land.

[3] Does not include the value of crops where crop-share leases are used.

[4] Includes the sale of other pelts, meat, and other products where a harvest is made to keep animal populations in balance.

Source: Compiled from U.S. Fish and Wildlife Service data.

APPENDIX TABLE 47. Wildlife Refuges: *Receipts and Disposition of Receipts from the Use of Lands, 1942-56 and Projections for 1960 and 1980*[1]

(in thousands of dollars)

Fiscal year	Total receipts	Refuge development and maintenance[2]	Payments to counties	Expenses of sales	Enforcement of Migratory Bird Treaty Act	General administrative expenses	General Fund
1942	103	...	23	11	...	...	69
43	104	...	25	4	...	...	75
44	189	...	43	16	...	...	130
1945	247	...	61	3	...	...	183
46	294	...	69	18	...	...	207
47	376	...	88	26	...	...	262
48	576	...	136	34	...	...	406
49	418	189	97	30	93	...	.
1950	376	159	88	23	105	...	.
51	460	185	108	27	98	...	.
52	1,051	145	254	32	119	21	.
53	1,617	926	396	30	161	36	.
54	1,912	1,484	470	30	134	99	.
1955	2,283	1,552	564	26	211	75	.
56	2,319	1,354	547	34	319	97	.
1960[3]	2,500						
1980[3]	3,000						

[1] Beginning with 1949, the disposition of receipts retained by the U.S. Fish and Wildlife Service is not accounted for in the same fiscal year as that in which the receipts were collected. These funds, largely expended in the following year, remain available to the agency in succeeding years as long as there is a balance.

[2] From fiscal year 1942 through 1948, 25 per cent of net proceeds from refuge receipts was appropriated for payment to counties. The remainder of receipts was credited to the General Fund of the Treasury. From fiscal year 1949 through 1955, 75 per cent of net proceeds from refuge receipts was appropriated for management of national wildlife refuges, for enforcement of the Migratory Bird Treaty Act; and 25 per cent for payments to counties.

[3] Projections of authors.

Source: Compiled from U.S. Fish and Wildlife Service data.

APPENDIX TABLE 48. Fish and Wildlife Service: *Receipts from Nonland Sources, 1942-56 and Projections for 1960 and 1980*

(in thousands of dollars)

Fiscal year	Total receipts	Sales of migratory waterfowl hunting stamps [1]	Excise tax on arms, etc.	Excise tax on fishing tackle [2]	Sale of sealskins and other products
1942	5,322	1,430	2,750	. . .	1,142
43	3,186	1,368	1,250	. . .	568
44	2,959	1,205	1,000	. . .	754
1945	3,079	1,498	900	. . .	681
46	4,138	1,766	1,000	. . .	1,372
47	9,275	4,222	2,500	. . .	2,553
48	15,561	5,178	9,031	. . .	1,352
49	15,319	2,185	11,276	. . .	1,858
1950	15,877	3,959	10,378	. . .	1,540
51	15,947	3,895	9,351	. . .	2,701
52	28,436	4,335	17,846	2,929	3,326
53	21,456	4,594	10,679	2,857	3,326
54	24,003	4,543	12,147	4,556	2,757
1955	22,302	4,363	10,266	4,625	3,048
56	29,869	4,668	15,094	5,347	4,760
1960 [3]	33,500	5,000	16,000	8,000	4,500
1980 [3]	53,000	6,000	25,000	15,000	7,000

[1] Commonly known as the "duck stamp."

[2] Excise tax on fishing tackle levied and appropriated, starting with fiscal year 1952.

[3] Projections of authors.

Source: Compiled from U.S. Fish and Wildlife Service data.

APPENDIX TABLE 49. Fish and Wildlife Service: *Disposition of Receipts from Nonland Sources, 1942-56*[1]

(in thousands of dollars)

Fiscal year	Receipts obligated	Wildlife refuges[2]		River basin studies[2]	Waterfowl management investigation[2]	Research on birds and mammals[2]	Federal aid to states[3]	Administration of game laws[4]	Administration of Pribilof Islands[5]	Administrative services[6]	Other[7]
		Land acquisition	Development and management								
1942	3,703	...	932	...	...	39	2,380	58	97	177	20
43	2,213	...	729	...	...	21	1,264	55	5	119	20
44	2,574	256	661	...	53	21	1,296	49	124	94	20
1945	2,589	980	608	...	51	28	672	60	91	79	20
46	3,005	632	956	44	63	33	981	84	97	90	25
47	4,772	692	1,333	19	103	74	1,965	143	226	192	25
48	9,454	648	1,400	...	130	104	6,440	184	212	311	25
49	12,146	472	1,434	...	195	94	8,883	195	418	425	30
1950	13,387	222	1,541	20	220	89	10,309	218	265	483	40
51	14,557	251	2,190	20	15	383	10,160	317	386	805	30
52	18,896	481	2,300	80	15	402	12,900	356	1,382	950	30
53	22,688	760	2,047	108	282	244	15,740	625	1,822	1,030	30
54	22,677	434	2,542	278	317	285	14,827	645	2,181	1,014	154
1955	21,796	766	4,134	340	375	425	12,467	680	1,262	1,178	169
56	22,683	710	3,247	283	373	460	14,452	659	1,316	1,066	117

[1] These receipts are part of those shown in appendix table 48. In some years, particularly during the war, not all these receipts were appropriated by the Congress. There is also a normal lag between time of receipt and time of obligation.

[2] Financed from the receipts of the sale of duck stamps, from unused federal-aid funds which revert, and since 1953 from a small portion of 25 per cent of the receipts from Pribilof Island sales.

[3] Financed from excise taxes on fishing tackle, arms, etc.

[4] Enforcement of the duck stamp law and the Migratory Bird Treaty Acts. Financed from the sale of duck stamps.

[5] Sixty per cent of the receipts of the preceding fiscal year from sale of products of the Pribilof Islands are appropriated for administration of the islands and protection and management of the fur seal herd. This arrangement began with the appropriation of funds in 1952.

[6] Pro rata share of expenses for activities shown on this table.

[7] Payments to Post Office Department for printing, distribution, sale, and accounting for duck stamps.

Source: Compiled from U.S. Fish and Wildlife Service data.

TABLE 50. Wildlife Refuges: Obligations Incurred with Annual (or Direct) Appropriations for Administration of Lands and Related Activities, 1942-56

(in thousands of dollars)

Fiscal year	Total obligations	Activities directly related to management of lands					Other activities		
		Total of management obligations	Mammal and bird reservations	Construction and land acquisition	Soil and moisture conservation	River basin studies	Administration of game laws	Research on birds and mammals	General administrative services [1]
1942	2,051	865	758	107	...	...	492	622	72
43	1,424	584	556	28	...	...	444	335	61
44	1,516	638	624	14	...	...	465	340	73
1945	1,561	700	700	...	...	...	485	310	66
46	1,528	752	752	...	...	...	495	219	62
47	2,150	998	998	...	...	100	556	411	85
48	2,546	949	949	...	...	194	991	317	95
49	3,124	1,664	1,664	...	...	148	607	473	232
1950	3,358	1,853	1,853	...	...	168	647	446	244
51	3,902	2,273	1,934	241	98	230	678	456	265
52	3,852	2,152	1,857	197	98	290	688	465	257
53	4,747	2,513	1,795	621	97	695	774	470	295
54	3,637	1,959	1,594	272	93	320	690	454	214
1955	2,378	982	838	46	98	269	605	375	147
56	2,816	1,221	952	171	98	375	633	443	144

[1] Pro rata share for activities shown on this table.

Source: Compiled from U.S. Fish and Wildlife Service data.

APPENDIX TABLE 51. Gross Cash Receipts and Net Cash Receipts into General Fund of U.S. Treasury by Major Types of Federal Land, 1905-56 and Projections for 1960 and 1980

(in millions of dollars)

Fiscal year	Gross cash receipts from					Net cash receipts [1] from				
	Total	National forests [2]	Public domain [3]	National parks [4]	Wildlife refuges [5]	Total	National forests	Public domain	National parks	Wildlife refuges
1905	—	0.1	7.0	…	…	—	0.1	—	…	…
06	—	0.8	7.6	…	…	—	0.7	—	…	…
07	—	1.5	11.6	…	…	—	1.4	—	…	…
08	—	1.8	12.7	…	…	—	1.3	—	…	…
09	—	1.8	12.2	…	…	—	1.3	—	…	…
1910	—	2.0	11.5	…	…	—	1.5	—	…	…
11	—	2.0	11.1	…	…	—	1.5	—	…	…
12	—	2.1	10.0	…	…	—	1.5	—	…	…
13	—	2.4	7.0	…	…	—	1.8	—	…	…
14	—	2.4	6.1	…	…	—	1.8	—	…	…
1915	—	2.5	5.4	…	…	—	1.8	—	…	…
16	—	2.8	5.4	…	…	—	2.1	—	…	…
17	—	3.5	6.1	—	…	—	2.5	—	—	…
18	—	3.6	5.4	—	…	—	2.6	—	—	…
19	—	4.4	4.3	—	…	—	3.2	—	—	…
1920	—	4.8	6.1	—	…	—	3.5	—	—	…
21	—	4.2	14.5	—	…	—	3.1	—	—	…
22	—	3.4	11.8	—	…	—	2.5	—	—	…
23	—	5.3	10.7	—	…	—	3.9	—	—	…
24	—	5.3	16.4	—	…	—	3.9	—	—	…
1925	—	5.0	10.8	—	…	—	3.7	—	—	…
26	—	5.2	11.4	—	…	—	3.9	—	—	…
27	—	5.2	9.2	—	…	—	3.9	—	—	…
28	—	5.4	6.7	—	…	—	4.0	—	—	…
29	—	6.3	6.2	—	…	—	4.7	—	—	…
1930	—	6.8	6.8	—	…	—	5.0	—	—	…
31	—	5.0	4.8	—	…	—	3.7	—	—	…
32	—	2.3	4.1	—	…	—	1.7	—	—	…
33	—	2.6	3.9	—	…	—	1.9	0.6	—	…
34	—	3.3	4.0	—	…	—	2.5	0.5	—	…

APPENDIX TABLE 51—continued

Fiscal year	Gross cash receipts from					Net cash receipts [1] from				
	Total	National forests [2]	Public domain [3]	National parks [4]	Wildlife refuges [5]	Total	National forests	Public domain	National parks	Wildlife refuges
1935	—	3.3	4.8	—	—	—	2.5	0.7	—	—
36	—	4.1	5.2	—	—	—	3.1	0.7	—	—
37	—	4.9	7.4	—	—	—	3.7	1.5	—	—
38	—	4.7	8.4	—	—	—	3.5	1.2	—	—
39	—	4.9	7.7	—	—	—	3.7	1.3	—	—
1940	—	5.9	7.5	1.9	—	—	4.4	1.6	1.9	—
41	—	6.6	8.7	2.1	—	—	5.0	1.9	2.1	—
42	19.2	7.2	9.9	2.0	0.1	9.7	5.5	2.1	2.0	0.1
43	21.7	10.1	10.5	1.0	0.1	11.0	7.6	2.3	1.0	0.1
44	31.8	15.9	14.9	0.8	0.2	15.5	11.5	3.0	0.8	0.2
1945	31.4	16.3	14.1	0.8	0.2	15.8	12.1	2.8	0.8	0.1
46	29.9	14.2	13.8	1.6	0.3	15.0	10.5	2.7	1.6	0.2
47	42.8	18.7	20.8	2.9	0.4	21.3	13.9	4.2	2.9	0.3
48	60.8	25.0	31.9	3.3	0.6	28.3	18.4	6.1	3.3	0.5
49	72.6	32.1	36.7	3.4	0.4	34.2	23.6	6.9	3.4	0.3
1950	74.3	34.6	35.8	3.5	0.4	36.6	25.5	7.3	3.5	0.3
51	109.9	57.6	48.3	3.5	0.5	56.4	42.5	10.0	3.5	0.4
52	139.3	71.5	63.1	3.6	1.1	72.8	52.8	15.7	3.5	0.8
53	146.8	76.0	65.0	4.2	1.6	77.3	56.6	15.4	4.1	1.2
54	150.3	69.0	75.1	4.3	1.9	73.2	51.0	16.6	4.2	1.4
1955	317.0	81.1	228.3	5.3	2.3	226.3	60.1	159.3	5.2	1.7
56	331.3	117.0	206.7	5.3	2.3	226.5	86.3	133.2	5.2	1.8
1960 [6]	399.3	148.8	241.0	7.0	2.5	238.5	108.6	121.0	7.0	1.9
1980 [6]	877.0	318.0	536.0	20.0	3.0	518.2	234.0	262.0	20.0	2.2

[1] Net cash receipts equal gross cash receipts minus payments to states, counties, and the Reclamation Fund. Both on cash basis, omitting revenues "in kind." Includes some minor items payable to miscellaneous funds. Includes that part of revenues available for expenditure. Is equal to difference between gross receipts as shown in this table and payments to states, counties, and Reclamation Fund shown in appendix table 52.

[2] Includes receipts from Tongass National Forest as well as from other national forests and land utilization areas, all shown in appendix table 5; also includes receipts from formerly controverted O & C lands as shown in appendix table 13.

[3] Data taken from appendix table 27; data shown above include O & C land (except controverted) and submerged areas, but exclude acquired land as to mineral receipts. Include receipts from Mineral Leasing Act, from national forests and other areas created out of original public domain.

[4] Receipts from entire national park system; see appendix table 37.

[5] Receipts from wildlife refuges only; see appendix table 47.

[6] Projections of authors.

APPENDIX TABLE 52. *Summary of Payments to States and Counties and to Reclamation Fund out of Receipts from Federal Lands, 1933-56 and Projections for 1960 and 1980*

(in millions of dollars)

Fiscal year		Payments out of receipts			To Recla-mation Fund from public domain lands [4]
		To states, territories, and counties			
	Total	From Forest Service receipts [1]	From wildlife refuge and park receipts [2]	From public domain and revested lands [3]	
1933	2.0	0.7	–	1.3	2.0
34	2.3	0.8	–	1.5	2.0
1935	2.6	0.8	–	1.8	2.3
36	3.0	1.0	–	2.0	2.5
37	4.1	1.2	–	2.9	3.0
38	4.8	1.2	–	3.6	3.6
39	4.2	1.2	–	3.0	3.4
1940	4.3	1.5	–	2.8	3.1
41	5.1	1.6	*	3.5	3.3
42	5.5	1.7	*	3.8	4.0
43	6.5	2.5	*	4.0	4.2
44	10.1	4.4	*	5.7	6.2
1945	9.7	4.2	0.1	5.4	5.9
46	9.0	3.7	0.1	5.2	5.9
47	12.9	4.8	0.1	8.0	8.6
48	18.7	6.6	0.1	12.0	13.8
49	21.9	8.5	0.1	13.3	16.5
1950	21.9	9.1	0.1	12.7	15.8
51	32.7	15.1	0.1	17.5	20.8
52	41.9	18.7	0.3	22.9	24.5
53	44.0	19.4	0.5	24.1	25.5
54	46.2	18.0	0.5	27.7	30.9
1955	54.7	21.0	0.6	33.1	35.9
56	67.9	30.7	0.6	36.6	36.9
1960 [5]	96.8	40.2	0.6	56.0	64.0
1980 [5]	209.8	84.0	0.8	125.0	149.0

[1] See appendix table 7 for data on national forests; to this has been added an estimated share paid to O & C counties out of escrowed receipts from formerly controverted O & C lands, for years earned rather than for years paid.
[2] See appendix tables 38 and 47.
[3] See appendix table 29; payments to O & C counties out of escrowed receipts from formerly controverted lands excluded.
[4] See appendix table 29.
[5] Projections of authors, based on projected revenues shown in other appendix tables, and on present law.

APPENDIX TABLE 53. Summary of Expenditures on Federal Lands With and Without Major Investment Items, 1940-56 and Projections for 1960 and 1980

(in millions of dollars)

Fiscal year	Expenditures for all purposes on					Expenditures, omitting major investment items, on				
	Total	National forests[1]	Public domain[2]	National park system[3]	Wildlife refuges[4]	Total	National forests[1]	Public domain[2]	National park system[3]	Wildlife refuges[4]
1942	55.6	33.8	5.2	14.8	1.8	35.9	22.9	5.2	6.1	1.7
43	39.6	27.5	5.1	5.7	1.3	36.2	24.5	5.1	5.3	1.3
44	41.2	29.6	5.2	4.8	1.6	38.2	26.9	5.2	4.8	1.3
1945	43.2	30.4	5.6	4.9	2.3	40.4	28.6	5.6	4.9	1.3
46	51.5	37.5	5.9	5.7	2.4	46.0	32.7	5.9	5.7	1.7
47	101.6	65.6	6.5	26.5	3.0	61.6	40.1	6.5	12.6	2.4
48	72.0	51.5	6.4	11.1	3.0	58.9	40.4	6.4	9.7	2.4
49	86.0	54.1	7.4	20.7	3.8	68.1	44.5	7.4	12.9	3.3
1950	99.5	58.5	9.1	28.1	3.8	76.9	48.7	9.1	15.5	3.6
51	111.3	62.1	10.0	34.3	4.9	78.2	47.0	9.9	16.9	4.4
52	115.8	68.7	13.9	28.1	5.1	84.0	49.2	13.0	17.4	4.4
53	123.2	67.6	16.3	33.0	6.3	88.1	49.2	15.2	18.8	4.9
54	141.2	85.6	17.3	31.9	6.4	93.6	54.0	15.1	18.8	5.7
1955	152.8	82.7	19.3	43.4	7.4	95.1	53.3	16.2	19.0	6.6
56	176.5	97.6	21.2	51.1	6.6	110.4	65.5	18.1	21.1	5.7
1960[5]	258.9	129.9	31.0	80.0	18.0	147.9	76.9	26.0	30.0	15.0
1980[5]	425.5	202.5	48.0	135.0	40.0	282.5	126.5	41.0	85.0	30.0

[1] Data taken from appendix tables 9 and 10. Include expenditures on formerly controverted O & C lands, Tongass National Forest, other national forests and land utilization areas. Include expenditures out of 10 per cent of receipts for roads and trails, and contributions made by timber users and others (K-V and other funds). Classification as to operating and investment expenditures made by Forest Service, and includes all investment.

[2] Data taken from appendix tables 31 and 34. Investment includes only construction of roads; other investment items cannot be separated out but are small. Expenditures on public domain and revested land (other than controverted), and mineral leasing on all acquired and on national forest and other areas created out of original public domain. Expenditures include those out of funds made available by private persons as shown in appendix table 34.

[3] Data taken from appendix table 41. Investment includes construction and property acquisition.

[4] Total expenditures include expenditures out of refuge receipts for refuge development and maintenance, and for expenses of sales, as shown in appendix table 47; expenditures out of duck stamp and other miscellaneous receipts, for land acquisition, and for development and management of mammal and bird reservations, as shown in appendix table 49; and expenditures out of direct appropriations for mammal and bird reservations, soil and moisture conservation, and construction and land acquisition, as shown in appendix table 50. Excludes share of general administrative expense for these items. Investment includes land acquisition and construction only.

[5] Projections of authors.

APPENDIX TABLE 54. *Net Balance of Gross Revenues and Expenditures by Major Types of Federal Land, 1940-56 and Projections for 1960 and 1980* [1]

(in millions of dollars)

Fiscal year	Net balance of gross revenues above all expenditures on					Net balance of gross revenues above expenditures, omitting major investment items, on				
	Total	National forests	Public domain	National park system	Wildlife refuges	Total	National forests	Public domain	National park system	Wildlife refuges
1942	− 34.7	− 25.3	+ 5.2	− 12.8	− 1.7	− 15.0	− 14.4	+ 5.2	− 4.1	− 1.6
43	− 16.7	− 16.5	+ 5.7	− 4.7	− 1.2	− 13.3	− 13.5	+ 5.7	− 4.3	− 1.2
44	− 8.0	− 12.6	+ 10.0	− 4.0	− 1.4	− 5.0	− 9.9	+ 10.0	− 4.0	− 1.1
1945	− 10.1	− 12.8	+ 8.9	− 4.1	− 2.1	− 7.3	− 11.0	+ 8.9	− 4.1	− 1.1
46	− 19.7	− 21.8	+ 8.3	− 4.1	− 2.1	− 14.2	− 17.0	+ 8.3	− 4.1	− 1.4
47	− 56.0	− 44.7	+ 14.9	− 23.6	− 2.6	− 16.0	− 19.2	+ 14.9	− 9.7	− 2.0
48	− 7.6	− 23.3	+ 25.9	− 7.8	− 2.4	− 5.5	− 12.2	+ 25.9	− 6.4	− 1.8
49	− 8.8	− 17.9	+ 29.8	− 17.3	− 3.4	− 9.1	− 8.3	+ 29.8	− 9.5	− 2.9
1950	− 19.5	− 19.7	+ 28.3	− 24.6	− 3.4	− 3.1	− 9.9	+ 28.3	− 12.0	− 3.2
51	+ 3.7	− 0.7	+ 39.5	− 30.8	− 4.4	+ 36.8	+ 14.4	+ 39.6	− 13.4	− 3.9
52	+ 30.6	+ 8.4	+ 50.7	− 24.5	− 4.0	+ 62.4	+ 27.9	+ 51.6	− 13.8	− 3.3
53	+ 32.4	+ 14.9	+ 51.1	− 28.8	− 4.7	+ 67.5	+ 33.3	+ 52.2	− 14.6	− 3.3
54	+ 19.6	− 8.4	+ 60.1	− 27.6	− 4.5	+ 67.2	+ 23.2	+ 62.3	− 14.5	− 3.8
1955	+ 176.1	+ 8.3	+ 211.0	− 38.1	− 5.1	+ 233.8	+ 37.7	+ 214.1	− 13.7	− 4.3
56	+ 166.5	+ 29.4	+ 187.2	− 45.8	− 4.3	+ 232.6	+ 61.5	+ 190.3	− 15.8	− 3.4
1960 [2]	+ 156.9	+ 32.4	+ 213.0	− 73.0	− 15.5	+ 267.9	+ 85.4	+ 218.0	− 23.0	− 12.5
1980 [2]	+ 473.5	+ 133.5	+ 492.0	− 115.0	− 37.0	+ 616.5	+ 209.5	+ 499.0	− 65.0	− 27.0

[1] Data come from appendix tables 51 and 53; in addition to the gross cash receipts shown in the former table, receipts "in kind" equal to expenditures from private funds, as shown for national forests in appendix table 6 and for public domain in appendix table 33, have been added to obtain gross revenues. Definitions of all terms shown in footnotes to source tables.

[2] Projections of authors.

APPENDIX TABLE 55. *Net Balance of Net Revenues and Expenditures by Major Types of Federal Land, 1940-56 and Projections for 1960 and 1980*[1]

(in millions of dollars)

Fiscal year	Net balance of net revenues above all expenditures on					Net balance of net revenues above expenditures, omitting major investment items, on				
	Total	National forests	Public domain	National park system	Wildlife refuges	Total	National forests	Public domain	National park system	Wildlife refuges
1942	− 44.2	− 27.0	2.6	− 12.8	− 1.7	− 24.5	− 16.1	2.6	− 4.1	− 1.6
43	− 27.4	− 19.0	2.5	− 4.7	− 1.2	− 24.0	− 16.0	2.5	− 4.3	− 1.2
44	− 24.3	− 17.0	1.9	− 4.0	− 1.4	− 21.3	− 14.3	1.9	− 4.0	− 1.1
1945	− 25.7	− 17.0	2.4	− 4.1	− 2.2	− 22.9	− 15.2	2.4	− 4.1	− 1.2
46	− 34.6	− 25.5	2.8	− 4.1	− 2.2	− 29.1	− 20.7	2.8	− 4.1	− 1.5
47	− 77.5	− 49.5	1.7	− 23.6	− 2.7	− 37.5	− 24.0	1.7	− 9.7	− 2.1
48	− 40.1	− 29.9	+ 0.1	− 7.8	− 2.5	− 27.0	− 18.8	+ 0.1	− 6.4	− 1.9
49	− 47.3	− 26.4	0	− 17.3	− 3.5	− 29.4	− 16.8	0	− 9.5	− 3.0
1950	− 57.2	− 28.8	0.2	− 24.6	− 3.5	− 34.6	− 19.0	0.2	− 12.0	− 3.3
51	− 49.8	− 15.8	+ 1.2	− 30.8	− 4.5	− 16.7	− 0.7	+ 1.3	− 13.4	− 4.0
52	− 35.9	− 10.3	+ 3.3	− 24.6	− 4.3	− 4.1	+ 9.2	+ 4.2	− 13.9	− 3.6
53	− 37.1	− 4.5	+ 1.5	− 28.9	− 5.1	− 2.0	+ 13.9	+ 2.6	− 14.7	− 3.7
54	− 57.5	− 26.4	+ 1.6	− 27.7	− 5.0	− 9.9	+ 5.2	+ 3.8	− 14.6	− 4.3
1955	+ 85.5	− 12.7	+ 142.1	− 38.2	− 5.7	+ 143.2	+ 16.7	+ 145.2	− 13.8	− 4.9
56	+ 61.7	− 1.3	+ 113.7	− 45.9	− 4.8	+ 127.8	+ 30.8	+ 116.8	− 15.9	− 3.9
1960 [2]	− 3.9	− 7.8	+ 93.0	− 73.0	− 16.1	+ 107.1	+ 45.2	+ 98.0	− 23.0	− 13.1
1980 [2]	+ 114.7	+ 49.5	+ 218.0	− 115.0	− 37.8	+ 257.7	+ 125.5	+ 225.0	− 65.0	− 27.8

[1] Data come from appendix tables 51 and 53; in addition to the net cash receipts shown in the former table, receipts "in kind" equal to expenditures from private funds, as shown for national forests in appendix table 6 and for public domain in appendix table 33, have been added to obtain net revenues. Definitions of all terms shown in footnotes to source tables.
[2] Projections of authors.

APPENDIX TABLE 56. Index of Farm Real Estate Taxes and Estimated Taxes on Federal Land in 11 Western States, 1938-55

State	1938	1939	1940	1941	1942	1943	1944	1945	1946	1947	1948	1949	1950	1951	1952	1953	1954	1955
1. Index of farm real estate taxes (1909-13 = 100)																		
Arizona	205	243	207	192	152	138	120	183	200	312	337	465	575	559	569	632	653	650
California	225	232	233	233	225	216	248	282	380	435	486	483	524	538	577	594	619	684
Colorado	172	175	179	183	178	180	189	211	233	269	291	306	318	338	386	396	416	439
Idaho	171	197	193	190	166	182	189	233	262	300	331	352	362	405	414	412	432	453
Montana	167	169	174	172	158	163	167	202	229	284	300	321	327	348	373	364	382	393
Nevada	209	248	230	227	221	201	217	215	216	231	259	269	264	255	263	255	254	255
New Mexico ..	204	211	208	219	239	232	235	249	309	322	342	376	403	386	409	404	395	406
Oregon	227	228	224	170	199	164	197	218	289	323	411	487	519	525	534	540	576	626
Utah	209	208	201	198	181	176	176	217	216	287	297	316	315	341	301	338	330	386
Washington ...	110	113	113	111	110	109	114	141	158	192	220	233	218	230	242	241	246	283
Wyoming	180	176	175	179	172	185	194	210	232	269	315	400	405	421	437	441	436	454
2. Total estimated tax on federal land (in thousands of dollars)																		
Arizona	767	910	774	718	568	517	449	685	747	1,167	1,262	1,740	2,150	2,090	2,130	2,365	2,445	2,430
California	12,340	12,720	12,780	12,780	12,340	11,840	13,600	15,460	20,850	23,650	26,629	26,500	28,700	29,500	31,600	32,550	33,900	37,500
Colorado	1,444	1,469	1,502	1,535	1,493	1,510	1,585	1,770	1,955	2,255	2,440	2,570	2,668	2,835	3,240	3,320	3,490	3,680
Idaho	1,540	1,775	1,740	1,712	1,496	1,640	1,704	2,100	2,360	2,705	2,983	3,170	3,260	3,650	3,728	3,710	3,890	4,080
Montana	1,415	1,435	1,475	1,458	1,340	1,382	1,415	1,714	1,943	2,410	2,543	2,725	2,772	2,950	3,165	3,090	3,240	3,330
Nevada	2,060	2,450	2,270	2,240	2,180	1,985	2,145	2,120	2,130	2,280	2,557	2,655	2,607	2,515	2,592	2,515	2,508	2,515
New Mexico ..	640	661	652	687	748	727	737	780	968	1,010	1,074	1,178	1,265	1,211	1,283	1,267	1,239	1,275
Oregon	8,200	8,240	8,090	6,140	7,190	5,925	7,115	7,870	10,440	11,680	14,833	17,600	18,750	18,970	19,300	19,520	20,800	22,640
Utah	2,030	2,020	1,950	1,925	1,755	1,708	1,708	2,108	2,095	2,785	2,885	3,070	3,055	3,310	2,920	3,280	3,205	3,750
Washington ...	6,220	6,480	6,480	6,270	6,220	6,160	6,445	7,970	8,930	10,850	12,433	13,160	12,330	13,000	13,680	13,620	13,900	16,010
Wyoming	1,262	1,235	1,228	1,255	1,207	1,296	1,360	1,473	1,627	1,886	2,206	2,805	2,840	2,950	3,065	3,090	3,055	3,185
Total	37,918	39,395	38,941	36,720	36,537	34,690	38,263	44,050	54,045	62,678	71,845	77,173	80,397	82,981	86,703	88,327	91,672	100,395

Source: Based upon data from Agricultural Finance Section, Production Economics Research Branch, Agricultural Research Service. Original data to one decimal place. Calculated by proportion between estimated taxes in 1948 (taken from table 13, p. 317) and index numbers in various years. Slide rule calculations.

APPENDIX TABLE 57. *Payments to 11 Western States and their Counties by the U.S. Forest Service and the Bureau of Land Management from Receipts, 1944-56*

(in thousands of dollars)

Fiscal year	Total, 11 western states	Arizona	California	Colorado	Idaho	Montana	Nevada	New Mexico	Oregon	Utah	Washington	Wyoming
1944	7,471	139	1,439	255	220	509	95	925	1,289	249	510	1,841
1945	8,186	189	1,619	316	272	356	92	1,001	1,597	274	853	1,617
46	7,707	177	1,664	517	263	407	87	956	1,310	254	643	1,429
47	10,494	195	2,364	867	272	463	103	1,405	2,058	337	401	2,029
48	15,336	224	3,102	1,411	324	547	54	1,837	3,181	360	742	3,554
49	17,638	269	3,587	1,791	418	663	56	1,859	3,475	485	838	4,197
1950	18,439	280	4,097	1,803	477	774	234	1,793	3,905	450	1,120	3,506
51	23,401	346	4,225	2,145	565	732	315	2,522	5,516	740	1,241	5,054
52	33,993	519	5,379	2,660	889	1,145	425	3,270	10,427	1,257	2,333	5,689
53	37,657	600	6,538	2,911	975	1,560	240	3,333	11,476	1,231	2,824	5,969
54	42,673	574	6,526	3,376	1,041	1,416	436	4,078	12,734	1,476	3,449	7,567
1955	50,990	481	6,514	3,646	1,060	1,470	746	4,596	19,356	1,599	2,850	8,672
56	59,671	708	8,865	4,124	1,810	2,141	498	4,931	21,506	1,630	4,338	9,120

Source: Compiled from the Reports of the Director of the Bureau of Land Management, Statistical Appendices, and U.S. Forest Service data.

APPENDIX TABLE 58. *County Tax Revenues from Private Property and the Combined Payments from Receipts from National Forest and O & C and Coos Bay Revested Lands in those Oregon Counties in Which Both Lands are Found, 1945-56[1]*

(in thousands of dollars)

County	1945	1946	1947	1948	1949	1950	1951	1952	1953	1954	1955[2]	1956
Total, 18 counties												
Taxes	22,876	25,128	31,280	39,579	51,614	59,781	63,861	71,491	76,120	82,407	91,218	–
Payments	1,291	1,095	2,041	3,363	3,280	3,217	5,891	9,363	10,363	9,975	18,105	18,514
Benton:												
Taxes	383	391	660	717	832	1,147	1,313	1,337	1,312	1,541	1,732	–
Payments	78	72	102	133	116	71	121	236	252	211	401	363
Clackamas:												
Taxes	1,521	1,660	2,122	2,389	3,330	3,887	4,224	4,555	4,908	5,363	5,851	–
Payments	59	63	137	176	186	195	410	566	759	675	1,149	1,270
Columbia:												
Taxes	567	606	749	775	1,169	1,202	1,285	1,331	1,415	1,459	1,538	–
Payments	18	14	30	46	36	38	66	125	133	113	213	187
Coos:												
Taxes	733	814	1,040	1,103	1,501	2,000	2,227	2,621	2,859	3,536	3,883	–
Payments	67	58	107	176	143	137	240	416	459	450	884	792
Curry:												
Taxes	65	125	217	220	312	402	256	394	453	511	666	–
Payments	15	25	29	42	51	40	157	129	125	276	608	683
Douglas:												
Taxes	623	863	1,103	1,467	1,932	3,055	2,906	3,010	3,696	4,506	4,703	–
Payments	337	258	495	831	862	776	1,395	2,209	2,249	2,283	4,196	4,194
Jackson:												
Taxes	894	842	1,236	1,588	2,149	2,581	2,685	2,926	3,328	3,190	3,765	–
Payments	168	129	273	418	346	395	714	1,282	1,361	1,235	2,381	2,088
Josephine:												
Taxes	274	449	702	749	952	1,068	1,228	1,250	1,254	1,327	1,358	–
Payments	106	85	140	210	221	158	333	520	545	707	1,940	1,606
Klamath:												
Taxes	1,182	1,376	1,747	1,989	2,426	3,184	2,881	3,215	3,071	2,934	3,128	–
Payments	78	55	77	145	165	175	389	443	492	548	790	819

APPENDIX TABLE 58—continued

County	1945	1946	1947	1948	1949	1950	1951	1952	1953	1954	1955 [2]	1956
Lane:												
Taxes	1,716	2,087	2,887	3,121	4,154	5,577	6,324	7,213	7,951	8,596	9,491	–
Payments	207	185	359	648	679	720	1,211	1,978	2,272	2,092	3,183	3,767
Lincoln:												
Taxes	365	479	668	748	1,012	1,257	1,478	1,495	1,573	1,687	1,841	–
Payments	13	21	30	52	26	39	46	117	138	99	229	331
Linn:												
Taxes	728	879	1,447	1,799	2,451	2,791	3,023	3,165	3,486	3,808	3,885	–
Payments	57	50	96	228	221	226	384	598	714	588	714	981
Marion:												
Taxes	1,516	1,644	1,916	2,417	3,397	3,996	4,068	4,558	4,512	5,465	5,687	–
Payments	26	22	49	80	92	96	171	260	319	259	358	452
Multnomah:												
Taxes	9,850	10,193	11,091	16,389	20,327	20,886	22,258	26,478	27,819	29,038	33,482	–
Payments	10	9	21	28	28	30	60	89	115	91	359	287
Polk:												
Taxes	451	441	701	807	952	1,220	1,174	1,303	1,380	1,497	1,419	–
Payments	24	20	42	64	51	53	91	175	186	157	299	262
Tillamook:												
Taxes	387	402	433	663	910	1,172	1,189	1,204	1,280	1,374	1,450	–
Payments	12	15	24	40	23	31	42	97	111	83	182	226
Washington:												
Taxes	968	1,143	1,616	1,615	2,327	2,619	3,319	3,524	3,731	4,279	4,930	–
Payments	7	5	12	18	14	15	26	50	53	44	90	77
Yamhill:												
Taxes	653	734	945	1,073	1,481	1,787	2,023	1,912	2,092	2,296	2,409	–
Payments	9	9	18	28	20	22	35	73	80	64	129	129

[1] Taxes shown are ad valorem taxes levied on property. City and town taxes and port taxes have been excluded. Special assessments have also been excluded.

[2] Payments for 1955 include the disbursement of funds accumulated over a period of years as receipts from lands, the jurisdiction of which was contested by Forest Service and Bureau of Land Management.

Source: Compiled from data from the Bureau of Land Management, U.S. Forest Service and Oregon State Tax Commission.

APPENDIX TABLE 59. *Estimated Value for Assessment Purposes of All
Tax-exempt Federal Property, in Each of 18 Counties
in Oregon with O & C Lands, 1946-54* [1]

(in thousands of dollars)

County	1946	1948	1950	1952	1954
Total, 18 O & C counties	247,427	256,397	282,168	299,813	306,260
Benton	1,660	1,454	1,798	1,751	2,738
Clackamas	21,447	22,371	35,500	23,000	23,000
Columbia	21	21	21	21	21
Coos	14,252	13,952	10,066	10,066	10,066
Curry	5,700	5,700	5,700	5,700	5,700
Douglas	30,747	30,672	87,570	22,770	22,800
Jackson	38,188	10,662	16,814	13,500	13,500
Josephine	3,324	4,120	5,580	2,870	2,941
Klamath	7,194	9,409	9,377	9,377	9,377
Lane	35,430	35,431	35,445	99,250	106,833
Lincoln	1,597	1,682	1,746	1,923	1,978
Linn	6,005	6,443	6,455	11,300	15,004
Marion	201	496	501	27,942	27,977
Multnomah	78,102	110,755	60,559	67,751	61,606
Polk	250	230	2,550	106	109
Tillamook	2,519	2,200	2,200	2,200	2,324
Washington	93	93	93	93	93
Yamhill	697	706	193	193	193

[1] Estimated by county assessors.

Source: Compiled from the biennial reports, Oregon State Tax Commission.

INDEX

Index

Acquired lands:
definition of, 31;
expenditures on, Figures, 285, 288;
and mineral development, 101;
Mineral Leasing Act, application to, 31, 223;
mineral-producing, disposition of receipts from, Table, 436–39;
miscellaneous mineral production, Table, 427;
oil and gas leases and production, Table, 426;
revenue:
cash receipts, summary, Table, 434–35;
distribution of, Figure, 282;
and expenditures, net balance of, Figure, 288;
forecast of, 278;
Mineral Leasing Act receipts, Tables, 276, 426;
miscellaneous mineral production, Table, 427
Administration of federal lands. *See* Administrative reorganization, Management, *and* United States Government agencies
Administrative reorganization, 81, 364–75;
and Bureau of Land Management, 370;

combination of departments of Agriculture and Interior, 369;
consolidation of all forests into the Forest Service, 369;
economies of, 374–75;
general outline of, 369–70;
limited role of, 370–72;
potentialities of, 374;
problems created by, 372–74;
proposals made but not adopted, 366–69;
summary, 375
Agricultural Conservation Program, 258
Agriculture: price reporting, 366; subsistence, 199
Agriculture, Department of. *See* Department of Agriculture
Alaska, 173, 448*n*; area of, owned by government, 36; excluded from this study, 13; extensive management of federal lands, 35; forests on public domain in, 92; homesteading in, 107, 108; national monuments in, 112; pulp mill, first in, 198; purchased from Russia, 18, 20; revenue from timber sales, forecast of, 279; submerged lands around, 102; timber, 65, 88, 421*n*; wildlife acreage in, 124; wildlife management, 299
American Association for the Advance-

477